CYCLING THROUGH FRANCE

Published by Freewheelin' Publications

Copyright © 2018 Paul Ward

Paul Ward has asserted his right
under the Copyright, Designs and Patents
Act 1988 to be identified as the author
of this work.

All rights reserved.

ISBN 978-1-72096-877-1

A catalogue record for this book
is available from the British Library and
the American Library of Congress

Also available as a Kindle ebook
ISBN 978-1-84396-513-8

No part of this publication may be reproduced,
stored in or introduced into a retrieval system or transmitted
in any form or by any means electronic, photomechanical,
photocopying, recording or otherwise without the prior
written permission of the publisher. Any person who
does any unauthorised act in relation to this publication
may be liable to criminal prosecution

Pre-press production
eBook Versions
27 Old Gloucester Street
London WC1N 3AX
www.ebookversions.com

CYCLING THROUGH FRANCE

Paul Ward

FREEWHEELIN' PUBLICATIONS

Contents

THE FIRST TRIP

1
Leaving England

6
Bretagne

42
Loire and Cher

86
Into the Massif Central: Puy De Dome

116
Volcans D'Auvergne

132
Across the Margeride

141
Le Puy En Velay

147
Cévennes

165
Ardeche

174
Ventoux

190
Rhone to the Gard

198
The Herault

203
Into the Haut Languedoc

209
The Aude

220
Corbiéres

233
Coté Vermeille

244
A Taste of the Pyrenees

263
Train Experiences, Gironde

268
Maritime Charente

273
Vendée

279
Low Land to Loire Atlantic

283
Into Morbihan, Finistére

THE SECOND TRIP

299
The Return: Bretagne Finistére

308
Bretagne Cotes D'Amor Veloroute 6

313
Illé et Vilaine

317
Loire Atlantic

320
Maine et Loire

325
Vienne

335
Indre

350
**Creuse. Into the Massif Central:
Gorges de la Sioule**

364
Gorges Chauvigny

370
Puy de Dome Monts Dore

382
Cantal Mountains

399
Haut Loire and The Beast of Gevaudan

413
The Stevenson Route: Velay

427
The Stevenson Route: Gevaudan

438
**The Stevenson Route:
Crossing Mt. Goulet and Mt. Lozére**

452
The Stevenson Route: The Valley of the Tarn

461
**The Stevenson Route:
Valley of the Mimente
Crossing the Desert
In Search of Modestine**

472
Corniche Des Cévennes

479
Gorges Du Tarn

484
Aveyron. Languedoc. Haut Languedoc.

491
Haut Languedoc

510
Corbiéres

518
Crossing the Pyrenees

590
Mountains to the Sea. Landes.

594
Gironde

602
Bretagne Return

THE FIRST TRIP

Leaving England

Drizzling rain accelerates fading light of evening, road signs direct through Plymouth towards Milbay Docks. The new ungainly wobbling experience of pedalling a loaded bike amongst endless overtaking vehicles spraying my feet and legs with rainwater and road grime.

Tall glass and modern steel lead to Edwardian rundown masonry. Dilapidated wall space shared between bill posters and graffiti. Floral weed display grows amongst ancient litter. Random arranged collection of burnt and dented commercial wheelie bins adorn alleyway and pavement. The only colour illumination comes from the Takeaway and Kebab shop windows getting ready to feed the hunger of late night drunken lager creatures. A roundabout signed 'Ferryport' directs through wide shallow puddles to join a handful of cars waiting at closed barriers. A lady appears in florescent green and waves me to my own personal lane under canopy shelter from the wet. She weaves between rows of cars administering smiling leaflet instruction.

Ahead, the large ferry. A white solitary maritime block of flats. Rows of windows lit from the inside makes its interior warm and inviting. Looking around at the other piers, Milbay seems no longer to be used. Stone greyness empty for years. Grass growth between broken concrete over old stone pier. Heavy steel streaks brown rust down to murky green water peppered in radiating rain circles in a low whispering hiss.

A polite smiling lady with a busy inaudible squawking two way radio issues a boarding card instructing me to follow the lane ending with all others at closed gates of a large metal shed where signs threatening deeds of woe to anyone daring to be unofficial. Cold. Only just May. A jovial man appears, unlocking the gate.

"Go on through and get down to the cafe. It's warm in there."

I open the door to a buzzing drinks machine, a few tables. Red glow standby of a silent television hanging from the wall. The other end home to a counter served by an office dispensing information to lorry drivers. Regular drivers are familiar with staff. One of the drivers reaches behind the counter and finds the TV remote pushing button after button ending in enlightened wisdom of turning it off. Televisual spell broken, people engage conversation. The driver sitting opposite tells me of European routes and the many places he has visited on his motorbike.

"Are you on that bicycle with the boxes on the back?"

I am.

"Are they off of a motorbike?"

I made them.

He recounts a story of having expensive panniers on his motorbike. Taking a short cut through a street with bollards and forgetting the extra width tearing off the hinges. Clothes and contents strewn across the cobbles. Much to the interest and amusement of passer's by.

"Where are you going. Around Brittany?"

"I hope to manage a little further. I want to travel through Brittany to get to a little place near the mouth of the Loire, called St. Marc-sur-mer. Then to St. Nazaire to follow La Loire upstream, cutting across and down the River Cher then over the Massif Central. Then I would like to go down through the Cevennes. Maybe then the Ardeche or Haut Languedoc. I would like to swim in the Mediterranean and then..... well. It all depends how long the money lasts."

"Are you serious?" He says, then adds. "France is a big country. Pedal all that way?"

He only half believes me. Further questions to validate my intentions.

"How long is it going to take and how are you going to get back?"

He has leant forward in anticipation of my answer. I tell him that I don't know and that nothing has been planned. All I have is a one way ticket across the Channel, one national map, plus three of old maps. Brittany, the Pyrenees, the other the Haut Languedoc. But I do have a compass.

Leaning back on the chair and smiling he tells me. "You're mad, you are. But have a good trip. The Tarn is a good river... If you ever get there."

He gets up and joins other drivers sauntering through the door talking and laughing amongst themselves. Voice collective fades bringing the room to silence, the only noise from outside. Through the rain streaked window sets of arrived headlights dazzle the blackness. The lady behind the counter informs boarding has commenced.

Outside I am the only bicycle amongst half a dozen

waiting motorbikes of different nationalities. Riders peer out of full face helmets that show only piggy squashed cheeks, eyes and eyebrows. All focus is ahead, engines revving in waiting anticipation. Next to the two wheeled queue, lines of waiting cars, caravans and motorhomes. Headlights trail out of view. I am waved over and directed to a path I must walk the bike up while queued headlights wait. My pedestrian progress enters the gaping mouth of the ships raised bow. Motorcycles follow. Behind them come the collective noise and fumes of big haulage. I finish securing my bike to a rail cheerfully assisted by of one of the French crew. I get my sleeping bag, note the deck number and finding the stairway climb repetitive flights opening the door to the restaurant.

Sounds of crockery being stacked, cutlery being sorted and industrious noises accompanied by cooking smells coming from a white lit kitchen. The place empty apart from one couple who somehow already have managed to get halfway through a big meal. Professional eaters. I close the door, leaving with the image of meat eating teeth and sawing knives.

The lounge smells of pastries and coffee. I hear the noise of an expresso machine, cups and saucers stacked in readiness to serve tonight's passengers. I search for my booked reclining seat I know I will not use. Dropping the sleeping bag, looking through the saltwater dulled window to observe the headlight procession into the ship. It is the first moment today free of apprehension of being to time or having the need to be doing anything.

Ships engines rumble, then the whole ship shudders. Crockery and cutlery rattle and chatter. The stationary lights of Plymouth move past the window as the ship reverses out with three blasts of deep funnel away from a shrinking dock. Vibration ceases. Engine pause for a moment resuming the shuddering with everything that can rattle, chatter or vibrate joining in as the ship spins to forward direction. City lights are replaced by featureless darkness of agricultural Cornish countryside. Engines smooth to a hum. I watch the passing lights of Kingsand and Cawsand. The ship slips from Plymouth Sound. One solitary navigation light goes by. I observe the shape of chapel topped Rame Head as a fading silhouette moving past the window. In nighttime blackness all view has gone. Goodbye England.

Bretagne

The sound of electric motors raising blinds give a cue to look into hazed dawn light. Low coast, a dark grey line above a pale grey sea below light grey sky. The ship quietly hums over flat water, bow intent on a singular coastal point.

Lounge steerage passengers without cabin or bed wake bleary to the smell of fresh coffee accompanied by noises of crockery. Smells of warm fresh bread, buttery croissant breakfast temptation. Scarecrow hairstyles rise from the floor half asleep drifting back and forth part spectral clutching toothbrush and toiletry bag, in the hope of making an acceptable appearance in front of a mirror for a return to daylight.

Window defines ribbons of yellow white sand, low hills, woodland rise. Distant church spires, the collective outline of rooftops. Detail increases with every minute nearing the coast.

The ship ghosts into a modern port of large stern trawlers individually coloured. Common only in brown rust over the stern from dragging dredges and hanging steel rectangular otter doors for keeping the net open. Nets coiled on large drums hang above the stern, opportunist seagulls busily scavenge a free meal pulling fish remnants trapped within the tight wound coil.

Ship engines vibrate and rattle everything returning to a

hum. The overnight passage to Roscoff ends in hydraulic noise of ship doors opening. Frantic exit to vehicle decks, crowding stairways rushing to wait collective in a fog of exhaust fumes. The crowd diminishes to a human trickle, I bid "Au revoir" to one of the café staff.

I push the bike. The steel painted deck wet, the rise of fish odour. Steel deck hydraulic noise. Vehicle fumes, electric hold lights exchanged for concrete slipway in early morning bright light. Vapours of cool hazed morning fresh sea air. The seagull squawk.

I join motorcyclists at Customs. The officer looks at my passport for half a second, hands it back and waves me on.

I am finally in France!

Rushing vehicles roar for the junction in mass noise stink up to the main D road. My slow wobbling plod takes the opposite, coasting into the town of Roscoff so quiet it seems yet to wake. The only people are market traders busy setting up for the day. Metallic clang steel tubing slides together assembling stalls. Chicken slow spin is cooked by the flame. Boxed colours of fruit and vegetables unload. Clothing on rails appears from the inside of a van. A trailer selling seafood is opening up.

I ride under a tall navigation lighthouse built square of creamy gold granite dominating the harbourside. Coasting to the far end of an inner harbour, a panorama of the town. Windows look over the waterfront, many colours of small boats. Bike leans against harbour granite, I find my packed breakfast.

A row of cannons, old harbour defence point at the fishing fleet moored along a modern pier. In lazy amusement, I line the fuse with my eye with the centre of the iron barrel and see what I can sink. A lady walks her dog.

"Bonjour" as she passes.

The greeting returned. A first communication.

Diesel engine roar changes focus to a ferry reversing and turning. Laden with goods and vehicles it weaves its way between boats on swing moorings. Its destination the offshore L'ile de Batz. Engine drone fades with distance, the wake travels in silence across the harbour upsetting the still composure of the water and slapping against the underside of boats putting each one in turn into sideways rocking. The wake reaches the steps below the railing I lean on. I watch it surge up over smooth worn granite, repeating, returning the water to stillness.

It would be nice to stay here all day, all week. In a state of cosy semi trance, doing not a lot. But I better get a map out and make a decision on where to go. I look at an old yellow Michelin map of 'Bretagne'. The next town that will give choice of direction is Morlaix. I might as well follow the map's red D road until I get there. How long it will take I do not know. I suddenly realise even with the planning I haven't a clue about France, the hills, distances on the map. The language. But what does it matter? I have no schedule and I have all day, every day.

I look the bike over. Everything secured for departure. I made simple aluminium water carriers that hold a two-litre bottle on each side of the front forks. The back tyre looks half squashed, but with all the weight of a tent, sleeping bag, clothes and cooking equipment. It will always be.

A turn of the pedals, a wobble and I am away.

A house looks as if it was once a fort with a round stone corner tower, small paned casement windows between shutters of white have peered for centuries through its large pale yellow granite blocks under thick slates that have resisted many stormy winters of Finistére. Palm tree green, flowering red bloom along the waterfront return to the market where the first customers of the day sort the produce.

The ferry terminal now empty, the final tie with England cut. The road faces inland, pointing south. Many miles are ahead. Untold views without expectation. Around a corner and the sea is gone.

A Sherman tank in Second World War decay sits on a workshop forecourt. Horrific times not long ago. Not experienced on the shores of England, spared by a few miles of water and one bad weather forecast. Wine booze discount warehouse proclaims 'best deal' enticing the euro. Back of town commerce, ramshackle shed. Garages sinking in bushes. Bright painted beach huts decorate manicured roundabout. Articulated haulage leads traffic from the new direction of left.

Arable fields wide without hedge, lines raked parallel, furrowed earth. I witness the watering with arrived steady rain backed with blustery wind. Downhill appears a heavy old bike painted black used for a sign display. Strings of onions hang about the handlebars and frame making an advert for a café. Stereotypical image. The onions selling Breton berry attired Johnnie Frenchman.

I stop at the empty roadside to zip up my waterproof jacket, pulling my hat down over my head as far as I can to keep rain out of the eyes.

Through the windblown swirling rain the road descends to the blurred outline of a bridge crossing high over an estuary creek. Colourless shapes of yachts veiled through rain in tethered rows follow estuary curve, obscured by grey hill peppered in blurred tree shape.

Rain blows into the eyes, wind shakes my cumbersome loaded bike. Vision blurred I am met with a hill to climb. Head down, face out of the wet. Shelter appears under a concrete bridge where I stop to undo the wrapper of a flapjack bar. The wrapper is showing an idealistic bright morning sunrise over a hill of green. A world away from the moment. Rain drips from the end of my nose, empty wrapper slips into the leaky side pocket of my jacket. This road has turned to dual carriageway. Looking at the old map it shows a single road.

I get the feeling I am not meant to be on here.

I cannot leave the road. Crash barriers form a fence to the opposite carriageway. Riding in the wet, the occasional passing car horn aimed at me. Orange flashing lights become a parked Highways van. I stop alongside and ask if this is motorway. 'Route National.' It is.

"Interdit pour velo." Accompanied with a sideways wagging finger.

"C`est combien kilometres le prochain sortie?" I ask.

"Demi," the reply. Half a km to the exit.

The driver leans over to the window and I have now become their morning amusement. With a half grin, he tells me. "Be quick! Make sure the police do not see you. Or it's a big fine and no bike."

"Merci." In flat reply.

I make the exit without arrest. Through the sleepy village of Henvic I find a blue cycle sign to follow. Where it goes I do not know. It becomes my only option. Out through fields the noise of the Route National runs somewhere to my tree obscured left. Its noise my direction guide. It has not been the best of starts. But it's a start.

Rain eases, sky brightens, day warms, drying when I get to Taule. A little nowhere place with a minimart that eats euros. The locals watch the outsider come out of the shop having purchased a bag of their food.

Under green spring woodland. Over busy noisy Route National. Rough country lane serenaded by background tyres and speeding engines louder crossing a footbridge over multi lane traffic, abandoning me in modern suburban housing silence.

The local bus shelter map gives direction. Somehow I have arrived above Morlaix.

Main road downhill to the harbour. Direction points 'Centre ville.' Yachts and boats held captive in watery calmness by dripping blackened lock gates. Release can only be when the tide fills the estuary creek.

Multicoloured flower baskets in bloom hang harbour railings. Half-timbered medieval buildings, granite and render facades flank both sides of a large open square with an ornate bandstand. Town buildings tumble steep hillside. Granite gable jumbled slate roofs and chimneys under green woodland clouded skyline. Overhead high railway bridge stone pillars taper to hold arches carrying a railway line high across town. A post against a wall holds a brown direction sign for camping. I look at my watch. Half twelve is too early to stop.

The old Bretagne map out of date is folded away. It has more detail but has caused trouble enough. My naive plan has just scrapped itself. The red cover of the new Michelin national map is opened. Without much detail, but enough for now. It can get me where I would like to go. It shows bike banned Route Nationals, including the one travelled. Main departmental red D and minor yellow D routes I am allowed on. Morlaix is shown in a green box as being 'pittoresque' and it has a campsite somewhere. I reason that other places green boxed on the map should also be nice and will have a campsite somewhere. The simple map backed by a compass heading for green boxed towns cobbles together an elementary travel plan. The Monts d`Arree south look good. Green boxed 'Huelgoat' is right in the middle. It takes a few minutes to work out the way to escape Morlaix.

Bumpy town street, busy cars and vans. A rattling bus changes gear enveloping me in a black diesel cloud. Traffic, bumper to bumper. Dodging potholes, weaving parked cars, oncoming vehicles. Opening car door, fingers cover the brakes.

Hard climb out of town, reaching for the waterbottle. Opening layer of clothes. Straight road climb, houses grow space between neighbours further from town. Houses give up to countryside. Wild flowers nod in long roadside grass, rough fenced fields. Isolated trees. A village of white houses, Plourin-les-Morlaix is without a solitary living soul. Bike trail crosses the road disappearing into woodland, a disused railway line is veloroute 1. The information board says it goes all the way to Huelgoat. It could be nice. A mountainbiker with helmet, sunglasses, Lycra top, Lycra leggings, clip pedal shoes, knee pads, elbow pads and water carrying backpack speeds past mud plastered. He has made my mind up. I stay on tarmac. Plougonven village. Peppering rain. Wet silver edged grey curtain veils broken sun. D9 wanders green countryside miles climbing to empty Lanneanou. Lands wild and heathered. Rough moorland, managed forestry's planted black block hill horizon over craggy woodland valley plunge.

D42 wild 'Parc Naturel d' Amorique. The middle of the Monts d' Arree. Solitude views fall steep. A feeling of calm. Sounds of river flow hide in the valley. Steep dense green rise to the skyline. Cows quietly saunter to their field gate opposite to see who has turned up. Noses busy inhaling, sniffing for the chance of food. Staring indifference, ears forward with mouths sideways chewing. No food, no interest, they wander off.

The loaded bike speeds downhill, weight adds momentum. Wet road smell, twisting green bough bends. Wide valley field, stone bridge crosses busy infant river. Eyes look to a steep climb through woodland. I see no one. All around birdsong joined by the sounds of secret trickling streams busy down the hillside in hurry to join the babbling meander. Secret spring woodland without breeze, quiet pattering raindrops on thousands of leaves unmoving in mass unison soft sound under a great canopy of green. Climbing tight bends savours wet woodland smell with every meaningful breath.

Woodland beauty finishes cresting at a junction signed 'Huelgoat.' Downhill to the start of town. Old houses narrow the road weaving to an old bridge of granite. I stop.

Smooth black lake changes to a mass broiling. Thundering under the bridge, tumbling through jumbled chaos boulders overhung by mossed woodland. Boulders the size of houses. Land of granite.

Municipal camping sign points to the lake. I follow it to find a tarmac car park for motorhomes, further around finds nothing.

Town square patisserie million calorie window. Corner supermarket saltwater tank of live crab and lobster. English couples dreamily stare in the estate agent window. Next door, Maison du Tourisme. I enter sweated on the inside and rainsoaked on the outside. The lady behind the counter dressed immaculate, perfumed with perfect hair. I politely ask if there is a campsite near Huelgoat. I am given directions to "Camping River Argent 3km on your right."

"Merci Madamme."

"Monsieur."

Freewheeling sweeping bends under great solid boughs of centuries old beech. Rocks, cliffs, cascade roar echoes the green valley. Campsite entrance.

One tent and one motorhome resident. The Accueil (reception) is closed. Through the window, last season chairs stacked on tables. Pots of paint and dustsheets tell of many hours of work getting ready for the season. I look around the buildings and find the Patron under a sink amongst plumbing tools and fittings. Without getting up he tells me to pitch by the river. It's the only part of the site open at the moment. Pay tomorrow. With a friendly nod he goes back to his work.

I am looking at the river. It is four feet down and running fast. The bank opposite rises very steep as wooded hillside dotted with rock. Birdsong echoes over water rumble tumbling downstream somewhere. My new tent pitched for the first night. I sprayed the tent pegs florescent orange not to leave any behind, or fall over them. The place peaceful in light fade late afternoon drizzle. Leaves on the many trees tint the light soft green. Wet lush grass and thick soft moss intense in colour. Gold grain sand colour challenge illuminates rocky riverbed below long swaying river weed.

Hot shower rebirth. Warmed blood hums the body after the day's mileage. Hungry. I cook a meal on my one ring stove.

Cosy in the sleeping bag with a full belly. Drizzle becomes pattering rain, a couple of hours later it becomes heavy rain. I wake in the middle of the night to torrential rain sounding as gravel hammering the thin outside sheet. The inside dry, for how long I do not know. I pull the sleeping bag over my head and in its warmth and comfort listen to the pelting racket falling to sleep.

90 km

The first sense is hearing. Eyes remain closed. Rain continues soft pattering the nylon sheet. Sleeping bag warm comfortable. The idyllic way to travel. Birds busy singing. Song seems to double, echoing back from the steep woodland. Downstream hissing rumble of the river tumbling over boulders more powerful than yesterday. The sound of rushing water nearby so clear, so detailed. Soft constant smooth swoosh of moving water in crystal chime along the riverbank. I do not think I have ever heard such a river before.

Contented in the peaceful surroundings. Legs stretch straight to wake the body. My legs push against the far end of the tent. I recoil them double quick against my chest with the cold sensation of icy water on my feet. Opening my eyes, putting my hands down on the groundsheet finds it dry, but floating. Ripples of watery rhythm pass under.

Clothes, camera, map and journal bundle into the sleeping bag. Crouched balance slowly unzipping the tent reveals a rising river within a couple of minutes of flooding my nylon home. One of my shoes has started a downstream voyage, the other has capsized and sunk within the tent porch. The stove stands in moving water defiant as a lighthouse. An empty tuna tin and a plastic biscuit wrapper have sailed off speedily downstream on a whitewater adrenalin trip in water too deep to contemplate a rescue. I am making for the covered dishwashing area, returning for shoes and the camping stove. I could have had 220v mains electricity in the tent. If ever there was a lesson against. This is it.

Standing in the rain, barefoot in cold ankle deep water pondering my empty submerged tent. How to move it in one go. A lady on her way back to the campervan comes over to have a look offering assistance. She holds the tent hoop at the shallow end while I pull out all the pegs. The suction of the water pulls heavy, its release leaves a feather to carry to as high ground as there is.

I thank her. I see the funny side to the whole event. I explain about waking in the tent oblivious to the outside rising flood. She does not find it amusing.

The bike is starting to be claimed by the river. I wheel it next to the tent. Opening the lid of the pannier box. Enduring the nighttime deluge everything has thankfully remained dry. Comforts of clean dry clothes in a wet world. Wringing the soggy end of the sleeping bag, hanging it to dry.

The campsite Patron returns. Standing looking at the river letting out a whistle of surprise at the submerged pitches. Hedges and bushes bend and shake overwhelmed in fast current.

I pay for two nights. Wet weather should stop later. Sunshine tomorrow!

Rain stops mid-afternoon. Thoughts of food and looking around Huelgoat. Plastic bags over dry socks slip into soggy cold shoes. Easy ride up to town. Supermarket promises a feast. Paying with notes and coins of unfamiliar currency.

Woodland road river roar. Steep steps descend to a fairytale world amongst great mossy boulders. Amidst woodland stillness overhanging tree branches sway in breeze generated by thundering baritone tumble. Atomised vapour rise inhalation invigorates. Beautiful, impressive. Because of the massive amount of water after the rain. Along the fairytale gorge, black pool water bubbles gold brown and foams white. Old tree thick furrowed bark. Deep green soft moss smother, growing repetitive years between huge round granite boulders. Long lengths of lichen trail green grey beard from overhanging boughs sprouting tree fern. Small evaporation clouds hang amongst green branch. The smell of saturated woodland. This place today, the true meaning of 'Enchanted Wood'.

It is understandable how rural Bretagne has direct connection to Celtic mystery and Arthurian legend.

A couple stand watching the powerful cascade tumble into a deep black pool.

"Bonjour."

I comment how beautiful it all is.

They wholly agree.

The sleeping bag retrieved near enough dry. I hope body heat will do the rest. I spend the evening eating, lazing around looking at a route for tomorrow. Bike light doubles as a torch.

In the blackness of night hard pelting rain wakes.

'Better check the tent.'

Last conscious thought is without deed.

6 km

The echoing woodland dawn chorus alarm in weak glow of dawn light, without rain. The sleeping bag goes back over the head wanting more hours of comfortable slumber.

Reaching from snug warmth everything is cold. Everything damp. Beads of silver hang above on the inside of the flysheet. The tent has not leaked, just humidity from the rain deluge. I push clothes down into the sleeping bag to warm for a few minutes before commencing routine horizontal tent dressing. Crouched spin around slips on old reef sandals and emerging to look at the new day with a stretch and the chill to the feet of silver dew cover.

River continues its flood, mist hang over fast flow. Hilly woodland, evaporation suspended wispy pale strokes of white from the dawn artist's brush. No breeze stirs the riverside. Overhead. Busy clouds silent, rolling over and over breaking to blue. Cloud edged gold, the morning sun yet to reach into the valley. Wet weather banished. Time to go.

I pack. Trying to make some order of how everything is placed. Yet to find routine. Dry socks slip into carrier bags into shoes still wet. The final look around to check nothing is left behind will become part of routine. My ear leads to the refurbished building following industrious metallic plumbing noises to find the Patron amongst pipework to thank him.

He tells a story of once travelling to Scotland by motorbike for an experience of two weeks touring in the rain. He gives me the best directions for today's route.

After the last couple of day's weather I am going south! Hoping for a drier experience. On the map, a little town. Le Faouet.

Gentle downhill forested road follows the River Argent. 'The river of silver.' Breaking cloud, fleeting sun lights trees with warming colour. Shortening shadow rolls beneath the wheels. The smell of felled resinous pinewood in the air through cleared forestry. Small bridges cross busy little rivers. Flash of silver chatter under sun weaving fields disappearing hushed secret into woodland.

Crossroads busy, main road D769 long climb into forest country. The Montagnes Noirs uphill harsh gradient down on the granny gear. 360 degree forest horizon, long straight road rolls big hills. Flying freewheel descent, the slow upward grovel payback all the way to Le Faouet.

Sun lights the village, coasting bumpy tarmac in lazy freewheel tick. Farm building dusty walls, part open large old work worn wooden doors, home to jumbled rusting metal farming equipment disappearing to a dusty blanket of interior shadow. Houses narrow. Ancient street. Corner reveals an open spacious town square of closed lunchtime shops. Bar parasols shade chattering diners. Open market hall. Oak posts on square cut granite. Low roof sweeps high equaling a three storey house. Centre an octagonal tower holds a clock. A bell shelters under a dome roof.

A group of amblers eye the bike pointing discussing and nodding moving at a pace of time killing saunter. Parked vans in the car park adorned with hippy artwork, rusty steel chimneys through the roof. The attraction to Le Faouet is its relaxed artistic feeling.

'Autre Directions' downhill flattens to fields. Grazing herds of white Charollais cattle. From the edge of the field a deer spooked near the road bounds evasive, back legs kick together into bushes for cover. The slow chewing cattle uninterested in melodrama.

D769 signs for Plouay, Arzano, Pont Scorff, Hennebont

and Lorient. The climb long, back to the granny gear plod up the inside white line. Large sign artistic impression of an otter advertises 'Vallee d'l'Elle.' Road steep, reaching for the waterbottle pushing the loaded bike weight. Hard shoulder shrinks to the verge. Sound of an approaching lorry struggling down through its gears. Louder, closer, moving alongside less than walking pace. World darkens closing its great shadow one side. Forest lined verge on the other. Steering straight trying not to wobble as the cab crawls past. Heat from the engine, the smell of gearbox oil and diesel fumes fill the lungs.

Noise vibrates through my chest in consuming temporary world of passing bedlam. I hear the whining of bearings and the whirring of inside spinning parts all under strain driving large slow spinning wheels. Tyres bulge, grabbing into the road. Dragging the great weight uphill. The lorry and its long squeaking trailer pass. Noise fade. An encore performance follows. The last lorry trailer pulls ahead. Back into daylight, breathing clean air. I had better get used to the big wheels. Gears change up through the box and they are gone. I must be nearing the top.

Forest hills level to patchwork fields. Industrial rooftops over the crash barrier. Flat road easy speed. Dual carriageway. The voice of the highways worker returns warning about cycling on Route National. The road without blue 'Interdit' signs for bikes returns to single carriageway. Signed exit. Pont Scorff. Adverts for a zoo. It seems worth a chance for a campsite.

Downhill junction. Dusty closed Bar Tabac. Opposite fades an information board. Pale icon for a campsite somewhere up the road. Mundane farm scenery, cold headwind, flat fields. Dust blown by oncoming trucks, a good sign. Dust means no rain. I push the pace in effort to warm from chilling headwind. Hills raise the body temperature. Fast down into Pont Scorff les bas. Over the pont 'bridge,' wild woodland river one side. The other a narrow estuary of peaceful boat reflection. Restored stone houses amongst bars and art galleries. A banner for a 'cycle sportif' between sixty and a hundred km. advertised.

Bends climb from the village. Streamlined Lycra clad roadriders sweep a bend. An all knowing nod of seriousness from behind the dark of sunglasses. Pont Scorff appears nearing the brow of a hill. Immaculate pristine clean cobbled streets, little shops, bright sunny walls. Two choices for camping. One directs over the brow of the hill towards a zoo. The other points between white walls to a sunny green meander along a winding leafy countryside lane, overhead dance white cumulus cotton wool clouds. An old blue sign reads 'Camping 100m.' Five hundred metres later, 'Camping 100m'. A repeat distance brings the roof of a caravan hiding noises of leisure.

Manicured campsite entrance. 'Camping Entre Terre et Mer.' 'Between land and sea.' The polite lady takes my money for one night's stay and shows me an expanse of grass which could hold half a dozen tents. But tonight, it's just for me.

Hard knocking overhead. Birds hammer the gnarled oak trunk, digging out grubs and flying off to return in further search of the bark. Busy great tits emerge their heads from nesting boxes placed high, a green woodpecker stoops in flight uttering its laughing cry making a woodland dash.

The sun gives a burning display of orange to fire red, lighting flat patches of cloud dying remnants of Finistére wet weather. Under the sunset, silhouetted shapes of distant trees across fields burn in setting glow. Country sound of donkeys braying across fields to each other lasts until the falling of dusk. **92km.**

Sun lights the tent warming the interior, sounds of breeze blowing through trees. Early breakfast. Undoing a carrier bag, wet clothes have acquired the odour of wet dog.

Before anyone wakes I rifle the laundry room finding some free sweet smelling wash liquid left in a cupboard. The liquid promises to transform my tramp odoured clothing into a fragrant floral spring meadow in which people jump through with ecstatic joy, having the most fantastic moment of their entire lives. So the picture on the plastic bottle implies. The reality is to plunge socks into hot bubbly blackening water to kill stink scrubbing in some sweetness.

Wrung washing blows sunny warm under a sky of blue decorated with summer white cloud breaking and rolling. It's warm enough to sit in a T shirt laying on the grass watching clouds shapes. Trying to light the gas with damp matches, the heads fall off of the sticks in small pasty lumps. The strike on the box falls to pieces in my hand. The last soggy physical memory of underwater camping.

"Bonjour" to a man lighting up a cigarette. Unknowingly to an Englishman from the Midlands. He is working, setting up mobile homes and chalets on sites living and working all over France and Spain for many years. Living here for the season with his wife, after moving from near the coast on a flight path of a twenty four hour airport.

Witnessing my matchbox pulp he offers a lighter. Many produced from his pocket prove no inconvenience of nicotinic pleasure. Between smokes he informs the weather has been good. Information on places. I am told cryptically, Lorient will not be easy on a bike. Decathalon store sells gas. Sealing my fate into city rush.

Pont Scorff sunny white buildings look over sparkling granite cobbles. Green country road. Jungle sounds passing the zoo. Busy supermarket sells food without gas. Towards Lorient. Under concrete shade the Route National race above. Surrounding traffic sweeps downhill to wander big store aisles.

Lorient 'Centre ville,' looking for clues to the town of Vannes. Signed direction, cityscape modern tall building glass. 'Vannes' sign swiftly delivers Route National. 'Interdit' for bikes. I double back to the railway station using 'La Gare' as reference. A different route signed 'Vannes' ends in a Route National blue sign. Red line through a bike. 'Interdit.' No signed alternative. Amongst the metallic whirl stink up, the voice from the campsite.

"Lorient will not be easy on a bike."

Compass blind weave through city streets. An old part of town should give escape using old roads. My map falls far short for city travel. Compass orientation northwest crosses the river. Car rush wide road. White line split, several lanes. Dirty city shopfronts under high tenement verandahs. Buildings throw block shade, cast shadow high wire cable criss cross. Road space fight against lane bullies. Two skinny wheels take on city spin.

Old city masonry. New steel skeleton clad in coloured tin. Out of town shopping land adorns grey complicated junction. Crash barriered slip roads feed roundabout traffic spin suspended on concrete over Route National rush. Bridge view, the minor road to Hennebont in direction for Vannes. Endless traffic bumper to bumper both ways next to four lane thrash

Route National. I have a drink pensive in traffic fumed noise watching a vehicle shopping jam early hot sunny afternoon. I have no appetite for it. Half way around the merry go round of madness I see a familiar D769, the route arrived on yesterday. I take it to get out. Signed exit. Caudan.

Route National concrete and vehicle bedlam fades to green cut verge. Manicured rose bloom speaks of civic pride. Green parkland, a bus shelter under leafy bough contains a map. I memorise direction. Thirty seconds later returning to memorise again, photographing for reference. Sleepy Caudan's well cared for street ends in direction towards Pont Scorff. I take the opposite. No more Lorient. Country lane signed 'Le Poteau Rouge' wanders old tree leaf shadow dancing the road in rustling breeze. Fields of oilseed yellow bloom under bright blue sky. Black and white cows slow graze fields of green. Chickens behind wire peck dirt turning the earth at the bottom of a smallholding worked by two people who look up smiling.

"Bonjour."

Woodland follows countryside roll. Main road points Hennebont. Bumps, patches, pothole dodge freewheel steep to town gables bill postered above traffic lights. Stone bridge crosses quiet water at the head of a creek.

Estuary sun sparkle breezy blue water. Yachts of different eras. 70's ugly aluminium peeling grey, hard angular. It's roof and deck decorated part white by resident seagulls. Glossy modern fibreglass racer pulls eager at the mooring rope, sharp bows, open wide stern. A graceful aged narrow 1920s/30s teak deck wooden yacht with the point of a canoe stern, motionless quiet. Cream paint fades, tall varnished wooden mast flaking, rope and rigging jumble. Corroded green brass. Portholes from the sides of a wood cabin roof.

D9 away from the estuary. Long quiet road, roundabout rise over Route National, wide flat land. Neglected stone barns have watched centuries of farming seasons roll over and over. One farm a hamlet in itself, narrow cartway between old stone agricultural buildings, labourers' cottages. In the middle, the grand farmhouse. Splendid, worklike. The large flower and vegetable garden muddied by the dust of farming's daily industry.

Ribbon development houses and shops. Flat land ride, the hills of Finistére long gone, a windy metal suspension bridge crosses saltwater inlet. The Étel. Bright animated clear view seaward, dark blue windy water, rooftops of the boating town of Étel. Upstream rocky islets between many secret finger creeks disappear from view under low distant tree lined landscape. Below, long rows of bright green seaweed covered submerged structures farming shellfish. People fish from the slipway. Sleeping little Erdeven amongst landscape flat. Town shops in a land of granite Neolithic Menhirs and stone rows. Winding country lane searches for the coast. Low houses, two old round stone towered windmills. One could still work. Sail frames complete with moveable roof to face to the wind. The circular stone structure lime rendered and washed white. Against the deep blue of the clear afternoon sky the white tower is impressive.

Blowing offshore wind propels toward the sea passing a campsite. Road ends in miles of sand dune view across long beach expanse. A weathered smooth great gold brown granite boulder Menhir half buried under sand looks over the dark blue expanse of Atlantic Ocean. Fast moving sails. Windsurfers plane at speed parallel to the shore taking advantage of strong constant wind. Sun glint sail makes a speeding smooth turn, 180 degree white wake carve into ultramarine blue flat windy sea. A race of return direction. Multicoloured sails of land yachts speed way down the beach. Families enjoy an afternoon of sandcastle repose. The campsite back from the beach behind sunny golden granite Gites for holiday rent. Campsite Accueil 'Ouvert.'

I am apologetically charged a pittance for my flat grassy pitch. A handful of people in caravans, the early season feeling of the place to myself. I pitch the tent tight to a hedge sheltering from strong blowing wind. The shower is the hottest. Sunset takes the wind leaving a reddened sky. Blackbird's evening summer serenade in South Bretagne.

62 km

6.30am. Sunday morning, clear cold, just off of frost. Breezy sounds exaggerated by rustling leaves T shirt warms inside the sleeping bag, fleece top denies chill. Outside sink cold shock wash catches the breath, waterproof delays cold dawn sting. Hands in pockets heading for the beach passing Les Gites and Breton gold brown granite houses next to modern perfectly square white neighbours. I see no one. Hear no vehicle. It takes five minutes of walking to be on the cold sand trickling between the toes. Sub horizon sun makes warming appearance. Orange glow throws my long black shadow across the sand expanse. Below tideline easier walking. Rippled hardened wet cold sand numbs the feet.

Low sun colour enrichment. Sea a deeper blue, tiny breaking waves crest and roll white tinted orange. Remnant of night a half moon in suspended fade to the west. Rock and reef glow orange. Distant figures walk a dog.

The end of the beach. Bare rock headland climb. Further bays gold warmed in risen sun. A small open blue boat. Solitary figure dressed in yellow bib and brace oilskins checks and re baits pots laid between rock reef fingers and jagged stone islets.

Coarse grass and pink blooms of sea thrift share the rocky headland with gorse yellow flower. Sand filled cove repeat melting to the curve coast horizon of far away Île de Groix. The panorama south of endless beach, far away villages hazed line to Quiberon. Belle Îsle silhouette tries to close the horizon. Hidden in the dunes concrete Nazi defence gun emplacements. Blast wrecked bunker decay looks seaward. The date of their slave construction reads 9,9,1942. Path above the beach roams dunes flanked by long dry pale grass and wildflower colour. The call of a cuckoo.

Car park holds one vehicle. A Renault van, converted to a camper housing an emerging family woken to this sunny morning. No one stirs from the Gites or houses. Soft morning rich colour tint rapidly replaced by rudeness of hard daylight.

Windsurfers arrive in cars and vans. Rigging sails, part shouting conversation to the café owner busy opening up the front of the wooden café and brushing away sand.

Kerhillio early in season has been perfect. I thank the Patron with my limited vocabulary.

Sunday people cycling. "Bonjour!"

Supermarket stop fuels the day. Carnac. The amazing number of Megaliths, Dolmen, stone rings and stone rows travel for miles. Hundreds of stone art architectural arrangements surrounded by rows of standing people.

A sign directs for Auray. Straight road flatland. D768 more stone wonderment. Woodland dense, black pool stillwater, ancient swamp and marsh. Restaurant decorated with many statues of animals, wood people play musical instruments made from twisted fallen tree boughs and bits of trunk fill the tabled garden. Under Route National, road numbers to Auray.

Old, beautiful, a town on the top of a hill of narrow cobbled streets, stone and half timbered buildings. Heavy black oak, block granite corbel overhang. Créperie bars, restaurants. White stone sun sparkling Hotel de Ville town hall. A slated domed belfry on circular pillars houses the town clock. Decorative ironwork on a large ceremonial balcony over main entrance doors, long small paned windows ornate between hanging flag colour.

Freewheeling over cobbles tumbling steep under seventeeth century doorways. Hanging signs artistic. Stone bridge to St. Goustan. An old coal port transformed now boasts quaint beauty selling trinkets between restaurant tables. D101 sunned views across fields to the Rivére de Auray. Estuary blue, boats of white set against fields bright yellow to a backdrop of darkened green woodland.

The estuary forms part of a great seawater inlet of the Golfe du Morbihan. Sunny road runs from the waterside into open rolling countryside, blue sparkle of the Golfe moment's return crossing an inlet to Le Moustoir. A church on the water, Penmern. Easy countryside ends steep climbing to Vannes.

Cash and carry, Bricolage (d.i.y.) stores of corrugated colour to a roundabout. Compulsory cycle lane so slow, tree roots push up the tarmac constantly banging the wheels of the loaded bike, I curse every encounter. The cycle lane shared with everyman including his wandering dog predicts a disastrous meeting. I take the road fast pace downhill to get out. Interdit or not.

Signs for the port. Crowded sunny waterfront, overhanging red and white striped blinds customer shade outside cafés and bars. Yachts float the watery mirror, perfectly spaced planted shady trees. Live jazz, sweet cooking smells, a pannier market crowded. Red London Routemaster bus parked amongst a great bustle of enjoyment under afternoon sun.

Crowd mass escape to empty mundane streets. I have missed the old town riding too far. How can you miss castle walls and towers? I have managed it. Roundabout roundabout, a small town. 'Sene.' Excursion to peninsula views across sparkling sunny water peppered with white sails to L' Île d' Arz part obscured by tree covered islets that are not small, but are dwarfed by the length of this main isle. Boats appear to disappear, masts and sails move between tree covered rocky islets reinforcing their perspective as islands, rather than a false view of vast lakeside. Trees overhang the water's edge, house gardens on fire with floral colour. A short hill under woodland joins traffic at Poulfanc. Two roundabouts, eight roads, I mess up. Signs for 'Nantes.' Hill plod sends smoked barbeque aromas from a garden inducing hunger grind. Route National. 'Interdit.' No bicycle alternative. Back down the hill, nostrils and stomach tortured by a barbeque smoke return. Over the bridge, uphill to a Route National industrial estate. Metal roofed corrugated shade, industrial walls in Sunday afternoon silence. Sunshine. Mirage campsite sign.

It is real. Arrow points to a bright flower garden entrance. I wait at the Accueil counter. The sounds of T.V. from a joining door. The everyday noises of a home. Amongst the colourful brochures a free campsite booklet details seven hundred sites throughout France. The Patron arrives and we fill in the forms. I go to pay. My last 10 euro note has fallen from my pocket. I carry no cash. I pay by travel money card, using it for the first time. Silent pause linger waiting for electronics. . . . 'Zipp zipp' relief buzz of a printing receipt. It works.

I am shown my grassy pitch between chalet lines and privacy hedge. The Patron corrects my French from 'Bon' to 'Bein.' I say 'Bein,' he corrects the tense to 'Bon.'

The tent is up. I shower in the 1950s under copper pipe trickle and spend a quality hour leisurely eating, finishing with soft ripe juice running apricots. In the warmth of evening sun, only the background traffic drone penetrates the quaint and peaceful oasis from the Route National.

75 km

Harsh background sounds, tyres and engines of different pitch speed both ways. Each speeding noise subjected to the falling tone of the Doppler Effect a hundred times a minute on rush hour Monday morning. Singing birds in the bushes in competition with constant internal combustion engine drone.

No Bretagne beach this morning with golden sand between the toes, no old boats full of flowers or soulful wanderings. My thoughts interrupted by water boiling for tea. The food box runs low, the need to fuel up somewhere. I pack slow, waiting for warming sun to dry a silver dew tent. Sitting on the grass waiting, there are noises from behind the hedge.

From a nearby chalet, obscured from view a door opens. Footsteps, noises of a rattling toolbox. The door opens again and a female voice gives muffled tones of instruction, answered by the husband. Soon the electric drill is busy, making holes for something. The wife comes into view and is looking at a neighbour's unoccupied chalet. She has her back to me, hands on hips of considerable beam, deep in study. The noise of drilling ceases, this breaks her concentration giving a cue for her to return behind the hedge and administer further muffled instruction. Then the closing of a door followed by half a minute of intermittent battery drilling sounds, followed by the noise of tools being returned into plastic boxes.

The husband appears. A man in his late sixties or early seventies wearing a baseball cap and check shirt. He greets me. "Bonjour."

I return the salutation. On seeing my loaded bike leant in the hedge he comes over, hands in pockets, soft voiced without hurry.

Where am I from?

Interested, looking over the bike, he asks about the panniers.

I reply. "Je en fait" etc. I made them.

Slowly nodding his head in their study, replies a smiling. "Tres practique."

From behind the hedge, he is caught and summoned back immediately to duties. I hear further muffled instructions given. A vehicle door opens, closes, a car engine starts. The chalet door closes and half a minute later the car pulls away. The chauffeur and the chauffeured.

I can see his life. A tether of near permanence to a mains cable, powering a drill, powering a lawnmower, with occasional promotion up a stepladder under permanent surveillance, presented with an infinite list of duties impossible to ever complete. The only parole, the job of being an obedient trolley pusher, shared with the near purgatory visits to d.i.y. 'Bricolage land.' Au revoir d.i.y. retirement slave of Theix!

A wave of thanks to the Patron at the office doorway. I have the noise of the Route National in my left ear and the sound of a tractor working a field in my right. Beautiful countryside under warm morning sun, great piles of greying firewood at the edge of fields. Crop green lines, sandy brown furrow, parallel corduroy pattern acres in size, broken by the focal point of a solitary battered old tree straining to produce leaves.

Noyalo has a few people shuffling around half empty sunny morning streets. Joinery workshop makes wood machinery sounds. Cut wood smell from open blue faded double doors. A window, the inside sawdust on the glazing bars. A brown version Dickensian snowed Christmas card.

Mini roundabouts signed to hidden one road villages, glimpses of the Golfe du Morbihan secret silent marsh reed creeks. Still water fingers of the Golfe hold apart fields. A final view across the island peppered expanse of water after St-Armel. Junction directions for Muzillac and La Roche Bernard. Arterial D20 inland wandering. It is difficult to follow a coastal route, the land so convoluted. Single road villages, river and creek watery barrier isolation. Communication faster by boat.

The road for Muzillac. Long straight, climbs subtle, descents hardly noticeable. Steady pace long distance pushes rhythm. Many kilometres fair exchange to the little coastal and rural villages missed. Long low climb into town. Supermarket stop. Coloured tin shed 'Bricolage land', under concrete carrying Route National. Roundabout delivers pretty sleepy town of granite cobble, red bloom and white wall sparkle. Closed for the afternoon. Flat road, building dwindle. Jammed in rusty corrugated iron patchwork fence repairs keep fussing chickens from escaping to the road through holey rusted fencing wire. Dropping through rolling field sweep. Shaded woodland stop under a great gnarled pine trunk flaking grey pink bark.

Winding road flanked wild yellow red bloom. Cereal crop sway waves rolling into dark green woodland. In the half hour I have stopped, the only passing traffic, a couple of cars and an old open blue 'Ford 200' tractor puffing vertical smoke trundling up the hill in engine note waver big tyre bounce.

Sweeping freewheel bends, the woodland canopy, isolated houses peep from the green. Uphill payback birdsong serenade, rising quiet village street. Three retired ladies walk up the hill, long dresses, large summer hats. 'Bonjours' with smiles. Two men work a fenced smallholding. One turns the ground part wrestling the handles of a smoking blue wheezing petrol rusty rotovator looking soon to turn its last. The other bent over plants lines of seeds next to growing rows of vegetables. The top of the hill. D774 points La Roche Bernard.

Metallic suspension bridge in tension spans 50m (150ft) above deep river anchored to far side grey cliff. Bright blue cable tethered sweep from skyward towers, road flexes under vehicle weight. Below, neat lined yachts follow wide river bend. Town roofs fall to deep waters edge. Upstream, single span arched concrete carries the metallic Route National flash.

La Roche Bernard leaves behind Bretagne for Loire Atlantique. An area taken from Bretagne by moving a line on the map and seeing the graffiti, some of the locals are not happy about stealing them away from Celtic identity.

A 50ft wooden trawler sits on a roundabout. Facing no

more storms or battering waves marooned on a sea of gravel surrounded in flowers. Roundabouts display old navigation buoys, painted bright colours name danger. An old set of sluice gates and a mockup lock keeper's cottage amongst flowerbeds lead through more boat roundabout decoration.

Roadside compounds brim with marine craft, lined yachts for sale on a maritime garage forecourt, polyester resin permeates the air. Behind chainlink, units build weekend fishing boats and big white cruisers formed in giant wax primed jellymoulds. Lines of empty hull sailing boats wait for completion.

Small town and village adverts proclaim why their heritage must be visited in a tempting diversion. A pair of thatched roadside cottages as if in Devon, England. They are in a state of near dilapidation, covered in years of road dirt. Grimed gloomy windows peel paint, thatch rots to green. Corner junction for the wild reed marsh wetland expanse of La Grande Briére disappears through trees. Fields shaded, meadow of lone ancient trees hold many horses. Close groups, the paired groom each other's manes in tail swish. Some stand motionless, staring at nothing in yellowing light of late afternoon.

Guérande old round windmill tower. Roundabout roads, human density swells traffic, people finish college. The evening commute masses leaving work. I fight for my space against bumper to bumper cars, campervans and trucks. Everybody in a hurry to get somewhere at the expense of everybody else, cars do not stop for pedestrians at crossings, run or be run down. Too many rats in the cage, attempts to stuff me into the kerb. Pacing the traffic, swept onto a merry go round maddened roundabout mutating to dual carriageway. Kamikaze traffic speed, pushing the pedals top gear. The edge white line dodging glass, wire and bolts fallen from the underside of vehicles. Ahead the exit from bedlam signed La Baule centre. It is looking like a city. I prepare for a pushed and bullied battle on two skinny wheels. The feeding roundabouts busy, I take my turn and do not give in to anyone.

Traffic calmed streets of modern glass frontage, polished stone pavement people busy. Tree lined brick paved roads. I stop in the centre. Big glass frontage. 'Maison du Tourisme.'

I wait to dry from the efforts of riding before walking in. I hold the door for two ladies.

"Merci Monsieur" waiting for my two second belated reply as I am trying to remember the formality muttering. "Je vous en prie, mes Dammes."

They look very pleased, whatever the true context of the sentence is. It is polite. I do not see any information on St. Marc and think what to say at the counter. The place people busy. I wait my turn.

"Bonjour Madame. Vous avez information pour les campings en St Marc-sur mer. Si vous plait?"

I am looked at for one second before a reply "Moment Monsieur."

I am not sure if I have got it right and while she is consulting with her colleague, I repeat over in my head what I had asked for. The two of them look on a desk, stare at me for one second and then both disappear behind one of many large wood doors into a walk in cupboard. They both appear and come to the counter together with brochures on cycle ways, La Baule and St Marc-sur-mer. One leaves to attend another customer while I am shown direction on the map from here, places ringed with a ballpoint pen, fussed over and given the address of a campsite just outside St. Marc called Fort de l'Eve. All this for free, all with genuine help and concern.

"Merci Madame."

She smiles and bids me goodbye, attending to the next person.

Slow ride evil speed bumps. The backside rattle keeps all traffic at walking pace. Pristine shops, people mass peacock strut, sunglasses. Smart casual emits fake cosmopolitan importance. Traffic lights, La Baule promenade panorama. Sea front white sand, shallow water sun sparkle over the blue, promenade railing shine miles each way along a wide curving bay watched by low rocky headland. Loiré Atlantique Riviéra. The smell of credit card lifestyles mixes cheap perfume and spray tan. Fine 19th century residence views swallowed by modern high rise concrete shapes. One shaped like a galleon, the square and the curved balcony overload boxed idealistic dream. Or a ten storey claustrophobic suffocating nightmare with beach access across the road. The whole town a grid plan joining many roads to the seafront, each with traffic light control. Pedestrian crossings from polished pavement to polished pavement between tall tended flower planters cycling a stop start cruise along Le Sunset Strip. The flip side is it's a perfect place to retire. All shops are nearby, the whole place flat, modern apartments give wonderful sea views without property maintenance worry. The day and evening promenade walks to café time post swim. It becomes very attractive. The developers have sold a dream.

Traffic light conversation with a man on a commuting bike, asking where I am from whilst waiting for the red change to green. A retired lady steps a foot on the crossing. I stop. A car speeds through, top down stereo boom not bothering to slow. Eyebrows raise. A roadrider on the opposite carriageway in all the latest expensive Lycra race colours with sunglasses, the serious frown and a very expensive bike. He has not been far, face devoid of expelled effort, no sweat stinging eyes or shiny facial glaze, no wet clothing toil and there will not be any. He is the same as the portly males dressed in the latest surfing clothes on the beach safely gazing out to sea waiting for summer waves that will never arrive. Lines of blocking sandbars far out to sea keep the wave a mile out sucking the power before reaching the shore. Its daily playtime for the happy poseurs of La Baule.

The end of the promenade. Colouful boats in the water, an offshore boulder harbour marina thousand mast sun breeze glint. Old town roundabout, gentle weave uphill amongst white painted house walls irregular old, late afternoon distorted shadow long across the tarmac. A cat sits in the sun, eyes closed, blissfully swaying to the point of sleeping sat upright. It's ears twitch, listening to everything happening around. It does not move its head or open an eye because it contently owns this neighbourhood.

The road to St. Margeurite. Detached grand houses set amongst old trees and pines. Entrance high pillared. Closed gateways too high to see over in absolute quiet privacy. This is what its adolescent fake gold plated neighbour aspires to. But will never achieve. A mind image of heyday. Long car bonnets of deep colour, brass and chrome over running boards. It is the 1920s. Chauffeured well dressed ladies, furs, hats and fashion fussing over some small groomed toy dog.

Between the boundary walls, walkway sounds of a choppy

sea blown against rock reef, the smell of seaweed mixes windblown with saltwater freshness. I ride past a huge house, a mansion of long time closed shutters fading paint, missing tiles from elegant roof sweep, rusting gutters grow long grass of decade emptiness. Abandonment. A few houses along, new apartments in concrete grow under a tower crane. Maybe it is death by concrete for the mansion. It would be a shame to lose this area, the architecture tells of the Great War and post Great War prosperity. Splendid houses from an era, of whose architecture will never be seen again.

Suburban seaside grandeur ends dropping steep to be faced with a climb. A bus stop map for a clue to how far to St. Marc.' Freewheeling bends, a little town of detached residence long garden shade. A sign 'St. Marc-sur-mer.' Artistic in impression of a beach, a surfboard and the silhouette of the comic film character. Monsieur Hulot. A passing glance at the sand covered road to the beach, a suburban climb looking for the campsite. Two hills, a large campsite opposite a complex of Second World War bunkers. 5.50pm the Accueil shuts at six. I pay the young student running the office double paid elsewhere. But it is the only game in town. I have a 'smilinghappycamperland' to myself. I am told I have to wear a band on my wrist to prove I am staying here, even though I am the only person resident. He is the only member of staff, and is about to go home.

It becomes a cold blustery evening, rain patter gives an excuse to go to bed. I hope tomorrow is fine as it has been a long wait to be here at St. Marc-sur-mer, the mouth of La Loiré. The great wild river of France.

101 km

The sound of arriving lorries at 7am. The drone of heavy goods passes close halting in groan. I hear tools and machinery dragged across the metal bed of a tipper truck, then the noise of a diesel compressor revving. I know what will follow and soon hear a jack hammer breaking up tarmac rattling through the ground. I could do with an alarm call, but something a little softer without the vibration. Not even the student could have thought of such a prank.

Empty 'smilinghappycamperland' occupants are mostly on the end of a shovel, which is something long term to avoid. I have a wash, shave, fill up my waterbottles, sauntering through a greasy cloud of diesel exhaust fumes, courtesy of the battered trailered shuddering nervous compressor. Tea is on the boil accompanied with a baguette washed down with more tea. In reasonable clothes I escape the din, walking down the mile to St. Marc-sur-mer plage. The stage for a famous comedy film. 'Les Vacances d M. Hulot.' By Jacques Tati. In which the character of Hulot causes general visual comic mayhem to the holidaying cast of the film based around the 'Hotel de la Plage.' The first of four films created for the hapless, accident prone satirical comic character of Hulot.

Walking down to St Marc,' I see many similarities to its grand neighbour of St. Marguerite. Fine houses, calm and quiet atmosphere, longtime an area of desirable residence. Narrow road shops lead to the Hotel de la Plage onto a sandy beach renamed 'Le Plage de M. Hulot.'

The 'Otel' is not 'O-pen.' Entrance steps chained. The hotel much used in the film. Beach views, a small stone breakwater, across the sea a horizon lighthouse on a distant reef. The scenic Point de Chémoulin, the film set for Hulot to somehow set light to a shed full of fireworks. Giving an impromptu display in the nighttime early hours bombarding the occupants of the hotel, waking everybody as he manages to do in different ways every night of his stay.

A statue of Hulot stands adjacent to a seating area. He is looking over the beach in perfect character stance leaning forward. Hands on back of hips, elbows angular, hat tipped forwards on his head and trademark long pipe coming from his mouth, unfortunately broken, now smoking a skinny 'roll up.'

Underneath, a man dressed in white waiter's jacket with a bow tie and black trousers is finishing sweeping the daily sand from the timber walkway restaurant entrance.

I ask if the restaurant is open for 'café?' Standing in front of him in a pair of shorts and casual shirt.

Yes it is. I am welcomed to a frightening sight of rows of white clothed silver laid tables, each having crystal wineglasses each side of fresh cut red roses placed in a tall glass vase. I am shown to a relaxed area of sofas for morning coffee.

People arrive for lunch greeted at the door, shown to the table with fuss and care in a very formal polite and pleasant way. I escape as the place fills. Smart suits, summer dresses to enjoy fine gastronomic fayre with a background hum of conversation.

My lunch plucked from a dim chiller shelf. Out of the dinge uphill saunter, shrink wrapped cake, apples and semi decomposing bananas even flies avoid.

The tent now marooned on its grassy island surrounded by steaming new laid tarmac. Lunch with aromatic boiled bitumen garnished with diesel exhaust. Road patching continues, an excuse to go back down to La Poste to send cards. The man behind the counter tells me the cost and I give the right money. Quite surprised, he says a rough translation of. "Not bad for the English!"

Walking back up the hill, an entrance to a large subterranean Second World War bunker below road level is someone's garden with a house on top. The gates to Fort de l'Eve bunkers are open. I wander in to a massive structure of reinforced concrete built into the cliff. One even has a false gable end with a chimney built to disguise it as a house. The feeling is of sombre unpleasantness defending the entrance to La Loiré and the shipyards of St. Nazaire. The campsite connected by tunnel under the road to a beach. Late afternoon is spent amongst the plant machinery serenaded by road repairs.

Evening campsite emptiness. Solitary lighthouse 'Grand Charpentier' comes to life distant under approaching night veil.

Loire and Cher

The tarmac gang have arrived further away, replaced by a loud diesel concrete laden rusted dumper truck crawling its way chug chugging down the site in smoking wheeze. Campsite, building site. Take your choice it is all the same today here early season at Fort de l'Eve.

Coming back from the 'sanitaires' a bike is leant against a tree. A touring bike bears the words 'DAWES Galaxy.'

"Bonjour." To the owner starting to pack.

"Dawes est le velo de l' Anglais." My cobbled together sentence.

"Par leevoo Inglais?" Is the reply from a student looking blank at me.

"Nice bike" My reply.

He has ridden back from Barcelona following canal paths to Bordeaux coming up the coast to get back to Cherbourg for the Portsmouth ferry, booked for tomorrow. 'Bonne chance! Monsieur.' That's a lot of Km to make under the pressure of time.

Directions through St. Nazaire to the Maison du Tourisme are given by the student host. Freewheeling to a seafront promenade of wide areas paved, gardens and trees spacious follow the seawall. Two war memorial stone pillars in the sea. One for liberation twice, detailing loss of life both times in both wars. A great bronze bird in flight carries a soldier on its back. The other is for the courageous Commando raid on the dry dock of the Second World War. Separate displayed is the gun from the English warship. The dock area and half the town are dominated by the huge concrete U boat pens. I spend a while looking up at them. Monstrous sad intrusions found at Brest, Lorient, Bordeaux, St. Nazaire and no doubt other ports. This is the first Sous Marine I have seen. Direction to the structure easy, towering over the waterside. Huge heavy built sombre concrete, long tunnel narrowed seaward entrance contains a rectangular dock. Interior cold dark, dim shadow natural light. Overhead netting catches falling concrete and rust from rotting heavy steel convoluted formwork over which many tonnes of concrete were poured to give an impenetrable mass.

The Maison du Tourisme glass fronted single storey building sits inside one of the vast pens dispensing information on the Loire a velo cycle route. I am given a sketchy leaflet detailing the route and am told I will first have to cross the huge bridge that spans La Loire.

It is higher than the tallest of ships allowing their passage unhindered up to and from upstream docklands.

I also ask about the attack on the dry shipbuilding dock by the Commandos.

I am told it is possible to view it from up on the roof the Sous Marine pens.

From the dismal concrete hole the warm bathe of sunlight. Long ramp to the rooftop, strange concrete shapes deflect the blast from air bombardment. Saturated by heavy bombs in an attempt to destroy the structure in daylight air raids by the Americans. The surrounding area pulverised to dust, the structure so over engineered, designed impenetrable still stands. 480,000m3 (x by 2.2 to give the tonnage) of concrete poured in its slave labour construction took nearly two years to complete. A retired submarine moored inside one of the pens is open to visit.

There are pictures of the young crews on the U Boats standing to attention and relaxed informal pictures showing them as just boys, their faces so young they look like they should still be in school. 30,000 men went to sea in the submarines, the terrible fate for just about all of them, to end up at the bottom of the Atlantic Ocean sealed up suffocated crushed in the remains of sunken U Boats.

A Tribute to the famous Commando dry dock raid at St. Nazaire recounts the suicide dock raid by ramming an old World War One ship, the Campbletown packed full of explosives into the dry dock gates. Many died, smaller boats landed to attack defences, boats landed full of Commandos, boats were hit and burning in the river in the attempt to protect passage of the bomb laden ship. Commandos leapt onto the dock to attack the defences. The story of a genade landing at the attackers feet to be kicked back amongst the Germans defenders who threw it. Eventually all were surrounded and captured before the ship blew up putting the dock out of action for the duration of the war. Having to pass under the armed mass of Fort de l'Eve must have been beyond terror. Rough translation into English of the tribute.

On the 28th March 1942
The port was neutralised in a decisive event of the battle of the Atlantic. An incredible exploit by Britain offered the first victory for the Allies that gave back hope. In reprisals, the occupants razed the old town.

With the cryptic information on how to leave St. Nazaire I make for the huge high bridge spanning La Loire.

Elbowing through traffic, straight road behind dock rail lines and fencing. Ship bows tower over buildings. Signs to Nantes looking for 'St. Brevin' to cross the bridge. A cycle lane, parked cars, alleyway broken bottles. Busy road, the click of an opening car door across my path mimmics a gun being cocked. A swerve dodges getting hit by a following car. Cycle lane leads to Route National. Misread direction to a sign gantry 'St. Brevin.' Bike sign under Route National sends me in opposite needed direction.

No more time wasting cryptic cycle paths, I get on the hard shoulder of the Route National for one junction and head at speed for the bridge hoping not to meet the police. Road slows Route National becomes D route bridge approach, cycle sign appears. The climb, sixty metres (180ft) between towers holding deck cables. It is beautiful artistically engineered viewed in full size appreciation on approach. A sign says I am under video surveillance. 'Sourir.'

Lorries, buses and cars race the bridge, accelerator floored engine scream, exhaust fume spiral, wheels of speed at elbows length. A sign 'No Stopping.' I don't intend to. Panoramic St. Nazaire. The river mouth, Port, Sous Marine pens and two new huge steel cruise ships of pale yellow rust. Twenty storeys high grow under blue spot arcs and spark cascade. All dwarfed by the bridge towers of red and white joining cables to the sky. New lands south swallowed blue in haze. Across the bridge the great wild river of La Loire disappears into soft horizon. Riverbank industry port lined with gantries and cranes unload the biggest cargo ships appearing at height as toys in a bath. Distant flaming petrol chemi candles of refinery amongst spacecraft gas terminals landed amongst giant metallic cubed tanks. Dockside fade, sulphurous industrial haze.

Nearside lane closed for four wheels, not for two. Carriageway freewheel view. The coast to St. Marc-sur-mer, headland silhouette, faraway lighthouse. Au revoir Monsieur Hulot!

Bottom of the bridge, Paimboeuf arrow exchanges traffic mayhem surveillance for quiet country amble.

The granite gold rolling rugged land of Bretagne has gone. La Loire sleepy soft growing countryside is kept apart by an oozing watery giant. Signs point 'Le Pellerin.'

Lazy freewheel zig zag, sun shaded deserted back streets of white painted houses, summer blue window shutters frame ornamented window vased flowers under patterned lace. Waterfront quayside, queued cars wait silent for the ferry arrival.

The river half the estuary width of St. Nazaire is still a thoroughfare for shipping. Tower cranes, big floating work platforms, a large boatlift. Upstream tall river lighthouse guards an island. Riverbank life slower than industrial buzz of St. Nazaire.

Modern white and grey painted ferry 'Lola' arrives. Name from a piece of famous French cinema, so the signboard informs. Powerful engines cope with strong flowing tidal current passing in whirlpool swirl to meet the sea. Hydraulic ramp drops to the slipway free of charge. Le Port Launay totals a bus stop and a few silent houses surrounded by trees. I watch the ferry load and leave, motoring the sparkle half spun by the strong current. Bow bites into the flow returning to Le Pellerin's quayside of red roofed mulicoloured house frontages huddled collective in window stare across the river.

Everybody gone, silent country cycle, the rooftops of Coueron. Grand nineteenth century houses of cut stone. Long window decorative ironwork, ornate roofs steep, slated square towers. Riverside park cycle path. Red brick abandonment, tall industry silent, brick chimneys lean cracked, split tops fallen. Across the tidal current a wooded riverbank, a fake sunken house sits for amusement amongst reeds. D107 signed Nantes. Through St. Herblain 4.30pm. I should be looking for a campsite, determined to get through Nantes. Hopefully something the other side of the city. I have no idea how big or complicated Nantes will be, or how many kilometres are left in the day's journey.

St. Herblain railway tracks to industry. The back end of Nantes. Industrial riverside behind walls. Fences spiked rusting tops coiled in barbed wire. Ground pounded under the heavy feet of industry for decades, worn earth left sterile. Plant growth relegated to neglected spoil. Nature has a hard time against scrap mountain's large caterpillar tracked cranes towering above ship bow and leviathan haulage. Landfill odour permeates.

High fenced dead end spaghetti rail tracks, graffitied wagons tethered in rows wait in dirtied sidings. Sign points

'Le coeur de Nantes.' 'The heart.' Not before witnessing a huge high bridge held on long rectangular concrete pillars taking the Route National high over La Loire. The deck of the bridge steel painted dark red in a curving arc hard against blue sky.

I stop underneath the great concrete structure for a drink before the impending journey through city traffic. The underside of the road so high does not intimidate overhead space, as disconnected with the ground as a passing aeroplane. My eyes follow the concrete column down to eye level, within a hands touch in front of me a poster of a missing girl. The details under her picture say she was last seen in March. The poster is peeling from the wall, starting to fade as if she is fading away as yesterday's news. Next to the girl 'NO AIRPORT' rally advertised to galvanise a protest at the 'outrage' of more aviation. I look again at the missing girl, her forgotten eyes are looking at me slowly fading trapped inside the decaying poster unable to be reached. It gives a shiver of unpleasantness. I hope she just decided to get the hell out from the steel scrap heaps, rail goods yards with a maze of spaghetti tracks all leading claustrophobic to a dead end. This dead end part of France. I hope she escaped it and her life is better.

Flyover shadow, pothole dodge, high steel roadside fences keep me in, or out. Cranes that could lift a church, silent motionless. Huge grab buckets sit waiting for cables to drop them into the rusting guts of ships. I pedal around broken bottles dodge sharp metal. Gravel and grime mixes with industrial smell from a flaming chimney. Massive silo complex old grey green weathered concrete, broken dirty windows one hundred foot rusting frames carry conveyors, convoluted pipes suspended to somewhere. Big darkening shadows fall from industrial structure. Brightness of graffitied walls and rail wagons. In a layby, parked cars of youth. The occupants leaning on the bonnet or sat inside with doors open, feet up on the open window, stereo booming, sunglasses, attitude. It is their moment, their turn to think they are 'IT.' The day for them is coming when they will find themselves sucked in, trapped and used up by tricks of the system, to toil inside the dark industrial surroundings, to be spat out as old men broken bodied, no longer useful no longer wanted. May they savour and enjoy their 'IT' moment, because it does not last, not for any of us.

The approach into the city. Blocks of tenement flats over kebab shops, multi cultured épiceries, dingy window cafés. A one way system around an iron railinged park echo's lost nineteenth century. Cityscape opens modern to river promenade, lanes of traffic endlessly join from the left. I have to use the appeared cycle lane. I keep the river in view to the right. As long as I can stay by the river I should not become lost amongst the many one way system junctions and traffic lights. Through heavy rush hour traffic riding slow. Bumper to bumper, road lanes cross tram lines, split cycle lane of three directions, traffic island crowds of pedestrians cross on light signal. Everyone is going home. The traffic tries to force me over a bridge across the river, battling into the centre stopping on a wide paved island surrounded by blurred vehicle whirl. I am looking around for possibilities of where I can go. Everybody knows where they are going except me. 'NANTES EST.' East goes up river.

I would like to spend time amongst the gracious buildings, appreciate the fine architecture of the city and maybe visit the large Cathedral, but not in rush hour with an itinerary of finding somewhere to stay out the other side of the city within the next hour or two. Obligatory cycle lane, slow speed road away from the river separated from my guide. Over a pavement, cobbled street, around a harbour tranquil with colourful boats, hanging flags, shining brass. Wooden masts and painted funnels opposite overhanging striped awnings of cafés and bars. Traffic noise replaced by people sound, eating, meeting with a social drink finishing the day of work under parasol shade. Roasting coffee beans blow sweet aromatic smoke, a slope rejoins traffic over and around the harbour heading back to the river, going east. I follow a suited office worker on an electric bike effortlessly propelling himself along, he disappears taking a junction. Compulsory cycle lane under a road through a tunnel into daylight, depositing on the edge of the river separated from the road. Rough path, alcoholic smashed bottles, carrier bag discarded cans, mud path sharp edged stones. Misread direction grinds to a bumpy halt just managing to keep heavy bike balance. Crossbar shuffle, legs either side fight a steep stony slope return to busy roadside. Towerblock living watches my comedic bike antics.

Signed out of town retail heaven directs traffic to Route National. 'Loire a velo' sign points to follow smooth tarmac alongside the peaceful riverbank. Speeding engine buzz replaced by birdsong and the lapping of water against the grassy edged bank. All my pre conceived imagined ideals of journeying along La Loire realise in the moment, complete in original thought naivety. The quiet traffic free route along the edge of a big flowing river, blue sky and birdsong, overhanging trees reach down to touch the river with leafy fingers. Trailing branches hide ducks swimming away vocally muttering ingratitude's of disturbance looking back with an indignant eye. Tree shadows lengthen with increasing hours, sunlight turns orange yellow of early evening.

A line of bollards stop vehicles entering the travelled way, a change to muddy path through overgrown bush and trees. Chain-link fencing, barking snarling dogs, shacks, caravans, dismembered washing machines, stripped out cars rammed full of scrap metal. Shotgun shacks, fishing boat hull, vans, smart caravans, chalets, on a ride through 'Banjo country.'

Pathway to meadow grass amongst broken woodland, watery glimpse. River sounds. A row of houses, people out stroll in conversation, runners, people cycling. Riverside woodland. Sign directs. 'CAMPING BELLE RIVIÉRE' St. Luce sur Loire.

Leafy lane side gate opens. I am not sure if I have accidently strayed into someone's garden. Grass kept as lawn, manicured hedge. The cabin Accueil open. I wait. Presently a well dressed lady of years and impeccable formality appears, smiling asking if I wish to stay. I tell her just for one night.

As I have arrived by bike I am told to sit down while an aperitif of chilled local fruited wine of my choice decants from a jug and is bought to me, complimentary. I am asked of my journey and recount my rush hour experience of Nantes, the best I can with my limited vocabulary. Much to the sympathetic amusement of the gracious lady. I fill in the forms while my glass is replenished. I offer to purchase a drink from the little bar to return the politeness. Hospitality is solely for her administration. The cost for one nights camping is very reasonable, the welcome given worth a thousand Euros.

95 km

* * *

First the cuckoo, then a cockerel signals every bird to make as much noise as possible. A donkey does not want to be left out joining whole hearted in serenade accompaniment of a nearby cow. It's 5.30am. A wind arrives, woodland amplifies breeze rush. Arriving rain patters the tent nylon postponing an early start. Unhurried packing forms rough routine. Thanks to the Patron. Through the gate, a parting wave.

No road, no traffic, no people. Meadow pathway, ancient wild marsh pollarded willow, the growing twisted tree. Green world tranquility, quiet riverside road points to Mauves-sur-Loire. 'Loire a velo' sign crossing the ironwork span, river wide, signs point to farm tracks weaving. Lone jogger burns patisserie guilt. Near distance rides a lady on a large brown horse in plod half asleep. They turn to follow wild hedgerow through waving grass, amble toward rooftops tree obscured.

First view of a Loire chateau. Square slated tower central, round towers end a façade. Each wear a conical slated witch hat.

Track ends, the road to Champtoceaux, a first climb since the bridge at St. Nazaire. Vineyards advertise the growing Muscadet vine at La Varenne. Views to the river Island 'Ile Moron.' One bank of the river flat land the other hills and cliff face. Views never the same, woodland road twist, village rooftops above, sandy riverside fields sprout crops below. Wheeled gantries creep sandy planted furrow. Smooth river tree green reflection, patchwork agriculture woodland skyline.

A cyclist has stopped. Puncture. The man in his sixties plus wears full roadracer clothing riding the latest carbon fibre machine not so thoroughbred laid in the bushes back end missing. "Creve Monsieur?"

"Oui, creve."

Puncture is fixed and the wheel replaced.

"Au revoir."

Champtoceaux. Walled fortress large squat brown stone towers guard an arched gateway. Arrow slits, plastic double glazed windows above. At the top of the wall openings big enough for holding many defenders shooting and pouring unpleasantness upon attackers.

Rain shower wet tarmac shine along empty one way street. Twelve o'clock. A population gone to ground. 'Midi'. Wooded hill freewheel under dripping tree overhang. Steep rocky drop corkscrew bends holds the smell of wet road. Flatland ride, river inlet giant pond.

Across the river to Ancenis. Bridge view the full width of La Loire. Current swirl boils grey, silent liquid movement pulls twenty four hours at stone bridge pillars. Downstream defiant tree covered islands split the river to channels. One channel for navigation, the other has stone piled weirs directing flow when water is low and doubling as an overflowing weir to slow winter flood.

Ancenis rises across a hill closed to traffic for the colourful weekly pannier market. Busy stalls, smoke curl enticing cooking smells drift over inaudible crowd hum, shouting touting traders, customers busy paw at the goods. The further up the narrowing hill the denser the crowd jumble. A moment absorbing the atmosphere leaving the noise of the people gathering to fade returning to the river. A small yard, sheltered riverbank slope home of many Loire river craft. A tubby steel sailing boat with a dented hull moored close to the shore. It has a short mast on a pivot that can be lowered by an antiquarian greased cogs for bridge navigation. The hull painted black, a white stripe around the deck over a porthole eye. The whole thing held together by large dome rivets gives the appearance and finesse of an iron boiler converted for pleasure.

Bridge crosses a tributary feeding La Loire, the cycle route back across the river. Road ride climbs boring featureless farmland, grey dotted industrial buildings rise. Drizzle fade, sun teased by lifting cloud, cold breeze drops. The river sparkle lures, down to a bridge crossing to the rooftops and spire of St. Florent-le-vieil. Loire a velo sign points to a narrow road along the river levee protection. Low lying wet farmland, wild tree livestock shade. Houses of isolation. Clouds travel inland in favour, but a wind blows down river headwind chill.

Static donkeys and a munching goat tethered to a long chain, green marsh meadow, ancient scarred pollarded willow. Straight road long distance, traffic calming twists keep drivers attentive to stop a racetrack rolling plummet from the steep levee. Many people cycle opposite direction, propelled by the wind hardly needing a turn of the pedal. I am on the drop bars ducking headwind.

Inland flood water smother, submerged growing green drowns in stillness turning dying yellow under dark marsh flood. Scoured roots reach deep along the flowing river edge. Mistletoe clump grown thick rustles leaves on bare branches of its host.

Wide pale orange sand banks, riverside town Le Fresne-sur-Loire. Tall stone spire, high wall protection. Mansion of stone boasts riverfront garden pruned perfection. Adjacent jumble riverfront houses fight for a view.

The river a wide mass of constant moving water. Attempts to control the flow to stop erosion by rock barrage and blackened wood groins. Wooded islands hide full river width.

Montjean-sur-Loire house quayside wanders to sheltering woodland breaking up the headwind. Old farms, narrow road steel bridge deck of wood to an island. 'La Basse Ile.' Big enough for farms and hamlets. Low pitched red tiled roofs, shuttered windows, walls of pale colour. Steps rise to high living, design practicalities in readiness for winter underwater. Bloomed colour, planted tubs of visual pleasure. Woodland shelter, open field headwind forces a low gear crawl. Sheltered cove under branch shade is home to many river punts. Flat bottoms, flat bows, straight sides, wood tarred. Square fishing boats, booms and steel winches, old sailing boats tubby. Lateral rudders oversize win control over the current.

Island escape by suspension bridge. Charlonnes -sur-Loire centuries old. Dominant church over jumble roofs tumble the hill. Houses built on the river, waterfront steps to the back door, tethered boats patient below.

Crack of thunder, heavy rain. Shelter hurriedly joined by others cramming under a canopy roof waiting for the shower end. Laughter shared about the soaking. Sunshine kills the cold blowing wind.

Route points across two bridge span crossing the wide river and its islands. D210 lane follows riverbank flood defence shelter protecting houses and lush countryside roll. Idyllic large woodland ponds hold small islands, tall trees squeeze a place to grow. Two swans, white arced wings framed by green disc lily pads in mirrored calm. Patient fishermen motionless under a large green umbrella, bodies hunched forward in attentive gaze to the florescent float. Riverside route changes to a path alongside sandy beach reed rustle under overhanging oak.

Purposeful rivercraft pulled dry beyond the grab of flowing current. A waterside bar fronts an empty municipal campsite.

It costs next to nothing for the night's accommodation. I spend a while talking to Oliviér over a beer. He has a sharp sense of humour. We talk in French/English with language correction. The barmaid joins in, she is Polish, making a three way language conversation.

The more beer Oliviér has the more he talks putting across a free spirit persona without care or ties, but underneath he has many worries for France. He doesn't know where France is going. What will happen with the economy, the euro and the world?

I am told to come back here in the autumn to watch the river reflect yellow orange and deep red under yellow autumn sun. His favourite season for a loved Loire.

I escape to pitch the tent and eat. The showers locked. Back to the bar to get the key without getting dragged back into the drinking. The crowded bar bounces with loud music. Making money out of the bar may have priority to the running of the campsite tonight. I get the feeling possibly every night.

Showers work on the principal of wash before you use, not after, the same for the 'Bac a vassille,' the sink for dishes. Judged by the left behind food scraps of considerable age. Daily chores, bed. Bass drum and brass music beat is excellent for drinking, but not so for sleeping. I eventually nod off waking around midnight to the metallic sounds of chains banging, metal squealing and clanking of rumbling goods train vibrating the ground plodding along the back of the campsite.

Music stops. Car door slam, engines leave. Silence. Solitary night song, a bird. I guess it is the nightingale, I would not

know. Many notes, unending in sweet melodic serenade.
91 km

Company in the peace of new morning. A tent has appeared, two mountain bikes with panniers lean against a tree. The ground silvered wet in dew, low rising sun mist veiled pales all colour to an atmospheric wash. Black hulled square fronted sailing punts, thick wood masts suspended over the watery mirror. River island floats in haze, a morning without horizon. The only movement the unending smooth current swirl boil in silence.

Cuckoo hoot repetitive, jay squawk. Blackbird alarm and panic. A sparrowhawk appears from inside the leaf cover of a tree, facial fearless menace stares deep for one second, launching with a small fluffy bundle gripped immovable in strong claws chased futile by a mob of shrieking blackbirds. The balance of nature. One loss feeds another's existence. We all eat and are eaten. Wise observational words from three thousand years ago. Easy words for the eaters.

Breeze dissipates mist revealing broken cloud, short moments of sun soft warm the skin in contrast of early morning chill. I pack, exchanging sentences with the travelling couple folding their tent. Breeze increase promises a day of headwind.

The mobile home of closed curtains houses the alcohol pickled. Not a movement or sound from the night revelers yet to surface from the flower decorated outside walls of accommodation brighter than the interior snoring occupants. Au revoir Sirens of La Loire. There will be no sweet song emitting from within caravan walls, no need to be tied to the mast, no luring to Loire rocks. La Poissonniére. The feelgood campsite with the ambience of a Sunday morning student house.

Signs direct under dripping railway tunnel climbing narrow village street. Melancholic lone church bell reverberates the air between strikes to the brass. A town official stops all vehicles directing different route. He tells me "cinq minute." I must wait because a funeral is taking place. Smart dressed people quietly appear, the village fills the church, a mood of hushed respect. I wait next to the official and ask how old the person was. "Quatre-vignt-dix ans." Ninety.

"Bien age." Both nodding in agreement.

When all are inside the church I am told it is alright to go, leaving with an exchange goodbye. The organ resonates through open heavy black doors. Narrow lanes under house gaze weave. Habitation replaced by parallel vine lines to an open skyline, field rolls below into deep shadow shelter. All pedalled height is lost, under rail line drip reuniting the riverside along a bumpy potholed track. Cyclists in opposite direction loaded and rattling. Stone ping rattles the mudguards.

Climbing wild countryside, overhanging trees keep the bubbling sound of running water in leaf covered secret. A narrow field, two goats chained look over a fence bleating. Tortured souls jog the steepened hill slow. All the movements of the jog lack forward motion. Backs show patches of wet exertion, faces red and glazed, slaves to the patisserie. Toiling in calorific sin, purging taste bud pleasure.

Mary and Jesus held behind bars gaze across a running trough growing slow spinning lily pads. Vine row neatness, high brick bared by fallen render. Hill drop to village immaculate. Restored houses finely decorated paved in cobbles, thick wood doors drown under basket flowering bloom. Narrow lane houses with river access, a feeling of selective wealth in the air. Desirable residence, commutable from the city of Angers.

River edge ride, beautiful parkland, a path flanked each side with trees form a leaf canopy, straight line illuminated tunnel of green. Behind the trees river water lap, the other side fields and farms distance across open flat land. Miles of bumpy woodland track, large lakes given to watersports. The eternal static optimists, seated fishermen perched attentive in mimic of an unwelcomed Heron adversary.

The city of Angers. Concrete waterfront ride. Loire a velo replaced with a green bike sign to who knows where. I have lost route direction in the park miles back. Lured false by the tree tunnel ride.

Boulangerie stop buys warm bread and cake sweetness, fresh, smelling good. Cold wind blows. Mentioned by a passerby, shoulders up and tense, hands deep in pockets of winter coat. I am in agreement. Oven heated bread warms cold fingers.

The city beautiful. Opposite a huge fort massive walled, great round towers protect a chateau palace immense, lost inside a fortified mass. The towers once higher, decapitation was ordered by the king, being bigger than his. Great spiked spire ornate over fortified castellation, river flow shadowed beneath.

Converted steel barges moored to a pontoon walkway. Tubby craft painted bright, potted deck flowers under varnished wood. Lace curtained window, homely stove pipe through an extended roof once a cargo hold makes alternative city living.

Fine carved stone, ornate arch bridges, many buses amongst

the bumper to bumper busy buzz rumble commute.

A man sat in a punt quietly fishing anchored central to the channel. Paradox surreal sat in calm meditative pursuit. The city sprung grown to smother all wild riverbank, walling him in while absorbed in angling concentration.

Plane tree perfect lines shade long avenue cobbles rolling slow under the wheels. People saunter unhurried chatter. A toddler runs head forward clumsy and laughing in new found ability. Leaf roar cold wind bends high branches, the iron bollard dodge. Avenue traffic free. River edge ride, looking for a Loire a velo sign. Nothing. Opposite bank commerce holds all the main traffic routes. I should be over on the opposite bank. I ride a tributary to somewhere. Thoughts of a back track through the city to battle traffic are annulled.

Building shapes fade, sun flooded path of long wild shoulder high grass running the edge of wild riverbank turns to follow a quiet slow moving river creek narrowing to a stone's throw in width. The opposite riverbank a scene from 'Wind in the Willows.' Red mud bank holed for a home at water level, ancient tree root grip, gnarled trunk, thick overhanging bough leafed branches wait out time shading the bank of Île St. Aubin. Rowing boat ferry and a hand pulled flat vehicle pontoon tethered by a cable. I watch a car pulled across. A gentle pull starts momentum from the carried weight. Once under way only the smallest effort is required for the pontoon to cross. The ferry made fast on reaching the far bank and the vehicle drives away. Timeless romantic work of green bough reflection centuries old resists modern 'efficient' replacement buried grey municipal under cold concrete.

Broken lane turns to tarmac, junction, fast D road. Compass

direction ninety degrees wrong, needing a bridge east over the imposter returning to La Loire.

Flat, fast D road, compulsory cycle lane ends in roundabout spin. East crosses a river, a moment of self congratulation. Road numbers on the map do not correspond with numbers on the road. Map wise now blind. Compass informs the road goes far from La Loire direction. Advert for a supermarket to find out where I am is direction to nowhere. A maze of tiny unnamed 'commune' places. Crossroad ramble, miles of flat countryside, woodland planted identical grey trunks in perfect spaced grid. Slow moving streams amble fallow meadow, marsh pool, black water smother floats water lilies. Overhead wheel brown birds of prey, large triangular forked tail, long wings end in feathered fingers. The Red Kite glide soars high without energy.

Thoughts of. 'Where am I?'

Green countryside plod. Kestrel delicate flutter over lunch, before dropping on it. A big bird of prey glides fields. Black and dark brown outstretched straight wings, feathers end in long spaced fingers, the tail as the red kite. The smaller black kite. Narrowed wings distort size perspective.

Miles later the Sarthe river. A town. 'Briollay.' Afternoon people removed for dejeuner. Town closed. Crossroads names to places passed two hours ago. East ramble in flatland agricultural silence. Fluttering red poppy carpet, verge bright yellow oilseed crop escapees, pale blue nodding flower. Isolated grouped houses marooned in crop sway.

Seiches-sur-Loir rooftops crossing the River Loir. An oozing slow moving junior of its near namesake. People! Supermarket! Without reason the entrance and exit on different roads. I travel unknowingly back toward the city of Angers. In suspicion I stop. The compass and signs for places opposite in direction from destination confirm what has happened. Long slog of wasted effort held captive on busy arterial road gets busier nearing the city. Strong headwind riding the gutter, fast straight road ends marooned on Route National roundabout. Barred all signed direction. The only option a coloured unit industrial estate. Freewheeling weave, concrete, haulage bays, a little road with a terrace of old houses. An old lane. Old way will lead somewhere. Country lane swallowed by housing, across traffic blur noise main roundabout. 'SAMUR 50km.'

Fast busy road, pace quick, scenery boring. Ribbon development stuck between light industry and agricultural storage tin. Piled wreckage grows weeds, the metal rust of farming amongst nettles. Empty haulage in rattling hurry to end the working day, the evening speed commute. White line ride around glass and bolts, 45kmph constant eats the kilometres. Chateau gates, manicured entrance. Long avenue trees shade gravel driveway.

Smallville names fall, junction for La Ménitré earns five tired minutes respite. Quiet country road leaves arterial rampage. Slowing headwind, signed joy. Municipal campsite direction straight on, hoping it's open. Old rusting Ford advertises scrap to be deposited on the flatbed. 'FER' rough painted letters. In the caravan dwells the metallic entrepreneur.

Roundabout tidy Ménitré. Stomach tired, head yawn, bleary vision looks for an information board of town direction interested only in a campsite icon. I find it. Junction direction Samur reunites calm river reflection. The welcome green of a campsite field below the earthwork levee, downhill to a site occupied by two caravans. The Patron gone home. Present

residents, a French couple and a Dutch couple democratically decide I should stay and settle up in the morning. Tent view across La Loire, the evening warm lit windows of a stately Abbey. Dark woodland rolls back to a dusk deepened skyline.
109 km

The cuckoo, then the cockerel, the shrill wavering laugh of the green woodpecker passing close. The late lazy riser fat woodpigeon in tuneless flat drone perched overhead. Drizzle patters soft on the tent. Saucepan's metallic chatter boiling for tea.

La Loire windless water reflects the Abbey nestled in soft surrounding wooded hills as perfect symmetry. Misty drizzle subdues colour to monochrome, absorbing shadow softens the edge of morning light. The sound of shotguns from woodland on the far riverbank echo across water expanse. Abbey bell response chimes nine o'clock.

The Patron arrives in an old minibus towing a rattling trailer of racked yellow plastic canoes. I pay him for my night of residence, wander a few paces to the river edge to photograph two Loire sailing boats. One is dinghy size. The other twenty feet long with a blunt rounded bow, long square windowed cabin and a folded mast. The rudder is set at an angle to keep the boat away from the riverbank using the constant river current to maintain opposing tension on the riverside mooring ropes. Simple and clever, showing knowledge of river ways. The craft completely of varnished wood looking brand new with carved figurehead, additional carvings along the top of the hull of leafed patterns, ornate carvings cover the stern.

A weatherbeaten figure, skin of old leather wears lived in

denim working clothes filling two big cans with river water. Simple conversation about the river and he asks where am I from and where am I going. Wishing me a "Bon voyage."

Wet tent pack up wandering if it will rain all day. I could stay here and sit it out, or progress up river. Lying to myself of stopping for the day if the rain comes down hard.

One more walk to the riverbank to enjoy the tranquil, picturesque view of La Loire. Upstream large commercial fishing punt with poles, ropes and winches moored silent. Craft moored in a misted line obscured by the river bend opposite a large wooded island. A fisherman poles a punt dropping traps with a splash reflected in silhouette against misted still pale grey.

Loire a velo directs along the top of the levee. The defending obstacle between swollen river devastation of flat land towns, villages and endless agriculture. Many times in history the river has drowned thousands in consuming flood.

Long bridge span from Le Rosiers-sur-Loire toward Gennes. The first houses and villages of white cut 'Tufa.' Buttery subterranean sandstone easily cut and shaped when first quarried, hardening drying slowly on exposure to air. Houses have their own cave, hillsides hold natural formed caverns. Subterranean holes exploited as garages, stores, a mushroom museum and an illuminated model village. Estate agents will sell them. A cave with a view.

Large residences private behind iron gates. Rose gardens, terrace of fine houses, manicured lawns, ornamental great conifers. Oriental twisted black trunk contrasts the luminosity of white stone façade through windless drizzle.

Déjeuner through the window pane. Lace hangs, a centrally

placed bottle of wine, a filled glass waits on the table next to the window. Cooked lunch is served from a steaming pot onto a waiting plate placed upon a tablecloth of white.

Riverside gardens, steps over the wall access the water. Small town épicerie, a half hearted minimart half empty shelved low quality produce double price. The exception being good fruit along with plastic strangled bread and one choice cold vacuum sealed sliced meat. A group of cyclists loaded with camping gear make for a busy café doorway. Windows run condensation. Blur shadows of seated people under diffused yellow bulb halo splashes reflection across a wet pavement.

Loire a velo route signed 'Samur.'

The city approach narrows through century's weathered stone glowing white under grey rain saturation. Nineteenth century suburban luxury town houses, four storey small pane windows elaborate frame with scrolled detail on wood and masonry under complicated roofs finished in ornate finial and ironwork twist.

Loire á velo sign invites to follow. The leaflet shows the route going right through Samur. River suburb. Retail park. Decathalon store. Veloroute sign through a large and beautiful green park of great old trees growing on grassy islands, some accessed by bridges over deep silent slow moving water. People are fishing under large umbrella shelter from steady windless rain. Loire a velo sign has gone. I have made a mistake. Back to the traffic Island finds the Loire a velo sign following direction to a green veloroute sign, there is nothing else. Under dripping bough soggy parkland to housing estate silence ends all patience. From now on I follow my own route.

Far away from La Loire, south in the suburbs of Samur

on a wet Saturday afternoon getting wetter. I need main road signage to the river. Across the street a wedding outside church doors. Black cars, white bouquets, people in suited clothes. All attention on the happy couple everyone smiles in celebration. Their day of new life direction photographed and proudly shared by many guests oblivious to the windless steady rain.

Downhill. Rain stings the eyes. Small shop illumination, vehicle headlights, shining wet city street. Bar Tabac awning shelters a handful of seated old men with a beer in their hand happily smoking watching the day's happenings pass. Well practiced in their art, years of experience of seated alcoholic observation whilst inhaling nicotine mixed with fine traffic fume garnish. I become a subject of their silent focus. I stop half way down the hill thinking I have missed the junction needed for the river. I turn around. Returning uphill. Tabac gazers repetition of observation.

In the cycle lane a loaded bike makes pitiful progress. A gap in the traffic gives opportunity to pass. 'Dawes Galaxy,' on the frame, the slow pedaling cyclist looks up in the rain. I say "Bonjour" and add "Ces le Velo d' Angleterre Monsieur."

The reply, "No com-prendeee."

English.

"Hello."

The rain now pouring.

He is looking for a campsite, about to head off on a main road on the direction toward far away Poitiers into agricultural campsite desert without chance of shower or tent pitch.

I ask why he has not gone to the river where there is always going to be somewhere to stay?

He replies. A lot of the time he has been pitching his tent

in fields, because he has not found many campsites in France.

I look at the map and guess a good bet for a site. I tell him of being left nowhere repeatedly by the Loire á velo signs. Sometimes there, sometimes just disappearing.

He has experienced the same coming downstream from Tours, meeting a group from Holland and two riders from Italy who have had similar experiences with the route. He is tired and just wants to stop somewhere and get out of this rain for the night. On the road for nearly three weeks and needing to get to Carcassonne within a month.

"How do you cycle these hills?"

What hills? I am in dismay.

"I bought my bike off the internet last month. It was cheap."

How much riding previous have you done?

"I didn't have to because I do a lot of walking.

The bike is the wrong size. Too long. Overstretched, his chin on the too low handlebars. Without clocking mileage in his muscles he is suffering with pushing the extra load. A beautiful bike, but not for him. He has made up his mind on his route and is going to walk his bike up the long hill of about half a mile.

He points one direction. I point the opposite. The blind lead the blind, both lost clueless.

I offer to go up to the top and go down the other side to see if there are any signs to named places for the chance of a campsite, then come back. All he has to do is wait at the top of the hill. Rain has soaked my crummy waterproof, cold wet trickles the neck and ribs pulling cold through to the body. I leave him to walk his laden bike up the hill.

Two people walk soaked to the skin, clothes stuck to their

bodies, shoulders stiff, arms by their sides. Faces screwed up resigned to the cold soggy dripping discomfort. I have the same expression, we nod a half laugh in mutual cold soaking.

Downhill slow brake squeeze, squint vision through rain bullets. Rainwater and grit taste, breathing open mouthed. The rain so heavy. Freewheeling chill through soaked clothing. The bottom of the hill, a roundabout. Signs proclaim nothing.

The return. Face tucked into a sodden jacket, uphill effort warms the body. Hill crest blur visible, tight across the white line gives room for passing cars. Metallic noise, escaping air hiss, back tyre wobbles to flat.

Laying bike onto a slippery grass bank. Cars pass close, spray lifted at speed. Looking back. Rusty wire is kicked into the hedge. Opening the pannier box finds a new tube. Fighting with the lid before everything becomes soaked. It will not close. A bowl is in the way. Have I used it? Not since Huelgoat. It is always in the way, I throw it. I get ready the new pump bought for this trip and remove the back wheel, the tube is out from the tyre, a new tube is in. Blackened wet hands work the tyre over the rim.

A car pulls in, a man gets out in the rain and asks. Do I need assistance?

I am touched by the kindness on this wet late afternoon. On finding that I am English he summons his daughter out of the car to ask questions and make perfect translation.

Questions of my journey. Where do I sleep? How many km in a day? He is impressed and asks how I do it?

I reply. I just pedal. We all laugh.

I now have some air in the tyre. He asks if I have fixed it.

I tell him it is done. I thank them genuinely for their kind concern and wave to faces looking out of the blurred back window until they are out of sight.

I pump air into a squashy soft tyre. The nozzle blows off of the hose the first time it is used. Pathetic quality. Sold as good from 'The' large English chainstore that sells car parts and 500 mile life bikes.

I have a spare pump. I undo the pump from the bike frame. On the first pump the handle comes off in my hand to the sound of escaping pressure from the tyre. I stand saturated at the roadside looking at both pathetic items that have let me down. The two pump remnants quickly find their way end over end into the bushes.

The oily chain fight, the back wheel in is tightened. Blackened hands are cleaned with a rag, wiping palms through cold wet grass. The heavy slow uphill push, a pudding soft tyre rolls sideways too flat to ride. Gutter stream runs over cold feet lifting heavy squelching shoes. Maybe I will find bike shop or a petrol station on the way. I have an adaptor for the valve to fit a garage airline. I will have to do it covert, no doubt 'Interdit.'

Solutions run through the mind pushing the bike accepting my fate of possibly walking at best one or at worst several hours. Down hill comes a roadrider. I him flag down. He does an arc across the road and stops next to me.

"Vous avez une pompe Monsieur? Mon pompe est nul, c'est fin. C'est dans la poubelle!...Bon marche nul." Have you a pump? Mine is rubbish, finished. Binned…. Cheap rubbish!

He laughs and says in perfect English I can use his pump.

The word 'Zefal' on a metal chrome tube puts the tyre up. I tell him I am going back into town to purchase one the same.

He tells me the store is open until 7pm giving direction.

I thank him from saving me from the long walk offering him enough for a drink of thanks.

He will not accept anything, saying he lives not far and it was no inconvenience. Then he is gone.

I remember to fiddle the brake wire into the calliper. Brakes being useful.

At the crest I find Mr. Dawes has long gone into agricultural wilderness looking forward to another night camped in puddled mud.

Rainy freewheel, headlight shine, thrown spray. Amongst city traffic. Thoughts of the puncture and pump incident fortunate. Better here than fifty miles from nowhere up a mountain with a day of pushing a bike to smallville closed.

Bridge arch spans above the park of directional misfortune. I find Decathalon. Clothes drip a trail, small puddles whenever I stop in the aisles. I produce soggy notes to pay, apologising for the soaking state of the cash offering to pay by card. Amused at my drenching, I am told it is no problem.

The people who came to my assistance this afternoon were all very kind, including the amused lady at the checkout. Outside the shop I see the Loire á velo sign and ride past it. In tarmac shine amongst headlights I become part of city traffic swept through a roundabout.

Pedestrian zone. Riding wet shining cobbles. Plate glass illumination, displays of colour reflect across rainsoaked pavement. Dressed windows enticement, shoppers purchases carried in coloured emblem carrier bags. Dressed in their best, playing cosmopolitan city image lifestyle. Soggy oiled and grotty. I do not aspire to fashion chic.

Three streets re unite the river flowing black below thick

stone. A beautiful multi arched bridge holds the headlight commuter jam. Riverbank road passes under palace fortress gaze of splendour. Round towers and battlement walls control river passage. White stone fairytale Chateaus show themselves as subterranean cave facade. Great stone block walls, cobbled sloping riverbank. Caravan roofs and tents across the river, the campsite for the city.

Samur wine adverts. Cave shops, cave hotel, block mass fortress, caves in the weeds to the most beautiful village. The main road through Candes St-Martin wide enough for one car. Buildings of white cut sandstone blocks yellow with the years, architecture ornate perfect. Waterside houses, fleeting river view narrow passage. Stone houses twist a narrow hill. Pretty street ends in roundabout. Rain stops, a campsite sign.

Down slow to the Accueil. Greeting smile and politeness. Showers are up a flight of steps with a winter depth marking of 6m! (18ft). Shivering peel of soaked clinging layers drop soggy to an uncaring heap. Hot shower flow warms muscle and blood. The pleasure of warm dry clothes. The evening in sleeping bag warmth. The only wet steams from the mug. I wonder how the rider on the Dawes bike ended the day. The church bell chimes 11pm. Please remove the batteries before midnight.

67 km

Hoo! Hoo! Hoooo! Overhead. In the darkness another owl answers from across the river. Do me a favour, go and join it. Owls keep the social hours of students. In partial dawn rain patters the outside of the tent. The excuse not to rise. The morning in and out of sleep in warmth and comfort. At midday I go to the Accueil, pay for another night and ask if I can use the tumble dryer. I am given a token 'jeton,' washing clothes in a sink to the amusement of two Spanish ladies resident and running a laundry business. With broken language conversation the older lady says that she is a devout Evangelist and is hoping to go to America in the future. For ten years they have been moving around Belgium, Germany and now France before going back to Spain.

I am asked. Why I do not use the washing machine?

They ask. Where am I from? Where am I going? How many children and where is my car? I don't have one.

Reliant on my bike as transport living in a small tent. They think that I am so poor.

Where do I eat?

In my tent, cooking on a one ring stove. They think I am some lost vagrant soul and are filled with pity for me!

How funny the perceptions of another's situation. Seeing only their interpretation. They live in a large caravan, have a car and TV. I have saved for a year to achieve the living standards of a tent dwelling vagrant propelled by bicycle. I find their interpretation amusing.

An hour later a call from outside the laundry room. The ladies set the dryer controls and tell me how long the drying will take. How pampered.

Rain ceases, brighter sky. Flecks of blue, drying breeze. I am called to collect warm dry washing.

Long grass home of many mosquitoes, dejeuner on my feet, ankles and shins.

Under pink evening sky a hunched grey Heron fishes the silent river, spear beak poised.

From my sleeping bag the last chimes on the evening

church bell heard are nine.

8am getaway, the place still asleep pedalling up the slope to join the road. The Patron puts his head out of the window, shouts a goodbye and wishes a good journey.

Mist. Humidity. Without breeze, without leaf stir. Green quiet views weave the River Vienne. D751 towards Chinon. Mist softened cliff fortress floats magical in block shadow, diffused light masks chateaus ten storeys in height. Turrets, square and conical roofs, tops obscured in part by low cloud fingers slow early morning roll. Stately buildings behind tall fortress walls formidable collective mass of defence. River silent, moving without disturbance, mist muted reflecting riverside town buildings huddle under imposing fortress ruin. A detour view from La Loire.

Compass direction, narrow country road. Village secret hidden amongst woodland near to nowhere. Narrow village street, épicerié stop. Pushing the sticking wood door scraping the floor. Buzzing refrigerator vibrates metallic irritation. Meat counter odour, fruit and veg opposite mixes fragrance to give the smell of an old grocers shop. In type nearly extinct. Old scratched lino, 1960s squares of patterned dinge reflect florescent ceiling repetitive flicker. The blue glow insect electrocuter fizz announces the demise of a fly. In the middle, shelves of biscuits, tinned food, wash powder and other uninteresting necessary products of everyday comfortable existence.

I greet the lady shopkeeper dressed in universal long nylon pale brown check shopkeepers coat busy in the arrangement of cheese.

'Bonjour' is returned with a voice that is not saying the

same as the mind is thinking.

I am under character study surveillance as I walk around the shop picking up things needed. Ham and potato salad, boxes of cookies, jam, cheese, packs of snacks. I ask for a baguette. On seeing the amount I wish to buy and cash to pay for it, a smile has appeared on her face. The multinational money smile of the shopkeeper. I am accepted by this purveyor of fine fayre as notes slide into the till and small change is returned.

"Au revoir Madame."

I am responded with a happy "Bonjourné!" As I pull the sticking door closed.

The village gone, bend weaves the downhill. Damp and darkening trees overhang steep mud bank ending at the watery lap of La Loire. Direction 'Tours.'

The beautiful stone block Chateau of Ussé. Many towers round with carved decorative corbels, battlements under slated roofs steep and conical. Finials of decorative ironwork. Chimney stacks banded dark red brick and white stone. Striped decoration rises above steep roof. The chateau not the largest, but of the most pleasing proportion and detail.

Narrow flat road farmland, neatly planted rows upon rows of trees between pond mirror green canopy. Cycling a reflected still green world. Birdsong, smells of stillwater pool. Flooded trunks, humid woodland. Out of the trees at speed, bright countryside, woodland falls to the river.

Villandry. Chateau of splendour asks an unfortunate entrance fee. I take an opportunist photograph balancing on one leg on top of a wood post to get a view over the purposely obscuring hedge. Many people, many cars, coached daily herds of room and garden strollers. Americans with a hired campervan take bikes off of a rear carrier. Seeing my bike saying.

"Check out these serious water carriers."

"We passed you a long way back and you're here already. How do you do it? We make 30km a day on circular routes."

I tell them my day has not really started. I want to get past Tours and hopefully visit Chennonceaux. So I am only stopping to get quick look and photo of this place.

They have a couple of days left exploring the Loire Valley. Then on to Geneva for a week before flying back home.

I wish them a good trip and head up the road.

Today's plan. Stay on this road until it ends. Work across the city of Tours not crossing the river until am well past the city maze. Houses to one side, caves on the other. Caves doors marked 'PRIVÉ.' Caves of privacy, for sale, viewings arranged.

The confluence of the River Cher. Goodbye La Loire.

Suburb Tours away from the city centre. East under Route National. Brown and orange tin Bricoler world. Poster offers easy term monthly manacles. Into The land of identical white apartment blocks. Double glazed plastic for identical people living out the grid plan. New area concrete featureless maze token green grass square designed without a heart. I need to find the old part. Old parts of town connect with forgotten D roads going places.

Through apartment land. Compass directs over eight lane speeding racetrack vehicle madness. As long as all those vehicles travel below they will not be on my route.

South. Aged D road. East out of town hugs the River Cher. Hill view countryside. River slips peaceful through soft green away from unchecked cell growth proliferation named 'Progress.' Traffic fade, rain. Leggings and shoe covers. Rain for the day.

Good speed, fast road, leg resting downhills. Hammering rain, descending through grey. Aptly named Bléré so wet I cannot see or breathe. Sheltering grey concrete bridge, looking for map direction to Chennonceaux. Two other cyclists, lightly loaded bikes share the shelter.

"Bonjour."

Americans, looking for the Chateau. The father and son are from Montana with hired bikes, detailed routes and accommodation arranged for them every day.

They ask. "Where are you staying?"

I don't know until I get there.

"Well where do you hope to get to today?"

South east somewhere. It's the opposite approach to theirs.

We ride talking. Railway crossing. Directions end in a car park for a Chateau crowded.

Having found the chateau they are off to find their accommodation, returning later for sightseeing.

Joining the herd parting with euros. A multinational shuffling corridor crowd awaits ticket inspection. Mob release runs wild over wide avenue of trees, Chateau keep and gardens. The great Chateau overcrowded with grouped guided narration of chosen language.

Magnificent gardens dulled by grey oppressive rain. Meticulous pattern lawns, paths and flowerbeds puddled. Chateau arcade spans the River Cher.

The building likes archways. The main gallery room spans the flowing river on many arches. Above is an arched ceiling and many large arched small pane decorated curved bay windows give a view out over the rain pelted river in which a lady of nobility once bathed daily so the crowd followed passing guide noted. She is not out there today.

Gold leaf, ridiculous fireplaces of pompous grandeur. Works of portrait art signed Van Dyke and Reubens. Kitchen profusion of polished copper pans hang about a great cast iron range on a stone flag floor. Spiral steps of perfect stone. More paintings, shining gold and splendour cared for perfection. The place still a palace, impressive to be enjoyed once. Used in the Second World War to smuggle and exchange people and information across the river. Mary Queen of Scots may have lived here for a while. Outside standing looking at white cut stone blocks making the Chateau structure. Round tower façade corners, grand entrance doorway overhead balcony balustrade. Carvings surround dormer windows, long windowed chapel of sculpted detail.

Car park meal. Cold ham plastic sealed salad, no shelter from the rain. Standing next to the bike eating and dripping. Half a box of cookies grow puddles in plastic packaging, biscuits crumble soggy. Cardboard gives up, turning to mush in my hand. Damp feast finished with flat cola and water. I am cold. Its windy, clothes are stuck to the skin. The flip side. I cannot get any wetter. With this reasoning and riding the method for warming. It is time to go.

Coach dodge crowd manoeuvres. Out of town, streaming soaked shining D road, rain in the face, spray rise doubles the soaking. The road flat and fast. Wind behind turns a pace of big gear speed. Riverside views through grey rain bullets, large monster shape looms dark from saturation. Montrichard. Under the great expanse of wall, military window gaze surveys.

Orange flashing through grey rain loom becomes the lead

vehicle to an entire school of children and teachers on bicycles. Today's lesson. Cycling. Waves, bell ringing and shouts of "Bon courage!"

Countryside colour washed grey, weather blurred focal shape indefinable, buildings in wet melancholy grey isolation. Odometer clocks 100km. Campsite icon directs left breaking the pace. Country road to houses. The silhouette of an old man looms through the rain shuffling along the street with a small furry bedraggled canine on a thin lead.

I politely ask if there is camping nearby?

He looks at me like an extra in a 1950s B movie monster film, taking a step back telling me "Non, non. Non comprende! Non!" Waving his arms and walks off. Stumpy old weirdo.

Isolated agriculture darkened in grey saturation. The tune 'Dueling banjos'. On the road to nowhere wrong end of the day for wasting daylight, energy and time. I turn round and leave the place to the hiding backwoods boys. Through misty grey rain, the shuffling shape of the same old weirdo with the ever yapping wet rag on a lead. He does not look, summing up the straw bale of a place.

Main road Roman ruins. Understanding fully why they had enough, packed quick and left without finishing the building work.

D976 away from the river, under grey streaked Route National. Rail goods yard, rain shapes tall, sombre brown half decayed concrete silos loom misted rain stained house unmoving fan blades in silence. Roundabout hand painted sign on a rainsoaked board advertises Camping a la Ferme. Camping a la Banjo? Hotel Motel Bricoler land check shirt truckers, junction signed 'St. Aignan.' I take it. Any chance of a change welcomed.

Old stone bridge crosses the River Cher watched by looming grey misted fortress on top of a hill. Direction sign points for a campsite. '4* á cote la riviére.' I follow, freewheeling into the entrance flanked by hard blowing flapping flags. Leaning my bike against steel bin fragrance finding money and passport, entering the Accueil drip dripping a wet trail to the counter. I am greeted by a polite lady who fills in the forms saying I can go wherever I like.

The pitch not too far from the showers, dodging puddles. Raised ground is chosen as a possible island next to a thick sheltering hedge banishing blustery gale gusts driving hard rain. I must thank the weather for getting me here and not turning to headwind. The bike is jammed in the hedge tied to a branch. Into sanitaire sanctuary. Clothes peel landing squelch on the floor. Blood warms, road grime spirals the plughole. Fresh clothes have stayed dry. Secured in tent luxury, hot food, laying on the sleeping bag. Outside the wind increases to a gale, driving rain sounding as pelting gravel. Hopeful thoughts of it blowing through tonight.

134 km

Light rain ceases at 9am. Wind gone, washing hangs, hazy sunshine dries. Gears and chain are oiled from yesterday's washout. The pack up, thanks to the Accueil. Into town in search of food, visual and cultural nourishment. Traffic light release amongst very old half timbered buildings. A big chateau fortress old and splendid. Tower gaze across town square modern car park converted. Spending time in this little town is worthwhile. Narrow streets, old buildings shuttered windows, decorative iron verandahs, rose covered walls. Long shadow roof overhang, shops, white stone, oak beam ruddy burnt twisted brick infill. A time worn town of many generations. The Cher not as lavish as the Loire.

Superette calorie fuel up. Downhill sunshine, following the river, undulating road, gardens of flowers, woodland shade. Rough agriculture fallow. Poppy carpet red glow amongst wild green. Flat road weave towards Selles-sur-Cher, distant bridge across the river. A short cut across farmed lands straight line to meet again with the river will save two curving days riding.

Many caravans in a field next to a muddy pond, a traveller's camp of African people. Footballs kicked high in the air, children play. Vans arrive as others leave. One man runs it, giving instruction. I take a right up a hill, direction signed 'Valencay.'

Fields, dotted areas of woodland to a village of strangeness. People do not greet as everywhere travelled. Stare of silence, eyes of emptiness, expression melancholy. The act of walking, a downcast shuffle along the street. The only business advertising is for agricultural machinery repairs. Scattered abandoned rusting farm machinery amongst long grass weeds and overgrown bushes. A house, a barking snarling dog lunging at the wobbling fence setting other neighbourhood dogs barking. Away from backwoods banjo village through flat land fields. Short turning descent, a bridge, woodland to copied village strangeness. I push the pedals to escape the insular remote weirdness. In the freedom of countryside I stop and tie washing over the pannier box to dry under hazy sunshine. A bend. Forét de Gátine, plunged into dark world forest silence.

The only sounds, humming tyres, my breathing over the

smooth chain link loop endlessly turning the sprockets. No creaking branches, no birdsong not a rustle from within the thousands of shadowy silent standing tree trunks. The only light permeates from above. Dull trunks absorbed in forest blackness. A floor littered. Fallen rotting limbs half submerged in isolated black unmoving pools, 360 degrees flat. Through the bottom of a deep wood canyon travelling captive straight road miles. Narrow strip of light my guide towards exit.

Roundabout deliverance. Majestic plane tree descent, pruned, cared for leaf canopy shade radiates a tint of green. Sunshine release to high iron gates. Chateau Valencay. Guard houses of imposing masonry stand sentry to a long driveway of splendour. Valencay is externally equal in splendour to Chennonceaux. Immaculate lawned gardens to an arched entrance centre to a facade of white stone. Ornate windows, sweeping squared roof, chimney stacks big as a house reach above the ridge. Round towers, conical roofs, proportion and balance to the elevation. Long wings hold many windows. Large round tower, mass slate, domed roof large centred belfry. The tower forms the corner for another wing, more towers of symmetry. Bygone wealth. Pompous impressive historical splendour. One hundred schoolchildren walk by in the grounds. In fresh memory of yesterday's crowds. I leave.

Twists of town direction, D960, farmland horizon, black outline faraway trees. Silent rural crossroads town of Vatan, spidery grid roads radiate. The main road closed. 'Route Barre.' 'Deviation.' Diversions blind from road numbers travelling a different route headed for a no name village. Empty plane tree avenue in the middle of nowhere. Grey concrete, under Route National. Narrow country lane parallel to four lane speed.

Compass points south. The plan. Find a road cutting south east to meet the River Cher.

Straight line undulating miles. Sole focal point, huge wind turbine blades 'swoosh swoosh' accompanied by speeding tyre grind and racing engine drone bound for Chateauroux.

Paired Kestrels on a fence fly repetitive circles to land same place in happy courting play. I apologise for my intrusion. They scatter in low field glide to gain height without wing flap effort.

Landscape of boredom. Empty road induced trance of leg and lung rhythm passes time. The up down rollercoaster. Surrounding flatland one crop monotony. Far distance car approach. Metallic dot of silence gains size on each seconds appearance on the brow of each road hump. Then, full sound full size. Nondescript driver peers through glass, nose over knuckles wheel grip. The coloured blur. Gone. Exhaust linger. Tarmac emptiness. Silence. The hum of the bicycle tyre.

Junction pause, direction signed to some place. A no detail commune road. Avoid. Flattening landscape. The sky has come down to claim everything. Agricultural featureless flatland void without focal point to gauge progress or pass time in ponder. I push a big gear, travel at good speed. Feeling tethered stationary, without a tick of time. No building rises to be seen. Waist high long green leafed waving desert of nothingness. Feeling of oppressive isolation intensified by the hidden distant traffic drone carried on the breeze. Miles and miles. Miles and miles. Same view.

Primary red silent speed through the green. Car roof travels straight line acute angle. Straight lines will intersect somewhere. Roads eventually meet. D8 release south east. Small agricultural 'La Champenoise' few rooftops. Big arable farming empty of people. Lines of large wheeled bright colour farm machinery patiently wait for purchase and mud. Sparse villages, road straight to the vanishing point. No mans land strip of tarmac separates cereal crop's 360 stretch. Pylon open arms hold curved droop satanic crackle power lines running out of sight across dulled green.

Vehicles high speed along straight tarmac. White stone verge edges the drain. Truck scream past. Bars gripped tight avoiding being blown into the ditch by the heavy goods blast. Roar of the engine. Diminishing rattle. Further into the landscape, smaller, smaller, vanished. Straight road crop silence. Sign points 'Issodun.'

Large white and red painted towers. Pylons against vast steely grey sky closer become huge dominating lattice structured steel spidery shapes. Maybe military, maybe a radio listening Cold War leftover. Towers surround low weird central building without presence or movement. Straight road miles of coil barbed wire fencing. Sinister military might is under siege from bright flower yellow oilseed.

Flatland monotony.

Outskirts of Issodun greets with drizzle, wasteland, brambles and a short climb to agricultural stores as big as aircraft hangers. Farmlands' concrete castles.

Corrugated retail bricoler land. Rainsoaked roundabout. Military tanker convoy and a little Renault van containing lawnmowers tries several times to shove me off of the road and into the kerb. I fight back with highway chess manoeuvres. Strategic gap squeeze in roundabout surge leaves the little van to wait. The feeling of small victory.

A suburban hill blueprint of an anywhere 1950s brick estate

town of bypass England. Fast traffic country road in speeding hurry home, headlights absorbed in faded grey half light. The further from town the quieter the road.

Woodland breaks agriculture softening landscape ambience. D9 splits quietly without telling. I cut across a rough lane. D9 toward Chateauneuf-sur-Cher, towards the river. Tarmac ribbon flat field weave. Aircraft beacon strobe, white wind turbines slow spin, background sky darkens angry. Drizzle fade, thickened air moisture keeps the road soaked. Wet tarmac smell, rain spots infrequent hit the skin. Road number change, road split. Compass informs D14 change to D18, further a direction sign 'Chateauneuf-sur-Cher' confirms. Black fir darkness exaggerated by tense electrical sky. Claustrophobic narrow road black trunk density. I meet no one. Out of the forest, fields of silence, isolated houses without light or life, unfriendly challenge solitary dog bark. Road bend, barking fades. Open space, road straight, a mile, a bend. Repetition. Small village campsite is advertised closed. Climbing bends descend to a junction. Ligniéres right. Bourges left. Left descends. Dark walled railway, dripping stone bridge. Chateauneuf-sur-Cher confronts with a big fortress walled Chateau controlling the river. The place alive, glow of lights, municipal sign points for camping. Backstreet direction. Open doorways, residential human voice, clanking kitchen pots. Tumbling river sound louder. Sign points to the riverside town park barred with a red and white entrance barrier.

The Accueil a chalet. The only other customer is paying for the night's facilities. A Dutch cyclist who is following the historic Meridian south to Carcassonne. A pleasant person with an old fashioned ridge tent of old fashioned quality and a very pleasing shape of how a tent should look. I fill in forms and pay a pittance to camp on the edge of lawned riverbank. Old majestic weeping willows delicate branch tease over smooth moving river weir tumble. Town rooftops decorated with spires, conical roofs and stone towers differing in size make a centuries old skyline. A town of age carrying good feeling.

The showers in a row of individual wood door cubicles containing one light bulb and piping hot water operated by a pulled string. Technology years adequate.

I had a feeling this place would be good looking at the map. The chance of camping a guess. I have been travelling in France for two weeks. The last two days the map has been folded many times giving great progress nearing the Massif Central.

In evening stillness River Cher oozes slow against houses and gardens tumbling the weir in satisfying roar.

123 km

Into the Massif Central: Puy De Dome

Bang. The tent pole breaks on emergence. Sorrowful droop lop sided. Jagged grey aluminium pole piercing green nylon gives appearance of limb break trauma. Packing involves a quick gaffer tape lashed tent peg repair. Breakfasting without the tent feels strange, having nowhere to laze. My neighbour from Holland rolls his tent in conversation. I leave him packing methodical and walk to La Poste using the cash machine. Town wandering looks for towers and spires seen from last night's residence.

Chateauneuf-sur-Cher is an underestimated town. Old, split between splendid and semi quaint dilapidation, not suffering prettified suspension in architectural formaldehyde. The Chateau is round towered plain without pomp. Town narrow streets rise to a church covered with sculptured art. White sandstone covered in beautiful intricate design. The quality of the masonry a credit to the extremely skilled masons who have sculpted figures of such lifelikeness it feels as if they could at any time leave their places and walk around the town. Faces of statues in everyday people. Stone eye gaze follows my walk, every fold in clothing looks as soft cloth material even to the intricacies of lace cuffs.

Ornate doorways into the church under three gothic arches. Large carved structural stone carry's facade and tower above. Elaborate carvings and balustrading, an octagonal belfry, a dome and spire. Fearsome griffon gargoyles throw rainwater from the building.

A town once of importance.

Entrances of houses medieval. History of the town Roman. Old doorways, centuries of wear. Half derelict round tower with battlements. Conical roof missing many slates, roof timbers open at the mercy of seasons.

The Dutchman appears on his bike. I will not find anywhere open selling bread etc. He has looked and found the boulangerie to be closed. Au revoir and he is gone.

There is always somewhere selling bread.

A woman passes carrying two warm fresh fragrant baguettes. I take up the scent trail. Sweet fan blown smells of cooking bread and pizza end at a window of displayed cakes, bread, croissants. Fruit and tarts brim with cream. The narrow door opens to several ladies looking and buying.

"Bonjour mes Dames."

Received with approval waiting while they browse the shelves.

Walking out with bread, fruit tarts, 'abricot' croissants and a heavy square hot pizza.

Quiet street ancient wall and window echoes a passing car. Hearing guides to the weir roar. Footbridge spans the river to the campsite now empty. The Patron gone.

A tubby man in a baseball hat, earmuffs and municipal overalls cuts the grass driving a ride on mower. His face wobbles with every bump, backside welded to the seat part man part machine, playing on his big green toy round and round making decreasing circles. I squeeze the bike through the locked entrance barrier. Au revoir Chateauneuf sur Cher.

D35 countryside follows chocolate brown slow moving ooze. Overhanging trees reflect calmness, the river wander slides through rough patchwork farmed land. I rise above speeding Route National on concrete lowering back to agriculture. Arterial D2144, the sleepy crossroads town of St. Amand Montrond. Described as the centre of France. Traffic lights, a few shops and shuffling shoppers. No one appears ecstatic about being the pivotal point of a nation.

Mundane street hill climb. Changing landscape, bigger hills 360 degrees. Wandering river recedes below. Smells of freshly cut sweet oak. Wood yards line the road. Timber seasoning piled, wood bundled and strapped, split offcuts form fence posts. Rough cut seasoned planks wait for transformation into joinery. Factory adverts for woodblock flooring.

Steep fields roll, tops wear wildwood bonnets. Tumbling hedges divide the growing green. Hills to ride up and hills to freewheel down. Villages of silence. People do not look or bother to acknowledge through nowhere town.

Hills grown. Direction sign. Montlucon. 45km. Miles back at St. Amand Montrond, Montlucon was signed 50km! More timber production between farms and smallholdings end with a view of a distant grey city under dull haze. Muti storey buildings, crammed rooftops cover a central hill. The 'Mont' of Montlucon. The long approach. Undulating hills, half built 'Bricolage land,' roundabouts without roads, new roads without directional purpose end in churned graded mud, stacks of drainage pipes sink in large puddles. Straight road ribbon development. Gut feeling about the place. Bad. Getting worse.

People stare saying nothing. A place used up industrial dirty. Straight road, old patched not patched pot holed, miles of grime dirtied facades. Overhead sagging cables in criss cross lash up hang from rust streak steel clinging to neglected masonry. I am held by the many traffic lights that delay my exit from this hole. People on the street are small and dumpy with round heads. The 'umpa loompa' song plays in my head. I keep following 'Clermond Ferr.' signs on D2144. Signs for 'Desertines.' Good advice for residents wishing self improvement. More traffic lights and pot holes, dodging sunken manhole covers, car wings and wheels nudge and nip my side. D2144 drops into dirty grey concrete exhaust captive ring road. Uphill racing cars and smoking haulage to traffic lights dulled in dirt. A filter lane gives reprieve south east side of town inhabited by many North African and Eastern European people. A small épicerié displays road soot fruit. I buy a Coke and chocolate bar from a polite North African teenager serving and running the shop by himself secondary to his main business of tapping frenetic at his mobile phone.

Outside shawled North African women slowly waddle side to side along broken pavement under large bill posters advertising expensive cars and cream guaranteeing endless youth. A world away from their lives carrying heavy shopping long armed to dilapidated hundred and fifty year old tenement residence rotting in human overuse. Two roomed compressed pig pens, the long stairway echo of people's lives. The chipped and scuffed door's wobbly worn handle bodged lock surrounded by a greasy knuckle stain from decades of opening. The ancient toilet bowl, tiles missing, the flaking enamel bath rust stain tideline. A lifetime of sweating out ailments cocooned under dingy ceiling lightbulb glow. The overhead chair scrape, kid's heavy feet running around, banging on the ceiling because their television is too loud. So far away from internet and satellite beamed western world of glitz promise. Migration ended here. No swimming pool balcony drinks lifestyle for you Montlucon.

Van passes. A goggle eyed white bald pigmy is shouting and jeering at me. I give the occupant a defining finger of meaning and hope he comes back for an in depth discussion of his actions. He does not.

Road split, no one gives. I need to cut across the lane. City traffic attempts the gutter push. I shove my way to escape. A hill climb ends dull dirt city experience. Road drops fast, descent slows to a long uphill under tall arches of a railway bridge. A bend shields the approach to the seeming endless 8km uphill to the Roman spa town of Neris le Bains. Climbing above the tops of adjacent trees, waist high barrier edge to a sheer drop. Passing cars close behind, horns sounded without reason. Verge appears as the hill catches up with bridge altitude straight line climb. Out from the fast oncoming downhill traffic an overtaking car accelerates head on, speed impossible to stop taking up the whole carriageway forcing me off of the road. I lean out over into the road giving a finger as it comes screaming past in blaring horn reply. I look back to see if the car will stop. It doesn't.

Nowhere nothing road ribbon villages. Little garden snarling dogs. Montlucon and its surroundings has left me sour, pushing the pedals harder knowing with every revolution I climb further away from the hole and its industrial lisping inhabitants. Large hill long climb descends not so far. Each hill makes altitude.

A place to stop under trees. Information board. I have made it into the Puy de Dome. It feels a major achievement. I look for something to eat in the pannier box, finding the forgotten pizza. Jackpot!

Long slog ends in hilltop dirt. Desolate used up Montaigut. Waiting at grime dulled traffic lights looking at brown peeling paint of a café window longtime closed down. Through dusty exhaust soot and road grime covered glass, a strange picture of people enjoying themselves with cavalier beards wearing tights. Depicting century's' old or maybe latest town fashion chic.

On the crossing, a man who was born to shuffle moves across the road on a stick. 'ting…ting… ting'. The hobbling goblin. Articulated bulk hauling trucks thunder through the street shaking the road and buildings in hurry to escape. Lights green, escape quick, long drop freewheel. Hills all around rise into St. Eloy-les-Mines. Big industrial chimneys painted red and white dominate. Everything brightens. Shops, lights, people. Adverts for canoeing and windsurfing on a lake. Signed destination for tonight. Menat 11km. The map puts Menat in a green box. So hopefully a campsite.

Steep forested domed hills hazed hilltop blue dominate. My first savouring grind. Steep twist forest road. Trees one side, edge drop the other increasing with altitude. Temperature cools helping the exertion at the end of a long day. The first hilltop view of many green blue covered round hills. Steep plunging dark forest black valley panoramic wild beauty. Down for 5km. Freewheeling on the drop bars, alternating the brakes prevents wheelrim overheat. Signs. 'Use engine brake.' Low cliff forested sweeping bends, long straight run drops and drops. I yawn. Nearly asleep on the bars imagining a soft pillow. Concentration. Keep awake. Squeezing grip on the brake levers. The road rolls steeper, levelling to a junction signed 'Menat'. An information board. A campsite near the little village, an alternative on the river at Menat-le-Pont. I decide to try down on the river and hope a pedal back is not needed. Following signs. Under the main road. Ancient winding lane, a fast flowing noisy river crossed by a cobbled Roman bridge. Narrow road houses. Parkland. Riverside campsite almost empty.

Accueil 'Fermé.' Wondering what to do whilst yawning, eyes watering with tiredness. The Accueil is open 8.00-9.00pm. A tall man appears in tidy country clothes, brimmed hat shades the eyes. An attentive black and white Collie stays glued to his side. I can pitch wherever I like. The Patron may be back tonight or tomorrow.

Soft grass pitch, unpacking the daily bundle. A surprise voice.

"Coffee is ready."

How kind and welcoming to be invited to sit and talk with new people.

The two men are old friends. The owner of the caravan and his wife have travelled from Holland to visit their longtime friends who live near here. The kind lady Patron arrives and we fill out the necessary forms before returning to the caravan where on learning that I am only staying for one night I am told the place is too beautiful for just a single night.

They are right. It takes little convincing that I should stay for two.

The site next to a flowing river is surrounded by forest

green. Steep craggy hill ruin castle surveys all. I spend the evening watching the light change on the castle. Form and colour temporary obscured by small cumulus cloud shadow dancing across forest hill surround. The lightshow continues. Hours lengthen shadow, mellow sun splashes castle walls pale pink orange, tree green deepens to black.

124 km

7am. Everything humid. Hanging mist above chattering turbulent flow. Moss covered gnarled bark of overhanging oak, long rich grass. Riverbank peppered with dew covered small wild flower blue and yellow.

Absorbed concentration of the moment broken in surprise.

"Bonjour" from a passing fisherman clomping past with intent.

Green waders and green gillet adorned with many purposeful filled pockets, carrying a fly rod and folded landing net.

I return the greeting adding "et bon peche." Received with a grateful smile.

"Merci!"

As he works a lay in the river where a fish could be enticed to the fly.

Castle walls float in the sky. Mist veil warmed to haze by climbing morning sun. Birds busy in song over river rumble. The ratchet of the fishing reel, observing the skilled flick of each lengthening fly cast. The line gently settling in an arc of silver momentarily on the smooth flow before retrieval further to be cast. Behind the fisherman, dense woodland full leaf tinted with risen sun. Tree covered steep rising hills, crest dominating black coniferous forest.

Easy ride to Menat. Old quiet village of narrow streets, worn stone, rendered façade. Shortening shadow rolls upward under overhanging eaves. A handful of shops. The boulangerie. Worn stone steps, opening the door. Small room filled with baking bread smell, the sweetness of pastries. Young lady serves baguettes. Pizza and three heavily filled fresh blackcurrant creamy fruit tarts are carefully boxed.

I deposit two of the tarts for the Patron and her friend to enjoy over coffee. Washing hangs dripping. The castle entices a walk across the cobbled Roman Bridge. Sun sparkling river in boiling constant roar. Downstream silhouettes. Half submerged fishermen cast the fly, the line arc sparkling streak hoping for a catch secondary to immersion in the surroundings.

Over the bridge, a handful of leaning houses. Green leaf high banked lane dapples sun reflection. Climb changing view across to the near empty campsite. A field of white Charollais cattle graze. A couple of farmhouses, narrowing tree tunnel track edges a climbing field. Horse shoe prints in damp mud betray favoured use. Between trees, isolated slated gables in the green. Insect mass hum, the busy drone 360 degrees surround in daily work.

Arriving to silence. An 11th century castle to explore. I own it for the time that I am here. Three big round towers, an iron barred subterranean dungeon, tall chimney flue to gaze up to a point of light high in stone towered darkness. A kitchen, large fireplace ovens under arches, stone staircase lit by natural light. Heavy floor bulk joists held by a great beam of oak spanning the room. There are arrow slits to peer through, above window views to forested steep domed hills and sheer cliff. The castle cliff edge view vertical over snake coil road dropping far again to winding river glint. Menat-le-Pont nestled centuries overpowered by natural steep surroundings.

Chateau Rocher was constructed in the 11th or 12th century by the Sires of Bourbon replacing a circular wooden fortification. Its function to control the communication between Montlucon and Clermond Ferrand via the Roman Bridge. The only crossing point for a great distance. The Chateau was owned by the family Blot after the nearby hamlet is named until it passed by marriage to the family Chouvigny until 1748 when it was abandoned, gradually falling to ruin partly aided by the enterprising locals using its masonry to construct houses in surrounding villages. In 1911 it became a National monument, restoration started in 1960. Its impressive structure imposes itself over the entire area. I leave it, giving up temporary ownership to whoever next may come along to lay claim.

The tree walk re trace, a familiar black and white Collie barks recognition, running up in welcome. I am trained in less than thirty seconds to throw sticks repetitive. In the eyes of a dog I must appear quite intelligent. I am welcomed and spend time looking around a task of barn renovation half way with a new roof with windows fitted and what it will look like completed. I can see it as a very beautiful place to live. Fine cliff river views across a meadow. A place to watch the changing four seasons. Fresh coffee halts building work. The dog gives duties of stick and ball throwing.

Walking the Roman bridge follows marching footsteps of Roman soldiers, Kings and armies. I become just another unrecorded pair of feet added to a thousand years of history.

I am greeted by a lady with an arm full of library books to look through about the 'Massif Central'. This thoughtful person has gone out of their way for me. Evening meal looking through the books of appealing landscape photography of mountainous areas.

Commotion. Two black dogs belonging to people in a chalet have come down to cause dog trouble resulting in a beating with a tree branch by an angry shouting Frenchman. In their mischief the canine duo have got into my tent and run away with my food bag scattering the contents as a trail in beaten retreat. There is little left un-mauled, enough for breakfast I had locked away on the bike but everything else stolen and ruined by the pooch mugger pair. One can hope the dried pasta and rice devoured will swell up and expand to bursting pain, while the bruising aches from the stick beating will stiffen them.

I have been invited for coffee in the awning of the caravan with the luxury of a chair. The attentive Collie lets out a displeased growl, picking up a scent. From the top of the bank two black dogs contemplate crime. It is as near as they wish to venture. The temperature warm, evening light fades appreciated with a refrigerated beer. Thanking the kind hospitality, I go to bed noticing the rear tyre is completely flat.

The hammering on a nearby tree by a woodpecker wakes me into packing. I eat the remainder of yesterday's baguette rubberised in mid toughening process washed down with swigs of flat coke. Not the usual calorie banquette. I have a vision of chewing a meaty drumstick of tenderised black dog. But first the puncture. The wheel is off, the culprit a stone imbedded in the elongating hole made by the wire puncture from Samur.

I patch the inside of the tyre with two patches and a piece of thin cardboard jamming as much rubber and glue into the hole from the outside as I can, then fit a new inner tube.

It feels difficult to leave Menat-le-Pont. I say farewell to the people in the caravan before seeing the lady Patron, thanking her for the thoughtful kindness shown. Up the slope, the few houses. Crossing the narrow cobbled Roman Bridge. Fishermen downstream waist deep in daily ritual fly in silver arc. From doorways, people prepare for a day's fishing. Riding the ancient road. Campsite view, tree shaded climb. Under watchful gaze of tower and rampart brings no main road this morning.

Road weave against quarried cliff, eye level treetop view. Stream cascades the secret hollow, light shafts pierce precipitous green. All height is lost re acquainting with white noise roaring River Sioule. Stone bridge, rooftop shine. Chateauneuf-le-Bains. My pen drops from the holey plastic map wallet. I stop to retrieve it, having to wait for a lone white plastic motorhome. I watch the pen as the rolling motorhome wheel squashes it once, finishing it with the weighted rear wheel grinding it into a hundred splintered pieces. The only encountered vehicle since leaving Menat this morning.

Forested coniferous gorge, great areas of sheer cliff in slow erosion hold fallen scree ending in river edge boulders. Road follows the riverbank, other times high climbing views over gorge boulder rapids between deep black moving calm. The Gorges de la Sioule. A remaining piece of gorge wilderness. Bridge brings a contour climb, feelings of disappointment leaving gorge beauty and friendly people of the River Sioule.

Climb drag, temperature rocket. Shadeless cover. Gained altitude 400m (1200ft). 'Manzat.' A memorial. My translation;

Here assassinated
by the Germans 2nd July 1944
The young patriot Antione
Monsignier aged 24yrs

There is small plaque with the young man's portrait commemorating the 60th anniversary of his murder surrounded by bushes and woodland. With the thoughts of the memorial filling my mind I have forgotten to visit a volcano crater lake and a giant Cedar tree. Road arrives interdit at Péage roundabout.

In need of fuel, shops of food opportunity closed after puncture delay. I have nothing but two litres of plastic tainted water. Downhill speed, smooth tarmac, wind roar. I jam on the brakes. Distant spherical planets have crashed into the French countryside half burying themselves on impact. Apart from one standing defiant spiked. Puy de Dome with added rocket shaped weather station. Many deep blue domes fade distant in heat haze.

I need Clermont Ferrand, descending the miles through Chatel Guyon. Food opportunity. Fermé, bar is without a menu, St. Hippolyte closed for dejeuner. The famous waters of Volvic. In the bottom of a bag, half a packet of melted gum sweets left over from Tours last week. They taste foul in a jelly lump but contain glycerol, easy converted energy. Fuel starvation into Volvic. A heavenly sign. 'Pizza Open!' Arrow points downhill delivering to a caravan. Pizza Closed.

Small town old narrow, tall tumble walls lean dark grey basalt, rendered facades topped in orange roofs. Everywhere closed, even the little cafés. Lunchtime has finished. The Euro minimarket has someone coming out of the door. Lights extinguish, the sound of a key turning the lock for the afternoon. A small bar, seated occupants stare unfriendly. The same look as Montlucon. On staring back they look amongst themselves in greasy smirk. Whatever causes them to be as they are, I hope is not in the water.

Main junction burning heat. Heat shimmer Riom radiates buildings far below, industrial 'Bricoler land' swarms distant metallic moving glints. I reason a good chance of an all day supermarket somewhere amongst the industrial maze. Water is low, less than a litre. I ride past the famous spring water factory closed for lunch. There is no water in Volvic.

Traffic lights release, downhill freewheel speed under high glare generates cool breeze. Traffic maze, looking for a supermarket. I could buy a bed, a car, surround sound, a washing machine. Through the vehicle bumper procession a big sign euro supermarket chain. Emerging with far too much and spend time trying to pack everything on the bike after drinking down a litre of chilled quenching cola. 'Never shop when hungry.' But I am always hungry.

A couple stop to ask. Where I have travelled from and where I am going? Polite and friendly, wishing. 'Bon courage!'

They leave. I spot a racket. A woman in a headscarf with walnut skin wearing a long black skirt to the floor is constantly talking on a mobile phone. She directs people to hassle what they can out of customers packing shopping in their cars. A man in his mid twenties with sweaty black hair and a cigarette between his knuckles comes over to me and asks if I have cigarettes for him as I am finishing tying the last of the shopping on top of the bike.

"Non!" The straight answer.

Another two join him gradually moving around to intimidate me. They ask for money. I am not in the mood.

"Non!! Vous trouvez Travail!" (No, you find Work!) Is my half shouted reply on unlocking the bike and slamming the chain down on top of the box and the shopping. I have had enough. Staring at them the sweat from the heat running down my face, they back away. They are not scared, but will not want the police. I leave the car park in anger, without care. Weaving traffic on the main D2009 for Clermont-Ferrand in big gear speed along a tree lined flat road. The shopping falls hanging to one side. I couldn't care less if it falls off. I am not stopping.

6km to Clermont-Ferrand. Block mass jumble city ahead, the road speeds up to dual carriageway, lorries thunder high speed, another cuts across my wheel taking an exit at speed blaring its horn. I have had enough, taking the first available exit slip road to a travellers camp. I put one and one together of the supermarket experience and keep going. Minor road modern housing, little lane offers small tree shade from intense high sun. I finally eat, but it is too late to benefit the body. I sit eating and pondering the map void of detail. I don't know how long I will be on the road to find a campsite or where one will be. Maybe the housing estate leads to the city, or maybe a modern designed dead end.

The reason for a city visit is to replace the breaking tent poles and see the famous Cathedral. I need an alternative route to the arterial racetrack. D road climb back up into hills turning north away from direction I wish to go. I grind to a pace slower than a walk. Intense heat, the body suffering from energy depletion. It is quicker to walk. For the first time I push the loaded bike for about 1km until gradient eases. A car full of imbeciles speeds downhill laughing screaming out the window at me. I freely give a most meaningful multilingual finger gesticulation reply. My finger feeling worn from overuse the last few days, I would like to put it away. Top of the hill ends in crossroads. Straight road countryside looking for signed Clermont-Ferrand and hopefully a campsite.

Scrapyards, car breakers, municipal tips, waste ground to countryside road junction. Clermont-Ferrand 7km. Volvic 7km, nearly back to where I started on the original planned route. Clermont-Ferrand gradual descend for miles, pothole dodge under trees, the road offers nothing, into busying suburbs. I try Durtol for a camping chance, riding up a steep pinch. Just a commuter suburb railway station, municipal office behind bars and views into countryside unknown. Main road return, conscious of losing height, not wanting another hill climb. A bus stop map offers nothing for a campsite. Tired ride right into the city centre busy terminus for buses, looking at the route maps. An icon for a campsite is shown out of town. Royat.

Find gives energy, bus route number on bus stop signs give methodical direction for Royat under sun yellowed busy evening commuter rush. It all goes uphill through Chamaliéres. Steep straight, shops and traffic lights. Pharmacy green flashes 27degree constant steepened climb, bus stop check guards against mistake. Shops end. Left turn under hotel gaze, campsite icon points steep through housing, brow of a hill, campsite icon directs a further climb. The city far hazed, a model from altitude view. Patient ascent, modern suburb, house building, spectacular view, road twist, campsite entrance. Accueil closed.

I am told. "Pitch wherever you like. Pay tomorrow."

The site full of expensive white plastic motorhomes. Identical grey aged people with identical vehicles have come from a thousand miles to stare at each other sitting in identical chairs under identical awnings. Ritual pushing of roll along water tanks and emptying toilet cassettes between digesting newspapers broken by an unhurried glass of Vin du Pays.

The site very smart, every pitch stony hard for a motorhome wheel. It is difficult to get the pegs into the ground without encountering rocks or tree roots. Spotless sanitaire shower gives grateful re birth from the road. Hot water runs over, the body quietens from long day exertion. I eat for a long time laid out watching large mozzies trying to get through the flyscreen while big wood ants run over the outside sheet.

I left a special place this morning. Gone are the woodpeckers, people peacefully fishing, the river noise running through steep rock gorge. I have exchanged it for a manufactured brochure cover. A dusty gravelled pitch for a motorhome, a campsite bar, chlorinated swimming pool noise and everywhere the sound of… Germans.

83 km

The dawn chorus wake up, watch hands glow a bleary 5am, falling back to sleep to the lone cuckoo call bouncing hill echo. 8am sky promises a hot day on the road. Milk holds the night chill complimenting slow breakfast. Paying a polite lady for the pitch gets helpful direction to La Pardieu where the Decathalon store will hopefully sell tent poles to replace the fracturing problems. My elbow feels uncomfortable, examination reveals a tic imbedding itself into my skin. Nice.

Motorhome occupants buried faces digest identical tabloids from identical chairs avoiding all communication. No one says goodbye or good morning wheeling to the entrance. Long steep downhill radiating flat city streets. Under high building gaze attentive for signed direction. The place will be out of town amongst modern tin shed concrete commerce. Tall city glass, 19th century ironwork, traffic, people noise chopped off by busy ring road. Compass chooses direction. Up and down pavement cycling ends in busy roundabout. Decathalon sign. Saturday traffic hypermarket rush, giant retail stores across the tram lines. I come out with four spare inner tubes. Replacement tent poles equal in dire quality.

Busy road return, the end of town where people from North and mid Africa mix with Eastern Europe. Cheapo minimart feeds the taste buds with quivering sun ripened fruit.

Brightening cosmopolitan centre. Long plate glass department stores, boutiques of chic, moments of music's muffled beat thump passing the door. Shops end at the Cathedral Square.

The huge Catherdal has imposed its mass over Clermont' since the 13th century. Volcanic black basalt towers above old and modern buildings. Black mass construction contrasts surrounding facades pale colours topped with tiled roofs of red. Shading striped awnings of bars, restaurant chairs and tables fill the pavement. Ancient narrow backstreets hold one roomed artist studios and bookshop intrigue. Crowd saunter visits shops, time killed wandering a pace of leisure under sunshine. I try to photograph the Cathedral. Not so easy because it is immense. Huge main doors ornate carved, painted red. Black stone gothic arch supports a huge circular tracery window stone carved between two massive black towers of sculpted decoration on a scale beyond grand. I could stay here and stare at the building for hours absorbing figure detail amongst patterned carvings hundreds of years old, there is so much. The hard blackness of its mass adds to its atmosphere of unmovable dominance.

Town buildings six storeys, blinds differ colour, shaded narrow descent people busy. Mid distance scattered red roofs, white rectangle houses buried amongst green of woodland to a skyline watched over by the dark forested mountain spike of Puy de Dome.

Downward cobble rattle to a large square. Plinth mounted statues. A triumphant man in battle dress waves a short sword galloping his muscular steed over some poor soul slain under the hoof. I have to wait for a drum procession, people parade in costume. The crowd observes patient behind lined barriers. A stage set for later entertainment. The effort made for a weekend enjoying lively happy city atmosphere.

Chamaléres repeat climb. D68. Town ends century's older. Street narrows under sleepy old house lean. Steep sinuous long ascent. The cycle pilgrimage road of Puy de Dome.

Silent countryside green, long hairpin bends. Tumbled rock wedged in deep roadside storm culvert.

I drink. Skin leaks from the grilling sun, black tarmac oven bakes from below. Humidity intensified, void of breeze. Backward and forwards gains altitude. Sole traffic, a passing scooter offers an encouraging wave and toot. The Tour de France historical battle above. A mountain duel to the top between Jaques Anquetil wearing the yellow jersey and Raymond Poulidor. Shoulders locked in combat, pushing each other toward the summit. Anquetil spurred on by an intense dislike of his opponent ran out of energy less than a minute from the summit finish.

Café near the top. The main road. Cold wind blows downward, heated draught blows upward. Views to the city swallowed in vast landscape. The great black stone Cathedral so small it could be delicately lifted by tweezers.

Large cold spots of rain from clear blue sky sting sweated skin interrupting a view across the Puys to faraway Monts Dore snowed spectacular. Surrounding blue coloured volcano shapes disappear forever into haze. Finally, Puy de Dome. Looking up at the great volcanic steep cone, the highest volcanic mountain chimney has no close relative mimicking its spectacular spiked form. I enjoy a minute of contemplation in strange cloudless rain.

From behind Puy de Dome a rush of black cloud envelopes the sky. A flash of lightning. Ground shaking thunder claims the mountain. The rock summit consumed in dark swirl steel blue cloak. Strong wind roar amplified through a thousand trees. Time to leave. I cannot outrun a storm, neither do I want to be chased off a mountain taken all afternoon to climb. Cloud darkens everything inside the great Cumulonimbus thunder cell on a metal bicycle on top of a hill dressed in static nylon. I escape the hill top through Montrodiex leaving the mountain.

Manson's modern houses lead to an old village square deserted.

Fountain in joyful tumble runs into a brimming trough. Chapel entrance of simplicity. I lean the bike. In strengthening wind and pelting rain walk to an open heavy wood doorway of a church empty, standing dripping on the threshold. A great clap of thunder nearby sends a pressure wave through the body. Spartan stone interior amplifies noise. Outside as dark as evening, watch points 5pm. Clothes drip, not wanting to leave a puddle inside the room. Standing in the doorway experiencing the simplicity that gives its beauty. Wind and lashing rain accompanied with lightning flashes and cracks of peeling thunder illuminate an interior of plain rendered walls. Rows of simple dark wood pughs lead the eyes to an altar of plain cloth. Placed central a red glass, inside a candle emits a glow of red. Coloured flickering shadow cast upon the wall bends from the outside blowing tempest. Placed either side part way to the end of the altar single candles in a clear glass give soft flickering glow of direct and reflected yellow light. Highlighted by the atmosphere of the storm it is a sight of simple timeless comfort, humbling yet uplifting.

The storm eases its violence, tense static charged air released. The storm moves in opposite direction back from where it came. I decide to ride out of the village and head for Laschamps deeper amongst the Puys.

Raining climbing plod twists past old houses, water pours off the hill. A massive horizontal flash of lightning hisses low overhead. Air around the static discharge superheats and expands, a ground shaking pressure wave bang reels across rooftops. Thundercloud envelopes, unleashing large hailstones so thick in number I cannot see, having to get off the bike, the only immediate shelter a lone closed brown garage door. Squeezed tight against metal, waterproof trousers around my shoulders dissipate the hailstones and cold deluge running down the body. Ice pelts bare legs purple cold, numb hands grip the bike. Gale gusts. Shoulders tense, hat pulled over the face.

Hailstone carpet covers the road pebble size elongated. Sleet eases the battering changing to torrential rain. A river of water runs over the frozen layer cascading downhill. I am on tip toe, heels against the door, out of the flow bringing mud, stones and rocks the size of a shoe rolling past joining the rain, hail and ice. Lightning hiss and thunder crack from all direction. A car creeps slower than walking pace, wipers as fast as can work, headlight beam absorbed in deluge. Face shape peers from the blurred rear window, red of tail lights, wheels bump and bounce over stones on a slow drive against downhill torrent.

What am I going to do if this the daily weather of the Puys? My tent will not cope with the pounding and neither would I wish to experience a repeat.

A moments easing. Time for escape.

Debris slows pace, rocks and gravel wash downhill in a road river of storm water. It is hard to see through the heavy rain vision blur. A wheel digger clears rocks and mud of a washed out bank, alongside works a soaked man with a long handled shovel desperately labouring to divert the muddy road torrent into a roadside culvert to save the planted growing crop. Temperature increase, lower land, rain ease. Vision returns, downhill spiral steep, toward Clermont-Ferrand. A sign for camping, a bend. Indigo campsite. Back to where I started.

I lean the bike against a bench, remove my saturated hat and walk dripping into the Accueil amongst dry people from another climate relaxing in summer clothes. Squelching to the counter meets the same lady serving this morning. I pay for another night's accommodation, explaining to her amusement why I am soaked from the storm up at Puy de Dome. She laughs and orders bread for the morning.

Shivering putting up the tent, hands white half numb. The shower walk. Soggy clothes peel from cold skin, hot water banishes body shiver. Background mountain rumble, thinking about options. I have been up to the road pass of Puy de Dome. I have no intention of going to the summit by bike or if 'Interdit,' by rail.

I look for an alternative travel route. The day's achievement has been to get a shopping loaded 45kg of bike up mountain roads. Weighing over six times heavier than modern Tour de France race bikes who employ someone to carry the shopping and mop the sweated brow. Weather wise I am here two or three weeks too early. The season later to start in colder higher altitudes. The temperature difference of lower land ahead in summer season is pulled upward, fueling the violent stationary storms.

In darkness sounds of rumbling thunder. Warm and cold gusts of wind race silent up and down the mountain. Across the blue lights of a chlorinated swimming pool the bar is busy filled with noise of Saturday night German revelers.... Oompah!

46 km

Bread waits at 8am. Party people are timidly silent after their night time alcoholic exuberance suffering with cranial sledgehammering fragile whimpering. I pack in atmospheric mist billowing cotton wool coolness across the motorhome village.

The somewhere above mountain hidden vapour veiled. Downhill chill ride towards Ceyrat. Cyclists' Sunday. Expensive beautiful gloss race machines pedal the gradient. Uphill, midway to the mountains, trees cut by obscuring hanging grey blanket drizzle.

Sign points Le Mont Dore. Steady climb, grey and wet that will carry on grey and wet for many miles. The chance appearance of a lower road below the raining cloud going south away from Clermont-Ferrand weaves volcanoes. Time frozen chimneys and craters amongst forest rise. Some have tops blown off, others suffered sides blown out. Towers born of violence, solidified rock top fantasy art castle ruin. Ornamental tree grows from the highest point in misted background. The ancient Chinese mountainscape silk painting. Lava flow frozen under nature's rock spell. Strange geological sculpture, natural formed monuments honour violence of molten creation 10,000 years ago. Silently observing progress and folly of the many species of man and will witness far beyond the two legged race's future.

Clouded climb to moorland plateau of ancient ruin, the siting of a strange monument. 'Caesars Fortress.' Panoramic view many miles, the Puys chopped by raincloud under high building Cumulus towers flattening to form Anvil top atomic bomb thunderclouds. Many stack against each other, massing a mountain attack. Visual weather forecast suggests stay low and try for the mountains tomorrow.

Narrow road, steep downward twisting lane. La Roche Blanche. Streets built narrow centuries before motor car requirement. Weatherworn render, black basalt rubble stone pointed in white lime under orange red tile roofs. Tangled streets, black stained chimneys poke skyward random. Pocket high walled gardens, wood window shutters, corroding iron balcony. Dwellings without sequence without repetition cling a descent of appealing chaos. At the bottom of the hill houses modern, wide road green lawned rectangular identical box living. Route National. Junction split first for Ambert shared Le Puy-en-Velay. The second, an option of the Cantal Mountains weather permitting. Landscape this side of the Allier valley volcanic and steep, endless climb. Old quiet Sunday village in leaning slumber. Compass navigates south, map blind of detail. The sun out. Go with it.

Two churches of size, very old, one without a tower. Rubble stone with great quarter circular buttresses along its length, roof shallow pitched orange tile, a bell hung between stone pillars. Circular terrace of tall rendered stone houses grown differing heights lean against each other, windows start half way up the building in ancient defence. Parts of the village Romanesque Middle Age style.

Rich landscape, white cows graze, waving crops, summer green woodland. Steep hill forest hides sleeping volcanoes. Molten rock broken castellated turret lookout across agricultural village. Stone built stores several storeys dwarfed to matchbox size under volcanic gaze. Across the Allier valley, distant high blue half outline domed Puys.

Steep sided woodland, sunshined hairpin bend. Across all landscape evaporation builds white cumulus towers thick against deep space blue. Thundercloud after thundercloud feeds off the heat engine of warmed land. Mini mountain road col. Panorama reward followed with a helter-skelter downward cooling freewheel deep in green agriculture.

In a field under shading of trees stand two donkeys. One long haired grey, the other short haired brown. Attentive ears forward looking to the gate. A small boy in a white shirt approaches, the donkeys run to meet him. Heads over the gate, both parties in greeting with each other.

I cycle past commenting. "Votre amis?"

"Oui Monsieur" the proud smiling reply.

Little river. stone bridge. Guarding chateau of gold brown stone. Four round corner towers, shallow conical roofs, red tile. In use as a residence. Flat fields, trees in centuries grown twisted lean. Black kite ascends the feathered wheel. Long wing vulture persona, far glides the thermal fuelled search soaring the miles without energy use.

Climbing fields, sturdy bough solid oak. Descending to Sauxillanges. Silent crossroads village. Forested Monts du Livradois rise. Direction of Issoire winding ascent. Cat sat to attention on the edge of bushes, twitching ears forward in concentration contemplating murderous deeds against small birds and rodents. Momentary eye contact, the guilty cat stare before returning to patient observation.

Peopleless agricultural sunshine, wood barn alone, wide open arable roll swaying with the breeze. Far away Issoire without detail. A turning advertises a village as 'One of the loveliest in France.' A climb. Large white Notre Damme peering through trees over a small church at Usson. I stop to enjoy the view. Yap yapping dog stands at a driveway entrance called by an equally annoying yapping woman. No attempt is made to walk thirty seconds to grab the canine windbag. After a minute of both mammals repetitive yabbering I give up. Back down the hill, noise fades with distance increase. D road steepens to the river valley. Temptation for freewheeling speed, weight gains momentum, caution applies the brakes. A bump sends my two remaining choc au pain snacks airborne from the handlebars never to be seen again. Hill ends in flatland ride, a small village tranquil under cloud dancing through the blue. A few people, a nod. Sign points Route National. Lane of green beckons countryside weave listening to Route National speeding buzz. Heat plod uphill. Shadeless bends, fading energy. Hot afternoon humid. Campsite sign offers reprieve, a driveway of shading trees ends with a fine stately residence.

A lady seated in darkened depths of the Accueil swiftly relieves my euros in exchange for a night's accommodation. Gliding spectral from behind the desk I must obediently follow as a canine.

I am shown with a dismissive hand where I may. "Stay!"

It is one of those meetings that should never really have to happen. The Lady is, or wants to be aristocracy, very intelligent, proficient in English with a plum in the mouth accent I find surprising. Too perfect for a French person. She stands in dressed casual elegance. I imagine she probably has a Rolls Royce or two in one of the stables. The contrast, I am a sweaty 'rostbif' who has pedalled up the driveway wearing a pair of shorts with a cheap cycle T shirt topped off with a bush hat. I am on a bicycle and will be staying in a tent, very much the peasant. My comparative language skill is of patheticness.

By fingertips I am handed a photocopy of campsite rules in French.

"So you can improve your understanding of the French language" I am told.

I can also order bread for the morning. I am to add my name on the list.

I decline, telling Marianne I usually take cake for breakfast. Petit dejeuner du bourgeois. My thoughts.

"Je vous merci Madame."

"Merci Monsieur."

"Je vous en prie Madame."

She liked that one. After a half bow one step back hat in hand in floorward gaze.

I have run out of French grovel vocabulary as the Lady glides back to the Accueil to deal with a couple from Holland who seem to have nomadic accommodation of a caravan attached to the back of their mass produced vehicle.

While putting up my tent under mosquito impaling I come to a chuckling reasoning that she still took the money out of the hand of the filthy proletariat and has to provide service to get it!

In all humanity how the obtaining of money has no divided boundaries of class, however repelling the extraction process for some may seemingly be. In life observation, when people decide they will hold themselves aloof, it seems a great personal torturous complicated struggle is needed to maintain the illusion of vain superiority. If all walks of life had to go around without the pretense of clothes, how the common labourer would physically appear to be the King.

I have been told. "I may walk the grounds and enjoy the view down across the river."

After finishing the ritual of the tent I endeavor the walk only to be beaten back by swarms of large mosquitos coming up from the disturbed grass in squadrons, attacking in formation with the noises of World War ll fighter planes. I retreat. Pursued back to the tent. Sieged from behind the flyscreen.

My assistance is called upon by the Dutch couple to help level their caravan by chocking the wheel up on two yellow plastic wedges. There is much pushing and handbraking before a pause. The result is acceptable for sleeping in my eyes, but not so for the occupants. Horizontal perfection must be achieved. A spirit level is produced signalling more expelled energy in the pursuance of the little bubble reading perfectly between the lines. A modern DIY tool version of 'The princess and the pea.'

Across the valley, lightning signals bombardment of the hazed Volcans D'Auvergne. The spectacle intensified under steel charged dark stormy sky.

I talk with the Dutch couple for a while who are on their way to Spain, staying here for one night. The man gets spiked by a large mosquito exclaiming. "Watch out for ze midgets. Zey bite!"

I spend a while wary of small angry people under bushes.

The search for a water tap. For two seconds I observe an open windowed scene. Between a pair of long tied back curtains, a white tablecloth, silver cutlery, large candles flickering, sparkling crystal wineglasses full. A waiter dressed in a white jacket with a serviette draped over his forearm held horizontally against his body, leant slightly forward. The pretend formal submissive waiter pose. To the left, a hand over the table with a shirt cuff of white, suit sleeve of dark blue with gold square cufflinks. To the right of the table. Painted long nails of elegant hands, a wrist decorated with gold and pearls. A fleeting insight to the values of others.

My search for a tap of unpolished brass ends at the car park. The rarity of a British made car. A 1970s Range Rover on French plates. The choice of royalty for the countryside and stately pursuits. It stands elegant corroded above surrounding younger French models painted up, plastic skirts, bland.

From the restaurant/bar communal kitchen back door appears a member of staff dressed smart in clean whites carefully carrying a large tray with a silver lid walking to the main residence. Perhaps gourmet 'poisonne et frites avec pois de mushy.'

Through the royal hedge maze a tap fills my two old plastic cola bottles. The Dutchman in surprise exclaims. "Zehr is noh toilet paper!"

I reply there never is in France and tell him if he wants a hot shower, let it run for a while as the boiler is a long way from the shower heads as I had found out.

My tent return zips the door to put an end to mosquito bloodletting. Before going to bed I find a tic walking up my forearm. I unzip the tent to put it out for the night trying not to let in the Dracula mosquito squadron assembled in formation patrolling the flyscreen.

Under thick humidity, thunder continues its roll across the valley.

65 km

Volcans D'Auvergne

Sleep totals twelve hours. Thundery shower pelts the thin tent, a rainy excuse for laziness until pattering ceases. I have run out of sleep, feeling I should be doing something. Starting with a historic French royal breakfast of cake followed by the English version, tea. Digestion of bread left for resident higher orders.

White cloud in heavy hang. Vapour streaks in slow heavenly rise. Mindful of a deluge return, packing is accelerated by mosquito squadron's spiking through clothing across my shoulders and now madly itching legs. I say goodbye to the Dutch couple. Wishing them well on their trip to western Spain, telling them of the Cantal Mountains not far away. They have never heard of them, preferring grey views of crash barrier blur.

The Range Rover has gone. I was going to stop at the Accueil to say a polite thank you for the stay. But it is probably not a good idea. Any communication an unwelcome intrusion. It would be better to pull my hat down over my eyes and not be there. It is what I do.

Freewheeling the driveway, thoughts wander back to the cold stuffy feudal reception not experienced in France. Too perfect spoken English and the English car.

How French was my stately experience?

Countryside tarmac strip snakes skyward, down on the granny gear. Fields fall away without ditch or hedge. The brown tint sun glare river way below. River and compass point south, empty road cycling meets a solitary roadrider.

Sunny morning 'Bonjour.'

Steep rise, busy village narrow streets where people have lived in high position of safety for an arm length of centuries. Lane twists the ancient habitations. Narrowed claustrophobic crest. Dead end alleys to confuse attackers, today cyclists, lead to ways of no escape. The lane turns 90 degrees weaving buildings to a countryside hairpin helter-skelter down and down. Terraced walls fallow, scrub grass and bushes. The roadrider on his upward return. A second of laughter shared on recognition.

Steel bridge crosses the River Allier, solitary fisherman nods greeting. Terminal metallic noise from the rear of the bike. I stop.

Leaning the bike against the bridge rail seeking the cause. The rear forks look fine, so do the wheel lugs. I bounce he bike to find the rack to which the panniers are attached has broken. I made separate aluminium brackets to help share the load. Now carrying the full load after the failing of the manufactured rack. Jubilee clip gaffer tape bodge stops a broken bar sticking through the spokes.

A noisy collective argument is happening in the reeds below. The makers of the incessant quarreling honk keep themselves hidden. Les Grenoulles. Frogs.

D214 follows the Allier sharing views to forested Monts du Livradois. Wide river crossing, through Jumeaux. Countryside to Brassac-les-Mines. Industry under tall brick built chimneys.

Country road climb, empty village birdsong chirp. Open window echoes reggae music bounce along sunny street walls.

Crossing Route National into Lempdes sur-Allagnon.

Little town is closed. The last frames of the pannier market stalls are packed into vehicles. Old town sunny street weave void of people at 'midi.' Short shadow, noise of river roar. The little gorge road lone companion to a turbulent river.

D909 'Gorges d l'Allagnon.' Proclaimed. The route chosen to ascend the Cantal Mountains. Just a line on the map. What a find! A gradual ascent against riverflow. A railway appears swapping sides disappearing subterranean to appear around a bend crossing on old bridges of iron, brick and stone. Rapids, wide bubbling shallows, clear deep pools. Controlling weirs power hydro electric taming a river in controlled cascade. Overhanging trees dance shade over the traffic free idyllic road. Parts of the gorge rocky narrow, opening to green singing woodland trapped against an elevated stone curtain. On top of a craggy vertical cliff, a ruin. Black stone square tower rises above half tumbled walls. I pass beneath. Watched by long black wings gliding from tower perch to ascend in spiral.

Clustered houses lean over winding bend. Two walkers wave a greeting sharing happiness to be in such a place. A girl roadrider pulls alongside on a gleaming roadbike asking me many questions as we ride.

Where are you from? Where are you going? Etc. She tells me this is where she lives and her love for the place. In the winter the snows are thick with the temperature going down to -20 degrees, sometimes continuously for weeks keeping villages isolated until snowdrifts can be cleared.

We talk for ten minutes, she is the most pleasant and

enthusiastic to meet. Another rider catches her up and she must go, increasing pace, increasing distance.

The river leaves a straightening road. Land wide enough for fields captive between forested volcanic ridge. Chimneys of rock high above trees, vertical cliff. Lava frozen in time. Isolated farmhouse, aged livestock barns empty.

Gorge narrows to end in rude noise and speed of Route National. Sign points Massiac. A notice on the door of a supermarket. 'Desolé. We are closed for a long holiday.'

Bumpy D road. Traffic heavy, straight line to town. Maison du Tourisme closed. Back lane supermarket closed. Other shops in town closed. Across the traffic blur a bar with tables offers a menu.

Inside to cool echoey dimness. Leaning on the bar, eyes adjust to interior light, background kitchen sounds.

'Desolé. The serving of food finished fifteen minutes ago at 3pm.'

I order a Coke and sit outside looking at the town pharmacy electronic sign '30 degrees' of sun glare.

Twenty motorcyclists sweat, wrestling into layers of black kevlar padding, black full face helmets and thick black leather clothing. They are off together somewhere and leave in a collective revving and great noise rumble to an appreciative audience. I follow a few minutes later. The click of a changing gear, silent, slow, without notice.

Direction St. Flour. Direction Murat. Underneath, campsite icon for a municipal site points to the Murat road. Edge of town camping. The back of a sports field. The Accueil a chalet. The Patron, a smiling man with glasses shows me my pitch in constant jovial mood with non-stop humour. One motorhome on Dutch plates the only other resident. My wet washing tree hung soaks up yellowing warmth of late afternoon sunshine.

Town wander finds the only trading shop. A Fromagerie. I open the door. Many large balls of cheese above little bottles wrapped in wicker tat dressed with straw enabling a charge of ridiculous price, and a rack containing bottles of emergency wine.

Cross purpose conversation with the shopkeeper.

I ask for some local Cantal cheese from cows rather than goats. Which would he recommend for taste introduction?

He picks up a whole round of great weight and offers it to me in the hope I will buy it. The thing is huge.

"Une tranche, sil vous plait. J'ai en velo" One slice please. I am on a bicycle.

He recommends "Moyen." Middle in strength.

The boule of cheese makes a satisfying heavy thump onto a worn wood board, gripping a handle pulls tension in the wire to cut one thick slice of creamy white solid Cantal cheese complete with the rind of crusted mould. Careful wrapping is folded in paper presentation. Walking back to the campsite I try some. Creamy, without grease, smooth richness, earthy in country taste. I do not notice the five minutes to the site gates. In intoxicating taste enjoyment I have pigged two thirds of my purchase.

Green iridescent lizards scurry to hide in grass rustle. Large docile ants as big as a thumbnail patrol around and over the tent. The River Alagnon tumbles rocky cliff gorge stepping back to a tree covered top. Thunder from a weir sends atomised haze skyward. The view to town ends in volcanic cliff. A chapel of St. Madeleine is perched precipitous looking ready to topple.

Vehicle noise, headlights. A Landrover arrives at dusk with a piled up roof rack towing a loaded trailer on English plates, setting up a large tent. I lay listening to cricket chirp. Mozzie welts on my legs, shoulders and head have swollen up angry and itching. I rub surgical spirit in the hope of cleansing the irritating souvenirs courtesy of Chateau Mozzie.

55 km

No rain, no thunder. Dry ground. Eating as much as I can stand of 'Brioche' sweet bread bun offering multi use as a pillow or a vehicle airbag, guaranteed to keep fresh for several years. The only choice available in the food bag this morning. Legs red blotched lumpy from the mozzies. My head full of lunar lumps cooled with a cold water wash. Bites swollen in mad irritation.

I meet the Landrover couple returning to England from Spain for the summer with their son. A toddler dictator who demands all attention.

Thanking the Patron. Riding up the driveway receiving a wave from a happy person living here for the summer with his dog.

Tuesday supermarket has open doors of replenishment. Returning past the Bar. Tables under energetic cleaning in readiness for the trading day. Direction passes the campsite completely empty. Two decorators paint the entrance pillars at municipal pace. Au revoir pleasant Camping Municipal de l'Allagnon.

Road climb to a twisting gorge. Sometimes open, sometimes narrowing. Shortening shadow tells of late morning. Breeze blows cool, steady climb. Rising cliffs tower beyond sight in brightness. Water trickle, pink and yellow flowers grow from fissure bringing bright delicate colour to dulled rock. Steep forest, volcanic sculpture towers pierce tree tops. Sometimes the river a little way below, other times long ascents hide the roar echo in tree smother. Birds of prey spiral to fly level with the cleaved cliff road. Rooftop glint of human habitation overwhelmed by natures surround. Green lizard bask on roadside rock. Red Squirrel betrayed by warning chatter. Long furry ears, chestnut ruddy brown. Smaller, daintier than the Grey.

Bulk timber carved sign. 'Parc Naturel Volcans d' Auvergne.' Greets steady climb away from the gorge to fields and cliffs of strange volcanic appearance. Twisting journey rise, a first view. Monts du Cantal push the horizon skyward. Covered summit winter snows regressed in season.

Traffic. I must be nearing town. The first view of grey stone Murat, part country village, part alpine town, looked over by a huge white Notre Damme on rounded volcanic cliff. Across the valley craggy ridge forest, summit chapel oversees. Background high ridge forest hills rise black, distant topped green, grey broken rock summit.

Downhill to Murat. Campsite signed direction, freewheeling slow through potholed industry. Green lane ride, campsite entrance shaded river trickle surrounded in trees. The Accueil closed. Sign invites to pitch and pay later.

The Patron takes next to nothing. I converse my broken French, the Patron prefers to practice his English. I ask the best direction for exploring the Puys. I am shown a contour map of the mountains and the most popular routes including the distances. He takes the trouble to check the weather tomorrow. I walk up to the 'Intermarche' under the sideways watchful eye of Notre Damme. 'Big Mary,' watches all. I return thinking of tomorrow's ascent to Puy Mary.

Evening yellow warm sun, chiming cowbell fields surround, campsite crickets, bleating meadow sheep across little river rush. Forested volcano view, horizon's snow dappled mountain rise. Overhead atomic bomb clouds contrast dense white against the primary blue. The heavyweights calm and dissipate as the cooling evening has switched off their heat fuel upward growth. Far away, higher land rumbles roll through snowed summits.

40 km

Donkey bray alarm echoes across the still valley. Thought of breakfast tempts a rise. 8am leaving the tent and carried weight behind for a dayride. Empty road. Town bypass rises steep gradient built for the internal combustion engine, not horse, cart, or bicycle. Slow grind. Maybe the brakes are stuck on. I feel shaky, not fully recovered from the day without food.

A herd of cows. Brown Cantal ladies peer down through the wire. One plays a tune from the bell hanging from a thick leather neck belt. Bypass roundabout furthers the climb, patient easy gear conserves energy. Cresting thin green amongst volcano chimneys. Road rolls over dropping. Large blue sign. PUY MARY. PASS DE PEYROL. 'OUVERT.' The mountain pass open.

Steep country lane freewheel, falling stream cascades rock, twisting ride under green. Rich meadow long valley rises steep into forest. Rooted veins of rock shoot vertical claiming the sky. Imposing brown grey mass, snow pocket, deepened fissure, twisted ridge rock. Little river babble, ancient stone bridge.

'Dienne.' Houses of heavy rubble stone. Lime walls, deep windows resist weather, stone slab roofs. Corners of each roof slab rounded resisting winter gale lift.

Long valley road. Mountain rise, semicircle dead end, mass volcanic high cliff. Isolated farms, small church of heavy stone. Simple arch windows under a slatted belfry, the spire of slated wood. House roofs huddle under. Sweeping fields to the valley home of a grazing herd shaded under mountain ridge. High summit's spidery iron crucifix. Puy de Peyre-Arse and Puy de Battaillouse lead far away to a mountainous dark dead end.

Tree covered road climb, steepened fields. Below, rich green sweep, cowbell sound. Thin evaporation in rapid tumble across peaks under pure blue morning. Today idyllic. Hard living in deep winter season. It is within two days of June. Stubborn remnant winter snow feeds meltwater streams. Vertical cascade vast silver tumble falls through emerald velvet green wandering the valley amongst the chiming herd.

Road steepens. Painted names. Tour de France riders. Shleck brothers, Cadel Evans, added words of encouragement, 'Come on!' Above, moorland. Boulders, cliff protrusion, fallow land. Commanding views across the volcanic Puys. Ancient molten flows frozen 10,000 years end in a rubble heap of scree sliding amongst clinging coniferous trees.

Fragrant yellow flowering roadside broom. Long grass refuge grows violet carpet of deep delicate blue. Cowbells on the breeze send a distant alpine chime.

Half snow covered Puy Mary. Distant road ascends under a long spined ridge. Dead end high jagged peaks, sparse trees on the edge of green. Snow drift shade sheltered by vertical chasm resists changing season. The ever long ascent loses early morning coolness replaced by sunny day heat. Steep pinching bends climb dead end rock. Zig zag steep, tight hairpin, scrubby trees without shade. Vallée du Mars rolls away blue swamped by haze. I keep from the broken verge, low stone post, rails missing no longer guard the long vertical drop.

Climb follows the rising tarmac contour cling tight under Puy Mary's summit. Shaded escarpment holds winter's snow. A ride under the ice drip, trickling stream chatter along giant rock mass. I crest the top, pipped by a red Lycra clad roadrider puffing away standing on the pedals straining to do it. For his own reasons he has to be first. There is no race today.

A café. Information centre plate glass. Blind rock bend, along the stone cleaved Pas de Peyrol downhill under steep rock ridge. Vertical drop either side far down into minute models of trees. Faraway mountains spectacular, wells the heart with joy.

New experience for the eyes and for the mind to savour and enjoy. Endless mountain cliffs, precipitous drops, thin ribbon twisting mountain road. One solitary dot of a car moves lost in the landscape, forests indiscernible blend featureless in vast panorama. Other views of long ridges surround a deep earth plunge big enough to swallow a city. Conical volcano mountains carpeted forest green, splashed in mass yellow and brown. Background mountain spikey featureless silhouettes hazy blue melts horizon with sky. I venture a way down a twisting road. A memorial of wartime written on plain slate.

To the memory
of the underground
of Mandailles
Killed the 19th June 1944

The few words are all that is said of fates of the participants of that day. Whether in battle stopping the advancement in response to the D Day landings or in cold murder I do not know. Cruel death stopping crazy idealism.

Returning to the 1589m (4700ft) Pas de Peyrol absorbed in landscape study riding in cold summit shade emerging to sun glare. Busy people between the information centre and café. I buy a coffee sitting at a wood picnic bench. The owners have forgotten people have legs. Many benches crammed maximise catering for the euro.

The view back to Puy Mary. Spine ridge reaches acute to a summit. Dots of colourful nylon hike to the top with a further descent over a long ridge to make a full day spectacular hike of immense view.

Different light and shadow upon the landscape constantly change detailed form of mountain panorama refreshing the visual spectacle of raw nature's massive scale.

The place busies. The arrival of rectangle motorhomes, motorcycles and cars all looking to park along limited road space. Vehicle occupants do the visitor centre circuit finishing in café refreshment.

Three roadriders arrive at speed on lightweight carbon machines giving a racing show around the corner to a café finish. A following large black Merc coupé stops a little way in front. The roadriders dismount, walk to the car, open the boot and take a drink from their bags carried in the boot. Pampered! They are off in downhill manic thrash. Merc chaperone follows in stereo beat airconditioned. Groups of cyclists arrive from either direction. Some calm, others sweat glazed hungry for breath after the ascent. All seek café sustenance. My coffee cup empty, a plate of crumbs in tastebud memory. Time to move over and through people crammed tables.

Slow freewheeling pace re traces the ascent through hairpins passing a walkers' Gite under summit watch. Residents emerge colourful in waterproofs with maps, sticks and wooly hats for the day's hiking.

Paired adders court in the sunshine at the roadside verge. The flat elongated square head grey. Black bead eye shines. Tongue tastes the air. The body grey, elongated diamonds, round black dots run to the tip of the tail. They travel side by side, in symmetry rear up tall together before returning flat to the ground. They are silent. I am silent. I do not bother them and they do not bother me.

Wave exchange. A lone cyclist long time on the road. Nut brown weatherbeaten. Grey tied back hair and beard contains a wide grin, riding a muddied touring bike loaded and road worn.

Cow symphony. Chiming and mooing without key or time, never reaching an end. Wild meadow muscly brown horses, white manes. Grazing amongst scrub bush.

The valley village of Dienne. Ancient stone beehive, a Burroner's hut many hundreds of years old with a stone tiled circular roof, an open ridge tile for a chimney vent and a small opening to crawl in through the wall. Ancient habitation for shepherds living with the summer flock.

Woodland return climbs the hilltop junction. An unhurried amble, freewheel speeding breeze, both brakes work hard. The entrance of the campsite. 3.30pm.

Routine chores washing the few carried clothes earns a happy laze. A feeling of every pedal turn to get from England

to the mountain panorama have been worth it. Evening passed sat on soft green watching the sky. Overhead orange is starting to burn, extinguished to a fireside glow behind black Cantal Mountain peaks.
64 km

The echoing bray donkey alarm. Today a rest day laze. The communal room horror chamber devices. T.V. and a phone. A walk into town finds La Poste to send cards of communication. An old ginger cat spherical, stiff in its back legs prowls the bushes. Silent wait. Reminiscing past great hunts and murders. It looks for a split second before returning to crouched concentration, front paws neatly together. The same visual focused anticipation of a fisherman.

Murat town. Winding uphill jumble under heavy slated roofs built steep, long stone chimney stacks centuries blackened. Narrow lane steps, twist and turn alleyway. Not one building the same. Five storey rise of heavy volcanic stone. Shutters shelter weathered windows peeping deep from stone reveals. Rooftop chequette windows shelter beneath carved oak bulk.

Single spout trickles into a semicircular trough sending unending ripples in a watery pattern dance. La Poste takes postcards, the patisserie sells sugar glaze fruit to enjoy exploring the narrow uphill. A couple of art galleries display work reaching extremity of standards. I pass an open glass door on my slow wandering.

"Bonjour" from an artist working a canvas.

The man reminds in appearance of Salvador Dali. The painted style is not.

The bloom of a florist, a cobbler. Gun shop hunting rifles

and knives big enough to dispatch elephants. Boutique shops internal muffled music, a bookshop of silence. Laughter from Bar Tabac. The pharmacy informs in digital green 27degrees. The top of town. Restaurant seating under awning shade. Chairs and tables polished in anticipation of lunchtime custom looked down on by 'Big Mary' completely in white holding the infant. Contrasting the black volcanic cliff on which she stands in open arm pose of blessing and welcome.

Spouts send water from metallic fish at the end of bearded face stone carvings around a circular post emptying to a round trough. Across the street, people sit for an aperitif looking through the menu. Shaded table holds arranged flowers of red.

The old road to Puy Mary and Salers twists narrow rising out of sight. Weathered black stone house facades roofed in heavy slate hold wrought iron snow guards. Bottle shape chimney pots patterned with cut outs have covered tops to stop snow dropping down the flue. Behind the houses black cliff face rises near vertical.

Winding shady lanes void of traffic. The quiet of France at lunchtime, sounds of people living their lives. I hear a sentence of conversation on passing an open window. The noise of a kitchen, pots, pans and cutlery. News through an open door, a radio. Everyday life at 12. Midi. Posters advertise a festival missed by days. The Fete de l'estive. Cattle are driven through the streets and up into the hills to mountain summer pasture. Celebrated by much drinking and eating. Winter at this altitude only just over. Back down in the Allier valley the first of the hay has already been cut, dried and turned in process of harvest.

Campsite return under the trees, the babbling river. A family picnic under overhanging shade.

Wishing "Bon Appetite."

A smiling "Merci."

From the Accueil, the Patron calls and asks of yesterday's journey.

I reply that it had exceeded anything I could have imagined and his given directions were excellent. I recount my mountain experiences up at Puy de Dome road pass. Resulting in laughter and being told the mountain had a reputation for anger and unpredictability. Hence the weather station and the Roman temple to the god Mercury.

Preparation for departure. Oiling ritual of chain, cables and gears. Everything runs silky smooth. The rear tyre is topped up, but when loaded always looks flat.

A German roadrider camping in his van offers the use of a foot pump. He has been riding many circular routes exploring the area for two weeks. Holiday ends tomorrow. He goes to his van returning with maps and shows the different places ridden over many years he has been coming to France. We sit down conversing between my occasional German and his few words of English throwing in some French. He shares valuable information about areas to future visit. Friendly, quiet and knowledgeable, achieving wonderful rides of the Gorges du Tarn and a lot of the Pyrenees. He returns to his van. Removing the awning shade, packing his table and chair before undoing the bike wheels in ritual closure to his holiday.

I pack the few necessities carried.

"Bonjour" to a retired French couple staying in their motorhome.

The Frenchman returns, he stops to ask me. Where am I from? Where am I going? How many kilometres in a day? Etc.

I answer his questions and get a "Bon courage!" reply.

He goes directly over to his neighbour sat outside a bike laden motorhome containing classic steel racing bikes and I am discussed between them. I do not hear what they say. Body language tells all.

The gossip is delivered pointing back over his shoulder towards me using his thumb, deep in animated conversation.

The neighbour looks surprised leaning sharply forward, then leans back in his chair tipping his baseball cap back on his head saying something. The Frenchman nods repeatedly in quick movements. At the same time together they turn and stare.

I raise a tin mug. Acknowledged.

The evening spent sat outside on the grass watching the sunset replay.

Across the Margeride

The daily donkey alarm at 5am is acknowledged only by the subconscious. 7am waking. Mist hangs the little flowing river, sun yet to break haze veil soft colour. I eat the remaining half butter cake, drink half a litre of milk and a litre of water whilst packing, nail the remaining half of yesterday's baguette in its vulcanising process spooning half a pot of 'abricot conserve' to save space.

8.15am, campsite occupants surface.

"Bon route" from the Frenchman.

"Wiedeshein! Gorges du Tarn, ok!" From the German roadrider.

A wave of farewell. The Accueil side window opens, the Patron waves and I thank him for a pleasant stay.

"Come back and see us again!"

Town wakes for daily business. Direction St. Flour naively thought as downhill as Murat is a mountain town.

Murat town absorbed further and further in rock and green land. Climbing a cliff cleaved road. Wired rock face sprouts bushes and wild yellow alpine flower. Heavy haulage in low gear whine with high revs. Gear change momentary pause before the shuddering and struggling engine grumble resumes the daily transport toil. Lorries pass slow, heat and oil engine smell, diesel exhaust spirals bits into my eyes. Holding breath resists a dirty lungful, eyes do the vision squint until the lorry passes. A few clean breaths. The approach of the next heavy hill crawler.

Thoughts of the happy campsite occupants in morning greeting enjoying breakfast in the mellow green. Sad to leave a good place? The journey has changed. Originally it was about places, the road the method. Secondary in importance. The road now the primary, always constant. Places ephemeral. Trust in the road. It is my guide.

Road levels, all hills have a top. The road to St. Flour travels small villages, isolated buildings of industry. Downward push, big gear roll towards town rooftops. Standard 'Bricolage land,' standard municipal roundabout. Standard tin industrial and glass front modern retail sheds will decant your commodity dream standard A.P.R.

Town busy road junction heads traffic away on a bypass. I ignore it. Shops, cafés and importantly a bank with a cash machine. Boulangerie sells an armful of fresh baked bread, cake and pizza. A large white stone Resistance monument dominates. A dying soldier cared for by the doctor. The doctor possibly one of the town inhabitants rounded up and shot. Either side are cut stone block walls contrasting black with the names of many inscribed in gold leaf. The Monument reads

Heroes
de la
Resistance
1944

St. Flour is strategic. Hillsides fall away quick to a far below river. I head down the bypass stopping next to white noise flowing water. Upward a town of turrets, spires, cliffs and defensive walls. The medieval town protected, controlling both river and important road route running under its gaze.

D road leaves town bustle. Little D990 away from arterial traffic into countryside. Singing birds, waving wildflower under late morning sunshine climbing across rolling farmland served by bright silent hamlets. Forest rise across far distant blue hills.

The Foret de la Margeride narrow lane twist. Steep continuous ascent under pinewood smelling heated and sweet. Rock edge road weaves the patient lives of countless silent trunks. Broken view tree cordon, dropping rocky steepness. Pine grows with twisted trunk and short bough, austere branch green needled. Bunched brown cone fruit dries under heat to split releasing the winged seed to flutter amongst many wild broad leaf trees. 15km of constant climbing affords fleeting views across Cantal Mountain contours left to travel in memory.

Rocky forest mountain trail conjures pioneer image romance. A place to live around the fire glow. Plantation fir escapees mix with wild pine. Above black needle branch high in the blue, birds of prey wheel. A different hill to the travelled slowly meets over dead end valley. Road snake wanders hairpins, journey into managed dense fir loses the sky. Smothered light deep shade silent. Flecks of blue seep, sun pierces in shafts, sky break through black tree canopy. Out of the forest. Bright hill wild rough. Fallow pasture. Boarded houses overgrown half dereliction. Agricultural buildings of stone quiet, empty, swamped in wild flower meadow consuming the grey oak post rotting out time. Rusting roadside stock fence redundant, no herds to wait for. No ownership to deliniate. A sign. 'Montchamp.' The Monts de la Margeride. Looking back to a final panorama. Blue Cantal Mountains patched white by defiant remnant snow.

The road ahead commits to blackened forestry. Light falls from a hemmed compressed corridor. Within grown density blackness nothing can flourish. Ground light starved twenty four hour darkness for decades yields a crop of euros from cheap construction softwood.

Full daylight, rooftops, into habitation of Pinols village. High rocky countryside leaves the Auvergne to a battle between Haut Loire and Haut Allier. Another monument to murder stands isolated at the roadside. In my translation it reads

Here
The graves of
F. Outour
Y. Leger
Assassinated
by the
Gestapo
The 27th May 1944
Deaths
for
France.

It is always with sobering surprise, because the areas are in isolation. Graves lonely feel forgotten. Away from social habitation. Monuments to sadness, monuments to outrage. A reminder of the darker side of the human mind, sinister capability. Destructive abnormality passed through genetics ever to plague the human race.

Narrow ribbon twists livestock pasture, locals busy munching grass, sideways chewing. The bovine disinterested gaze of a thirty month lifespan of all day grass digestion could produce. Pasture surrounded by wild moorland purples amongst deep yellow splash. Altitude cools temperature. Fir tree smother, dense compressed silence.

Road roll in freewheel. Lumber lorries of great size built for purpose. A powered unit with a short articulated back haul great long loads of cut fir trunks, separate bogie trailer fastened supports the load. The leviathans travel opposite direction along the narrow forest road sucking up dust with bits of flying bark and wood chips. I hold my breath squinting eyes in clouded airborne wood dirt blizzard. The lorry convoy roars past leaving me dirtied fragrant with earth and sawdust. Areas of forest cleared by tractor units. Hydraulic arm grab motion. Shadowed prehistoric herbivorous creatures munching in dark forgotten forest world dining on limbs and trunks. Others nose the ground, uprooting stumps in daily sustenance.

Half the forest replaced by grass meadow of green in full daylight. Steep land dropping far beyond sight. Trees thin to a ribbon, then no more. Aeroplane views, far distant valley. Surrounding hills of advancing fir held back from lowering land by soft deciduous green wood fringing steep pasture. Dotted grazing livestock served by lone farm isolation. 'Gorges d'Allier' proclaimed on a sign naming the waiting long helter-skelter ride to re unite with a river crossed five days ago.

Freewheel speed, contour hill roll. Low stone walls retain the road from a suede green drop off near vertical. I pull off of the road, wheel rims too hot to touch need to cool. Impressive views, open hillside journeyed reaches up in sweeping climb claimed by high forest smother. Sunshine heat of lower land softer to the skin, warmed air fragrant to breathe.

Across a wide valley and hazed hill horizon somewhere is Le Puy-en-velay. Destination for tomorrow.

Rooftops far below straddle the River Allier. The town of Langeac. It would be a good place to stop. On the map, no green box. Without a campsite it will be a long day.

Downhill breeze freeride alternating the brakes, leaning the bends, controlling speed. Two cyclists make their way up the long climb.

Rolling towards Langeac. 'Canoe Forest Adventureland.' Without mention of a campsite. Along the walled riverside, town information board blank. No municipal camping.

Langeac has a very old church looking over the River Allier. It is all I see. Main town occupation is sitting on a bench staring at the flowing river. Across the bridge reveals nothing for a campsite. A couple sat in the shade on a parked Harley Davidson shout "Allez!" Both laughing.

'Vallee des Volcans.' Permanent uphill. A picturesque village commands a hill amongst many wooded surrounding. High walls to old house cluster. Orange red roofs, church central, square tower walls. Under arches hang shining bells.

Road twist green woodland smother. Looking for a turning. Have I missed it, maybe the road numbers are different to the map?

Road finishes busy. Main N route. Le Puy-en-velay 40km away uphill. I plod the white line.

Rising busy main road in afternoon heat without breeze.

Heated tarmac glistens bubbles of melted black. A tractor rattles past. If he is allowed on this road, then so am I. Many cars and trucks thunder close. Every vehicle in France is going to Le Puy.' Noise and smell from hundreds of exhaust pipes. Long straight ascent. Vanishing point moves further distant. Long plod to a bend offering more climbing. I yawn, my eyes would like to shut. Legs push, wheels dodge bolts, glass and wire shed along the white line. The common junk and dirt of unmerciful main road. A rectangular sign too distant to read. Hopefully favourable. Even a garage shop selling more than fanbelts and oil would be welcome.

The sign. 'Camping 3 star. Ouvert.'

A turning to a country lane. Sign directs a destination 2.5km away. Bike wobble. Back tyre goes down rapid flat. I stop, throw off the sleeping bag and get out a tube, lay the bike over and take the back wheel off yawning. Feeling very relaxed with my mind wandering to search for a pillow. The puncture a slit in the tyre. Glass. With nothing stuck in the tyre I do a temporary halfhearted effort. I shall be putting up my tent and enjoying a hot shower to relax the body and awaken the mind for the evening. The site has a bar. I look forward to an ice cold beer reward. I half pump up the tyre, fit the wheel back in, flip on the chain using the specialist tool under the saddle, an old sock saves oily hands. Freewheeling, back tyre rolls soft as brioche bun, watching the odometer km looking for a campsite sign. Down to a small village. If this is a dud it has cost height. The odo' 2.5km. Sign directs up a steep potholed road by a farm. I come to a closed gate advertising the campsite entrance. Behind a hedge caravan roofs.

Opening the gate, up the slope looking for the Accueil.

Grass freshly cut smelling sweet, the place looks empty. I walk to an entrance of large patio doors to find the bar closed. Chairs on tables through dusty glass. The place not open. The front of the house, knocking the door. No one is home.

I will pitch the tent in defiance of leaving. If someone comes back I will argue the sign advertises the site. 'Ouvert.' If no one appears I am in anyway. I have finished my riding for today, the body refuses to do any more. The mind in tired agreement.

The tent goes up, the sleeping bag inside ready for a comfortable nights rest. I get the tyre fixed. Car noise pulls up to the house. I walk to the front door and knock. The door opens slightly and a lady in her sixties half peers around the gap.

I politely ask if I can stay, having seen the sign saying open. I am on a bicycle, have my tent set up and show her some money in my hand happy to pay for my night's accommodation.

She tells me they have not got around to opening the showers yet.

I don't mind. I ask if she has a working tap outside.

She comes out, shows me the tap and telling me I can stay. But will not accept any money because there is no service.

I tell her I have come today from Murat in the Auvergne of which she is quite taken aback and thank her for letting me stay.

She is apologetic that nothing is working.

The tap is all I need.

I fill my two plastic cola bottles with the cold water and cook food. The upturned lid of the pannier box becomes a makeshift bathtub. Road grime sweat is sponged away alfresco bathing.

Birdsong from surrounding trees dominated by the

blackbird's familiar summer tune is accompanied background by cricket's rhythmic chirp in my own personal country campsite beneath hilly flower meadow. Short hill horizon shows deepening colours of evening. Cotton clouds hang pink without movement.

106 km.

Le Puy En Velay

I wake in my own personal campsite in a village. The name I have no idea of. It is the most peaceful, without leaf rustle. Birds in chorus, heckled by a squirrel in territorial squawk, the vocal character remains hidden. Early morning freshness cold to the skin. With not much to pack, final things slip in the panniers.

I intend to leave the lady 5 euros for my night's occupancy. I write a note reading. 'Merci.' Selecting two large white perfect daisies to accompany the note and money. I am walking to the gate to place the payment when the lady comes out. I thank her placing the simple flowers in one hand, her face lights with delight, the other hand I place the money under protest.

Downhill twist through the sleeping village, crosses a single track railway. Farm lane ride, compass points South East, direction for Le Puy-en-velay

The smell of dairy farming. Leaf lane ride, flanked farm buildings. Milking parlour noise one side, a tractor busy scraping the opposite yard. Gate closes behind the last of the dairy herd ambling the field after routine morning's work.

Road split climbing. Sign points 'Loudes.' It's on the map. Twisting road brings far high tree horizon closer with every bend. Steep fields, river noise tumbles a valley. Woodland encroaches meadowland. Altitude increase.

Below. The farmed head of a valley, a tractor chugs bouncing down a rough lane with an attentive collie knowing routine. The dog sprints the field separated by a hedge. Stopping, listening for the tractor. Characteristics of the wolf. Head and tail held low in tiptoe walk towards a farm building.

Tight turns require straight leg push, gradient ease, 7km climb, tended agriculture, crossroads direct. Dotted villages, fields to far distance, long descent without need to pedal. High views across crops green paled to dry yellow. Forest fir mid distance, domed hills rough and volcanic. Beyond, a lowland ocean of white vapour, misted hills float as islands, the far shore high jagged deep blue mountainous horizon. The distant Cevennes. Excitement of new land to travel.

The morning not yet 10am, day heat yet to burn the haze. No need to touch the pedals, many miles of downhill countryside roll beneath the wheels. Farmworkers lean on a gate talking. A nod. "Bonjour".

The narrow built street of Loudes. Busy minimart colourful boxed fruit oozes taste. One street shops open to fields flattening to a main road junction. Direction. Le Puy-en-velay. Jet fighter behind a fence, 'Y' shaped tail. 1960s military no longer used announces an airfield.

Main roundabout. Exit for Le Puy-en-velay.

Le Puy-en-velay starts without beauty. Dropping into narrow busy city streets potholed bumpy and patched from never ending vehicle city spin. Street cast shadow from long time lived in friendly buildings, long windowed cast iron verandah scroll, large open eaves red tiled roof city. A feel of the south. Between buildings, the gigantic white statue of

Joseph holding infant Jesus stands on a pillar of rock. Busy traffic deeper into the city. Signed direction 'centre.' Busy traffic without impatience. Stop and re start traffic light command to the centre of town. An open air market, rolling waves of people. Pushing the bike, blending with the human jumble, mass filled pedestrian streets on shop jammed Saturday morning.

Three pack donkeys with wooden cradled carrying panniers patiently stand advertising their hire for trekking the Cévennes. I would like to stop to get a photograph, all the shop fronts are glass one after the other. The shoulder to shoulder moving crowd offers nowhere to lean the loaded bike. The little city breathes a unique happy ambience. Side street to a busy indoor and outdoor market. A saxophone and trumpet band with a bass drum plays brash music with Arabic scales mixed with jazz runs of notes makes exciting happy music. Good musicians, timing tight, sharing enjoyment creativity to a crowd of applauding onlookers under sunshine. People hand leaflets for political candidates, one being Mr. Prat. Politician name perfect. Fresh cooking smells of bread, quiet side street boulangerie. I open a narrow wood and glass door, stepping down into a small shop centuries old. Fresh sweet delight fragrant wait under glass. Cakes and bread for lunch, wandering tall building shade. Buildings' individual design, stone faced, some rendered, pillared. Architectural detail, long windows, shutters. Street lanterns hang off scrolled iron above the cobbled twist. Narrowed snaking lane, multicolored building maze on the side of a hill.

I wanted to visit Le Puy-en-velay to see the huge Notre Damme of France. A 23m (70ft) statue of Mary with a golden crown of stars holding the infant Jesus looking out over the city all in pink rusting cast iron made from melted cannons captured from the Russians during the Crimean war. The problem I have is the lady is having a makeover, covered from head to foot in scaffolding and denying all callers. The next spectacle stands on top of a towering volcanic spiked pinnacle. The ancient chapel of St. Michel, vertiginous high over the city. Built in AD961. Financed by a Bishop who felt it was his calling to build after experiencing the St Diago de Compostella pilgrimage to Spain. Testament to its quality is that it is over a thousand years old. I sit under the pinnacle of volcanic rock straining my neck in vertical upward view. The sun intense. Opposite. The municipal campsite Motorhome busy. I haven't done many miles, but cave under the clear heat. Mr. Prat in a van with speakers on the roof postered with portrait, name in capitals drives past in vocal campaign.

The campsite is open. I am told must wait until 1pm or the computer will charge for two nights. The chime of one buys a pitch. Tent routine. Washing hangs on the luxury of a communal drying line. 32 degrees of windless sunshine bakes wet clothes crisp.

Three revving motorcycles are directed arranged at set distance by the Patron. English plates bring familiar language tones busy removing helmets, unpacking tents, shedding sweated armoured jackets and padded over trousers in boil up. They are surprised to find me English and to be so far south. One crawls into his tent falling asleep, the other two head off into town in search of beer food and more beer.

Towering cumulus clouds gang up to surround the city late afternoon. Reaching temperature limit, gaining density becoming Cumulonimbus. Lightning flash, ground shaking rumble closes in to bombard a half hour deluge. Dry inside the tent, pelting rain on thin nylon, dozing on sleeping bag comfort. It clears leaving freshness. Smell of wet grass, steaming tarmac evaporation fast dries to start repeat cloud building.

Camped nearby, a cyclist from Switzerland going east to west, wanting to end up at the Atlantic coast. Problems of running out of energy cured by pasta. I agree with him, craving the stuff every night. He intends to travel the same route reverse direction to the Cantal Mountains.

Conversation of distance attainable. Monts de la Margeride spectacular views and the impending downhill fun to St. Flour and the ride to Murat. I recount how I could not find a campsite at Langeac.

He tells me. "All campsites are on my phone, it tells me everything. It is also my map.

Having no compass I ask how does he cope if the battery goes flat?

Computers, phones, communication. This journey is important to dispense with complication. Simplicity. A bike, tent and a paper map. Sole travel. Soul travel.

Later the Swiss man comes past on his bike going into town. He stops and explains how the gears on his bike are hub gears and superior.

"Imagine I am at traffic lights, I just do this." (Twisting of the wrist) "It is so easy." Nodding his head looking for a nod response.

I oblige while the mind thinks. 'I couldn't really care less.'

A couple arrive on loaded bikes both wet from the stormy downpour. Mid evening appears a loaded mountain bike. The rider has the appearance of a Red Indian. Brown weather beaten, looking to have been on the road for years.

Light gives way to late evening. Talking with the English motorcyclists.

I am asked. "How long have you been out from England and where are you going?"

I think it is over three weeks so far and I will be travelling through some of the Cevennes, after that I do not know, it depends on the day.

Do I want to know the news from England? No.

Would I like to see some film of today's riding?

Bike mounted cameras face front and back, able to switch between. Tales of speeding past a dozing Gendarme startling the man out of his skin open mouthed in his parked car a hundred miles an hour on a straight country road. Six days to get as much riding in as possible before catching the ferry from Cherbourg back to England looking for as many bends as possible.

I show photographs from the Cantal Mountains. Maps are produced and road numbers noted for the full Route des Cretes winding volcanic lands.

Chapel above is spectacular illuminated. The main features of the tower float in night sky. Notre Damme du France sadly veiled in blackness covered by matchstick scaffolding. The tower on the Cathedral shines gold in electric glow. Deepened evening sky produces a full moon.

A dozen loaded bikes have pedalled into the busy campsite. Le Puy en velay an ancient meeting point on the pilgrimage route to St. Diago de Compostella in Spain keeps the city in steady visitor flow.

32 km

The Cévennes

Someone makes as much noise as possible to wake everybody. The night had been of broken sleep which must be accepted in a city environment. This is the early Réveille Matin and at 5am there is no sleep return. I slip on clothes to investigate the identity of the early morning imbecile. I find many people doing the same and there he is. Monsieur Mouth. Hands on hips, the buttons on his stretched check shirt about to terminally submit to straining stomach containment. He is very pleased with himself looking through thick glasses. 'If I am up, everybody is up.' is the expression on his face.

Maybe a relative of Mr. Prat.

Dawn light broken cloud has a thick darkened blanket following. Cooler than yesterday, a feeling of rain later. I decide to pack dry rather than in rain. The motorcyclists roll tents and pack panniers. My tent down and rolled watching them sneak out of the gate locked for four wheels. Their noisy departure summons the Patron from his residence in a pair of shorts bleary eyed. There is supposed to be no noise before 7am. Tell that to Monsieur Mouth who has caused the early rising of a third of the campsite. Five minutes after the motorcyclists' departure I make silent escape, following signs for 'Valence.'

Traffic lights red, road empty. I must wait for no one. Sleeping streets silent. The pleasure of roads void of haulage and impatient weekday cars. A ride through potholed 'Bricolage land' direction for Le Monastier. River crossing. Brives Charensac. Old little town. Upstream broken bridge high arch of stone next to house walls forming the riverside. Sign proclaims 'La Loire.' Sandbanks and boulder wide flow. The river a junior version of itself many miles north and west. Downstream pillars of concrete rise from the riverbed. Reinforcing bars stand proud waiting patiently for deck construction to complete a new bridge. Suburban climb white wall modern village feels connected to the city. Agriculture replaces housing, fields gently roll around forested volcanoes. Cones of rock poke bare above black blanket trees. Gradient steepens, high woodland. 'Haut Loire' altitude agriculture, covered hills of black fir. Le Monastier appears out of moorland broken by rock and cliff. Views of wandering roads coiling hill rugged contour. Sub mountainous wilderness. A world away from soft feel Le Puy-en-velay.

Le Monastier sits on top of steep hillside tumbling into a gorge where the River Gazeille noisily runs several hundred feet below giving the town its full name of Le Monastier-sur-Gazeille. Opposite valley steep forested. Cliffs poke through trees.

9am. Ancient town narrow streets, sombre colours. Monastic church, deep burgundy and black stone buttressed walls. Large semicircular arched windows. Alternate black and white cut stone contains stained glass windows above heavy wood doors framed in deepening arches. Eaves decorated carved stone animals and people of early medieval style laid up and down the gable. Dog, horse, rat, cat, dog, hare, and donkey. The other side being made up of strange caricatured people, monsters, lizards, dragons and dogs or wolves. Strange creature carvings adorn an arch above centre stained glass.

The street sign reads Place de la Abbatail, 'The place of the abbey.' A circular narrow street, cobbled gutters built before the needs of the motor car, wide enough for horse and cart. Most buildings three storeys, some having additional rooftop rooms, black rubble walling, others rendered with arch windows, shutters and iron verandahs. All around the town piped reggae music at low volume from speakers tied to lampposts. The top end of the town black rubble walled stone chateau of four round towers, added small windows peer. Old drinking fountain centuries trickling to a trough. Reggae music directs to busy people setting up stalls for a Sunday pannier market. Crafts, baskets and pictures for sale. An old tractor chugs into the market pulling a trailer looking as an agricultural carnival float having leafed branches laid along the sides of the trailer that brush on the floor. The trailer covered in the fake grass of a grocer shop display. Bales of hay, a chicken coup containing fussing hens advertise fresh eggs and local cheese for sale. The happy feel from Le Puy-en-velay reaches isolated old Le Monastier-sur-Gazcille. A photographer's framed card studies depict the natural beauty and wildlife of this area. Trees and flowers, waterfalls. Bird of prey stands on a sun illuminated ragged crag against steely dark background. The work shows appreciation and artistic love for an area lived in.

Cars arrive directed to parking by a florescent green man. I have not come for the market, but for Robert Louis Stevenson and his book that starts here written in 1879. 'Travels with a Donkey in the Cevennes.' Here he spends a month getting ready to make a journey south across the Cevennes purchasing a small donkey to carry his pack over the hills of the wild Cévennes land.

He names the donkey Modestine. The two of them set out on the journey. The donkey proving to be a formidable servant to Mr. Stevenson knowing nothing about the species, experiencing a very steep learning curve on the ways of the ass. Stevenson meets quirky characters on the journey experiencing misery and beauty of the unfolding wilderness on a wandering zig zag south.

Le Monastier' so old. Not much has changed within the centre of the town. I see the streets and buildings the same as Stevenson's eyes, walking the streets where his feet trod. It is as close as I can get to observe living description of his book.

Wooden Icons of Mary and Jesus sheltered in alcove shrines in walls about the town. Medieval style of sculpture naïve, says they are many hundreds of years old. Beauty within simplicity.

Pushing the bike around town ends the same way as arrived, finding the convergence of the road junctions to put me on direction for 'Pradelles.' A town traversed by Mr. Stevenson. On the map it is at the end of a tight twisting D road that is marked as scenic.

I pass a man is leading two donkeys on ropes. Along the road over a rough steel framed fenced gate in a field of bright green stands a red brown donkey. Alert and staring. Too mischievous to be trusted. It puts its head over then kicks the gate scraping the floor with its hoof. Its extra long ears up facing me bright eyed almost with a smile, pushing at the gate. Standing still before a repeat. I tear half a baguette and throw it to the animal. The donkey picks it up and eats it in enjoyment. As I get on the bike it looks and brays. The animal brays over and over, sound diminishes with parting distance increase. The calling sends an echo across the valley.

Main junction road numbers different to the map. Three roads differ direction. One invites to drop into a gorge disappearing with the river through wild woodland and cliffs signed for Solignac-sur-Loire. Compass directs different. South.

Town rooftops float in the air from a dropping hillside. Crossing the river tumble, road splits. D500 Pradelles.

Climbing leaves the pleasing noise echoing River Gazeille. Pines and green wood views of Le Monastier. 180 degree change weaves tree canopy shelter. Bridged rock fissure climb. Road cleaved steep hillside, wet smelling tarmac, wet earth, drizzling mist rain freshness. Relief from 30 degree lower land heat. Soft rain on a thousand leaves, background whisper to birdsong. Faint rumble of distant river, hilly pasture to singing woodland. If I am to follow Stevenson's route exactly I need to turn for St. Martin des Fugéres. I stay on the D500, the map lacks detail. I leave the footprints of Mr. Stevenson for a while, he travelled the valley I travel the hill. The road more direct will reacquaint at Pradelles. I have no idea of how long it will take, knowing route map squiggles mean hill climbing.

Rain mist. Big droplets collected from many leafed branches drip. Wind stirs the trees, waterproofs needed. Open pastureland, wet grey monotony blanket rain cloud speeds the sky. Flattened reprieve resumes the climb. A roadside field. Three horses spooked by my silent approach run into a corner in panic. The bike incomprehensible, a monster come to eat them. I call, they calm returning to the centre in a walk, watching my progress. Cows stare across rusting electric fence with unconcerned sleepy gaze. Wind subsides in the lea of a hill, rain falls vertical. Bend reunites with blustery gusts. New view high wild land, dropping steep forested cliff lined gorge. River glimpse through mist rise.

A woman in yellow oilskins with two busy quartering collie dogs herds trotting goats along a rough track to a milking barn. I am ready with the camera. The animals walk into the scene, the battery goes flat and the camera shuts itself down. The moment gone. The picture stays in the mind. Being able to witness what must be mundane routine to one is enjoyed as privileged observation by another.

Helter skelter freewheel, rocky dark moorland pasture. Wild trees, bushes burst yellow sweet floral fragrant. Downward weaving road, isolated heavy stone houses, strong farm buildings tiled roofs add colour to raw grey. Speeding through hamlets, wet sodden lanes rise to clustered red rooftops. Secret villages shrouded under skyward forest black. Road plummet twist between rugged tree covered cliffs bring an everyday new surprise.

Yesterday the chapel, today a bridge over 30m (100ft) crossing a gorge of high wild land looking at a giants forest garden split by great slabs of grey cliff projection. Clear weave passage of dark brown edged water deepens to black. A reuniting with La Loire. Upstream water moves deep unhurried in cold calmness held by beaches of sand and boulders fringed with small trees doomed to flood. Behind elevated grow mixed leafy trees. Higher amongst rocky boulders mixed with slipping scree firs dominate twisted pines. Beneath the bridge, serenity flowing is broken by large boulders. Whitewater thunder rushes to pool deep downstream. Small river cascades cliffs landing foaming white over boulders in a hurry to join the enfant terrible Loire. Cliffs rise high. Fir clad vertiginous gorge sides. If the river had not been signed as La Loire, I would not have associated this small picturesque gorge flow with the ocean bound wild giant. There are not many miles left to the wild rivers beginnings across the hills to the marshy wellings of Gerbier de Jonc. The bridge crossed at St. Nazaire is the last, where La Loire mixes waters with salt of the Atlantic Ocean. There can be few crossing points in the remaining miles from here to its source.

Two vehicles in the last hour and apart from the Shepherdess, no people. All my height gained from the long upward road from Le Monastier has been squandered and must now be repaid.

Upward twisting forest road promises endless bends. A break in the trees affords final view to the gorge rumble steaming vapour rising to escape above forested cliffs grown to claim most of the sky. Built across the gorge three stone semicircular arches on tall pillars delicately span the river. The bridge has circular openings in the masonry between arches to reduce the weight of the structure mass carried on the slender stone vertical pillars giving pleasing aesthetic. This is my last upstream view of this infant that grows to support cities, palaces and many busy towns to its estuary mouth of world shipping.

Stevenson crossed La Loire lower downstream further back at Goudet with its buildings and people, chastising the pack carrying donkey feigning slow progress.

Silence. Rain. The upward journey. Thin road cling to gorge sides. Tree shelter steep long forest ascent. I have no donkey to carry my pack having to carry my own, therefore I am both donkey and driver. It takes more effort to propel the load by pedalling than steering. By simple percentage/effort mathematics I reason that I must be more donkey.

Twisting climb open pastureland. Rain dulls colours of what must be full vibrant greens and yellows in fair weather. Short descent, new valley view. Climb above a small river. Land rocky, sparse rough green. A few livestock graze in a diminishing triangular field. Low cliff rise above, old stunted pines grow deep root anchor far reaching into fissured rock. Ascent to managed fields and pastureland blurred through sheets of grey dragging cloud. Rain dulled livestock sheds appear. I pass close to a cow isolated from the rest of the herd happily tucking into hay together through bars in the shelter of the large modern steel unit. The lonely cow relegated to a small strip of grassed area next to the road surrounded by electric fence. It has a bad leg. Raw beef bloody, unable to put weight onto the shaky limb. The animal looks sad and lonely in its separation from its lifetime as one of the herd to silently stand alone in the wind and rain. I say hello. It looks up and follows me with a gaze as I pass by. It is probably going to be a sad end for the animal. You can almost see the knowing and fateful acceptance in the brown pool honest bovine eyes.

Rain constant. Wind driven bullets in the face, breathing open mouthed. Pulled down hat shelters the eyes. The upward plod. 'Haut Loire 1150 m' proclaims a road post. The land feels raw. Junction points straight on for Pradelles. Up close to the sign to see how far away the town may be, the distance number long gone. Not even a trace outline of the digit visible. Road flattens, rain pelt, hard gusts. Waterproofs no longer waterproof cling wet cold to the skin transmitting chilling wind. Sign loom, through grey blowing drear. 'Pradelles 4.'

I expect to see the Beast of Gevaudan leap from the blackness of surrounding wood constriction. The Beast a legend, the wolf that Stevenson remarked killed over a hundred people back in the mid-1700s. Killing shepherdesses, pursuing soldiers on horseback, eating children, no one was safe, apart from sheep.

It is so miserable. I would not want it any other way, the atmosphere suits book narration perfectly.

Main N route, long closed building signed 'GRILL RESTAURANT' and 'HOTEL.' Dusty road dirt stained windows loom grey wet. A feeling of grim inhospitality added to by speeding cars throwing spray from a wide black shining road. I stop. Switch on the bike lights, push the pedals in a big gear for speed on a gradual descending road.

Dull soaked land, greyed outline of faint high far away hills. A large lake looms long way below looking a grey hole through earth blackness.

Junction for Pradelles. Crossing the main route into town back alongside Mr. Stevenson, seeing the high landscape. Thoughts of lights, warmth and a town busy with people.

I am confronted by half a dozen large white plastic motorhomes parked on hard gravel behind a barrier. No welcome for tents or bikes. Too high and exposed for a tent pitch. Going through the main street brings a feeling of woe. The weather does not enliven ambience, it may be a different place a couple of streets in. Wind. Hard rain. Buildings rain streaked, melancholy desolate town closed on Sunday afternoon. Cold soaked enough to extinguish the flame of the most dedicated's enthusiasm. A sign says 'Vous ici' 'You are here.' I would rather not be.

Low on a wall a municipal sign for camping. 'Rue de la Gare, a cote la cimetére.' A tent pitch shared with the dead. I follow its lead down a bumpy track next to the cemetery. A wreck of an old corrugated Citroen van, piled rusting machinery drowns in undergrowth. There will be no campsite here. I go back up the lane and take a left, the main road. The campsite closed since last year. Through the padlocked bars, grass grows up the sides of green mould streaked caravans. The swimming pool has long been empty apart from puddled green stagnant slime collected in the bottom. Thirty seconds I am away fast downhill on a main road shining in the rain towards the next town on Stevenson's journey, Langogne.

Stevenson talked of people working in the sunny fields turning and collecting the second cut of hay. Today I see nothing through eye stinging rain bullets needing all concentration to keep on the road. Through road spray a miserable soul is pedalling up the hill with a bike loaded with panniers and bags. Happy inaudible shouts and waves of futile encouragement between unknown fellow sufferers. A sign shining running wet in passing daylight headlights advertises. 'Happy camping a coté du lac.' Complete with a smiling sun. That would do, situated on the other side of town by the lake. Into Langogne crossing the bridge, dodging puddles, uneven patches, killer potholes. On a wall a standard municipal sign for camping. That means cheap, open and tucked away. Lakeside camping annulled. Three minutes riding flat country lane misted drear sees two soggy 'randonneur' silhouettes with large rucksacks disappear through a gateway. Following leads to the campsite

Accueil containing a smiling helpful happy Patron who is everybody's friend. Genuine.

The site is clean, quiet. Hot showers and a charge of next to nothing. A tree gives something to lean the bike against. Two tents are resident. I can hear a river running down the far end of the site. Cuckoos call and donkeys bray in an adjacent field.

Warm, dry. Laying on the sleeping bag. Home tent comfort, plenty to eat. The outside chatter of tea on the boil. Rain hammers the tent. I think of the places ridden through today. Well, Mr. Stevenson. You pick some desolate, isolated areas to travel through. Lands wild and scenery big.

68 km

Drizzling mist dissolves. High white cumulus cloud roll, twist, fold over and over in wind hurry. Sunlight islands in chase across the ground warm the skin. It is time to pack. Air fresh, everything fast dries. The birth of a fine day.

Lost in the green empty field a tiny tent is being dismantled. A lady in her sixties carry's a small rucksack on which the thin rolled tent is tied.

"Bonjour." As she walks by.

The look of a St. Diago de Compostella pilgrim. Someone who has not slept between walls for many nights. Healthy weathered, walking alone with purpose. Scallop shell hangs from the rucksack.

10am. Country lane amble ends busy in Langogne town. I find La Poste to send cards waiting in the queue. The lady serving offers me a choice of several large postcard covering commemorative stamps.

"Les timbres de bleau. S'il vous plait." Regular boring blue stamps please.

Much to her disappointment. I leave her to serve everybody in a very slow enthusiastic complicated way.

Stream trickle. Jumble backs of buildings, main street shops. Town traffic busy. Car horn, stop start patience. Café tables busy under morning sun. All open on a Monday!

D906. For Villefort. Back streets end the town. Countryside roam follows familiar River Allier busy in chatter. River road beautiful. Easy flat ride. Rocky low cliff protrudes the greenness.

Stevenson travels parallel over the hill getting lost with no help from the local inhabitants. Fruitless wanderings lead him in a gale of rain sleeping in a wooded hollow. The next day Stevenson pushed his four legged vehicle to Cheylard before making it up to a village named Luc.

Luc sits under a steep high forested hill. Ruin chateau holds a little square chapel, its bell hung from an iron frame. On the roof sits white Notre Damme of maybe 6m (18ft) hands together in prayer wearing a metal crown looking over the part walled village. Remarked upon by Stevenson as being brand new, the cast iron lady has weathered well standing white against dulled pastures' black forest horizon. Steep hills, valley ride. Adjacent runs a single a railway line. The River Allier can be crossed tiptoe on stepping stones. Last week crossing the Allier would have meant a frantic swim across a fast moving mass dragged several miles in the attempt or drowned. This highland area, birthplace of The Tarn, Lot, Allier and Loire.

La Bastide village houses lean from both sides of the street. The Allier runs clear brown and gold behind sunny walls. A church, a bend. Village gone. Road climbs, a roundabout, I prepare for the Cévennes long uphill slog. The road decides to run gentle. I look for the turning to the Monastery of Notre Damme des Nieges (Our Lady of the Snows) where Stevenson stayed with Monks of silence. Direction missed back at the roundabout.

Planted forest, countryside road drops. A push for speed to get enough momentum to make it easily up the other side. Col du Thort. Brakes go on hard. I stop. Farmland one side, a distant huge gorge with mountainous ridges to the other. Surprise view granite cliffs disappearing down out of sight, trees sparse grow gripping plunging slopes. Sun illuminates speeding cloud roll curling, dappling the view in galloping island shade. New perspective, vast panorama. The raw Ardeche.

A farm dog barks methodical cows into a dairy. Cows slow in routine, unconcerned about canine orders. One stops. They all stop. Head turn watches my progress. The dog runs up and down barking furious. They resume unhurried pace. Road bend. The fade of barking carry's on the wind.

Farmland goes fast. Deep wood valley roll into the centre of the earth. Above craggy cliff resists tumble. Green bare moorland ridge spined craggy. Cliff collision raw giants capped black in fir forest. Folded hills compressed over and over end far rocky blue.

River Chassezac enslaved by man to power hydro electricity. Cliffs of shattered stone, road rises through blasted rock splinter. Downhill fast. Ridge ride amongst wild raw blue folded Ardéche. Opposite lands tower green mountainous. The Lozére.

Amongst hills alpine blue a barrage holds a manmade lake holding the Chassezac. Behind the lake, village tumbles a snaking valley climbing to a rugged peak swathed black in fir. Black thread footpath ancient trails ascend a ridge over Montagne du Goudet.

Downward. Hairpin rocky bends. High sun, strong blowing dry wind bleaches the face. Wild land excitement invigorates the soul. Open world, void of shelter. No false comfort, only the rawness of nature. I accept my insignificance, my mortal fragility amongst giant rock wilderness. From within, a moment of change. Renewed energies buzz wild.

Railway tracks subterranean dark holed under cliff face emerging to disappear back into a rock darkened journey.

Silent plateau. Habitation walled fortified with turrets. Jumbled roofs on the edge of nothing. Towering cliff drop. Mass white rectangular blocks stacked to disappear vertical from view. A sign reads 'Belvidere du Chassezac.' Arrow points direction. Speeding left leans the bend. Narrow lane, braking hard to stop in a dusty empty car park. Low cliff edge barriers easy to hop. The altitude 855m above sea level, vertical drop maybe 400m (1200ft) to a boulder strewn River Chassezac foaming baritone roar. Edge clamber over granite boulders until I have to jump from one to the other, earth between gone, replaced by leafed branches between nothing solid. I peer vertical far into the gorge. Strong wind gusts from behind making the deed more interesting.

It takes a few minutes to comprehend size and depth.

I ask myself. "What country am I in?"

Vertical granite crags squeeze the river roar boiling out of sight darkened by cliff shade appearing back into light tumbling through green scrub forest. Whitewater under sun glint changes to mercury silver slipping between silhouetted hard edged giants melting distant to blue. Raw terrain beyond the spoil of man.

I walk back to the bike open mouthed, shaking my head. Every day a surprise, something amazing and unpredictable to experience.

The fortified village of La Guarde Guérin belongs in a 'Spaghetti Western.' Betrayed by modern reality. A parked line of air conditioned tinted glass euro coaches.

Flat land ends dropping on a corniche road. Cliff rise above, ribbon passage cut from rock. Low wall, a drop far into nothing. Water noise rises from the boulder strewn Chassezac, tarmac ribbon follows its course. A tiny metal rectangle drives the river road. Viewed distant, a flea in the wilderness. Lone summit building. The chapel of St. Loup, (the wolf) stands on grey granite surrounded by stubby trees. Yellow colour splash across background giant green suede mountain.

Fast freewheel road hugs rock contour, strong headwind helps slow downhill speed. Slow through the last tight hairpin bend. A cyclist on a loaded bike starts the upward grind. A shared wave on passing.

Flat road across a dam holds man made Lac de Villefort's long dead end valley of water. Forest smother sweep, bare rock and cliff face, steep swathes of green. Black fir clinging to steep hill giant forms a fringed horizon. The first people since Langogne. Fishermen cast silver line trails in a settling arc onto the water from a grassy bank.

Lake ends, junction options. Of which to take?

A climb up to Le Bleymard will meet with Mr. Stevenson. From Le Bleymard I would travel on to Le Pont de Montvert ending up at St. Jean-du-Gard. Travelling back up the Corniche des Cevennes to meet the River Tarn. My other option. To leave

Stevenson and follow the final ride of English cyclist Tommy Simpson up Mt. Ventoux in Provence, via the Ardeche.

I will have to return to follow Mr. Stevenson in the most detail of his route from start to finish. Mont Ventoux beckons. 'The giant of Provence.' The most feared mountain of Le Tour de France.

Into little Villefort. Houses reflect in clear pools of river trickle spanned by roman or medieval high arch of stone. River runs hushed over large slabs of rock, edges smoothed rounded from centuries of water wear. Tumbling deep pools in green tint from overhanging trees between ancient dwellings.

2pm Monday. Villefort is closed. I have no idea of how high the hills will be or where I will end up. A few snacks in the bag the only fuel.

Steep climb high above rooftops. Sign advertises 'Super U' supermarket. Experience says it could be miles from direction.

Roundabout of three roads. Two run level half height along a great opening valley, the other disappears overhead through trees signed for 'Les Vans.' The direction.

Snake road hairpins up up up. Pine cling vertical growing from dust. 'Parc Natural d' Monts d'Ardéche. The panorama too big for vision to see at once, having to look down the valley bowl then up to view the forested mountain hills of faraway Montagne du Bougés and Mont Lozére. Endless forest black plantation, dark green carpet separated by dull yellow running spill across great hillsides. Travelling pools of sun illuminate white clustered dots connected by black cotton threads telling of villages and roads across a great widening wilderness valley.

My progress sinuous, rising. Hairpin bend chance view through treetop break to far below.

Cevennés steep peaks blue ragged rolling into each other to the horizon. Excitement to know I will future travel the wild blue giants.

A sign proclaims 'Rhone Alps.' Cresting Col Mas de l'Ayre of 846m, a little more than half Pas de Peyrol of last week still feels a mountain to climb.

Abandoned houses boarded, stone walls sink in dereliction. Across a hilltop plateau. Spectacular views into the Monts d' Ardéche blue mazed rocky endless folds. Valleys arid, bare dusted rock, trees grow sparse.

No need to touch the pedals descending through forest bends. Windows through the green. Far below lands of steep domed rock. Summit village, high cliff drop. Black shade valley falls beyond view.

I stop amongst ruins. Roof caved, broken bleached timbers hang, red heaps of fallen roof tiles swallowed by growing nature. A young family busy in repair of abandoned property making it fit for habitation. A dusty parked car with a trailer full of building materials to complete a dream. Their view into a steep valley from an aviator's window.

New lands for the eyes, so different from where I have travelled. Dry dusty hills rolling away to hazed lowland. Descending road, softening feeling. Villages dotted in the hillsides, rock stacks vertical. The cutting mountain wind of the Cévennes bannished by soft enveloping warmth inviting easy living. It must be the climate of the Mediterranean. Views without feature, blue pointed far away shapes rise from flattened land. Hills of the Luberon and Vaucluse bow to a mountain like no other. Mont Ventoux.

Helter skelter! Hairpin bends, speeding past farm orchards

of cherries. Sweet crop advertised for sale. Stone houses grow purple blue bloom across pale sun bleached walls. A few people, a little traffic, descending leaning bends, speeding the straights.

A reluctant return to civilisation. Campsites, into Les Vans. Freeride over, flattening into town. Everything closed apart from busy Bar Tabac. 'Joyeuse' supermarket direction. I enter daily mundane shopping world joining the people queue. Mind buzz still rides the hills.

Direction for camping. Suburban lane climb. Dusty track drops to sunny flat field ending at the barriered Accueil of an expensive campsite. Plastic motorhomes, luxury caravans, a steak restaurant. Fat unconscious old ladies lay around a swimming pool on white plastic loungers frying flab in the sun.

The campsite is expensive. Clean, quiet, spacious with a red hot shower to wash away the day's roadwork. Gorge river strange carved caves. Smoothed slab sculpture from the birth of the world. Reunited with the Chassezac.

Washing under bright sun hangs between trees. A Dutchman walks over, says hello and hands me a beer, asking of my journey.

On answering a question. He confirms I have made it to the Mediterranean.

79 km

Ardeche

I open my eyes. A tent lit by Mediterranean sunshine. Packing dry under dappled shade dusted ground to the soft white noise of the running Chassezac. I walk across to the caravan wishing the Dutchman and his wife a pleasant holiday.

Life around this part of the country not so house proud or cosmopolitan. A feeling of humanity. Things take their time in the south.

Supermarket stop, Les Vans for cash. The place busy. Coffee next to the jazz posters, tabled customer talk. Relaxed news digestion, seated town watching. I make my exit on a climb looking down onto the campsite, the rocky winding Chassezac behind.

Hilltop plateau spartan. Rock outcrops, stubby trees, white bleached stone scattered. Remains of dry stone walls under reclamation by nature. Ruin tumbled dusty stone building, dark green stumpy gnarled trees. Whiteness makes a sky deepen the blue. Lone cotton wool cumulus floats unhurried. Flat road ends in wooded hill. Green wandering road. Junction signed Vallon-pont-d'Arc. Downhill dusty cliff piled shale joins a flattened landscape parched yellow. Crops half drown under poppy blood red. Background view Ardeche rises a fortress maze of blued wild rockscape.

Headwind push low to the bars. Signed wonderments proclaim, 'Le Naturel Champignons.' A cave of lime deposits in the shape of mushrooms. Ecstatic visions await the fungal sculpture tourist.

Dark green vine parallel lined to Ardeche blue. The vine grip broken by waving yellow pocket crop, open growing land. White villages of wine, oasis in agriculture bake under sun glare. Dusty river edge campsites for the masses. Fat European bodies oiled sizzle on sunbeds by a pool under straw umbrellas next to fake palms. Living the magazine cover lifestyle complete with plastic umbrella drink, only today's magazine models carry an extra five stone.

Houses change architecture. Long low roofs, large overhangs covered with roman tiles. Windows smaller in size peer from thickened walls, rough thick window shutters. Some houses lime rendered in sun dazzle, others of rough stone walling. Gardens grow a lone black flame Cypress tree, a feeling of famous paintings. Van Gogh. Cézanne. Expressions of climate.

Busy traffic, busy junction. Bridge link for 'Camping Oasis 3 star.' Cliffs grow, the River Adduce wide running and shallow, beach expanse of sand and pebble bank amongst permanence of rock. Whole splintered tree trunks stuck out at angles jammed into rock shows violence of speeding water in swollen winter flood.

Road patched, potholed worn bounces and hammers the bike wheels. Flat fast road weaves the river. Cliffs recede, signs point for the famous gorge. Camping overload between outbreaks of canoe plastic. Orange, yellow, purple, green.

Paddle pleasure stacked on trailers, racks, stood up against log cabins and containers advertising hire. Minibuses full of happy faces tow trailers racked full of canoes returning from downstream adventure.

Compulsory cycle lane contains compulsory rocks and broken glass, riding the white line avoids punctures and the chance of a crash. 'Smilinghappycamperland' is looking older. The more established campsites hold premium river frontage. Start of the main gorge in view between trees. Road narrows. Rough layby with an information board gives an idea of the area. Caves of Neolithic art portraying lions hunting. 32000 years of wall art. Caves closed to the public, too precious to risk.

High cliff smooth water worn rising straight. Overhang loom before a skyward thrust. Low stone wall, river flow below. Rock tunnel meetings with large Euro coaches seven days busy to see the famous gorge. Viewpoint cram. Campsite crowded coloured tents. Large car park bursts with cars and coaches, places sell food, people sit eating. A crowd tiptoe on a viewing platform straining necks to look. It must be the famous Pont d'Arc, the natural great arch of limestone through which the River Ardéche passes.

Around a bend parked traffic ceases. A campsite, a small sign. 'Plage access 0.2km.' Path next to chainlink fencing keeps the campers in. Bumpy mud lane ride ducking under trees until it gets too stony for the wheels, pushing the bike to a beach. The famous arch appears. It is the beach from which nearly every published Arc picture is taken. The place busy, echoes of laughter and enjoyment reverberate surrounding white sunny cliffs. I lay the bike over and enjoy the view.

The arch solid. Magnificent. A great opening spanning the

width of the river. White rock sides form the river bend. One great mass of rock. Trees grow from the sides wherever they can get a hold adding decoration to the great white water worn rock.

The beach runs from the arch on a curve ending in rock outcrop. Shading trees, sharp white stones lead down to a sandy curve along the river edge. Water clear, tinted green in shallows drop into deepwater blackness. Opposite beach, white sand, tree cling vertical towering rock. Fantasy rock battlements against clear deep sky. Cliffs take the curving gorge beyond view. An endless daily procession of orange and yellow plastic kayaks parade the downstream drift. People swim smiling, splashing in the river.

A couple say. "Hello."

They have come here for a few days after attending their friend's wedding in the region of La Loire.

"What are you doing here?"

I tell them of my journey. I am offered a glass of wine and sit talking for half an hour.

Hot sun encourages a swim. River temperature fresh but not cold, against constant current emerging refreshed from the heat.

A rope swing tied from a tree growing next to the arc has a revolving queue of children swinging to plunge into the river. Sometimes frozen to the rope returning to the bank to try again under shouted instruction and encouragement with added waving of arms from the queuing participants who are the main audience. It's about the maximum swing, the biggest leap. The midair acrobatic contortion that command the biggest shouts. The style of youth in common multinational approval.

Farewells exchanged. I walk over and pick up the bike. Across the stones, a last look. Families enjoy lunch under shading trees. Plates of colourful food. Wine bottle glint, blankets and folding chairs. Children leap from the rope swing, the parading smiling plastic kayak carousel drifts under Pont d'Arc.

Road rocky bends. Garden hotel luxury on rare pieces of land. Multinational coach procession. The same portly driver, sunglasses, white shirt and tie giving running commentary. There have been no hills until now. Steep climb straight ascent. Rock escarpment under dead end high cliffs. Pace slows to a patient crawl. Long steep tarmac drag under hot afternoon sun. Road 180 degrees sharp, grinds ascent.

Cool darkness rock tunnel climb, daylight exit. The ascent must be 330m (1000ft) in less than a mile. Views spectacular. High precipitous limestone cliff forested in miles of scrubby trees under heat shimmer. Far down dark green and blackness of the river, edged bends of sandy beach. Shallowing rapids send lines in radiating V for canoe and kayak coloured dots to encounter.

Dropping road gains speed, a car pulls alongside. Driver shouts. "Chasseurs!" Pointing a thumb backwards. I stop. Looking back to see my old reef sandals on the road. Under a car, wheels miss. A coach follows. Footwear disappears beneath many big crushing wheels to appear unscathed. My only spare footwear.

Climbs and descents within the top third of the gorge. Spectacular views to the depths. Rocks named, signs proclaim. A great stack stands alone, defiant to millennial erosion. Cliff overhang. Caves marooned half way. Mud streak red stain down the whiteness. The river shaded by gorge narrows looking to close the river. Further cliffs widen, sun sparkle surface dance lights up shallow green edged sandbanks, beaches of pale yellow glow white. Woodland covers mass fallen banks of diagonal scree until cliffs rise vertical. At one point the gorge takes a 180 degree turn back on itself giving the biggest view across faraway bends.

Landscape lowers, road descent sweeping turns. Campsite adverts. 'Camping Naturaliste.' Amongst thorny bushes. 'Eco site,' Canoe camping at the bottom of the gorge. Auberge directions point to rough tracks through scrub. People at distance appear on the edge looking to leap from great height on which they stand. Closer they are safely behind railings. Cliffs of halved height. Road straightens, gorge widens. Cliff top buildings in afternoon sun haze. Road drops meeting widened river with a tree lined bank. Canoes and kayaks land in shallows ending gorge adventure. Low stone island where people sit, feet dangle in the water. Behind on the sloping hill, a campsite.

The day's canoe trade has come to its end. Cabin shutters dropped and locked ready for tomorrow. A peaceful scene of early evening yellowing light. People wade to and from the island, the sound of laughter. Excited children shout to each other. Campsite Accueil. Buying two nights riverside repose.

The campsite holds many people, terraced up a wooded hill and equipped with swimming pool, restaurant and shop. I pitch on a quiet part a couple of places away from other tents, get a shower and enjoy a big meal. Later on fifty young people arrive from their day's adventure. Surrounded by Germans. Not a single smooth French accent to be heard anywhere, everyone 'spracken und sprechen.' Even a family in an old Mercedes campervan a couple of pitches along are German. I fall asleep to traditional volks music songs in the Kline Fatherland of St. Martin-d'Ardeche.

82 km

A day off to celebrate a month in France. Rather than a mighty sporting deed to mark the occasion. I shall do nothing. Maybe sit by the river with a book. First is going through everything carried, throwing as much as possible, putting all items of no use into a carrier bag for disposal. Possessions. The traveller's ball and chain, a useless weight to drag. I find two tops never worn, the useless waterproof that is not waterproof. Spare cheap tent pegs, the useless side stand that will not support the weight of the bike. I tear off half a cycle guide book finished with, way out of date. That is 3kg not have to slog up hills and less weight pounding the rear wheel. Bonus. More space, not to fill but to make packing easier.

The Germans arrive back from morning activities, a good time to amble to the riverside. A weighty carrier bag drops into 'Les Poubelles.' The satisfying thud joins the rubbish.

'Kayak adventure.' Sign board informs of downstream excitement the length of the gorge over two days for about a week's pay of minimum wage, supplying kayak and equipment. The route marked on a map. Rapids gauged one to four on a scale of difficulty. A night's camping is shown mid way down and the cost includes food. It's tempting, especially paddling under the Pont d'Arc. Maybe another time I will grasp the paddle.

Within view of the river, open air restaurants prepare for a day's trade. The chair scrape drag, wiping tables double speed, chequered tablecloth floats down smoothed free of a crease. Entrance steps display the menu. Colourful growing bloom hangs the whole frontage to snag passing custom.

The riverside silent, canoes and kayaks yet to arrive. From the smooth white rocks water moves in mass flow uninterrupted blackness.

Silver flash betrays the presence of fish. Eyes focus seeing a shoal against the current, waiting for opportunist food. Upstream river disappears around a bend, cliff towers hide the river from view. Cliffs opposite end in great diagonal banks of scree. Bushes and trees cover green. Downstream the gorge ends. The clifftop walled town of beauty, Aiguéze. Towers look over defensive stone. The first man made claim for many miles since Vallon Pont d'Arc.

It is a day to let somebody else do the cooking. Ordering lunch with a house wine from the 'restaurant.' A café with a tarpaulin roof. The seating. The worldwide white plastic chairs that adorn patio and balcony. There are areas to sit for a drink and areas delineated by a gap between rows to sit to eat. Additional clientele are two retired people munching salad, a couple of daytime drinkers in suits having a little bit of food with the tableful of fast emptying wine bottles. Two very large eating machines wearing flowery shirts demolish the menu line by line.

The daily flow of paddled plastic appears upstream. Laughter and tired looking individuals all ages and nationalities paddling a single stroke to glide.

Evening sun yellows across a near empty campsite, the Germans all seem to have vanished. The only occupants are my

German neighbours watching Asterix projected between rust streaks onto the side of their ancient once white Mercedes van.

Ventoux

6.30am. The day's temperature already on the rise. Yellow sun lights trees, a final look at the river. Flat empty road has half lane luxury for cycling.

On top of the cliff, fortified Aiguéze. Picturesque walled. Square keep, stone towers. Church spires peer over in atmospheric soft light.

Fast ride crosses the river at Pont St. Esprit. Old ruin bridge of two arches, the missing third lays submerged.

The great River Rhone is crossed on multi arches. Pebble and boulder beaches, wild trees, grey river flow in unfriendly mass menace swirl.

Straight line Plane tree green tunnel, giants peel bark in silvered renewal. Road ends busy, roundabout traffic, a sign 'Rhone lez Provence.' Provence!

Army trucks full of soldiers wave approval. Across a bridge. Under flows the broad Rhone canal contained in sloping concrete. Town habitation fade. Plane tree avenues quieten to the vine. Wine country cicada buzz. Flat country ride looks to the Dentelles de Montmirail. Ragged rock sub mountain range. Behind imposing over all mountain pretenders. Mount Ventoux.

Flat land hazed blur undefined, distance empty. Parallel line vines to the vanishing point grow from pale dusted soil. Geometric farming tended by primary colour tractors. Spray bars above the rear of the cab, mist envelopes the vine killing destructive spores and the gnawing pest. Square metal gantries of spinning blades chop sprouting runners focusing growth energy to swell the grape.

Roadside conifer home to the strange buzz cicada music. D8 pedal under sunshine. 'Carpentras' D7. Flat open land dedicated to the vine. Big sky side wind. Fighting gusts blowing across the road. Direction change brings headwind. Gears knocked low to a crawl.

Wind. An invisible hill funnelled by the mountain increases strength. Drop bar grind keeps me low, the inner white line hypnotic gaze leaves the body to get on with the work. Imposing rock tooth gaze of 'Dentelles' de Montmirial. A sleeping roadside town. Back view high cliffs coasting downhill. The wind vanished.

Traffic outskirts of Carpentras. Old lived in. I buy last minute lunch. Noise of the door locking behind. Sun diffused plane tree shade both sides of the street. Three storey town houses thick walls, window frames gloss black, either side colourful window shutters pale green, purple. Colours of long summers. Poster pole adverts. Jazz nights. Political candidate's slogan for change.

Over a wall behind large wooden doors a tall narrow square church tower has a bell hung from ornate ironwork adorned with coloured bulbs. Across the road people sit for lunch. Meeting, greeting with 'la bise,' chatting under shading blinds of half busy cafés. Timeless moments of lunchtime France.

Downhill rattle. Tin box buidings of industry into countryside green. Brick plate glass intrusion. Corporate wine empire with easy parking brags vanities of 'success wealth and status.' The necessary truth of stainless steel mass production to fill supermarket shelves. Opposing the wine label image of traditional wood barrels of a single farmer tending vines quiet on a sunny hillside. I thought the brick mass was a motel.

Sign for Ventoux. New dual carriageway shrinks to a bumpy potholed old road directing mountain direction. I have left the ring road too early, lured by signs. Directions on the D150 disappear, crossroads possibilities without numbers. Decision time. Mormoiron.

Lane coils around a hill. Isolated stone houses, scrub bush twisted trees stunted, pollarded cherries full ripe fruit. Small area vines on ancient stone terrace amongst wildscape. I make a lot of height. Dentelles de Montmirail dwarfed by an expanding mass of Mont Ventoux. I crest the hill losing all gained height through sharp hairpin bends arriving on a back road into little Mormoiron. Crossroads through town dug up, 'deviation.' Without destination. Compass gives a two road choice. One will run to Bédoin. The other to Villes-sur-Auzon. I sit astride the bike pondering. Two cyclists carry nothing. I assume they are local or know the area. I ask in French direction for Villes-sur-Auzon.

"We are going towards the main road and can put you in the right direction."

The couple English have local knowledge.

Following, making conversation up a hill pushing 45kg while they push less than 7kg with over 70km in my legs today under 30 degree sun bleach. We go down country lanes I would never had known about and end up at a small lake.....lost. It looks good for fishing.

Unanimous decision. "Never go back." Compass sets direction. Ten minutes riding crosses to a rough lane, rooftops. The back of Villes-sur-Auzon. I am told scenery spectacular awaits toward Sault and Mount Ventoux. But not today. I thank them both for their help.

"We were coming this way as part of our ride."

They have been visiting this area for the last six years, their campervan parked at Bédoin for a couple of weeks.

Opposite. The brown municipal sign directs for camping. Shops in long shadow, daily life echo between narrow street walls. Gateway entrance. The Accueil. I pay a happy Patron for a night's accommodation in clear view to Mont Ventoux. A great mass of darkened blue wears a crown of white schist stone. Long square tower tops the summit.

A Dutchman asks me about the bike and my home made panniers, half amused. Telling of a wish to do something similar. In the past he met with an English rider pedalling around Europe, only to meet again a thousand miles later.

Quiet peaceful site, filled with caravans. A brash English Midland voice busy complaining. I hope not to meet it. After nightfall violent lightning and thunder. Sporadic heavy rain. Tree roar in the blackness amplifies the noise. Silent lightning, wind vanishes. Calm.

86 km

7am. The mind full of intent. Sky breathes no wind. A few low cumulus break small size, high cirrostratus cloud interspersed with flecks of blue. Lower cloud travels different direction to the high level. Two winds. Stormy? Or the remnants of stormy last night. Thick cloud bank. The mountain yet to wake, slumbering under a quilt of fluffy cloud midway, summit obscured.

I decide to go. If the weather is bad I can return. A box of cookies my fuel until I get to Sault to find a boulangerie. I wheel the bike through a silent campsite. Locked gate sign says it will be opened at 8am. The bike is too heavy to contemplate a lift over. A jogger comes to my rescue at 7.45am punching in code release.

Short climb. Into the Gorges de la Nesque. Olive bush, stumpy oak. Box trees, smooth rock slab. Patchy sky increases blue, mist veil softens everything on this agreeable new morning. The deepening gorge, lower areas tree covered. Scrubby vegetation claims the travelled level. Skyline dominated by white schist rock. Road just wide enough for a two car squeeze. I cycle the outside edge. Verge gorge drop over a little wall. Easy climb under rock towers. Precipitous drop, no second chance of a fall looking into ever diminishing size of tree tops. Cliffs grow height, everything gets bigger. Caves marooned high in smoothed cliffs, some of great size. Streaking long lines orange stained rock glow.

It is difficult to contemplate how these huge gorges are made by trickling water dragging stones to rattle, wear and carve through mass rock on geological timescale in comparison of man's finite 25500 day lifetime.

Twisting corniche road, fissures bridged by stone wall and infill. Sections of knee high wall have fallen. Thin air drop an arm length away. Every turn the view more impressive, too big for the camera lens. Great white cliffs control over half the height of the gorge, rock sculpture towers castellated tops, others smooth in defying overhang grow vertical sprouting tree fringe tops. Blind bends. Short rock tunnels, one held by a giant diminishing table leg. A flat piece of ground tight against cliff grow trees amongst alpine bloom. Nature's tended wild garden.

Tracks drop to the dry wooded gorge for walking. More bends, a view ever changing ever climbing. A house tucked against cliff. Rescue vehicle roped and ready for a call parked at the side. Many miles to the nearest neighbour.

I stop to take a photograph, a lone mountain bike appears. "Bonjour."

The only person I have seen in the gorge. Further stops absorb panoramic view. Mountain bike rider now an orange shirt dot lost amongst gorge cliffs.

Gorge ride ends. Gentle descent through fields, campervans parked around a small lake. The other side cliffs, scrubby trees, an old village built on a ledge up against cliff, the church tower steep and pointed of old stone. Chateau ruin surveys the village. Flat ride, a climb, space for crops, pale green pasture, mountain fringe. Rows of lavender maroon a derelict stone farm building. Rocks placed on the orange verge roof tiles resist the lift of winter gale. Isolated house focal point amongst fields. Grazing horses, lavender rows. Sault sited strategic above high stone defence.

Climbing hairpins to a pretty town of lively shops. Opening the boulangerie door. Smells of cooking bread, glass counter fresh delight. I am served by a boy in his school uniform working early before family trade is exchanged for state education.

Out of Sault. Road split. Downward through pasture weaving a hill dedicated to lavender. Cabins advertise lavender for sale, an old flat cart waits to display produce. Farm houses, fields of lavender grow on white gravelled beds. The blue purple delicate flower send appealing scent throughout magical countryside.

The road promises permanent uphill for the next 25km. Bend on bend, a canopy of oak mixes with twisted pine. Hairpin, straight, hairpin, straight, steady rise. It is tempting to push a bigger gear knowing it will steepen later. This road is going to be a slow burner.

Long climb. A fading sign. 'Le Chalet Raynard.' Promise of fine food and a bar. Woodland altitude favours beech and overhanging pine. Cones litter the verge of a cracked, patched, bumpy road.

From behind, the company of roadriders in team colours hyped for a mountain battle. Competitive vanity to overtake. Commencing only from the high village of Sault. Once ahead riders slow gaining very little distance. There is still a long way to go. The noise of a bike getting closer, the rider alongside standing on the pedals, behind the sunglasses a look of intent. Sat on the seat with one hand on the bars I offer him a boiled sweet in an act of part humour.

"Non non!" shaking his head in seriousness.

His accomplice also refuses, denied by his watchful leader. I go up a gear without getting off of the seat, push a little harder through my legs forcing the rider to work hard to pass, of which he must. He has already committed vein pride to the act.

Easy pace, enjoying the woodland beauty. Sun diffused rays through leafed branches throw long complex patterns of shade across tarmac. I contemplate the ride of Mr. Simpson on 13th July on the Tour de France 1967 that will end the final moments of his life.

A mountain biker overtakes. Thin legs thrashing, burning energies soon to be needed, the grind yet to start. Woodland soil replaced by shale, the white schist stone cap worn by the mountain. Alkaline smell edged with sulphur.

Deciduous trees have a hard time of surviving the altitude, stubby coniferous bushes and lone fir. The mountain biker stopped at the side of the road busy shovelling a sachet of energy gel down his sweat glazed throat, he carries so little drink. A couple of bends Mr. "Non non" to a bon bon has a puncture.

"Creve." Is spoken melancholy with a shrugging of the shoulders.

On a wide bend. Chalet Reynard. Ten roadbikes, a couple of parked coaches, a few cars. A rider assembles his bike from the back of his car for a summit sprint. Riders fly down the mountain tucked low in speeding blur. High price carbon fibre feather. Gloss flash.

From Chalet Reynard the mountain road steepens. Soft cover woodland gone. White scree. Solitary alpine yellow flower. Violets force soft flowers through dry rubble. Tall yellow and black snow poles mark the steep drop from the black tarmac thread. White stone steep mountainside, an uphill desert. The ascent now follows Tom Simpson's wheel.

Cyclists speed down the hill. Tyre hum, mechanical freewheel whizz. Cyclists slog grinding the gradient, a wheezing delivery lorry overtakes followed by a couple of droning cars. An entrepreneurial photographer waits on a steep bend. The photograph, the handed card, a code and an address. The road increases gradient, the granny gear plod, same pace, slower than some is without the tormented facial expression carried by Monsieur Alpha who must pass! Some keep a pace questing a personal time to beat, most do not. More opportunist photographers turn the place into a circus. I pull my sweat sodden hat down over my eyes in noncompliance being only able to see the front wheel and handlebars defiant of the pointed lens. People burned and blown, pushing bikes toward the summit leaning on a two wheeled walking aid. Cars parked at the road edge have bought sightseers shouting encouragement, taking photos and clapping. An obscure gathering in the misted silence.

I lift my soggy hat in pantomime to the audience which gets a laugh. It is only a hill, an extremely big hill, but just a hill somewhere above in the cloud will have a top possibly celestial, with gates.

Cloud rolling as smoke, mountainside tumbles steep. Opposite, the primary reason for coming up here. The memorial to the death of Tommy Simpson. English world champion roadrider who collapsed and died on this spot from exhaustion trying to chase the leading Tour de France group to the summit. I stop and lean the bike against the steep mountainside and make my way up the few steps to the memorial. I stagger two steps backwards dizzy, needing to take a few breaths grabbing oxygen out of the thinned air in surprise.

A car pulls up on Belgian plates. A flustering woman gets out, the engine ticking over. She runs up the steps and tells me to. "Go! You go!" Waving the back of her hand to shoo me away. She wants a photograph. I tell her I have cycled from England and up the mountain to be here today. She gets her photo, waddles back to her car and leaves.

The monument is cut from stone in the shape of the mountain having Tom Simpson's profile riding his bike highlighted in polished stone. Words in gold leaf cut into the stone read.

> *To the memory*
> *of TOM SIMPSON*
> *medalled Olympic champion of the world*
> *ambassador for British sport*
> *Died 13th July (Tour de France1967)*
> *Your friends the cyclists of Great Britain.*

There are little tributes left by people at the monument, including two small plaques from his family with written thoughts of privacy. I walk to the bike meeting a human looking in the most beat fatigued state possible. This man is running up Mont Ventoux! Was running. Reduced painful sweat glazed foot scuff. Tiny steps of ankle shuffle, elbows barely move, face near purple, eyes hollowed and red. I offer him a sugary boiled sweet of which he gratefully accepts as if a banquet has been presented. I pass him on the final upward km, cruelly steep on the last bend, twisting back on itself under a weather station before finally releasing the summit.

Underneath the weather station in a building more a bunker I buy a drink and a chocolate bar along with postcards and a small souvenir. Silent swirling cloud obscures eerie spectral half silhouetted crowd through sound absorbing vapour grey. Moments of parting cloud allow fleeting views of people cycling the last of both sides before greyness envelopes. A hole in the cloud shows a distant pattern of sunny fields looking out from an aeroplane window. The view soon masked by silent vapour. Vans and minibuses parked receive cyclists arrived from their toil.

An American lady crying. "Oh my oh my! I actually did it!"

She is wrapped in turkey foil and led to a minibus fully prepared for thanksgiving.

It is cool up here, but it is not polar. A waterproof is all most people slip on while waiting their turn to be photographed at the summit proclaiming 1912m (about 6000ft). I am asked if I can take a picture for two ladies who have made the climb from Sault. They have pictures together and individually. One holding her carbon bike above her head in triumph. I am told it is my turn and hand over the camera, receiving a nice picture chopping my legs. I would try holding the bike over my head, but would end up going over backwards rolling like a boulder down the mountain with the weight carried.

The emotional state of surrounding hugging people is getting too much. As I am leaving I see a sweated beaming face wrapped in a blanket who gives a wave. The runner. He made it!

Downhill! I have the additional distance of the gorge route over all the other cyclists here that will make it a freewheel distance of 57km! Why the Americans ride up and drive back down. It would be more fun the other way around.

Brake release, no need to pedal. Wind roar speed, whirring freewheel gear. Anguished souls toil hours of uphill suffering. Ahead, a car stopped with a shredded tyre, all contents are out of the car, including a fridge, bags of clothes and a baby bath. No one has stopped, not even fellow car drivers.

I ask an anxious looking family if they need assistance. They do.

They are from Belgium and the chap cannot get the wheel

off with the brace.

He shows me using his hands telling me it is. "No possible."

His wife, child and baby look anxious as they are broken down in a cloud up a mountain.

I put the wheel brace over the nut, stand on the bar spinning the nuts lose on the wheel. I tell him to put the car in gear and the handbrake on while I get a large rock and jam it under the other rear wheel to stop the car rolling backwards.

The jack goes under and soon the wheel is changed. The car back on the road ready to go apart from the packing.

"I never change before." A look of relief on his face.

They want to pay me. I do not accept.

Get a new tyre with the money.

I consider it deed payback from the cyclist who leant me a pump in rainy Samur weeks ago.

Down the mountain as fast as I dare. The café in parked coach blur. Into the woods. Straights, bends over and over. Tree green blur, concentration lean. Dodge the rough, the potholes, other riders, all the way through the lavender fields softer and warmer. Day heat radiates from softened land. The climb into Sault. Half numb legs push pedals. Boulangerie is still open!

With a bag full of pastries and warm cereal bread in sunshine sat on a wall watching the town. Body thaws from cold mountain temperature. The end of the ride for most of the cyclists. I have the mileage to ride again.

Bends out of town, horses in meadow graze. Lavender field fragrance under sun, the cliff village. A short climb draws shaky energy from somewhere. The top part of the gorge, stopping to enjoy immense views from Belvidere de Castellaras. Panorama along the great rocky gorge length flooded in sunshine.

A Frenchman selling vegetables from the back of his car asks. "Have you been up the mountain."

"Oui Monsieur"

"Bon courage!"

Lazy downhill. Single pedal turn keeps momentum. Return view perspective. Tunnel. The lone house silent. A cyclist or two enjoy the gorge to Sault. Freewheel to the campsite gate.

The Patron comes across the campsite from roping a pitch reservation.

"Ah, it is you! I was wandering why an empty tent was left?"

I pay for another night, enjoy a shower and fall asleep on the grass with my body declining to make any attempt of movement apart from necessity of breathing. Waking in the sunshine of early evening hungry looking up at the cleared view mountain. 'The Giant of Provence.'

A Dutchman asks me. "What was your time up the mountain? The hours."

"No idea. Who cares!"

115 km

The top of the mountain cloud free, guaranteeing a temperature rise for ascending riders. Yesterday lacked the famous panorama but I would not swap cloud cool for today's clear beating sun.

Goodbyes to people and the Patron, busy taping off pitches. Épicerie fuels the day, euro delight in the shopkeeper's eyes. One way system narrow street merry go round. Uniformed club cyclists café stop.

Toward Carpentras back west, looking to cross the Rhone maybe tomorrow. I have no idea of the km today. Hopefully somewhere in direction of Avignon.

Sun shine. Headwind to Carpentras. Big one way system. Direction radiates from centre ville. Compulsory cycle lane mystery tour of pavements, car parks and glass strewn gutters. Town pretty without need for manicure. Roman in age, generations lived old tall buildings, sun verandah. Green shade streets of old plane trees. Looking for 'Cavaillon.' Traffic lights, out of town 'Bricolage tin.' Showroom Porsche, ride on lawnmower, new bed surrounded by chipboard wardrobes.

Cheap European supermarket. Interior melancholy half lit, half alive. Potato salad, passable fruit, a sad brand of foul cola amongst rows of open cardboard boxes. Checkout bleep sad shuffle.

Road works to Cavaillon. 'Traveaux'. Dug up. Bumpy, slow. Potholes a car could fall into. Lumpy tarmac, manhole covers raised, rocks, glass, railway lines run the street for bike wheel destruction. Concrete lumpy, concrete broken. 'Deviation.' Sparkling smooth black tarmac 'Traveaux.' Interdit. Diversion zig zag through small town. People sit under bar shade relaxing, a full glass, deep focus discussion sorting out the world.

Compass guides along a wide old road without traffic. 'D31' map confirms south. Flat land endless one side. The other. The Vaucluse rising hills in softening green, focal distraction to harsh transitory journey. The legs have loosened and have had plenty to fuel. The leg engine runs well. Hot road busy, hard shoulder cycle plays dodge the glass, nuts and bolts, nails and scrap, weaving around half a lorry tyre. Stalls sell exhaust soot peaches. Land of many olive trees, fields of purple lavender lines. Wine growing sparse in comparison with the opposite side of Mont Ventoux. Roundabouts, 'Bricolage land.' A bridge climb over, a road goes under.

Bridge stop checks the map. The road race happening below could cut out an arc in the day's journey, replacing it straight line. It will be unpleasant, but functional. D900 goes west from city entrapment of Avignon. I take a deep breath, the last clean one for a while. Slip road builds speed to join busy hot noise stink of arterial progress.

Concrete bridges. railways. Travellers camp, burned out caravans. Roadside dump, broken farmland, wasteground. Enough to look within for new energies to get out. In favour the road is flat and fast. The River Durance rolls under the wheels on a long multi arched bridge traversing marshland and river channels. Great heaped pebble banks wetted by water born from the Alps. Arterial criss crossing. Noves. Quiet D28 to Chateaurenard. Ruin chateau in afternoon burn looks over its namesake. Signs through bumpy town street read Tarascon.

Countryside ride flat without interest.

'Graveson' bypass. 'Tarascon' D970 straight line in the company of railway tracks. Miles and miles of easy ride. Lowland stagnant stillwater smell. Road under rail bridge. Tarascon town. Shops closed for the evening. Town feeling is open and pleasant. 'Camping.' Signed arrows end at a large fortress chateau on a river.

Under fortress tower shadow. River frontage camping on the banks of The Rhone. I book in, pitch and have a beer in a large bar area opening to a terrace. The people friendly, absorbed in T.V. Rugby. One of the teams, Ireland. The other probably France. The audience in enthusiastic bounce on the bar stools, the tension of spectating in fixed screen gaze.

Fading light on the Rhone. Current fast, silent, mass unison movement. Falling in there is no getting out. Water spins smooth menace, windless mirror reflection of fortress tower battlements. Past conflict repaired bridge arches downstream, lights of crossing traffic in busy procession. Navigation lights under bridge arch directs river freight. My legs feed many large mosquitos in full feast.

Ears unfortunately subjected to Saturday night French talent singing. Warbling flat strained echoing, sickly gooey and toe curling. It could be a long night. Someone is wringing the life out of 'Yellow river' not paying much attention to the key, with additional dubbed accordions. Dusty Springfield is on helium with partial hearing loss. Elvis is groaning with an accordion 'post mort' finishing with a realistic duet of 'evening cats.' I fall asleep head buried hard under the sleeping bag.

85 km

Rhone to the Gard

Deep rumbling engine going upstream provides the alarm call. A walk past the fortress into town searching for a Sunday morning Patisserie. Backway lanes narrow, cobbles, buildings of yellow stone. An old man is painting his simple front door at a very Sunday Tarascon pace. He may nearly finish it one day. Things take their time. Tarascon pace.

Colourful window boxed bloom, iron gated doors. Notre Damme sits wooden over arched walkway. People with under arm baguettes. A patisserie, a fruit shop. Back street saunter, main town finds cashpoint funds.

Chateau fortress yellow block square mass of strength, round towered corners, iron bar windows. Tower tops corbelled out to prevent climbing up over. One side lower, defensive wall squat square towers guard portcullis entrance reached by a bridge over deep dug rough marshy ground. Window surround peppered with bullet holes. Shell scarred tower walls prove its tough modern strategic position on the Rhone.

On the campsite I talk with a small lady of more than seventy years living out of a very small single tent, delightful. She is walking the 'St Jacques' St. Diago de Compostella pilgrimage to Spain, having come this far from Valence. Resting a few days before carrying on with her two hiking sticks, baseball cap and rucksack funded by weekly pension money. There is a caravan nearby owned by a French couple.

I am asked. Where are you going?

Pont du Gard is my next stop. Across the Haut Languedoc eventually to Carcassonne.

I am given places to visit, the Frenchman takes the time to mark places on my map that I might like to see. Tarascon atmosphere is relaxed, the old town beautiful, the chateau impressive and the people met friendly and kind.

Wheeling out of the site I have left boiled sweets for the walking lady. She looks in the carrier bag, finds them and gives a great wave.

"Bon Chance Madame".

The Patron leans from the bar area taking a break from his cleaning to give a wave with a cigarette smile. Crossing the Rhone. Under passes 1000 tonnes of black hull rumbling low in the water pushing a further loaded unit downstream.

Bridge delivers to Beaucaire. Harbour terminates. A canal in lock gated shelter from the Rhone. Boats still, unmoving oily water. Fibreglass cruisers, converted riveted iron barge homes. Market has finished, stall holder's vehicles leave, the place crowded. Through the people mass looking for clues to Pont du Gard. Compass decision.

Low lying roads, stagnant ponds flank the verge. Unhealthy smelling marshland sponge. Thunder rumble behind obscuring trees louder and louder. Barrage de Vallabrégues controls the height of the Rhone. Huge steel doors raised or lowered from the riverbed on quarter circle pivot. Millions of tonnes of murky grey green cascade bubbles brown. Gated lock empty waits to transport 1000 ton barges. Road runs across the structure. Cars tiny travel the barrage giving scale to the engineering controlling the flowing mass.

Signs for Pont du Gard. D981 to a campsite amongst pines. The site divided into many areas giving a friendly feeling. I pitch the tent and fall asleep, waking late afternoon.

Access for Pont du Gard, a walk of a few minutes. Path follows the River Gard to a marvel of Roman symmetrical stone crafted beauty rivalling any modern sculpture for size and delicate design. A great aqueduct high above the river, once carrying fresh spring drinking water from Uzés 30km to Nimes for the city inhabitants. An honoured status for a Roman city, not granted for any town by Rome.

The aqueduct of three tiers, each reduce in height and width. Arch spans semicircular end central over vertical pillar support. The use of semicircular arches transfer the carried load vertical to foundation rock. Steps climb to view the structure. Large slabs of hard weathering stone are placed across the top of the aqueduct. Carved overhangs throw off rainwater preventing weathering damage to the structure. Repeated on the below tier for the same protection. Signs and a high fence stops the enjoyment of an unguarded top tier walk.

An added bridge butted to the side copies the aqueduct in its span. The names of masons and surveyors who made repairs are carved into the bridge parapet wall, '1783 and 1839' with line carvings of trade tools. The main material dense yellow sandstone, easy to shape, being able to achieve the incredibly accurate precision of the workmanship. Joints between are very finely grouted in lime, being only a few millimetres (1/8") thick and only just visible. Blocks are laid in such a way as the sedimentary stone grain is horizontal to load, compressing the layers, stopping stone from laminating to pieces. Square holes left high up at the start of each arch from its construction enable wooden arch formers to be fitted for support during future repairs and since made use of. New stone replacement blocks can be seen within the structure. It is impressive. Its quality proven by its 2000 year past and future longevity.

Flat slabs of the river's edge. The water looks inviting in its silent unrippled running blackness, little areas of collected sand beaches. A pretty scene framed by the wooded valley rise.

Aqueduct reflects full symmetry over the flowing river looking as intended art. Subtle yellow stone intensified gold in evening light against river blackness. I imagine the architects and people who built it standing in this same spot 2000 years ago staring in wonderment at the new creation 50m high and 275m long.

23 km

Bread appears at 8am. "Bonjour." From happy pinewood campers.

9.15am on the road. D19 little Remoulins in bustle. D918 Uzés. Apricot orchards, heavy branches strain ripened fruit. Windfall strewn oranged glowing ground. Uzés slow incline. Two roads in same direction without numbers or names local. 'Nimes' or 'Ales.' Town square map clue 'Rue de la Sauve.' For the next town.

Twisting drop sun glare, climbing under tree shade. D982 farmland pasture, black laden cherry fruit, sun orange apricot. Growing countryside oozes sweet fragrance. Small town sleeping, old main road wide and empty. Traffic speeds above on Route National.

The map shows opposite D8, there is no road. Further down D7 is not D8. Wide tall tree lined ghost road. Tumbleweed town is without name. No through traffic trade, the money flow dried up now passes overhead on a concrete flyover. The place silent, deserted. D8 guarded by a dead cat, tongue hanging out. Disused municipal dereliction sun bakes a stiff roadside dead cat. A corner tidy garden, a recently trimmed perfect hedge. Outside, a dead cat with a broken eye. No place for felines. Countryside beckons from thrice cat ritual.

Slow climb rising, horizon spikey and blue. Recognition of the Cévennes. High rugged hills frame a basin expanse of vineyards, endless rows of parallel tethered vine limbs stretch post and wire. A tractor works patiently between long green lines. Soil changes from lime and chalk smell of the Gard to a mixture of earthy stone aroma. Soil influences the grape, differing the taste of the wine.

Land fast changing. D8 crossroads, a small leaning dusty sign points 'Sauve.' A man is sat dozing in the shade of an old brown timber stall selling apricots, peaches and vegetables in the middle of nowhere.

Dusty tarmac track, wide enough for cars to pass in road verge dirt. Land of dry twisted trees pulsing in heat shimmer cicada buzz. Rock, dirt and dust. Wild sun bleached islands amongst a sea of growing wine.

Cévennes closer. Part forested cliff and escarpment, rounded rocky tops. Castleated towers rise over scrubby forest, ridges diagonal fold repeat, giant subsided steps. Jumble hills grow taller, peering over preceding rocky ridge lost in hot blue horizon.

Sauve. Unique jumble clings to a rocky dome shaped hill rising from a half dried river. Several arches span a summer dry trickle running between bush and pebble bank. The town a designed ideal by the artistic drawing skills of a five year old. Terraces of houses narrow old and tall four to five storeys without order or design similarity. Windows placed anywhere. Houses lean on each other united in effort to stay up. Orange tile roofs at any angle. Extra storey added within the roof. Chimney lean random look skyward. Church spires, castellated chateau ruin. Rocky summit home of a lone square tower.

D999. St. Hippolyte du fort. Road skirts a rocky domed hill. Everything changes. Land opens, long road straight in dropping steps. Either side scrub, box trees, rock protrudes. Wild dusty land. Heat haze distortion. Approaching vehicle's shimmer skim on a road of mercury. Parallel lined road, rock sub mountain horizon.

Descent weave, wild grown hills, St. Hippolyte du Fort lost amongst giants. A sign for camping points through town. Plane tree shade, lined shop windows. Narrow side street, tall old leaning uncared for houses lead from the bustle. Municipal depot, climbing road. Modern gated suburban housing's blue filled fibreglass status swimming pools, not one in use. Climbing a stone giant, sinuous contour weave, scrub box bush. Dark stunted sinew trunks grow from white fissured rock under windless blue bake. Heat doubled by tarmac reflection. Nailed to a twisted trunk, campsite sign tells me to keep going for 3km. Road rolls over, winding bends drop a long way out of town. Faith and patience. Campsite entrance steep country lane. Petrol strimmer's spinning blade attacks tree branches and undergrowth. The day's labour strewn across the lane as a hundred puncture opportunities.

I nod "Bonjour."

The Accueil closed. Caravans unmoved from last season. The Patron appears from his war against the bushes. Sweat glazed, leaf shred and splinter dusted. A smiling part out of breath greeting. He unlocks the door. Accueil lights flicker florescent over computer screen formalities. The chiller cabinet invites frosted plastic bottled Sangria.

A sloping field has five tents resident. River noise secret at the bottom of the field amongst dense trees. The shower is in a shed. Opening the wood door, steps into bathroom brochure luxury. Peaceful birdsong and river flow broken by mountain rumblings. Air becomes still, singing of the cuckoo and the blackbird cease. Time suspended unmoving silence.

Mauve streak across the sky. Hiss, thunder crackle, shaking the ground echoing through the hills. Ice cold droplets sting warm skin. I lash the bike tight to the bushes and check the tent pegs are immovable. Rain hits in deluge, wind increases to a gale. Judgment from the heavens for drinking cheap Spanish plastic bottle import over local Vin du Pays.

Rain lightens, birds resume evening's song. Thunder a distant rumble over somebody else's tent.

Clouds dissipate. Fading light reveals stars infinite, constellations visible. No town for many miles. No light pollution. The pristine night sky Milky Way visible as a greying sparkling mass long hazy smoke line. Uncountable number of stars are hung to shine through the universe. I wonder how many of the stars measured in time are gone. Only their light reaching my eyes and how many have been created, presence yet to be announced. The more I look, the more I can see. Until

there are more stars than empty space.
79 km

The Herault

Soft light through the green nylon. Outside veiled lines of silky mist low across trees, surrounding valley land suspended in stillness. Beyond. Milky veil shapes overhead roll silent. Water evaporates, the air holds coolness upon inhalation. I collect the obligatory baguette. Breakfast ponders the day's route.

Breeze brings the sun. A drying tent. Overhead cloud in swift race to the Cévennes.

Accueil stop goodbye to the cheerful Patron and his wife, the most hospitable of people. Cycling the steep lane receives a parting wave. Thoughts of buying the day's food re trace direction for St. Hippolyte.'

A panorama of spike peaks compressed looking impossible to traverse. Lower slopes clothed dark green in scrub woodland, colour tone change by cloud shadow speed. Busy town. Busy road. Supermarket stop. Needing to replace my plastic dinner plate. The middle fell out leaving only a saintly circular rim. Food without plate dictates more heathen saucepan eating.

Direction 'Ganges.'

Yesterday's campsite climb sets an open mind for today's road. Low roll weave between sub mountains. Spaghetti Western dusty hills, rock outcrop. High craggy cliff white and grey. Overhead vapour islands charge the blue.

Hills funnel headwind, speed slows, grinding climb, drop bar grip. Rocky towers cast shortening shadow of midday.

Hilltop views. Stone chapel rises over the road, a simple tower, two pillars hang a single bell. Cypress tree flame shape, long boundary walls surround. Land wild and rocky.

Town huddle under steep escarpment, spikey rock summits pierce underside of moving cloud. Ganges. Crossroads town, plain functional.

D986 through little Valmarie. A river gorge of Laroque. Church fortified built half into a pinnacle commands narrowed road between cliff and river. Traffic light release follows the wide River Herault. Water of darkest ink blue runs over and between large flat slabs of rock dropping in steps. Differing heights boil rapids between.

A canoe nears a tumbling staircase in whitewater roar. Unequal sizes boulders and slabs need skilled navigation. The craft disappears under the turbulent water corking to the surface, bouncing sideways on collision course with a giant boulder. Paddle spin, the craft in turbulence backwards misses the rock. Paddle dig. 180 spin. Frontways drop through bubbling white rapids with ease. I judged the situation as an amateur. The craft was always in the control of a master.

Away from the river through St. Bauzille-de-Putois. Basil the skunk? From the village cliffs rise to a hill of subterranean deep caves containing bad fairies. Grotte des Demoiselles.

Narrow D108E crosses the Herault on a bouncy suspension bridge. A few houses named Valrac. Road follows the river. Campsites and canoe hire. Rocky lands grow, tree darkened green smother. Narrow stone bridge with a single high arch crosses the sun sparkling Herault. Twisting narrow road climbs to a simple stone chapel looking roman. Three pillars join two arches hanging a bell in each under a stone gable.

Sparkling deep blue green flowing between white limestone overhung by dark green stunted oak. River edge beach of white sand under shading trees. Background rises great layered limestone crags part wooded.

Climbing road twists fragmented limestone outcrops shattered full of holes. Fissures encroached upon by twisted gnarled tinder dry box trees deep rooted in rock splinter. Gorge below flows deep green. Skyward limestone needle. Cathedral spired nature.

Long ascent to a rock plateau of box trees. Straight line tarmac line in jumping steps. Views across Montagne de la Sérrane. Behind tower the Cevennes. More mountainous than ever.

Straight line rise. Shadeless afternoon sun baking hard stony landscape. Rooftop shimmer in dusted scrubland. Crossroads village. Causse de-la-Selle names the plateau. Silence. 360 degree emptiness. Sign direction. St. Guilhem-le-Desert. Speeding drop helter skelter freewheel blur. Cracked cliffs grow, piles of boulders slip unstable on scree. Stumpy tree cling, falling giants fractured to pieces, road cracked holed, moonscape worn to dust. The first vehicle since St. Bauzille-de-Putois.

Flat ride rejoins the river. The gorge more than doubled in height. Pines grow on slopes under towering limestone. Long lined shallow diagonal layers, convoluted fold compressed by geological pressure. How much power is needed to fold rock? River flow slow, road twist and turn holds a thousand photo opportunities. Bird of prey patrol. Heavy body, thick wings, the Buzzard raptor glides, changing height and direction with a single twitch of wings. Fan of tail feathers expels no energy looking for opportunity. Lizards scurry for cover in the bushes.

Progress has been level for a while, waiting for the uphill payback amongst the giants, metres and feet marked in hundreds. Gorge bend, the river controlled by a man made weir powers hydroelectricity. Streams babble and cascade the gorge to join the Herault. The river drastically changes becoming narrow and deep wandering through strange stone spikes, spouted grottos and smooth blue pool constriction.

St. Guilhem-le-Desert is anything but. Every space occupied by parked coaches overrun by tourists. The ancient Pont du Diable. Gorge span single stone arch high over a deep blue pool framed by impressive rising rock. The bridge fenced is 'interdit.' The Devil's Bridge dates back to the eleventh century. He was to be given the first soul of whoever crossed it. The wily locals sent across a cat. Cat ritual again.

A beach in the shape of a horseshoe. Families sit in afternoon sun, children splash the sandy shallows.

D road rude return. Cars and trucks through Aniane. Flat D32. Busy streets of Gignac. A delivery lorry starts up, driver looks me in the eye and cuts the road off nearly running head on into a police car. Out of the town for St. Andre de Sangous. Road split unsigned. Uneasy for a couple of minutes I stop. I am not sure if this is the road to Ceyras. Compass decides it is not. Direction sign a km up the road. Ceyras. Under Route National for Clermont l'Hérault. Hopefully todays stop. On the map above Clermont l'Hérault is shown a large lake. My guess for a campsite.

Clermont l'Hérault permanent uphill. Ancient church crumble centuries eroded. Long straight climb under old buildings. Balconies of hung washing dry colours in the heat. Folded arms on balcony rails watch the late afternoon traffic commute.

Out of town, sign for the lake. Suburb climb. Building sites to countryside to broken moorland. Brow of a hill reveals large Lac du Salagou ending red mountainous. Languedoc red. Vivid contrast against blue water. Many hills fade to high lands. Freewheel to the lakeside. Windsurfers blast across the lake in the stiff evening breeze, cutting through choppy water silhouetted by low sun sparkle blind.

The lakeside municipal campsite. Pitches stony for motorhomes. The place is large. Caravans permanent. Green algae decorates with grass growing up the doors. A caravan home to a large family of cats growling at each other. I stop at an empty pitch reasoning it is as good as it will get, a corner having some long wild grass growing to pitch the tent over.

Shower, eat. A walk in breezy evening sunshine at Lac du Salagou. The lake big enough to have day yachts pulling at their moorings slapped by choppy water in strengthening wind. The lake seems to go for miles, the dam out of sight. Spiked rocky hills and far covering trees make it feel centuries gone untamed.

It would take a day to sail the lake in one of the little yachts. This evening it is enjoyed fully by kite and windsurfers speeding silhouettes back and forth across the water in constant strong wind. Cast shadows thrown from fast moving golden clouds advance from hills lengthening shadow in lowering evening sun.

88 km

Into the Haut Languedoc

The bin lorry réveillier matin. Not the preferred waking, but it starts routine. I leave this strange campsite that could be a most amazing place in France, if the green mouldy caravans were flame throwered. A gem of a place, cursed with melancholy dull residents.

Busy early morning Accueil gives a happy wave. Hill climb from the lake. New day light. Red hills glow. Blue water bright. Colour intensity.

Long freewheel, warm wind. Clermont Herault busy. La Poste sends cards kept since Mont Ventoux. Sign directs upstairs to a temporary office. Piped music of drills, sawing and hammering relayed from ground floor refurbishment.

The town of Clermont l'Hérault so very old. Pretty square holds many cafés, shaded seating under the pollarded plane. People meet for coffee, greeting before sitting. Boulangerie door opens to heat and homely baking smells. Shop busy, noisy with custom. An exchange of coins for rich taste baked gold. Three ladies serve the many. Breakfast sat watching happy town streets in bright summer glare.

Map points to climb the main road. D908 for Bedarieux to Le Haut Languedoc wine and wilderness. Under dusty façade gaze leaving town into countryside, ascending nonstop rocky bends. Roadside yellow broom sprouts fragrant from red stone dust. Far away tiny white building tops summit crag. Mini vineyard cram, pocket agriculture on rare precious soil. Limestone tower stack, steep escarpment, great craggy hill. Petrified stone city has received a cataclysm against it. Fantasy battlements of 'Le Cirque de Moureze.' A view down to morning blue Lac du Salagou surrounded by hills of red.

Above the tree line, a small plateau reprieve preludes a long time grind. The white summit building now level occupies an adjacent peak. New views of enormous limestone crags. Le Monts de l'espinouse, part of Le Haut Languedoc. Rocky peaks fall hazy blue away to first views of Mediterranean coast. Mini city sprawl. Behind white strip glare, soft blue Mediterranean sea. Direction signs for Beziers and Montpellier. Flat land easy route misses these wild spectacular hills.

In front, a great sweep of steepness. Far below forested black cleave falls beyond sight. Steep upward giants forested in fir. Impenetrable mountainous land.

The height spent expelling great effort to obtain is about to be lost on a drop for miles. Brake release speeds rock bends, surrounding land grows to command the sky. Areas bare, dust, crags, rock drop look down. Roundabout sculpture. The giant ant of steel streaks rust. Valley steep wooded drops into Bédarieux.

Long main street narrowed by tall worn buildings, plain rendered facades. Full length windows open blow curtains in hot breeze. Rusting verandahs hang washing, people sit watching the day. The whole town a staggered crossroads crazy one way system. Signs 'Autre Directions.' Traffic busy. Fighting against bumper and wheel attempts to push me into dead end gaps between lined parked cars. No direction west. 'Autre directions' again and again. I am dragged over the River Orb in the middle of a vehicle scrum. 'Autre directions' release to a riverside main road. Travel direction against the river flow confuses. Slip road offers a break. Tree shade benches at the riverside wait for picnickers. The tumble over small weirs overpowers the main road drone. The cooling trance of water mesmerisation broken when people arrive for shaded dejeuner.

Headwind, long shallow climb leaves industry and town buzz for parched land. A sign for St. Gervais-sur-Mare is on the opposite side to where it should be. The final event confirms suspicions. I travel opposite to wanted direction, battling headwind for nothing. Compass confirms north. I turn around. Wind propels downhill. The same faces lunch at the riverside bench. Town bustle, a sign for Lamalou-les-Bains. Flat bumpy traffic laden road offers easy speed. Health spa bill posters sell pampered bliss with hot stone healing water rejuvenation.

Dusty crossroads stop, needing a drink. It could be a long day ride. Thoughts of 'Where for tonight?' Trust in the road. Things will fall into place. A French cyclist on a mountain bike pulls up.

"Bonjour."

His bike has aluminium boxes either side of the front forks, handlebars wide for comfort. On the back of the bike a cross shape of old floorboards bolted through the rear carrier. Fading blue pannier bags from an Italian motor scooter are slung each side. A long space between the bags can support a tent. A bike for journeys. Journeys that have taken him all over France, into Spain.

"I did some of the St. Diago de Compostella route. I don't believe in all that stuff, but you say a prayer, a few euros a night gets a bed and good food."

I ask if he prayed for his supper. Going something like "Please let the food be plentiful with a little wine."

"Oui!" He laughs. "I went to Morocco. Wild country!"

Then he asks of my journey, interested in my route. Where I have been and the destinations hoped for. Soft spoken natural calmness of personality. A natural inhabitant from many generations of this area.

I find the people of the south easier to understand. Words slower, drawn pronunciation, sounds flow. With my limited language skills and his limited English we manage conversation, swapping between the two, around words to find words.

Employment is only for the morning, the rest of his day is free.

And how does he spend his time?

Enjoying the mountains, walking high forest land, swimming rivers, climbing the crags and cliffs. The bike is his transport and tending a garden gives nine months of food for free. A vegetarian. Meat bought only for his English Border collie of which he works to round sheep. Commands given to the dog work best in English! Spoken in French the commands too soft.

"We go this way."

The old road. A new replacement chops out 's' bends. A climb. Stone tumbled barns, verge tiles blown away by the winter winds worst. Rock land.

"Wait until we go around the corner."

Rock cliff vertical climb pierces blue sky. Moving clouds

appear from crags. A few km to a gorge tumble waterfall filling a sparkle pool.

I am bid farewell with information.

"Go to Mons. Take the old railway line, it runs for more than 40km. No cars and very beautiful. There is camping at St. Pons right in front, on the road. Au revoir!"

Gone up a twisting lane into the mountains. The wild man of Haut Languedoc. Vanished into homely rock landscape.

A majestic view into a gorge over lined planted vines. Rich green leaves shade ripening swelling fruit.

'Mons' signed. Short steepness delivers a disused railway line by a little row of shops. A railway without tracks under green bough shade. 'Voir vert.' Parallel above the road through hill cuttings, over bridges, through villages. I stop on a bridge. Tree shades reflection over slow flowing water shallow over glowing riverbed stones further to tumble through a woodland valley.

Short road deviation brings 'voir vert' return. Golden Notre Damme high on clifftop escarpment. Shading woodland birdsong. People on a slow afternoon walk, couples riding bikes. Long tunnel ride lights up overhead to extinguish behind. Two hours traffic free riding. Leaving the trail before St. Pons for the campsite.

Welcoming campsite Patron orders bread for the morning. The site expensive immaculate, a swimming pool for those with regulation costume. Shorts Interdit. No swim.

River noise flows at the bottom of the site, the other side a precipitous rise to cliff tops in forested fringe. Oranged rock catches the sun's last warm ray splash, trees soft yellow deepen to black.

The dropping curtain of darkness cue for stars to be lit.
95 km

The Aude

Dew thick on the grass runs cold between the toes, ground waits for the evaporating heat of morning sun to rise over high cliff ending campsite sleepy dawn.

St. Pons. Food stop buys for a long day to Carcassonne. I could go along the old railway to Mazamat taking a main traffic route into Carcassonne. The map shows a quieter route direct over the Montagne Noire ending in lower country. Squiggles on the map and the word 'Montagne.' Clues to a lot of climbing.

St. Pons de Thomiéres captive in a valley. Pleasant, unremarkable, I do not explore. Straight road splits. Uphill amongst big crawling wheels, haulage loaded with dusty aggregates close. I get off the road for the crawling leviathans to pass unhindered and there are a lot of them. Struggling engine sounds to burst into a thousand strained metallic pieces if pushed harder. Whining gears turn the wheels in steep straight line ascent ending on high crest.

Down through countryside green. Silver snake river glides sleepy to Corniou. Narrow tarmac lane climbs woodland, jumble rooftop view across the back of town ends habitation. Twisting D920 steep through thick green. Overhead thousand fanned boughs hide the light. Height lost through many bends, a look through a window in the green. High views, tree covered steepness valley plunge, an uninhabited world since creation. Stone ridge smothering forest, rock stacks rise jagged grey.

Steep road splits. Simple wood sign points 'Carcassonne.' Forested valley hidden village. Old house huddle around a church. Bridged river flows quiet in summer season. Rock strewn bank wreckage speaks of cold season capability. The village, Verreries de Moussans, the river. 'La Thore'.

Green shade forest climb, stream gurgle at the side of darkened shadow road smells of wet earth. Tree dense green leaf sky. Long forest ride rises to a clearing, rooftops against tree smother. Ancient hamlet weatherworn walls. Opposite side of the road hangs sunned lined washing. No human sound from little Galinié. Around a bend uptown cluster of old houses, a chapel in long grass. Hay cart, gnarled wood painted bright blue, decorated with hanging baskets. Pride in the little village of Aymard. Not a soul is seen. Woodland return, singing birds, scurries race away in the undergrowth. In the peace of nature I am faced with a murder memorial.

IN THESE PLACES
the 15 JUNE 1944
The looting Germans
after having pillaged and burned
the hamlet of Col de Serieres
then assassinated
Margurite ICHE 58yrs
Amie ICHE 28yrs
Francois VALEIRE 43yrs
of Col de Serieres

Roger GAUBIL 23yrs
of Labastide Rouairoux
Andre Houles 21yrs
of Mazamet.
Members of FFI
PASSER YOU REMEMBER
Their deaths for you to live
FREE!

In the churchyard, in a main town or a city a memorial is a memorial. Here, now, unexpected amongst the hung washing and flowers, so far from city crowds and politics. It shocks. Maybe not so much from inside the personal transported space of the motor car bubble. But under the sky by bike or foot propelled silent in calmness it becomes darkly poignant. It starts with politics and ends with politics. For pathetic ideals many must die horribly, mostly young people betrayed and robbed of their lives by verbal tricks of the mad old. Political devils wear suits.

Narrow green climb follows contour cling. Woodland release to squinting daylight. Many forested hills. Sunshine road upward twist and turn. 'Roc Suzadou.' Picnic bench beckons. 'Observation point' directs between rocks to be met with a drop vertical far down a cliff face with an open view across a valley. Foreground mountainous hill tumbles red soil and scree from its pointed summit, behind stretch many steep shaped forested hills in half fade heat haze. Southward panorama. Hills open. Lower land flattening wide and featureless until numerous convolutions of blue grow faraway into mass hazed snowcapped giants. The eyes focus to absorb the first atmospheric view to the Pyrenees frontier with Spain. Hours spent under woodland constriction intensifies the spectacle.

Forested ascent. Openings let in the blue. Lizards on the road run to undergrowth cover, kites wheel over the hill on hot rising air. Sat on a tree branch a bird of prey, the heaviest looking buzzard with a short neck, head blue grey. My silent approach, the bird is yet to see me. A close meeting with a honey buzzard surveying its forested domain from a hidden perch. I am spotted. The bird drops from the branch unhurried. Wings open, upward fanned finger wing tips, gliding without effort to disappear. A springing branch the only evidence of presence. The great raptor feeds on such small things as wasp and bee larvae, grubs, small birds and lizards.

I make the crest of a hill. Road turns to find another. Temperature cools the higher I climb. Lone house long garden ends in a large fenced run with a kennel. Against the fence together lay a pack of small beagle hounds. Asleep in the heat under bright sun. My quiet passing stirs only one to look through bleary eyes returning the weight of its sleepy head onto the comfort of its neighbour's belly joining the mass panting. It is too hot to bark.

Fields of long meadow grass vibrant green share the acreage with colouring wild flower. Years fallow without livestock. An abandoned farm long boarded up. Half buried under wild grass sits a red rusted plough in vain wait to be pulled by generation's gone horses. Weathered bleached fence posts flake brittle under the sun holding wire rusted to rotting remnants.

Cycling under wild green, the altitude 1000m (3000ft) proclaimed at Col de Salette on Montagne Noire. Where I never saw a soul.

The Haut Languedoc ends in new region. 'The Aude.' Named from the mountain river. Famous for the land of castles occupied by the exterminated Cathars. Road changes its number to D620. Down on a fast twisting bumpy patched tarmac shake about through sharp barriered bends along sides of cliff. Views through trees to steep forested hills. A village far below. Square church tower wears a hip roof bonnet of sun silvered slate surrounded by house jumble roofs clinging to a ridge. Hills tumble steep falling out of sight. The landscape too precipitous to hold a crop. Rock cling trees hold fissured cliff grip.

Twisting cliff edge bends, houses tight against the rock open doors to the road. Speed blur ride past sun brightened walls of white, shutters sunny blue. Open sky, village buildings so old. Dusty windowed shop closed. Centuries old rough stone church, roman numeral hands point 2.15. I started climbing this morning before 11 at Courniou. Less the ten minutes on this downward run point to three hours dedicated to the granny gear slow grind skyward and now I dare not ease the brake grip.

The village Lespinassiére tumbles down a ridge. Road clings steep, flash of rock. Tree blur speed roar in the ears, joining valley follows an infant river. Temperature increase, the heat of the Midi easier than the raw Haut Languedoc hills. Downward bends under black chateau ruin, towered broken castellation guards vertical cliff edge against background pure blue. The village of Citou, bleached bright. Old, lived in, alive with people. Small shop's primary fruit colours displayed amongst the dust. Steep tumbling land ancient growing terrace. Streams merge unified making the Argent Double a river of volume to be noticed, filling the valley in tumbling noise. Houses across the roar accessed by simple arched footbridge over the roar.

Fast road follows many river bends, exciting to travel. Steep valley flanked by dry rock towers sparse covered by growing flame cypress. The rocky hills hidden behind blank walls of Caunes Minervois. Main road junction finishes the fun, the river carried away under the road flowing from sight. People at a bar opposite enjoy afternoon sunshine where nothing much happens.

D620. Flat land shared with easy downhill makes 50 kph. Side wind pace unhindered. Open landscape, faraway hill detail absorbed in haze. Out of town directions for camping do not lure. Determination for Carcassonne. Carrefour des Bresssons main crossroads sweeps around busy traffic bend. A sign directing 'Canal du Midi.' Across a busy road, rough track drops to a grass edged towpath. Slow moving silent thick water sleepy saunter under shading plane trees. Pace of the day changes to the pace of the canal. Slow easy ride follows the narrow path. Tree shadows over soupy mirror water.

Canal locks step up in three, rising a total of maybe 8m. A boat waits to ascend. Two are in the process of passing each other through the locks. Hydraulic sluice doors let water out from the top lock lowering the downward boat. Water runs into the centre lock raising the upward journeying boat. The two locks equal in height, gates open, boats change place. The process repeated, boats sail away on new levels.

The mind romanticises the ideal, expecting someone to be winding a ticking greased cog mechanism by hand letting the water in and out, followed by an unhurried gate swing whilst smoking a long clay pipe. Things seem to have progressed from the 1700's with hydraulics and electric button pushing sat on a chair in a little steel and glass air conditioned tower. All the romantic notions have died with hydraulic oil and electricity. The same with the boats. No more wood or decorated iron barges transporting cargo having families living on board tending potted flower gardens amongst the hanging washing moving at human pace. No more sedate sails grace the countryside. Plastic fibreglass cruisers with diesel engines hired to the amateur provides entertainment as two boats negotiate passing each other in the confinement of the lock. Whoever is driving the Carcassonne voyaging craft is finding boats do not have a brake pedal after revving up and shooting forwards. The person on the bow has to quickly rope the boat to the side of the lock to stop the craft crashing headlong into the towering gates. The effort needed is nearly enough to be sent bodily through the small mooring ring as processed sausage contents. Panic shouts between bow rope operative and boat operator.

As the water is let from one lock to the other, turbulence boils water with instability. Unless the boats are held tight against the sides of the lock by ropes held and fed through the mooring rings, craft get swirled, shaken and battered against the stone lock wall. Either way seems to involve ropes wet and algal slime shaded walls dripping a darkened cold brown.

The canal is carried over a river running under at right angles. Beyond the opposite bank, modern traffic buzz. Into the city along the 17th century tree lined superhighway. Grass area of people watching the canal in afternoon sun. Low bridge, the canal passes underneath a road ending the travelled path.

Busy road crosses to a canal quay of moored pleasure. Fiberglass cruisers gently nose against converted steel barges painted black hulls, white funnels. Appealing cabins of varnished wood. Flag hangs from a short varnished pole surrounded in geranium bloom.

Wherever there are boats, a certain type of person appears. Dressed well with sunglasses, wearing light cream draped over the shoulders and something Breton striped or rugby, who hang around boats in association. Parading on show, never doing anything apart from pointing at some part of a craft with body language of all knowledge, waving a foot sideways dismissive whilst keeping hands firmly in pockets. Here today on quay patrol.

The canal continues as the 'Lateral.' Riverbank bend out of sight. Further on a lock staircase raises craft up a hill travelling far to Toulouse changing its name to Canal Garonne to Bordeaux, joining the Atlantic Ocean via the Gironde estuary. The other direction follows flat lands through the midi to Agde, changing name to join with the River Rhone flowing into the Mediteranean.

Across the main road into busy narrow city streets under tall building shade. Glimpses of 'La Cite.' The medieval walled city separate to newer Carcassonne. Shoppers summer clothed chic. Boutiques of thumping beats, savoury aromas drift between streets. Plate glass mannequin, branded gimmick image.

Out of place pushing my bicycle. No sports car, no expensive shirt showing gold, no pointed leather shoes. Tired body, black oily legs sweat dried, mind buzz from the day not available in the shops.

City gate, empty square. Carousel spins children on a bright musical ride. The children's moment for serving the day's sentence of busy shopping. The onlooking bag laden parents turn to wait. City grid plan direction to 'La Cite.'

The traffic stop start one way system crosses the River Aude. Under the walled city. Coned round turrets, castellated towers impressive. A municipal campsite sign to a hotel style desk Accueil. Booking for two nights gives a rest day for medieval wandering.

The large campsite contains a shop, restaurant bar, swimming pool and barbecue areas. A hundred plastic motorhome and caravan cables trail between gas barbeques and sun chairs. Satellite dishes poke above plastic roofs for a signal from deep space. Tents totalling six are pitched under trees against a tall perimeter fence.

79km

Lazy sunny morning, a wandering from the campsite follows alongside water slow moving. The shaded tree walk shared with joggers in various physical states counteracting the effects of wonderful french food. For some the appearance is effortless, for others it is not so. Bright red with bulging blood vessel eyes, lungs desperate oxygen grab in state of near collapse.

Path ends opposite medieval cité wall turrets. The entrance climbs a wide cobbled pathway high under holes for pouring hot unpleasantness through and slits for the firing of sharp things. I go through a portcullis expecting the entrance but instead I am under more defence walls, towers, holes and slits. If I was an attacker I would be finished. The path climbs high outside castle walls to a gated keep. If this was closed and the portcullis dropped behind all would be trapped and done for as over the wall is a long way down.

The other side of the gate opens to medieval gift shops,

medieval restaurants, medieval jewellers, hotels, bars, etc. But the view out across the rooftops of the modern city is worth the walk. Far across tiled roof red orange maze to heat haze views. High buildings, shaded streets, city traffic miniscule lines bumper to bumper queued across the river bridge.

Medieval streets overrun by a money laden tourist mob. Vendors fend them off with tat trinkets, plastic swords and alcohol beverage. Many a euro is shed across the counter in a day's campaign withdrawing in truce at night to re arm the tat ready for the repeat daily invasion.

Old timbered overhang, cobbled back streets. Much has been added and expanded by different occupants of Gallo Romans, Visigoths, Franks and medieval French nobility to make a formidable fortress. The cone roofed turrets and additional battlements were added by ideas of a 19th century architect Viollet-le-Duc. A striking church houses noble bones. A wandering hour between streets. Battlement gaze to yesterday's Haut Languedoc far black horizon around to blued hills and mountain lands to future travel.

Stone bridge crosses the Aude. Pedestrian cobbles, overhead lanterns hang central from ornate iron scrolled black and gold. River rumble accompanies turret view. Many nationalities cross the bridge drawn to 'La Cité.' The slow amble waterside walk.

White plastic motorhomes at the campsite barrier wait for dejeuner to finish. Swimming pool splash and laughter. Bar stool spectators watch big screen football holding a beer. 'Frites' arrive at the table.

Tents arrived, bikes outside. A lady lives under a tree. The tent joined to a tarpaulin wrapped around the trunk. At the sides bags are piled, a polythene sheet covers. She sits to the side of her habitation on a folding plastic chair reading. About her feet is a small dog less than the size of a cat wanting to continuously play, but ignored. After getting no attention it takes to wandering, making for the direction of anybody. The realisation of the dog's absence results in its calling over and over ending in walking the campsite looking for the animal picking it up with one hand and returning to the tent. Reading sat in the chair resumes. The bored dog is off again, friends with somebody else.

The dog follows me to the shower block getting itself let into the building much to the amusement of people getting ready for their evening. The thing wanders wagging its tail looking pleased with itself. Outside its name is being called without concern from the dog. Someone opens the door, putting it outside.

People jog along the path and walk dogs the other side of the fence. The little dog wanders away from the tent to the fence letting out canine abuse to a German shepherd, a Rottweiler and various other dogs happily minding their own business. The thing can hardly jump to the knee high wall. It's squeaking and yapping vocal abuse cause other dogs to lunge barking. Dogs pulling owners and owners pulling dogs in the middle joggers try not to fall over the animal tangle of crossed leads. Mayhem from the canine midget. The calling of the dog is followed by the walk, picking up the animal in denial of chaos caused. The entertainment repeated again and again on the unsuspecting public out for a quiet evening stroll.

Corbiéres

I take a time to pack throwing out a book along with anything not needed. I think about throwing away more clothes, but I carry so little, enough for a couple of days in case of rain. I cannot throw anything else. Which is disappointing.

I nod hello to a Swiss couple camped with bikes. They are returning to Switzerland from Spain on their mountain bikes and ask of my journey and are looking for a quiet route to leave the area. They look at an old map I carry. I tell them they can keep it. The man returns with a pound coin found on the road in Spain. I tell him that I will put it towards a beer when I get back to England. It is their rest day wanting to look around La Cite after chores of washing and sorting.

I pedal past the bag woman reading her book. The dog seeks the company of people washing breakfast dishes.

Main road traffic, busy multilane junction. Signs for an airport, direction for Route National. Going south using the compass. City speed condensed humanity swapped for farmland and birdsong.

Dusty lane, village street. People talk, baguette under arm. Time passes slow under the sun in Lavalette. In the middle of the village a small crowd are around a car. An elderly lady driver is trying to start the vehicle. The gathered crowd decide a push will get it going, shouting instruction amongst laughter. A smoking grumble splutters into life. A cheer of victory, triumphant pushers. Everyone a car expert. Mutual congratulation amongst participating generations.

Climb wanders sunny woodland. Signs forbid the picking of champignons on private property act as advertising. 'Do not climb the thin wire to pick the succulent delicacies growing here.' A car parked on the woodland edge. In the woods people scratch the ground and undergrowth, bag in hand. Hilltop view. Heat shimmer blue dusty hills. Road signs to nowhere. Limoux 23km. Cooling freewheel, fast single track through bright fields and sun drenched trees. Village rooftops. Distant blue snowcapped giants.

D118 fast and straight. Limoux floral displays flank the road. Shopfronts. 'Deviation.' Wide road, plane tree cafés. Pharmacy digital 33 degrees of shade. Tour de France images decorate a roundabout. Cut outs of riders on time trial bikes in yellow, green, orange suspended revolving around floral display. Signs advertise 'Tour de France en Limoux 15 July.' Boulangerie open on a Saturday at 12.30!

Easy ride in company of the River Aude. Steep wooded hills meet the road. Alet-le-Bains old bridge points to medieval half timber town. Canoe country advertises hire. 'Aire du repose.' Picnic bench shade offers respite from intensified heat. Lunch under a shading bough. Tree lined green reflection flows over gold glowing stone amongst the boulder rock.

Green lizard dart, iridescent flash. Hidden rustle in riverbank grass. A missile above the river. Speed speed. Head of black, white neck, pale speckled chest with dark grey wings held half folded. Nature's jet fighter has a black tail. Focused intent. The Peregrine falcon observed by chance, gone in a second. Privileged moment.

Turning, I am hit in the eye by a clumsy flying may bug. Two flying extremes. The amateur insect and the precision expert Falcon.

Short shade old terraced houses, dusty hot Couiza. The Frenchman at Tarascon recommended Rennes-le-chateau. Signed narrow lane snakes upward working around a hill. Bend after bend, earth dusty red, temperature bake. Windless hot sun. Halfway views far to an abandoned chateau ruin, towering walls fallen, solitary on top of a dusty hill. Wild land spartan, dark spindly trees amongst scrub. Distant great forested sub mountain. Cliffs and spiked crags skyward. Solitary white cloud slow pace suspended in blue backdrop. Hot dry climb, short hairpin bend. Silence. I wonder if the place exists. Bends to a car park, a panorama of hills. Far away villages swallowed hazed under Pyrenees Mountain. Climb ends against a stone wall with a mountaintop view across below fields dropping to far forest. Villages amongst agricultural sea joined by twisting ribbon roads threading the hills to faraway spikey deep blue Corbiéres. Next to the wall a castle keep restored perfect. A small round turret on the corner of its square shape complete with gothic arched leaded glassed window under battlements. I hear music.

Jazz saxophone ascending runs and cascades of notes. A guitar plays percussive comping chords to keep structure and rhythm unhurried, filling the village with music mood perfect for dry afternoon Mediterranean heat. The music follows to café shade. Created by two musicians bonded in thought improvisation. An appreciative audience sit relaxed, people about the place sat reading in the shade with a drink.

Pedestrian path to a chapel dedicated to Maria Magdalena. Strange inscriptions over the door in Latin. DOMUS MEA DOMUS TERRIBILIS EST ORATIONIS VOCABITUR. 'Terrible/fearsome things happened / said here?' Ornate carvings. Wood icon dedicated to the lady. Inside offers cool sanctuary from the heat. The arched roof is beautifully decorated leading to the semicircular Apse. The ceiling dark blue with stars and night time clouds over a round stained glass window of delicate perfection.

The body achieves calm in the coolness. In a half daze I wander into the bright afternoon furnace. A curious place. There is no one here under fifty five. A quiet crowd up in the middle of nowhere reading books. I did not see the dragon the Tarascon Frenchman told me about. Plastic ones are available from the souvenir shop.

Downhill ride hairdryer hot breeze, road bend red dust and orange earth. Lower land sun parched. Small triangular field holds cows of indifference.

High views lost to hills. Main road follows the river. A lane into back of Quillan town, stopping on an old bridge. The scenery has just got bigger. Towering vertical cliff rock and dense forest scrub encircle the town half shaded by stone giants. Upstream river noisy over boulders and slabs, rapids flank a black flowing channel. Canoeing youth rush over rapids, digging the paddle to spin banging into each other laughing, racing each other upstream through the channel to be first for a repeat ride. Downstream river widens and shallows, bubbling over stones to pools and wide channels. A man half immersed dressed in bib waders patiently fishes.

Sunny town square. A fountain. Chairs surround laid tables, customers enjoy an afternoon treat. Streets narrow, buildings shade afternoon shadow. Voice echo between buildings quiet. Too hot for effort. Sunday closed shops. Quiet café conversation. Cash machine dispenses needed funds. People sit out on chairs in front of doorways talking. Children in play on the pavement. The world goes slowly by. Sign points an exit weave through tall shaded streets. Main road for Axat.

Large rocky hills close the sky rising 1000m (3000ft). Village elevated swallowed in surrounding rock land. Flat road follows the River Aude. Rocky chasm squeeze, river roar captive volume reverberates vertical cliff. A sign, 'Defile de Pierre-Lys.' Bends weave, under rock arch. Concrete wall separates the road from the tumbling river gorge drop. Screams of laughter rise from below. Through the gorge seven people in a round rubber dinghy are bouncing along the fast flowing river dressed in wetsuits, lifejackets and helmets. Three to a side, one steers from the back giving watchful instruction. Downstream shrieks still audible above the noise tumble.

Rock tunnels shrink the road to one lane, high cliff walls so narrow looking to close together on the next bend. Hydroelectricity controls the flow born of mountains. Gorge steep rolls back. Roundabout. The entrance to a campsite. Coasting down a slope to camp pitches along the riverside. I book in, pitch the tent and stand bare feet in mountain ice water flow chilling the blood from midi heat. A sign 'Baignade Interdit.'

Wild grass under trees, river chatters the shallows, deep channel speed feeds the gorge. Cliff surround brings evening shade early, creeping shadow up the rockface. Tree dwelling cicadas overhead buzz. The evening deepens, cicadas quieten. Chattering river's lullaby.

92 km

Turbulent roar. No leaf moves. Stillness in a narrow rocky world. Haze veils a warming day guaranteed Mediterranean hot.

A tent without dew makes for a quick pack. Roadside sells oranges and apricots, vendors busy with crates arrange produce for display. Road climb. Cliff tops wear a cap of mist roll silence, masking the heat of background blue. The river ceases its companionship. Rock road rises, dusty view of a railway cut in and out of the cliff crossing the road. Train sound. Barrier race to beat the bells. A yellow engine in diesel drone. The descent into Lapradelle.

High stone ridge commands the valley. Ruined Cathar fortress of Puilaurens 800 year gaze from 700m (2100ft). Castellated stone walled keep, battlement walls to a large round tower.

Solid limestone crags. Small ruin castle on a pinnacle summit rises from a rock hill. Parched fields, pollarded olives, vine parallel lines. Narrow rocky defile. Signed 'Clue de la Fou' half hidden in escarpment black shade.

St-Paul-de-Fenouillet. Roadside stalls sell apricots, peaches, cherries. Roasting piglet on a spit is rotated in flame.

Traffic lights. D7 weaves a narrow street. Washing hangs, daily life sounds bounce wall to wall. Uphill dusty fields flatten to an airfield. Single engined planes, sun glint on cockpit glass. Rock and dusty scrub. Rusting car wreck dumped in the dust, engine missing. Wheel amputation. Stubby dark box trunk amongst rock, road climb along steepening valley side. An oncoming car of young people toot a thumbs up.

Looking down into tops of trees. Road bend to another world. Waterworn deep gorge rises, river roars below out of sight, echo trapped by rock. Single lane weave, passing place cliff squeeze. Road tunnel to overhanging towering limestone denies the sun.

Below hermitage in tight vertigo cling against a rock face next to the chapel of St- Antoine-de-Galamus. Terraced garden's precipitous zig zag path disappears to the river.

Someone tries to drive a van too big for the low cliff overhangs around the narrowing bends resulting in traffic chaos. A French motorcyclist wearing mirrored sunglasses stops and waits for the traffic.

"Espaniol Tourists!" Exclaimed. Hands in the air, smiling and shaking his head.

"Oh l'Espaniols!" I reply nodding with a tut. Without giving away my Englishness.

He controls the traffic. Telling cars to wait before waving others on. An English car creeps along apologetically thanking everybody including me.

"Bloody English" Through their car window. Releasing their tension to laughter.

Pantomime ends. The motorcyclist gives a part wave, part salute upon departure.

Many sharp twists and bends, flat road through rock world. Stepped cascades rise in roar to road level. Wall gap. A narrow rough path to the river's edge. I walk the bike, taking dejeuner through the bushes, jumping stepping stones to sit on a slab mid river. Deep pools, small cascade tumble. Clear green tint shimmers reflection. Salmon swim on the edge of the current waiting for downstream food to arrive. Fish forearm in length move between pools. Small bits of bread thrown upstream float toward the fish. Attacking the bread, making no attempt to follow remnants downstream, preferring to wait to see what comes next.

Traffic vanished. Silent ride. Cubiéres-sur-cinoble. Nobody. Signs of human habitation but not of human life. Faraway Corbiéres mountain rock dominates the skyline looking crashed from outerspace. Its contemplation takes the mind off the climb under clear sky heat risen to the mid thirties. Soulatgé in afternoon desertion. Thin road snakes dry countryside. Rooftop heat shimmer buildings of Rouffiac-des-Corbiéres.

Towering slab cliffs 400m high (1200ft). Expanse of ruin fortress walls run the length of a great rocky outcrop. Facade of high stone, round towers crumble, points of shining light through window openings contrast black shade castle mass. If it was not for the windows, I would not recognise the ruin as manmade. Long patient climb, steep pinch push watching the changing chateau elevations. Road crest view to long line jagged rocky escarpment burning in heat haze. Below village of Duilhac grows cypress trees. An artist study ideal.

Road fast loses the toiled height. Through pretty Duilhac. Pinky terracotta, pale lemon and white houses, orange roofs under sun bleach. Down and down, dust scrub junction. Duilhac now high above, pulsing in heat shimmer. The sign for Chateau Peyrepertuse points dusty skyward. Shadeless plod, sun glare hairpins. Ice cream, lollies and cold drinks. A poster of a glass filled with ice, a cold refreshing drink about to be poured. A shaded bar, people sat cooled. Bottle crate rattle. Grind sinuous, treeless dusty landscape, pace to near standstill, the bends quicker to walk, riding the straight. Two thirds up is just quicker to walk. No matter how much I drink it cannot satisfy thirst. My watch says 2.30pm, cloudless vast blue stillness. Car passes kicking up dust, engine drones the steep ascent. Cooling fan whine.

Baking without breeze, sweat runs soaking the body. My old hat drip dripping. I do not look up any more, watching my footsteps one at a time push and drip the ascent, stopping every five minutes slows a pounding pulse. Cars pass struggling with the gradient. Solitary tree offers short shadowed shade, a few minutes to cool. Carry on pushing, salt sweat stinging eyes. One hour of saddle and foot to the entrance steps. Bike is chained to the information post to stop it from running downhill. Tepid plastic drink unsatisfying. Waiting for the slowing pulse, trying to compose a soggy self. Every movement leaks a river. People arrive by vehicle. Sunglasses for the brightness, smart clothes adjustment, brushing creases from sitting in air conditioned vehicles.

Body temperature soggy but stable. Glass fronted Accueil takes payment. The rivers run again. Relief to get outside.

A French lady tells me. "You're Australian!"

I smile. "Anglais."

An English couple amused by my climb. "You made it then."

I had become their afternoon's entertainment.

Chateau entrance is not obvious. I walk over smoothed limestone. Under stone gaze around the rear elevation treading the worn path of a people vanished. Steps through bushes, high stone walls, portcullis entrance, steps rise under defensive wall gaze. Vertical drop three sides from high overhanging cliffs. Attempts to scale the chateau useless, the flip side being as an occupant, once driven up to this point there is no way out. You're finished. The higher part of the chateau gives most enjoyment, a view across lower ruins to its church remains. Loose laid ropes form a halfhearted barrier easy to cross, the edge with toes over straight down to the tiny tops of full grown trees. Window gaze to the snowcapped Pyrenees.

Different views. Opening valley of many hills. Le Salses to Port Bacarés. White hills. Far thin line glare immersed in Mediterranean blue.

How many eyes over the two thousand year history have looked upon the same views from this place? I am just another. Looking from curious interest and not from siege, attack and impending murder as the fate of the Cathars. Who were the attackers, the armies that laid siege to these fortresses? From the little knowledge learned it was Simon de Montfort. Plus a few other grab what you can noblemen. Under the name of 'The Albigensian Crusade.' Orders from the King of France and the Vatican. Their religious path was became too popular. First persuasion to convert, second inquisition. Finally a campaign of extermination after Cathar revenge against a Catholic stronghold where Cathar people were held in inquisition.

"Get rid of them, the spoils are yours. Your sins are pardoned before you commit them." From Rome.

From a Cathar head priest. "Kill them. God recognises his own."

A people systematically wiped out. Converted nobility, men, women and children all put to sword or burned alive on communal pyres. De Montfort a French nobleman and also the Duke of Leicester grabbed much but lost it all with his life during the campaign against Toulouse. He is believed buried in La Cité. Carcassonne. Give it a name. Crusades. Final solution. New world order, whatever title. The history, the revival, over and over. Greed and death masked by invented cause. Past, future. Never to change.

It is 4pm. I am not sure how many more hills to exit the high rock.

Time to leave this magical place inhabited once by the Romans, Cathars and later border fortress between France and Spain, until the border moved back into the mountains leaving not much to guard. Used later for royal and political exile to keep a few living quietly out of the way.

Stone steps to an aircraft panorama. Miniature village under great limestone ridge spine running far out of sight. A few light clouds appear with a hint of welcomed breeze. A final look up to the fortress in its magnificence. Defying Popes and Kings.

Brake grip. Many bends steep and sharp gain speed. Welcomed warm breeze, passing the shaded bar. Direction for Chateau Queribus. Looking impossible to reach.

Dust, rock, cicada buzz. Windmill hilltop village of Cucugnan. Chateau Queribus above a long spine ridge on a skyward great finger of rock. Defensive walls built to the edge. Zig zag path below stone mass walls. Intact tower shaped to rock angles on which it is built. Light and shade alters detail view with the twists of the road. Out of time to visit. Little specs of colour make their way around the walls giving human size to quantify its mass. No one ever managed a successful attack on Queribus. It was sieged for a couple of years finally giving up to surrender. Some of the sieged occupants managed to flee over the Spanish frontier.

Distant sea views. Road turn 180 degrees. Jagged cliffs, rock mountain ridge. Background snow giants look into Spain. The amazing panorama, silhouetted giants blue softened in haze, size difficult to quantify. Beauty in the late afternoon, the sun's bright daytime sting softened, tinted gold land.

Freewheeling speed through bends, down and down. A pool full of splashing children, families sat around. Maury wine growing town greets with wall murals. False doors and images of Les Vignobles. The Vinyards. An old municipal camping sign directs main road. D117. Re united from this morning. Out of town entrance, a little tree lined campsite. Accueil closed for an hour.

I pitch next to a tree, big ants up and down the trunk. The Patron arrives in her car, opens the Accueil and takes the money for a night. Showers immaculate and welcomed after the fluid drain dusty day. The place relaxed. Municipal friendly, quaint. Homely pleasant.

A retired French couple are in their campervan. The Frenchman seeing me changed and clean asks if I feel refreshed looking amused at the little pot boiling on the stove. Wishing. "Bon appetite."

He is looking at the bike and nodding reminiscent thought. A few lines of conversation. Back to his van unhurried, hands in pockets to watch evening T.V.

A man carries a box of apricots stopping at every pitch asking people just to 'Take some.'

Delicious juice bursts on touching. The evening is spent eating and drinking as much as possible to replenish lost fluid and energy. Orange sun sets the rocky ridge ablaze sinking behind in firey red. Light gone I get into the tent. Ants have to climb something. This evening big ants go for the record of how many can climb a tent.

70 km

Coté Vermeille

Speeding drone internal combustion alarm stamps on morning serenity. Fresh flowers in the washroom window, the place already cleaned as thorough as a tidy home. Personal touches welcoming to the heart. I pack without breakfast. "Au revoir" to the campervan couple. The Patron discusses tidying the campsite grounds with a man dressed in full strimmer uniform of orange plastic hat, visor, overalls and harness. Five second thank you to the Patron. Saying how clean and agreeable the place is. Is appreciated. Return to Maury for the boulangerie.

Streets random weave climb narrow and so very old. Away from the tourist pull of coastal towns. Humble, lived in. Working lives tend the bottle. Above every street Chateau Queribus reminds Maury of feudal control from fortress gaze. Boulangerie 'Ferme'. 'It's Monday.' I was told. If closed. Try Bar Tabac. On the main road corner a shop selling everything. I get bread squeezing past half of Maury in busy gossip exchange. 9.30am. Sun poised behind cooling haze is ready to turn up the blue burn.

Chateau Queribus visible from everywhere. Ridge rock grey, walls of a wide valley filled with green parallel line famous Corbiéres wine. River Maury. Dry rock filled, docile summer trickle. Little Estagel. Food stop. The shopkeeper and a wiry weatherworn old man in deep discussion. My bonjour returned with a nod, engrossed in hushed conversation.

Country lane will dodge Rivesaltes and Perpignan one way systems and big town cycle lanes. D1 ancient way narrow. House walls serenaded by summer trickle. Retired men dressed in worn suit jackets over bib and brace overalls. Flat hats shade deep creased faces. Sat together on the wall. Curled fingers resting on sticks. I become a moment's interest.

I am wished a happy "Bonjour."

Hilly lane over the rooftops, pocket vineyards amongst rock. Old dusty car, digging and hoeing tools lean against. An old man busy pruning vine runners stops work to bid. "Bonjour."

Hill crest unveils wide low flat land. Many miles to a haze coastline. Black mountain ridge ends plunging into Mediterranean blue. Mountain range snowcapped background, lower forested peaks. The sight fills the vision. Small white rectangular clusters lost in steep dark landscape make villages.

Long easy freewheel, the outskirts of habitation, smalltown signs. Roundabout flatland. Crossroads. Traffic laden speed. Backway lane quiet. Pézilla-la-Riviére. Le Soler. Ponteilla. Trouillas. Villemolaque. Banyuls-des-Aspres. Names sing of sun. Boulder strewn half dried River Tech arrives from high mountain frontier. Dusty side road plod parallel to busy 'interdit' main road. Bumps and potholes, scrub and birdsong. The redundant road somehow ends up in backway maze of Argelés-sur-Mer. Shop lined street half busy with smart dressed wanderers. Yacht masts above roadside trees, the smell of the sea. Palm trees, colours bloom either side of a wide road.

Bright sunshine, busy coastline. Racou Plage has an outbreak of 'Happycamperland.' to avoid.

The corniche route, little coastal towns. Fort Miradou, the sea colour cerulean blue. Windblown choppy waves break against dark brown rock. Above buildings white, a luminescence. Tiled roofs of orange vibrance contrast dark olive green land rising steeply from the sea.

Behind on a rock sits an old chapel, a solitary bell under an arch. Facing the sea a large black crucifix. Stone pier shelter. The start of famous Collioure.

Curved bay home to cafés and restaurants. Waterfront crowded people parade. The bay sweep, a restaurant on a promontory. Fake masts with sails attached advertise the place. Fort dominates a little harbour. Stone tower reflection in sun glint water. Traffic, palm trees, people mass crowded restaurants. Pavement spill into the road. Hill leaves the crowds, dropping to Port Vendres quayside. Dockside ship bow. Fishing fleet quayside silent. Colourful hull reflection in glass blue.

A large motor yacht is moored at the quay. The young deckhand dressed in white carefully washes the hull with a large soft broom keeping the sparkle. Across the road, shaded café aperatif. People try to look associated with the large craft wearing yachting clothes. Commercial dock noise unloading a ship. A balance of normality to played magazine lifestyle of waterfront bars.

Hillside climbs inland, dropping steep to a town suffering 1970s/80s architectural taste depletion. Banyuls-sur-mer dusty beach of grey sand. Walking up on the pavement, an old man with a huge flabby belly wearing turquoise tiny bathers and flip flops. No need! The disturbing sight finds new energies to climb out of town.

Landscape wilder, steep rocky hills. Green vineyard vibrance against rich blue sea. Tight bends, high cliff headland, a viewing area.

Timber building sells famous Banyuls wine. The last touristy place extracting the euro from the holidaymaker. The vendor and his employees are busy practicing their craft of ensuring the buyer feels special parting with their money in exchange for a bottle of wine. People behave foolish snobby, the reality. They have just bought a bottle of plonk from a man in a shed in a rough dust car park. Van parked waits for the re stock. The vendor eyes me sideways for a second. Experience tells him. No money, no sale, don't bother. He waits for the next people carrier and big four wheel drive to arrive dripping with euros.

Down the coast, the start of little town Cerbére. The headland of Cap Cerbére. The frontier with Spain. Coastal curve of a different country. Cap de Creus ends land horizon. Cerbére. The south of the South of France. The last town.

Below on a headland, a large block of flats or a hotel. It could be worth a look for somewhere to camp.

Vineyards green amongst barren rock, hairpin freewheel. The block of flats. Small building, large painted letters across the wall. 'CAMPING.' Dusty, looking abandoned. Weeds and bushes grow from the bottom of walls. My kind of place. 'Camping municipal Cap Peyrefite. Cerbére.' Is open! It is the Accueil. Inside finds the young Patron in part chaos of papers, paint pots and brushes. The place just opened for the season. A strewn desk. Whirring electric fan shakes its cooling head repetitive saying. 'No. No.' I am invited to sit on old chair comfort while administration is completed. I can go anywhere under the pines.

I ask of the building. Hotel or flats?

It is a specialist hospital and respite center for children and their families.

Bright dusty lane, pines below. A sports ground with rugby posts on the headland. Under pine shade, the ground terraced follows land contour. Shaded cool keeps away the blowtorch sun. Through twisting trunks Mediterranean sea.

Clearing rocks and sticks. Flat area luxury just big enough for the tent. Iron ground resists the pegs. Bike chained to a trunk stops it rolling. Through shading dark green, vivid blue sea spectacular. Dusty road bake exchanged for sea smell temptation.

Narrow path weaves flowers and fragrant wild rosemary. Millpond flat deep water invites. Goat track down the cliff finishes in rocky clamber. Between the rocks, a deep water gully. A dusty hot body launches into a cool Mediterranean blue baptism. Clear water depth to an emerald jewel underwater garden. Laying floating, blood cools refreshed. Tranquil lap against the coast. The freedom of sea swimming.

Sun sting gone, haze blurred horizon, windless water sky mirror. Cliff colour reflection in deep green symmetry. I have stumbled upon a gem for people with simple pleasures. Forgotten coast. Long overlooked by false reputation glitzy motor yacht money sucking towns pedaling plastic package dreams to the tourist drone.

I return to the rocks. Delicate sponges and soft coral below the surface. Heat from the early evening sun warms a cooled body. Sun warmed rock retains heat from the day. I pick my way up the cliff through the wild rosemary path. Delicate yellow petals of bunch bloom cacti grow round fleshy spikes.

Yesterday I had woken in a gorge next to a river, experienced spectacular fortress castles. Today I have travelled the area inhabited by the 'modern' fauvist artist colony of the early 20th century, experienced glitz town and have experienced a swim in the Mediterranean in my own private cove. There are half a dozen tents spaced about the large pine woodland. Back down the coast plastic 'happycamperland' crowds are being packed sardine tight and paying five times as much for the privilege.

94 km

Thoughts of Cerbére town early to beat the heat. Dusty corniche road hugs rocky hill contour. Sea view town buildings start with a garage busy, the noise of spanners, air tools and the smell of auto paint sprayed somewhere in dark interior. Road drops into town. Hotel of elaborately shaped concrete built in 1928. Art deco balcony views across a sheltered crescent bay of town building colour.

Cerbére was a railway town. Its heyday before and just after the Second World War when the train was the transport for long distance travel for the masses. A motor vehicle victim. Route National Euro route has starved passing trade. Palm tree fronted houses date from the turn of the 20th century. Long windows open to ornate aged verandahs. Climbing tree bursts vibrant purple to cascade the pink wall. Branched bloom twist over door and window. Sun faded blue shutters. The little fishing port. Bright painted rust streaked trawlers sheltered by a sea wall of interlocking concrete shape. Open fishing boats, small yachts moored in stillwater silence. Harbour road hilly bends to Spain. Diving centre advertises lessons. Trips explore an undersea garden near the campsite, a protected marine reserve.

The beachfront is opposite the small town square. Morning coffee served at the café restaurant. People's voices over the noise of the motor car makes a timeless ambience.

On the beach a lady arranges clothes and towel, bathing cap adjustments before placing a toe into calm water. A few more steps to the depth of the knee, the scooping of water first over the arms, the shoulders and then the final scoops run down her back. The swimmers ritual. Unwritten but practiced everywhere wherever people swim. River, lake or sea. She walks in up to her waist, then pushes off with a few strokes. Half a minute for the breath to relax and settle. Natural rhythmic glide enjoyment of a morning swim.

Street corner épicérie bright fruit display entices, the shop crammed with everything needed. 'La Poste' sends cards. An open sailing boat leaves the harbour. A beautiful boat of wood. Mast in forward lean. A spar starts from the bow rising near 45 degree angle high above the stern. Cream canvas hangs, the foot of the sail loose, controlled by a rope from the clew (back corner) of the sail. A lateen rig traditional barque catalanes.

Campsite pine shelter. I am stalked by a staring woodpigeon. Birds do not show fear around people. Sparrows and a blackbird within arm's length, looking for food. The woodpigeon walks a repeated circuit under the pines.

Late afternoon beckons the cliff climb repeat swim. Looking back to vines planted neat, terraced up the sides of great rocky hills end high country. Monts Alberes.

Pot washers view. The rocky coast of Spain, hazy Cap

Creus. Concentration is broken by clattering plates, cutlery and the sound of water from the tap filling the sink.

A Dutchman says hello. Asking. How long I will be staying? Only for another day.

A young French couple camped down the hill walk past. "Bonsoir."

The man says he saw me swimming and that they have both been in today over at a little beach by the hospital. They are out for the evening. Bidding 'Bonsoiree.'

Hospital tuneless karaoke, applause and laughter.

Early hours waking. Violent flashes of lightning, great thunder rumblings. In the darkness pegs part pushed into the ground are makeshift reinforced with rocks in case the wind gets up. Falling asleep to storm sounds high behind the hills.

7 km

Low rising sun, pine tree shapes on the tent. Outside dry and dusty. The storm stayed in the hills, not bothering to rain out the campsite. The woodpigeon walks its rounds, two quarrelsome magpies try to rule the place attempting to chase off a bird I have never seen before. A hoopoe busy poking around in the dirt with its long spear of a beak. Black and white patterned wings, pink and sandy brown back, white undersides and long dull orange and black feathers on top of its head that open into a fanned crest when chased by the magpie. Only to settle again to poke around for food. Making a cry the same as its name. It walks back refusing to leave. Magpies watch, chattering a grumble.

Unhurried chores staying out of the heat cleaning and oiling the bike. Shaded pine book repose waits for burn reprieve.

Lunchtime wash up bumps into the vocal Dutchman.

"Yes I come to this place, before I stay in Argels-sur-mer with no space, too many people. Here is very nice. It is a good place to get rid of my stress. All the time with my work, stress, computers and every day city driving is not good. Stress.

I drive here from Holland. This driving is a different stress and in a few days I must return. It is a very long drive. I think maybe I enjoy this stress."

I ask him. "What work do you do?"

He replies. "I work in the Public Library."

Stress?!!

Always latching onto a problem, uptight. A walking heart attack. He carries on.

"I think I am going to explore the hills on my mountain bike, lots of trails. I have been swimming on the beach near the hospital. Have you been swimming?"

"Yes, down the cliff under the headland, out through the rocks."

He tells me. "No. It is very dangerous."

I was going to say that was part of the appeal, but I do not bother. It would be without comprehension. I reply a dismissive shrug.

He gives directions to the correct swimming beach. The cove under the hospital.

"Have you read the signs?"

"Yes, about the place being a marine nature reserve."

He tells me "There is no taking fruits de la mer." etc. etc. Then midway through, he changes to. "I have a problem with my phone, the battery is empty. There is no electric here."

I tell him the shaver points in the sanitairs are mains and

I charge up my camera batteries using them. Another problem is produced.

"What if someone steals my phone?"

I shrug my shoulders.

He says "I will stay here for two hours and wait."

I leave him standing outside of the door guarding his phone on a campsite of maybe ten people who are mostly out for the day and have probably not come all this way for the chance of stealing a phone.

A while later I wander up to the bins with some rubbish, passing a painter in part concentration carefully glossing a window on the shower block.

"Bonjour."

On the way back. Lone figure stands phone sentry outside the shower block.

Sun relents magnifying glass burn. The cliff path toward the hospital, concrete platform steps lead into the sea. Rough path alongside the hospital fence.

I step aside for a young girl on crutches, two assistants look after her. She has a look of concentration, pain and determined intent. Trying to walk. I wait for them to pass. Polite greeting. The realisation taken for granted of being physically able.

Her goal. Just be able to put one foot in front of the other without sticks. The life goal may never happen. A young man is sat in a wheelchair, his neck, arm and leg in permanent twist, sat with his mother looking out to sea.

Path ends in easy clamber to a beach evident of many fires and good times. Shoaling fry glint in the shallows. Time spent watching the sea without thought. The focal point of a yacht distant off the headland in slow direction toward Argels-sur-mer. White hull and sails hold yellow tint reflected sun.

Bikes on the campsite. An American couple have ridden from Spain. Destination Céret tomorrow. They comment on the sea. I give them direction to the steps and the little swimming beach. The lady comes back from the shower block in petit trauma. "No toilet paper!"

The young French couple are back at their tent. The man comes over and talks about snorkelling over the rocks, proudly producing urchin shells collected. His lady arrives with wine, pouring me out a good measure of Muscadet. They ask of my journey, wanting to see photos. Conversation, the information place exchange. Chateauneuf-sur-Cher is recognised. They live just outside of the town. I had passed within a couple of km of their front door which causes surprised amusement.

Fans of English cinema discussing films and interests over wine under evening yellow. Beautiful people, most welcoming and open, typical of French people met. They go out for an evening meal. I start to pack. Tomorrow I leave this forgotten corner of France.

A Taste of the Pyrenees

Fond farewells to my French friends. A gift of two surplus bottles of beer are well received. The Americans gone. A place difficult to leave. A wave to the Accueil, a ride to Cerbére.

Patisserie window brims cycle energy joy. Fresh baguettes, a pizza glows colour. Maison du Tourisme information for 'La Route des Cols'. It is the first day of work for the young student opening the shop, still to find where everything is. Looking through cupboard shelves for pamphlets. Nothing doing.

We discuss Cerbére, my home, the openness of French people, England. My French bad, understood and with the lady's broken English we manage.

The day heats. Last look at the little town, the small bay. I pedal the hill, garage sound of air drill and compressor hiss. Campsite view, pines to a mirror blue sea hazed blur horizon.

Winding road hot tarmac magnifies heat, drink replaces fluid loss. Legs feel good, pace increase settles into work. Back in travelling mindset, the road the only permanence, the places ephemeral. Thoughts of the next town. Port-Vendres climb, steep brown dusty hill. A car passes giving a toot on the horn with a waving arm. The French couple. I wave back. The lady leant out of the window waving until the car goes out of sight.

Freewheeling into Collioure money pit. Traffic solid, seafront crowd café bar overflow. Climb close to the glass strewn gutter letting crammed traffic pass unhindered. Nearing the top, back wheel hiss. Puncture. I pull the bike across a busy pavement dragging it next to a flowerbed away from busy people traffic. Spare repaired tube replaces the discarded flat, washing my hands with precious drinking water. Breeze downhill cools the body.

Boat masts, palm trees. Argels-sur-mer. Ahead the two Americans, I stop to say hello. They are studying the map and want to get to Céret, a mountainside village famous for modern art. I am headed similar direction. Planning to go out the way I came in picking up D2. The old road across the bottom of the mountains. Bikes are 'interdit' on the arterial road leaving little choice. They decide there is another way flatter and pedal off toward city Perpignan. I gnaw my flipper size pizza thinking about the line of conversation. 'It will be flatter.' However far up Céret is and whichever way you choose to go, you still have to arrive at its altitude. Short may not be sweet. But it is short.

Main road roundabout. Flowers, traffic, people sound, old bustling shops. 'D2' high on a wall for the benefit of traffic in opposite direction. The back of old town, modern low housing. Over dual carriageway leaves town buzz and main road roar for parched countryside grasshopper rasp. Palm tree and conifer share flat land. Road to Soréde.

Undulating road, wild tree foothills ascend mountainous ridge towering. Little towns and villages timid lost in the green of Montagnes Alberes. Village narrow one vehicle squeeze. Romanesque church, ancient house lean. Midday short shadow, bright narrow cobbled ways echo daily life. Open wine countryside. Arterial D618 shatters country romance. Cycle path through a concrete tunnel offers shading cool respite. I lean against the cold tunnel wall cooling the blood for fifteen minutes breathing exhaust fumes from non-stop speed rush. Busy route into the town of Le Boulou. D115 crossroads, narrow lane signed 'Vives.' Sleeping village silence rises through cork oak woodland. Hundreds of trees stripped bands of bark in regrowth. Dates of bark harvest painted on the bare trunk. Trees a hundred years plus service the bottle. Fanned bough shade winding climb to Llauro. Trees and brush, panoramic view across Mediterranean flatland to an endless sandy white ribbon. Views across into blue Pyrenees Orientals. Chateau Queribus. Rather than the portrayed refuge stands as an upright finger of horizon defiance.

'Oms' twisting streets. Old houses around a church, maybe a hundred people inhabit the village. Stickers on pick up trucks say hunting is popular. Sign ceramic, handmade glazed proclaims 'Oms cite des Aspres.' Bar Tabac is closed until 4pm. By the door an old man sat on a bench enjoying the day. "Bonjour."

He asks if I want to go in.

Opening the place up, filling my waterbottle with cold water. I buy an ice chilled coke sitting in a cool shaded stone built room. The swallowed chill runs through the body cooling my insides. The return to piercing hard burn. A farewell wave from the Patron returning to the bench to wait for the next customer.

Farm building climb through Mas Cantuern. Calmeilles loses height, valley view to far away hazed sprawl of Perpignan. A climb to Col Fortou 646m (1950ft). Buildings lost to forest black fir. Background Massif du Canigou. Bumpy road twists the edge of steep wooded hill. The top of a dead end valley, a chapel. The back tyre is rolling off of the wheelrim.

I stop opposite the chapel. Doors closed, no one. Absolute silence of forest hills. Sounds only of my pulse and breath. The back tyre a pneumatic pudding. A pump up resembles circular. I have the feeling it is a long way to Prades. Not wanting to waste time changing tubes, I hope leakage of air is slow.

Sharp woodland climb crests Col Xatard at 752m (2250ft) the air hot cold alternating breeze, road sign direct to nearby Spain. Climb, climb, unrelenting bends. The village of La Bastide fortified village crests a hill. Overseeing church square tower. Narrow windows, semicircular arches. The clock points 5.35pm.

Climbing road into pocket farmland, waving meadow grass shared with wild stumpy woodland. A small campsite is tempting. I want to push for Prades. The few people at the campsite are the only ones seen since Bar Tabac at Oms. I climb nearer the great peak. Snow covers the summit of Pic du Canigou towering at 2784m (8000ft) giving focus to the climb to Col Palomére 1036m (3000ft). Mountain cloud silent swirl veils the summit rolling and curling in windless motion. A grumble of thunder from the mountain in an emotion of evening displeasure. It is cooler, still twenty something degrees, no longer the burn. Later day told by lengthening shadow.

Rumbling mountain cloud. Glimpses through trees to a long rock valley. Maybe the way out of the hills. Road drops across valley top, water tumbles under the road. Back to climbing. Slower and slower plod cresting above an open valley. Sharp drop weaves wooded contours. Fast steep forest blur, sharp bend road squeeze. A bend. Precipitous edge. The only car for hours cuts the bend off head on, oblivious driver is looking sideways at the view. I squeeze past in the grit and stones leaning over the edge of a freefall to angel wings, the vehicle on Dutch plates just misses in a blur. Too fast to slow, look or think.

Chateau ruin watches from high rock under snowcapped dark towering Pic du Canigou rumbling and crackling. Over a flowing tumbling river, far view down a long rocky valley. Through Valmanya in a flash braking hard, dropping on steep rock road excitement. Sinuous ribbon weave halfway height of a wide gorge under cliff towers. The road has stones periodically placed on the outside drop off. The width enough for one vehicle. Temperature warms in lower altitude, drop down ride, high twisting road 'Baillestavy'. Village clings to the smallest plateau halfway along the gorge. The tyre rolls like dough, steering wobble fight around sharp bends with vertical drops. I stop where I can get off the road, pump up the tyre and take off my sweat soaked shirt. Wind from the speed dries the skin, late sun without burn. Helter skelter blind rock bend sweep around cliffs. The view down 30m (100ft), a stone constructed leat of many centuries takes water to somewhere for drinking and irrigation. It's a longer drop again to the rumbling River Lentilla in the gorge bottom. Bend after bend, down and down. Hills part, cliffs recede. Low sloping areas of fields head high growing a soft green crop. The road on a low descending gradient runs straight, looked over by high ridge Pyrenees Catalans. Fast through the village of Vinca. Rolling back tyre fights the steering. Around a bend, two men carry a heavy wardrobe on its side shuffling slow across the middle of the sleepy narrow street. They look surprised at my speeding entrance to the scene, not being able to decide on which way to hastily go to avoid the collision. Too late to brake. Tight to the road edge squeezing behind the large wood antique avoiding a cartoon hole shape through the family heirloom. The tyre hard down on the rim. I coast to a halt out of sight from the furniture removals. A quick attempt pumps enough air hopefully to last until Prades.

Tall crops fill a wide sweeping valley to the main road junction. Sun turns cold grey high ridge warmed orange. Headwind. Direction signed Prades. A railway line next to the road, over the line a long narrow lake into which the River Lentilla adds itself. Toward Prades the tyre goes completely flat. The bike is laid on its side, a new inner tube is found. Tube change throws the discarded in contempt, landing directly across the rail of the train line. I meekly remove it without being seen and put it away. Grubby hands add to the encrusted road dirt and a day's sweat. Dead straight dusty road under orange sun glow, half wild from a day's adventure.

Boring headwind strengthens, gusts slow to near standstill. Road's stepped climb up a long narrowing valley. Roadside village, parked cars and people. Business serves passing traffic. 'Prades 7.' The village of Eus tumbles steep up a rocky hill. I was told to visit its beauty. The daylight ebb and no chance of cycling after stopping I pass it by.

More climbing. Thermal headwind rushes to lower land. Prades arrives into view. Bypass runs downhill. A lake next to a park. Main road junction signs to Andorra. Opposite points to town. A municipal sign for camping, busy sports centre crowded with people. I get directions from a Gendarme. Old town backs of buildings elevated. Fenced campsite, an entrance barrier. The Accueil closed. The campsite guardian shows me a pitch and tells me to pay in the morning, keeping my passport as security.

It is 8.20pm when I put up the tent and walk to the showers to wash the tiring mountain miles off my body. I cook my evening meal making a pasta mountain to devour and drink plenty. I had been using sodium electrolyte dissolved to replenish sweated lost salts and to stop the muscles from seizing. It has worked well. My body hungry for more after today's 5 litre consumption.

Two cyclists roll in at gone 9pm. I saw them in Cerbére early morning. Looking sun starved and English.

I go to bed still on the road, the body will not quieten. People playing football and having barbeques enjoying a late evening. The nearby church bell keeps chiming every quarter of an hour and fully on the hour. It is comfortable in the sleeping bag, laid out feeling as heavy as lead reflecting on the hard ride. But you would not expect mountain roads to be anything else.
137 km

I wake at 3.30am. Stomach craves food and water. Sleep partial, the body refuses to quieten feeling if it is still riding. A packet of biscuits are consumed between gulps from a full drink bottle of water laced with sodium electrolyte. The nearby church bell strikes once on the quarter of the hour, ears and mind have tuned in to the ritual chiming. The strike adds one on each full hour reached reminding me of the sleep I should be getting. I tell myself not to be so daft as to do so many km in the heat. Four strikes of melancholy droning bell, then five after the lonely quarters. The ground stony, a motorhome pitch. The grassed tent area is on the other side of the campsite, direction from which a pig can be heard happily snoring. The eyes aching tired, the body is not. The tent lightens with the colours of dawn. I fall into sleep.

Outside conversation is the first sense upon waking, eyeballs feel sandpapered and I do not want to open them but it is time to emerge into the brightness, feed the hunger and travel. I talk to an Englishman and his wife who are on holiday. A steel framed roadbike fitted with an enormous rear sprocket for mountain gradients hangs from a carrier on the back of their trusty rear engine Volkswagen camper. Cycling, climbing and walking the mountains at sixty nine can only be interrupted by canoeing. They are a pleasure to speak to.

I go to the Accueil and pay the friendly French lady municipal rates for my night's accommodation retrieving my passport. The place very relaxed, people camped under and around shading trees talking, eating breakfast. Its own little village of relaxation. People say hello, it is very friendly. I am just getting a feel for the place, but it is time to go. I pack up and see two pale sun deprived cyclists taking down their tents, they stand out as English. I say hello. They tell me they are crossing the Pyrenees to time after arriving on the train yesterday and need to get back home. Already hurrying to leave the country upon arriving.

I am asked. "When do you go back home?"
I reply. "I have not really thought about it."
"The hills are brutal, we are drained!"
My reply. "You are not the only ones!"
They show me a cycling guide. Telling me. "This book is

too rosy and misses out so much."

I wish them good luck.

"Bon courage!" from the holidaying residents.

Upward through twisting backstreets. Workshops, the open doors of houses, radio and T.V. chatter floats from darkened interior. Two teenagers on mopeds are stopped in the middle of the lane having a conversation. Narrow corner opens into a busy square. Prades pretty town. Centuries old crossroads for Andorra and high altitude frontier towns. Gateway to Spain. Imposed upon by snow-capped black rock Pic de Canigou.

Mountain roads skirt around but not over the untouchable rock entirety of Massif de Canigou. If you want to get there, you have to walk or climb.

Minimart queue busy in the morning hushed gossip exchange. Welcoming smells of hot fresh baking bread draw to join the purchasing jumble in the boulangerie. Outside waiting chairs and tables fill with morning coffee and conversation. Delivery vehicles roll by in routine. Everyday morning in Prades.

Over the river looking for 'La Route des Cols.' Direction for 'Molitg les Bains.' School building noise busy, road narrows. Houses with fine views of Massif de Canigou. The red ribbon rooftop of Prades town dwarfed by the giant celebrated in festival every year.

Steepness under bright sun. Green rocky countryside falls fast over waist high stone wall. Prades a memory. Molitg les Bains neat little spa resort. Every building connected to healing waters and beneficial rest. Spa village view, rooftops shimmering bright in morning sun shrink further in green tumbling landscape with every turn of the crank. The continuous climb, patient plod through bends. Village above 'Mossat.' Sun bleached and weatherbeaten orange roofs shelter old stone and rendered facades perched above a defensive wall of stone. Buildings tumble skyward in collective triangle. Storeys added to command the tallest view in rival to the church's square tower and a nave of bare stone mass. High windows watch my patient progress. Climbing the quiet main street between bright jumbled buildings returns back to the green.

Boulders hang on a steep hillside's weatherworn rugged land, earth ridged. Mini mountain rocky protrusion. Hill summit bald rounded, grass and stunted bush. Hillside woodland loses its green grip to altitude. Hills behind rise black forested obscured in part by boulder strewn neighbours. A farm half lost in the hill watches my low geared pace. Watchful gaze continued by a solitary house. The road lost between slopes ascending into silent cloudscape lowering with every turn of the pedal. Hairpin bend on hairpin. Lone house, sounds of talking and laughter.

The view travelled is of a long opening valley, lower slopes green with wild woodland under blue sun haze. I cannot see the bends to ascend, maybe I am nearing the top. A vehicle somewhere below makes the climb, turning to the house. Engine running, the opening and closing of a door. On the move, getting louder. The yellow of a La Poste van passes in low engine tone. I watch its shape zig zag several times above my head, smaller on each appearance, engine muffled.

Surrounding silence. Top of the hairpins, into old wood forest. Large trunks. Overhanging boughs offer islands of cooling shade. Sun has heated the day. Without breeze tarmac throws heat without reprieve from the sun beating. Sounds travel far reaching. Background serenade of singing birds and nearby scurries of small creatures spooked by my slow plod presence.

Water tumbles shy. Streams of a moments showing hurry under the road running away into covered forest lead to a cascade tumbling to a granite pool. Rock tint deep gold brown, white bubbles rise from clear black foaming in hurry away under the road. The little cascade surrounded by green moisture dependant plants who nod their frail green stems in appreciation of rising vapours. I join in their agreement with fresh bread and salad. Further up the road the boot of a car open. Chequered cloth is spread over a picnic table. Dejeuner with a centrally sat bottle of wine and two waiting glasses.

The tumbling stream hypnotic, cooling vapours serene in the heat. Cupped hands of ice clear water wash dried salt from the face, sending a waking message to the body. Rest spell broken resumes the climb. The lunching couple raise a hand.

"Bon appetite." Accepted with a nod.

There is only one gear needed to climb mountain roads, the lowest. I keep looking for another but twenty eight teeth are what I have on the rear sprocket, it would be nice to have a few more. Riding a bend is so slow, pushing everything through the pedals. It is quicker to walk the bend. Road straightens. Gradient constant steep. From behind the approach of voices trying to get a few words between grabbing breaths. The two English riders from Prades slowly catch me. They level, standing on the pedals to pass grinning and complaining about the "Killer hill!" Carrying on in duel slowly going out of sight. Exclamations of anguish echo the woodland. Road steepens. I slow to a stop, get off and push the bike over the steep roll, climb back on to continue the ascending plod. The forest is getting lighter, brightening between trunks. Very slowly the release to Col de Jau 1531m (4600ft) finds three smiling slumped bodies. The two English riders are accompanied by a French roadrider on a carbon fibre feather. The English riders busy push energy gels down their throats before making a loaf sandwich filled with ham and salad. Watched in amusement by the Frenchman who is out for his dayride.

The col view to forest and green scant stony hills in shade consumed by dull grey blanket swirl. The body cools from the soaked clothing drip. Waterproof jackets are on for a wind chilled descent. The Frenchman goes first. Speed of local knowledge, the two English riders trying to match pace on loaded bikes. I follow the dropping road. Misted monochrome forest, winter battered and potholed. Bends strewn with stones and gravel mix with water flowing across tarmac looking for streams chattering steepened forest. I slow before each bend. Ahead echoes the worried tones of inaudible exclamation. The isolation of mountain roads are not a place to wrap your bike around a tree. The vehicle carries all necessary worldly possessions. The three are gone from hearing range. Road bottoms out starting the payback climb. Another long woodland plod arrives into daylight at Roquefort de Sault to a gurgling drinking fountain endlessly filling a trough. The village silent, a sign advertises camping. I ride on. Field homes to staring cattle, growing winter feed waves tall. A climb through Bouscouet roadside farm habitation. Under dull blanket sky into half light woodland. Hairpin climb slow patient plod.

From behind, familiar sounds, the two English riders catch me up and ask.

"Don't you ever stop?"

"I thought you had gone on."

"We needed to stop for a drink and a rest."

They ride on settling to a similar pace gaining no further distance. The speed of the mountain climb of which there are two. One is for the racing bike, the other for the loaded bike. Ahead appears a familiar brown sign. The end of the climb. The two English riders stop, I follow a minute behind. Col de Garavel 1265m (3800ft). Other cyclists have stopped, travelling the long way to Prades.

Camping should be available at Escoloubre and Escoloubre les Bains not too far away. Short climb. Col de Moulis. An American cyclist has a bike frame made from bamboo. It is spectacular in its natural brown colour, glazed over with space age carbon cloth glossed in epoxy resin. A couple of other riders join him, all travel in an organised group taking a hundred hours of riding to cross the Pyrenees on a set route. All their luggage and food are carried in a van passing with a toot and a wave.

I stop and look over the edge to a valley floor far below, mountain river fast constant hum fills forested valley sides. The roof of a building lost against the forest, an old hydro-electricity weir. The road cut steep into hillside. Surroundings grow quickly around, losing height into a dull green world valley junction for Escoloubre les Bains. Everything green, growing moss and mould. The roar of the river all consuming in sound. Nothing stirs. Commerce sign. Nothing for camping. Downstream direction for 'La Route des Cols' travels the Pyrenees. A few houses tucked against a cliff, walls greened with grown algae. The place nowhere.

Further along the road, direction sign for camping. Roquefort de Sault. Back up the steep mountainous hill, back over the col and down through the hairpins is not going to happen. Options. Options?

D68. Over a bridge steep climbs over a ruin black chateau. I stop looking at the map. No chance of reaching the next campsite in the guide over two mountain roads having cols of 1600m and 2015m high with the possibility of a further one at 1565m. Without energy, without daylight. Too late for an attempt today. Maybe find a place to camp in the woods away from the sight of the road. I could get water from the river for a wash and I still have water left for cooking and drinking. Forest vertical, nowhere flat enough to pitch a tent. Nothing. An overgrown terrace full of brambles is impossible to get the bike through. Daylight is ticking away. The river goes somewhere. I have enough energy for hills, but not for mountains. I cannot be bothered to study the map.

Over the bridge up through the gears follows a thundering river through a rocky gorge widening spectacular. Grim desperation becomes broad grin elation. Speed ride under rocky towering cliffs. River boils white crashing into boulders tumbling over smooth slab. Trapped echoes captive between rock tower overhangs. Many bends, flat out speed racing through the Gorges St. George.

From a blind bend appears a tall white coach on German plates. Driver misjudges the sharpness of the bend. Too quick, arms frenetic pull at the steering to get the wheels to turn. Lurched over on my side of the carriageway it's going to be tight for both of us. There may be enough gap to avoid a head on slam. A moment not to touch brakes or falter, waist high wall tight, leg inches away, the other side a long drop onto hard rocks, tree trunks and a roaring river. A white flash, the wing, the low glass headlight, heavy spinning black wheel hard into the wheel arch, the blurred white side of the coach, the wall, the gap, a second, the moment. Woo Hoo!!! I do not slow or care.

Temperature warms. Softening feeling of lower land. Hydro-electricity attempts to tame the river with a weir. Sky brightens, the parting of cliffs. The continued drop with the river. Under a railway bridge, through a town. Old men sit with a drink watching the warm evening. Camping signed straight on. Brakes hard pulled for a roundabout. Campsite signed opposite. Wheeling the bike down a gorge campsite entrance. Axat. The same site stayed a week ago on my way to the Cathar Chateaus.

The bike is leant against a wall. I open the Accueil door, booking for a night, exchanging a few simple pleasantries with the lady behind the desk. I buy a few things from the shelves and pitch next to the fast flowing river. A hot shower washes the road off of my back. Refreshed. Cooking under shaded cliffs, pink stained by the setting Mediterranean sun.

Sat by the river with a beer reflecting on the day. The mountains. What shall I do? I could cycle back up the gorge to continue. Or?

Sleep on it. This is all meant to be enjoyable and it will be.
84 km

Haze hangs the river. Grass damp, cool to the feet. Sitting at the river's edge waiting for the Accueil to open. Warm crusty bread at 8am. Sun breaks across the crags working colour into the rock lighting up the river in freshness of new morning. I take my baguette, jam and mug of tea to a picnic bench enjoying a riverside breakfast whilst looking at the map route through the Pyrenees.

I have ridden the Pyrenees Orientals. I will return next year. The mountain route needs more planning to run smooth. The experiences of the last two days have given earned knowledge and an appetite for more. I pack, push the loaded bike past the Accueil giving the reception a wave. I stop, look back to the mountain river. The mind makes a pact to return.

For the first time a feeling of familiarity, re tracing the path of my wheels through the Défilé de Pierre-Lys. Canoers unload plastic yellow craft from roof racks and trailers ready for a Saturday of whitewater adventure. Further through the twisting rock gorge a club run for cyclists wear the same colours. All ages, all sizes. Waves and 'Bonjours.' Fifty riders go opposite direction riding space age carbon, others ride dependable steel of many years.

Almost out of cash. Stopping at Quillan bustling on a Saturday. I can get money out, but cannot check the balance. Head for Carcassonne and try the banks there.

Bright sunshine day, stopping at the bottom of a gated driveway at the edge of the road for a drink of cola. The lady owner is on her way out in her car.

"Bonjour"

She replies. "Not to drink the stuff! It is bad, terrible. I would do better to stop at the organic store and buy something better."

I am looking at the ingredients listed on the side of the bottle.

"Pour it away." A smile with the instruction as she drives

off. I consider myself told… I keep it.

Junction for Alet-les-Bains. Multi arched bridge of age spans the wide shallow River Aude. Narrow streets of stone. Overhanging beams of ancient half timbered houses quaint architecture. Lane maze streets lead to the town square. Protective walled gated entrance at the back of the town. Portcullis gone gives free passage to and from an ancient way into the heat blued Corbiéres. Floral displays about town add colour enchantment. Festoon lights cross the square to add fairytale nighttime ambience.

Tour de France adverts. Limoux town. Boulangerie closed! Apple tartlets denied!

River Aude silver in high sun. Dual carriageway city traffic rush. Carcassonne. Under Route National. Recognition of where I am. One junction. Camping Municipal entrance, the door into the Accueil. Booking for one night.

I walk into town passing under 'La Cité' round turrets and long castleated walls. Ornate bridge to tall city streets. Cash machine gives money, but no balance. Another cash machine. No balance. The moral. Pen and paper arithmetic list is more reliable than the computer screen. Trying to reckon the amount left in the account. I decide to head to La Gare to see what my options are. The lady at the enquiries desk draws blank after blank, but there is a favourable option of getting me to Bordeaux for tomorrow afternoon with the bike. Travel the West Coast. Sounds a good plan. Coté d'Argent famous beaches for surfing. The wine country of Bordeaux. The Atlantic Ocean. Bretagne for the ferry. Leaving La Gare, tickets in hand.

The afternoon under the trees forms a west coast plan. New lands, new roads and a train journey. A small barking dog says hello. Escaped from the bag woman sat outside of her tent reading.

People arrive and leave their pitches. The bag woman wanders over with the dog to the vacated pitch, checking picnic tables on return. A new found half cigarette is lit and some left over fruit retrieved. Then back to the book and the chair.

Two English riders in their sixties are camped nearby. A sightseeing rest day on their way to Montpellier taking the 'Bike Bus' back home. Survivors of a group travelling the canal from Bordeaux, the others returned home part way through the trip. Work and marriage parole expired.

Both are seasoned travellers of France by bicycle. Rides through the Pyrenees, La Loire and the Lozére brutal hills and brutal weather. They have encountered several days of torrential rain. Holed up in a cheap bad hotel the wrong end of Bordeaux, waiting for the weather to pass.

A strange folding bike, little wheels and drop handlebars stands next to a tiny tent. The rider retired and allowed four weeks a year to cycle in France before the matrimonial leash is recoiled.

He tells me how the little wheels and the gearing mean he can spin his legs and creep up any mountain at a crawling pace.

I tell him the Pyrenees had me crawling without the spinning.

His journey along Canal du Midi from Bordeaux ends at Narbonne. Speeding home on the TGV. Folded bikes allowed. Ordinary bikes. TGV. Interdit.

"I will be experiencing SNCF tomorrow."

"They hang the bikes high on hooks in a carriage compartment." I am told.

Sounds like a horror film.

I give away an old map finished with. Receiving information on Bordeaux. Cryptic directions to a campsite 'Du Lac.' Involves tram lines, a submarine base, docks and cycle paths.

If do not like the thought of the meat hook train. I will not bother.

The bag lady and happy canine companion walk past with half a bottle of red wine liberated from the bin.

84 km

Train Experiences, Gironde

Rough sleep. Floodlights, all night city traffic, a firework display, road racing, skids and squeals topped off with an outdoor pop concert. It all seemed to add up! Packing slow has all morning. The Montpellier riders are ready to leave. One rides a new touring bike. The other rides a made up bike of purpose, steel frame of quality hand painted detracts from its worth. Wheels, crank and saddle of top quality. Large rear sprocket gives a granny crawler for the steepest hills. The bike is so loaded. Tent and bags tied on with bungee cords topped off with the comfort of a folding chair look like a weekend trip to the tip.

The folding bike rides off. Little wheels look set to collapse under the load carried.

I tell him of easy main road to the coast under the Cathar chateaus, but he is sticking to the canal. With a wave he is gone.

The bag woman has been looking, when I leave she will be over. I make sure there is something. I have a bag of small cent coins, totalling maybe a couple of euros. I place the coins in a spiral around the tree for gleaning.

High sun reflects silver off of turret roofed La Cité. Over the bridge to the last view of the River Aude. Closed Sunday shops empty town silence. La Gare wait of an hour. My ticket is gnawed by a small yellow machine. I look for a lift down to the underpass for the opposite platform. There is no lift. The bike bump slowly down each step, along a tunnel faces a heavy bump and drag one step at a time up to the platform.

The emptiness of a train station. Slow wait, the silent people gather. A sudden mass of silver noise. A great engine roars into the station. Carriage blur along the platform ends in air brake squeal. Doors open in crowd exchange. I use the opportunity to ask where the carriage for carrying bikes will be. The platform guard looks at my ticket, takes it to his train staff colleagues. A moment of tipping back hats, scratching heads, drawing in breath.

"Come with me, you are on this train to Bordeaux."

Carriage door up a vertical set of steps. Bike squeeze through the narrow doorway hampered by the automated compartment door repeatedly closing against the bike trying to pull the thing into the carriage. The guard ties the bike. Train underway rocks side to side crossing points making speed.

He tells me the ticket office had not put me on a train with accommodation for cycles, only from Toulouse onward. The ticket was useless. The train scheduled was in an hour's time. The mistake has gained two hours journey time on a straight through service to Bordeaux helped kindly by the train guard and his colleague, bending the rules for me. In France, unhurried politeness goes a long way.

The 'Inter Cite.' Through the window countryside flashes by. Land change. No distant blue spikey mountains. Big sky follows the Canal du Midi. Towpath of walkers and cyclists. The occasional chugging hire boat on a soupy green voyage. A future route to travel. The train flies into Toulouse station waiting with a patient tick.

City falls to flattening fields, sky change. The intense Mediterranean blue paled in milky haze softness floating small hanging cotton wool clouds. Two bikes in the train carriage get ready to leave at Bordeaux. Through the window the platform slows to a halt. Guards vanish. The task of getting the loaded bike down the ladder. I tell the two cyclists to go first. They are from South Wales completing a ride to Carcassonne from Bordeaux along the scenic canal and on the return home.

Their bikes go first down the ladder. I hand their bags receiving help with my bike. People crowd in all direction. Tiled tunnel light and adverts. The bump bump, slowly up steps. Station ticket hall echoing hum. A thousand clattering shoes drowned by loudspeaker announcement. Door deliverance to South West France sunshine. Billboard map. The name of an opposite street. Decision by compass. Five minutes city riding. River Garonne waterside breeze. Famous palatial buildings. Children's joyful shriek under fountain spray. Deep river serves docks. Tall bow between the cranes, areas worn industrial. Sous marine base decaying concrete monument to slave labour. Tram lined road. Signs for Du Lac order to a cycle lane separating the road. Direction signs vanish.

Away from where I want to go, split by the Route National. Cycle path to a North African travellers camp. Sprawled dirty caravans, rusting panel vans. Parked polished expensive modern shining cars. Mercedes badge gleams next to stinking rubbish piled. Smell of sun baking human crap along the bushes. Children play amongst half burned rubbish smoulder. The whole area stinks, a pop up squatter village. Two or three hundred people live here. I have to get off of the cycle path into the rubbish dodging cars driving along the bike path to the squat camp. Long concrete bike tunnel to homeless tent habitation. Graffiti wall bridge traffic crosses breezy dark blue River Garonne. Tunnel double back to a junction of cycle ways. Lakeside stop to eat and drink. Sailing dinghies on a grassy bank. 'Camping International Du Lac.' Rammed full of campervans and caravans. Wandering crowds look as gated inmates daring not to venture past the perimeter. High season, busy people mass without space. I will try further up the coast.

Four roundabout diversion to a sports stadium velodrome dead end, looking for direction 'Blanquefort.' Signed only from opposite side.

Blanquefort is well named. Faceless industrial haulage depot in Sunday silence. Boring compulsory cycle lane headwind. Roundabout to roundabouts. 'D2' straight line ride. Outlying city grip release through old villages quiet and sleepy. A Sunday afternoon mirage. Boulangerie open! Walking out with an armful. Landscape softens. The historic vineyards of Bordeaux.

Vines rich in summer season. Rows arrow straight, pruned perfection holds a single neat red rosebush in bloom at the start of each vine row. First line defence detection of pest and mildew attack. The rose bed verge for miles. Between areas of vines, chateaus of status less pompous than La Loire. Impressive in white cut stone. Walls of privacy run far. Villages serving vineyards. Civic pride care for neatness. Whole area smells of money. Centuries of wine, the deep reds. Famous Claret.

The Gironde. A wide tidal mass of water separated by large islands growing woodland. An estuary so wide the far bank appears as land horizon. Leoville surrounded by vineyards overseen by a fine church spire's delicate sculpted stone patterned as lace.

Pauillac sign. Camping municipal points through town. Lush pitches and access to riverbank lined pole jetty cabins with winch down flat square fishing nets. 'Les Pecheries.' A few photos on a short walk, the evening meal peaceful. Sun sets on a cooler evening. The wind vanished.

The Gironde estuary Medoc inland shore of pine forested Landes. Opposite shoreline. 'The Coté d'Argent,' the Atlantic Ocean. Compass journey points North.

68 km

Maritime Charente

Croak croak. A frog is next to my head the other side of the tent. It croaks, stops. Croaks all night. Watch says 3am. Shining a torch out of the tent does nothing, neither does banging the ground. I am too tired to get out and throw the thing away, even if I could catch it. Falling back to sleep waking at half six with a fuzzy head. Thick Atlantic fog rolls the river.

Pushing my bike out of the gate before anyone has risen.

An old man asks me what direction I am going.

"North" I reply.

"The ferry is at Blaye" (back south)

"I go north to Royan".

"The ferry is at Blaye."

I get on the bike. I repeat, then he repeats. I say goodbye and he tries to hold my arm with a pinch. Personal space invaded. Let go.

I leave the weirdo of the marshes standing in the road. The French version of. 'Care in the community.' A fading silhouette to the mist.

Early morning town illumination. A supermarket amongst the normal. The road leaves another town behind. Pharmacy green numbers 26.5 degrees. Fog is burned to mist by the great hidden ball. Pleasant cycle in grey Atlantic drear.

Vineyards, rosebushes. The famous Rothschild vineyards pristine. Fine residence.

Monday morning traffic commute. Lesparre Medoc. D1215. Mist lift to a clouded day. Compass points north. Flat straight road to the vanishing point. Travelling fast feels stationary. Forest surround without a point of focus. Tucked down on the bars. Legs push rhythm. Edge white line ride. Signs for Talais. Soulac-sur-mer. Zone Portuaire. Le Verdon-sur-mer colourful beach holiday shops. Bike hire garage rents wide bar cruisers. Ferry terminal entrance, paying a few euros to wait for the boat.

The black hull of the ferry releases its cargo of vehicles in noisy procession. A minute's wait before a wave onto the deck. The ferry fills to capacity. Engine roar slips from the dock leaving Landes crossing the wide Gironde estuary for Royan. I get my first and last view of the white sandy beach running near continuous all the way to the Spanish border. The ferry rumbles the wide rivermouth. Many currents swirl and boil. Swell slow rolls the hull. The hazed town of Royan.

Harbour smells. Green seaweed and mussels hang the piles in wait for the tide rise. Dark water lap, sounds of seagulls. It has been half an hour between boarding and riding off the ferry. Half an hour at a good speed to cross the wide mouth of the Gironde Estuary.

'Autre directions.' Out of town following the coast road. Bucket and spade seaside shops. Suburb area of desirable detached residence. Fresh cut lawns over neat hedges, municipal grass verge and trees between path and road. Access lanes to the sea. An area where people who have done well or have done people well all their lives choose to live.

Lane ends in slipway to an empty beach. Late lunch view across the rivermouth, wide sea horizon. Familiarities of the Atlantic return. I accept leaving the Mediterranean with reluctant resignation. Places no longer have the letter X in their name or sing of sunshine.

Beach solitude ends. The rattling arrival of a small boy of three on a little bike with wide round tyres and stabilisers under watch of his father who nods in greeting. The little boy rides round and round on the hard sand before coming to a halt, getting off and walking back up the beach. His father tells him to fetch his bike. Protests with headshaking. The request is repeated and this time he throws himself onto his little knees before going face down into the sand in pure theatre. It's a moment of comedy practiced by everyone in their first years. They walk hand in hand to the little bicycle, the father picks it up and they make their way from the beach. The child now happy. Incident forgotten.

Mobile home campsite land. Manacled to slow compulsory cycle lanes. Elevated coast road, golden sand beaches of La Grande Coté. Woodland sandy landscape to La Palmyre. Car parks burst cars and coaches. People swarm in hurry to a zoo entrance. 'The Pirate Island' plastic themed 'Happycamperlands' catering for families sardine packed into a tin chalet complete with key to open for two weeks. D11E offers a way out. Cycle lanes busy with sauntering bodies and dogs on long retractable leads. A group of people appear around a hedged corner looking in the opposite direction to where they are going. The safety of the road exchanges crowds for countryside until Arvert. Cycle lanes filled with wobbling slow motion. Signs to La Tremblade.

D25 flat land. Estuary. Wide, muddy, full of shell fisheries. Marshland drain featureless land stretches to low cloud grey horizon. It all stinks at basse mer.

Large black spire dominates town rooftops of Marennes. Signs for the Ile d'Oleron. Marennes bypass busy traffic light junction battles road space. Narrow D3 delivers quiet countryside, winding fields reclaimed from the tide. Grazing herds of black and white cows captive on watery islands. Sluices and drains criss cross a maze of mud waiting for the tide. Rough edged old canals. Round timber bulk driven vertical deep into the mud, five or six together in a row keeping hulls from mud banks centered to the channel. Timber shack land bright painted colour, small boats pulled up. The pungent smell of processing shellfish. Work worn coloured plastic boxes await to be filled.

Road rises to the small village of Hiers Brouage. Wild tree rough land to large thick stone wall defences of La Brouage 17th century waterside fort. The port silted two centuries gone. Marooned in grassland defending brambles. Everything inside the fortified village is stone. Crowds wander the cobbles in souvenir saunter.

Wild marsh silence, scrub bush, long grass, twisted trees. A climb to village streets. Soubise approach to the secret naval town of Rochefort. Upstream and out of sight on the River Charente quietly building and servicing the ships of the French navy from the seventeenth century. I head for La Renaissance in search of a mechanical wonderment to Rochefort. The Pont Transborder.

The Carcassonne cyclist with the crazy folding bike told me how I should experience a ride on the mechanical marvel. A small sign points direction down a little country lane adjacent to the noise of Route National concrete bridge full of high racing traffic. The river's edge. Birds sing from the tree lined slow flowing marshland river. A large ironwork gantry spans high over the river held by framed iron columns. Cables hang supporting a suspended wood deck about 10m2 (30ft2) moving silent ferrying people across the river. The platform arrives, gates are opened. A shelter of painted wood each side. The varnished wood and glass cabin wheelhouse controls operation. Gates are closed, the polished brass bell is rung and the platform glides silently to the opposite riverbank. Rails and wheels high above traverse the gantry high enough for a sailing ship to pass freely under. It is as if the platform floats on air. Everybody smiles at the pleasurable experience. The only disappointment, the ride comes to an end too soon. A café with parasol shade looks over the National Monument.

Into busy town streets. "Bien! Bien!" Shouted encouragement as I cycle past. Camping Municipal sign. Friendly town site.

People passing wish "Bonsoir."

Retired men look at the bike passing comment between themselves as I eat and laze away the evening on the comfort of the sleeping bag.

130 km

Vendée

I wake not wanting to move. Random drips run down the outside sheet. An arm reaches from sleeping bag comfort to unzip the tent door. Outside the day misted grey cool. Water boils steaming chatter for tea. Bribery from prone contentment. Four choc au pains compliment a waking body. The pack. The Accueil stop. Bustling office friendly and full of humour take payment and produce a gift. A note pad printed with the campsite name 'Camping Le Reyon, Rochefort.'

10am. One way system town. 'Toute directions' magical mystery tour needs the compass to guide every junction, without it I would be blind. I find D911 congratulating myself on my navigation. D911 vanishes. Back to the compass.

Ship hull rust between warehouses and wharfs. Booms of cranes look over stacks of timber say the port is still important and in use. Yacht marinas, captive gated locks guarded by modern glass balcony apartments. Citadel forts of stone designed 17thC by Colbert. Lock gates and a swing bridge. A hideaway military town out of reach of the British navy. History mixes with modern industry 20km inland surrounded by the marshlands of Charente Maritime.

D911 again, splits in a V without telling. Compass decides,

numbers change D137. Thundering haulage in flatland speed past on one side. Busy Route National on the other. Diminishing road angles collide in junction. Climbing on concrete over four speeding traffic lanes delivers sunshine. Straight road points north. D5 flat land ride flanked by trees. Drained green agriculture, stillwater canals, floating green lily pad cover. Towpaths through tall grass. Water reflection, big sky over low green countryside. Straight grey road green miles end in roundabout.

Signs for La Rochelle, flat road straight. Air permeated with fibreglass resin from open factory doors, large racing catamaran hulls stacked. Countryside. Single storey ribbon development, houses mix with small industry. Traffic busies approaching La Rochelle. Sun heats the day turning up the temperature dial.

Shop stop finds shelves half empty, the buzzing flickering near dead chiller unit barren. A sad place, low quality high price. An inconvenience store. A few things to keep me going, fruit woeful. Half mouldy reflected ambience. How I miss the fresh fruit of the Mediterranean. A sneery man, the small minding shopkeepers' six day week penny grabbing world. A relief to get outside into sunshine.

I head for the coast. Town approach busying road. Car showrooms tin and glass. Slogans sell desirable living on uneasy credit for a life term. Under bare sun, Route National metallic flash thunders constant overhead, a fast merry-go-roundabout spins under… No. I turn around back up the hill taking a quietening country road of singing birds hopefully the back way around the busy town.

Through nowhere. Between fields of parched yellow. Rubble tips, haulage depots, a concrete plant, disused canals, a tall concrete silo. Wild woodland. Under the heat pulse into a village of silence. Every soul removed, every vehicle parked and emptied of life. Not even a neighbourhood dog bark. I should end up crossing the Route National and carry on to the coast. I go over the Route National to face a sign 'Route Barre.' Usually a bike squeeze through using the path. Not today. The whole of the road dug up from wall to wall to stop such convenience. The diversion is the Route National which is no good for me. Maybe I should have persevered with La Rochelle and its greenway. I am here now. It is what it is.

Tarmac lane runs empty alongside Route National to a main D road. Compass points north away from the coast. The only map option for now. Signs for Nantes, St. Nazaire and Paris. The first time I have seen these names for weeks, reminding me of northern progress. I ride the white line, trucks and cars speed past in battering gusts of engine heat. Straight line for a long time, the arterial D137 eases down over low hills. Roundabout. Little D20 shuts out main road noise replacing with breeze rustling long grass. Blackbird sings summer song from deep green countryside hush. Quiet wander towards the coast over railway lines and Canal Rochelle. D9 in sight of flat sea horizon. I stop for my lunch next to a still and fermenting black pool, not a movement. Decaying black branches, a fading crisp packet floating slow spin amongst dead leaves.

Land drains and marsh. Crossroads. Swing bridge over the canal. Straight road, lorry approaches distant at speed. Car overtakes, filling the road, travelling fast, head on, not slowing or caring. I get onto the grass verge, an upright finger is for the driver's sheepish sideways glance. Knowing what he is doing. Neck and neck car flash past races the lorry rumble, diminishing haulage rattle distant. Empty road exhaust fumes. Breeze soft rush sways tall grass. Single bird sings over the silence.

Flatland crop low wide expanse. Puyravault. A sign. The Vendee. Through Champagné-les-Marais. The village of Triaize. Single storey houses stone and render. Colourful window shutters. Maritime ornaments mix floral window display. Towards the coast, pancake flat. All around vast blue sky devoid of cloud, an ocean of wind waves across open swaying fields. Headwind through St. Michel-en-l'Herm. L'Aigullon-sur-mer. Straight black tarmac. Approaching vehicles shimmering slide across heat pool of sky reflecting mercury.

Chalet campsites. Lined single colour repetition. Two week city people get their reprieve from daily routine. Self catering behind chain-link 'Happycamping' convenience.

Le Tranche-sur-mer. Main street pretty town white sunny walls, bright blue and red window shutters under red tiled roofs. Woodland ride inland climb. A hill! Farmland, woodland, happycamperland. Les Vacances overload. Woodland one side, a few houses on the other. Longeville-sur-mer following the coast. A hill to quiet St. Vincent-sur-Jard seeming to snore it is so peaceful. Municipal camping sign. The peacefulness and heat fatigue cave me to submission.

A street of low houses finds a large empty pine woodland campsite with a small Accueil. The young student Patron computes administration.

"Go anywhere. Just come back with the pitch number."

There must be three to five hundred pitches residing two tents and a caravan.

I tell the lady pitch number 30.

"You cannot have that. It is the only reservation on the

whole site!"

I move my choice a distance away. The site clean. The lady soap scrubs everything with intent, or hoses it down. The student is the receptionist, cleaner, overnight security guard and dynamo person fuelled by a blue haze of cigarette smoke.

I am stopping for two days not having a full day off since leaving Cerbére on the Spanish border. Legs having pedalled over 300km since. It is 30 degrees. I hope for the same tomorrow. I use the rest of the afternoon to enjoy a cleansing from the road.

Washing hangs on a line between the bike and a great pine tree covered in large ants, busy in up and down transit. Food. Journal. Sleep.

130 km

Morning haze. Sweet smelling pine. The village square finds one shop open, the épicerié. The campsite Patron waits for Presse/Bar Tabac to open for the day's cigarettes. Back to the tent, a packet of cold meat is slipped under the groundsheet folding the sleeping bag on top as insulation from the burn.

To the beach.

Smart houses to shading pine woods. Trunks twisted, dry flaking grey bark tinges the air resinous sweet. A path under trees ends on a pebble bank. Pale cream sand bright under sun glare. Waves break small over a shallow flat reef to form a little point break wave peeling neat lines. Further view. The breakwater of Jard-sur-Mer. Inside holds many masts pointing skyward into the blue.

Sand near burns the feet walking the empty beach. World War Two bunkers in hiding, gun slits face the sea. Continuous whitened sand to Pointe du Grouin du Cou several miles away. Out in front a low sand strip with a lighthouse ends Ile de Ré.

Small waves along the point. Seaward rip current marked by buoys watched over by a closed up lifeguard hut on top of a seawall. Five or six people along the long beach enjoy the peace, venturing for a swim, cooling the blood from the heat. Sailing boats pulled high on sun bleached sand. Sails striped blue and orange flap in the breeze.

Legs immerse in Atlantic cool, wading the shallows, launching into temperature half of the Mediterranean. A set of waves break over a shallow rock and pebble reef. Half an hour bodysurfing small crumbly wave enjoyment.

Sails venture to the water. Small catamarans speed parallel to the beach in offshore blowing wind. Day heat intensifies with the climbed sun. White sand burns the feet. The silica content in the sand makes a whistling sound scuffing the dry running grains. A slow amble, thoughts of shade. Amongst beachside pines a large famous residence of Georges Clemenceau. Statesman. Thinker. Friend and advocate of the painter Claude Monet.

Afternoon under a pine follows its cast patch of shade. A caravan arrives to occupy reserved No.30. Their car cannot reverse the uneven ground. I help the retired couple push their caravan into place.

The Vendee has proven its reputation as being second in heat to the Mediterranean. The evening spent packing for tomorrow's early start. Alarm hands point 6.30am.

Low Land
to Loire Atlantic

Awake before the alarm. A minute of nothing tells the body to wake. Thick mist cools skin humming from yesterday's sun. Deep breaths of moisture laden air. Silent exit around the gate. Sleeping St.Vincent-sur-Jard.

I put on a visibility vest and the bike lights. Sea mist rolls tumbling vapour waves inland. I head for St.Jard-sur-Mer. Sound of a solitary cockerel. Tyre hum. Silent road.

Jard-sur-Mer never appears. Road turns inland, crops through the mist, low hills. Isolated village an oasis in farmland. The bypass of Talmont St.Hilaire has the machines and plant parked up from its new construction. Modern transit efficiency bypasses a town experience. Signs for an 'Musee automobile Vendee' breaks endless farmland. The block shape approach to Les Sables d'Olonne. Misted Bricolage sheds. Long straight road, shops asleep, no one around. Boulangerie closed blinds interior lights of busy baking. One way system waking commuter traffic. Road cut through passes La Gare. Rail sidings and metal remnants piled in heavy oil greasy railway smell. Roundabout points out of town. Motor cruisers and yachts. Estuary mid tide mud, grey water lined boats point same direction.

D32. Ollone-sur-Mer on top of a hill. Straight road. Buildings a hundred years old dominated by the tall grey block silhouette loom of a church tower. Morning mist monochrome. Patisserie window glows an orange colour challenge. Breakfast of sugar glazed sweetness on the bike.

Concentration through town junctions. D38 to the coast. Thick sea mist rolling cool lessens the reach for the drink bottle. Marshland flatland, stillwater smell, blank vapour view. Sluices control heights of canals and land drains. Mist billow rolls smoke from the sea. The coast's name. 'Cote de Lumiére,' Coast of light.

Brem-sur-Mer, 'Happycamperland,' Brétignolls-sur-'Happycamperland.' A street lined with old surf and windsurf board signs advertising the famous reef break of La Sauzaie. Today breaks only mushy ankle slappers onto the rock that gives the wave its famous shape.

St.Gilles-Croix-de-Vie seaside town has St. Hillare-de-Riez joined at the hip. Countryside, woodland. Wandering masses of St.Jean-de-Monts happycamperland brimming gift shops. Coloured plastic buckets, inflatable green smiling dinosaur rubber rings, blow up boats and inflatable blue dolphins. Supermarket stop, busy roundabout. Straight countryside road will cut a corner of misted coast's vapour view. D51 runs straight north. Silent crossroad house void of life. Flat reclaimed marsh sponge emptiness devoid of time. Miles and miles of reclaimed nothing meet the coastal route.

Land rise crosses a tidal canal. Banks full of pecheries huts, many nets hang over the water. Death row for a fish.

Beauvoir-sur-Mer. 'Les marais salants.' Marshland sea salt. An excavated shallow tidal lake maze of rectangular joining pools slowly trap the salt from sea water through seasonal evaporation. Hundreds of years old. The only way of preserving food for marching armies and voyaging navies before the invention canning and refrigeration. Whoever had salt, held gold. Stalls and vans advertise pure sea salt.

Bourgneuf-en-Retz leaves behind the misty Vendee for a return to Loire Atlantique crossed out with black aerosol paint. Replaced by 'BRETAGNE' deeply considered so by some.

'Aire du repose' is next to 'Aire camping car'. A picnic bench faces a long line of white plastic motorhomes. A campervan arrives stopping over a grid. The driver gets out and goes to a little rectangular door situated in the side of the vehicle where a grey cassette is pulled out after unscrewing. It is taken to the building and emptied before returning and replacing. Next a great gushing from beneath the vehicle as the waste water empties. The van parks next to its identical and has lunch, passenger spinning the seat to face the table. Another motorhome arrives and follows the same grey water ritual, parking then having lunch. A while later another arrives and etc. I like the way the person travelling can go from passenger to lunch table in a single 180 degree movement with the pull of a lever. But it all seems gizmo complicated.

I get back on the bike, leaving the rituals of van conversion to the converted. Bourgeneuf-en-Retz is closed because it is lunchtime. Streets empty. The back of town finds D5 running north on quiet country road.

Low hills roll fields, hedges, deciduous tree full leaf whisper in breeze, summer cereal crops sway mass unison. The road straight for miles. Tricky zig zag through sleepy Arton-en-Retz. The only characters are outside Bar Tabac. Curly long mullet haircuts in moustached 80's timewarp. Compass guides direction. Fork split re-emerges as D5.

Land deeper green looks regressed a season. No longer climate like the south. It is weather within four seasons of Atlantic influence. Chauvé, pretty L'Auviére totals a couple of shops. People hushed in conversation on quiet sunny street corner.

Hill climb through fields to St. Pére-en-Retz. The place a crossroads. Last chance direction decision. East to pretty Le Pellerin and the ferry Lola' across La Loire into Bretagne. Or St. Brevin-les-Pins taking on the mad traffic high bridge to St. Nazaire. Danger holds the shortest route.

'St.Brevin-l'Ocean 3km. 'Campings.' Underneath, 'Route Barre 2km'!

The suburb of St. Brevin-les-Pins to industrial land under Route National. Large busy 'Happycamperland' Accueil. Pitching amongst people mass shouts and screams near the banks of La Loire. Planning an early morning perimeter escape over Le Grand Pont to St. Nazaire. Thoughts of it being windy up so high, the traffic at touch distance speeding past. But that is tomorrow.

145 km

Into Morbihan, Finistére.

6am. Tea chatters on the flame as I pack. Out of the gate before anyone wakes. Early morning just off of darkness. Slip road to Route National. I see no interdit bicycle sign, riding the hard shoulder. Car horn. Passenger stares a frown. I should not be on here. Too late to change. I want to make the bridge. Apprehensive of apprehension ensures the quickest pace. Speed limit drops, slip road joins from town. The road I should have arrived on.

Under video surveillance, the bridge climb over La Loire. Hard shoulder narrows to nothing more than bike width shared with bolts, wire, plastic wheel trim and glass for the instant puncture. Early dawn refuses to yield to strengthening daylight. Paired vehicle lights in upward procession. Gusts strengthen the higher I climb. Glass and fallen metal, the lorry pass shake around. Diesel exhaust, bits into the eyes. Wind blows from the sea, blustery gust shake. A look down to the river 60m (180ft). Long black fingers of wind race over blown white flecked cold grey. Dark grey cloud bank stretches across the sky. Sunrise behind lights cloud edge holes gold. The riverside landscape kept in darkness. Paired headlights queue. The five day ribbon fairy light work procession to time lights main traffic routes around St. Nazaire. Bottom of the bridge traffic fight refuses space.

Directions for Montoir-de-Bretagne away from St. Nazaire. Signs to La Grande-Briére the freshwater reed and marsh wild area the other side of aerospace factories. Through large open doors of orange lit hangars commercial aviation under construction. Busy places amongst flat grey serving roads, rubbish and industry behind fences crowned in barbed wire spiral. All directions head Nantes pointing Route National. The back of Montoir-de-Bretagne, marooned surrounded by creeping growth industry under Route National buzz.

Early morning road quiet La Grand-Briére wetland, country greenery. Birdsong, glimpses of reeds, black still water, overgrown wild hedgerow. Flat road above watery landscape rising to small villages drops to wild reed marsh. Dredged waterways, wild grassy islands. Small black flat bottomed heavy pointed punts for fishing and shooting moored against posts, some half sunk, others slowly fill by leakage or rainwater. Motionless still water reflecting mirror grass banks, tall reeds and the twisted bough. Gold morning clouds blow over background fresh broken blue.

La Grande-Briére does not hold the marshland smell of its Vendee neighbour. Richer in growth, colours vibrant. A heron takes off. A fish eating vintage flying boat, long beak, coiled neck, big square ended wings flap curled downward in an arc slowly gaining height over the watery runway. I spook a cormorant, it breaks into a rapid flapping dash splashing across the water disappearing along one of the ancient channels cut from reed mass. The most pleasant cycle, nature and the cool greenness I have not experienced for weeks. A short climb brings the marshes of La Briére to a close. Surroundings of lush green pasture divided fields, hamlets of stone hold thatched roofs. Through the town of Herbignac. La Roche Bernard at river level. Many masts of moored yachts, neat lines same direction looked over by a great rock from which I imagine the town takes its name. Winding hill rises over river. Atmospheric medieval half timbered houses, surrounding cobbled ways. Old painted canons glossed black decorated in vivid red floral bloom. Stone facade of age, narrow twisting street shadowed between old buildings. The top of town, buildings jump a couple of century's. I have not seen such a pretty town since Alet-les-Bains in the Corbiéres.

From stone elevated steps a man shouts, arms waving. "Ou partir d'ou, Vous Francais?" Where are you from. You are French?

"Je Anglais!" my reply.

The man jumping up and down with enthusiasm.

A return over the suspension bridge spanning high across the river to Bretagne. Junctions on roundabouts all similar, without detail on the map it's tricky. Under Route National concrete watching the compass. D774 hilly farmland ride to Rochefort-en-Terre. Pretty village meeting of three main routes. Country lane bigger rolling hills. Sweeping bend drop to the Nantes-Brest canal. Pretty Malestroit in slow pace, void of time. Tree lined canal bank green. Boats chug slow along mirror reflection. Five road junction needs Josselin. D764 under Route National. Country ride without traffic. Long green climb, twisting road. D4 steep hill headwind. Huge wind turbines in a line, the great rotating blade swoosh slices the air in electrical rotation. The hilltop flat. Tree covered patchwork countryside, steep descent ends in medieval Josselin bridging the Nantes-Brest canal. Narrow streets low doorways, ancient stone dwelling. People sat at a riverside bar overlook the smooth windless canal. Fine chateau in watery reflection. Hanging basket colour, floral display. Vibrant reds over flowing green.

Round turrets, half fortress half pompous mansion. Three big round towers, castellated walls between. Tower roofs sweep steep conical, miniature towers grace each side. Windows line vertical over four tall storeys. Stone ornate carvings, elaborate finials. A corner of La Cité Carcassonne, adds fairytale beauty to this meticulous medieval town.

I walk the bike down the riverside one way street. The local Gendarmes drive up the narrow road. It is one of the few times I have not ridden along a one way street. Road halo replaces early morning Route National devil horns.

Flower beds, willow trees touch the water, people stroll along a woodland riverbank walk. Main street quiet houses and closed shops. Sign for camping points to cross the river. 'Le Bas de la Land' Accueil sells a pitch for the night. Clean, smiling friendly and municipal, so it is cheap. Grass riverbank holds the canalised river moving equal to walking pace towards town. Efforts of the day catch up, the body wants its bed. Tomorrow's route looks lumpy. Tired eyes put down the map when the light goes. Dusk temperature half of two days ago.

120 km

On the road before 8am crossing the river misted in morning quiet. A no traffic easy route of straight direction will run to main town Pontivy.

Mist vanishes, land warms. Lush fields roll, the road

climbing under full green leaf shading rough furrowed bark of ancient tree. Limbs long fallen, the oval wound healed cracked. Silent battle scars of Atlantic gales across Morbihan and Finistére. Boughs throw long islands of shade across the road, a weakened yellow tint of early morning sun. Cows sideways chewing stare, crops sway. Ripening corn nods its approval of summer morning breeze. Crossroads without traffic, hamlets silent without people, a few climbs and descents. Long hill down to the buildings of Pontivy.

Many people make a buzz, busy shops. Corner stop, patisserie smell lure. Sweet fruited sticky delicacies waken the taste buds. I leave the bike to walk cobbled streets of pret á port clothing next to art galleries. Pictures on easels outside under the cover of overhanging buildings. The most pleasant of towns to visit, more utilitarian than its little tourist neighbour of Josselin. The place feels unnoticed. Cobbled square surrounded by granite block half timbered buildings, thick slated roofs jumbled steep. A tree grows central overhanging the crowded pannier market. More paintings, clothes, food, a children's ride decorated bright revolves. Crowd amble paws over things for sale. The Maison du Tourisme floats. A red and white barge named 'Duchesse Anne' after Breton historical nobility, moored against the canalside floral promenade. Over a bridge climbing out of town. The Canal flow further and further below. Quiet tree covered countryside drops into Guémene-s-Scorff.

Marshalls in florescent green signal to stop while the participants of a cycle race fly across the crossroads. I am waved through a gap in the racing. Through the trees down to the River Scorff.

A family on bikes with camping gear cycle along the river

path. Mum, Dad, ten year old and lagging behind, a boy of no more than six makes frantic wobbling progress rattling on a little fat spongy wheeled hand me down.

Road number change. D1 climbs for miles, hilly patchwork fields rise to managed woodland. Ancient fern and thick green moss grow damp under roadside shade. Little springs along a water worn gutter flow over stones polished by constant flow babbling in gurgle busy downhill. Woodland ends, hilltop pasture breeze sway. Cotton wool bundles grow across the sky switching the sun on and off to a glimpse of background blue. Cloud shadow rush across straight road to the vanishing point. The farming village of Plouray. Directions to Gourin. Woodland. Flat road straight line ride into the Montagnes Noir. One car breaks road emptiness.

Lonely roadside houses, junctions signed to nowhere. 'Groas-Loas' country lane promises Carhaix. Narrow and winding D21 wild hilly country. Forest behind moorland. Granite breaks the ground sprouting swathes of purple heather between sprawling yellow gorse flower to a silent crossroads hamlet asleep in the sun. The staggered crossing empty of traffic points downhill faster and faster, the village of Plévin a long green blur, freewheeling twists to the Nantes Brest canal. Main road uphill through industry. Town bypass. Supermarket. 'Bricolage land.' I decide to head for Huelgoat. It is a long way.

Tree shaded layby has picnic benches. I eat any food I can find. Cold sardines and biscuit remnants make a strange menu. I top up the waterbottles for a tired ride.

Downhill junction. Signs for Roscoff 'continental ferry port.' Huelgoat D764. Uphill riding misses the junction. Realisation after ten minutes climbing long slow grind of half energy. Cars pass. Engines utter flat dwindling monotone searching for lower gears to make the hill. Fields, forest, cliff face. Adverts for Huelgoat. Road drag into the Parc Naturel d'Amorique. Out of water and energy. The slow climb grind, slower and slower into the Monts d'Aree.

Signs for Huelgoat point to a little road. I take it, stopping at an Aire du repose where empty picnic benches offer cool shade trees. I am out of all energy. Ten minutes of body slump bring thoughts of open shops and a campsite bribing the body to move. Grateful downhill surprise. The entrance of the town square. People happily browse the prices of property. The property obsessed English.

Into the small corner supermarket, large tanks of live seafood, aisles of food. Purchasing an enthusiastic amount for evening demolition.

Downhill bends. Great tree bough green world, waterfall tumbles in steep valley echo. The driveway to the Accueil. A couple of tents in residence. I pay for the night, pitching the tent away from the river. The Patron busy on a tractor mower cutting the damp lush green. Wet summer grass smell fills the air.

The River d'Argent flows under trees, sun yellowed in evening glow. The welcomed shower after the long days ride. Walking back to the tent refreshed the Patron exclaims. "You come back!"

130 km

A feeling of having returned home even though there are plenty of kilometres to ride to the ferry port. Everything damp in silver bead dew.

A Dutch couple who are on a two week holiday cycling around Finistére enduring nearly two weeks of rain and wind.

"Yesterday it did not rain and we go to a headland on the coast to enjoy the famous view."

Was it good? I ask.

"It was fog. We see nothing!"

They have only a couple of days left either to enjoy or endure Finistere weather, which is forecast dry for a day or two.

Packed by 10am. Goodbye to the Dutch couple.

Easy climb under green canopy beech trees. Town square illuminated million calorie patisserie window lures to purchase taste bud art.

Bridge crosses the cauldron roar. A footpath under trees to the boulder strewn valley. River rushes deep subterranean to appear from secrecy the other side of town flowing past the campsite. I watch a group of people take a flight of steps below ground to view the subterranean river darkened course. Signs remind people to stay on the paths, to prevent slipping down the holes between giant boulders never to be seen again. Fern and moss creep, trees skyward struggle amongst granite chaos. Boulders worn round were deposited by ice. Smaller rocks and earth eroded were carried away by the river now running below suspended house sized granite remnants. Reasoning has just killed centuries of legend. Sorry. Morning sun shines through trees splashing dancing colour across boulders and trunks.

Signs for 'Camp d'Artus' King Arthur's camp. Village of Berrien. D769 will run all the way to Morlaix. Into the Monts d'Aree. Woodland, fallow ground. Low granite moorland, outcrop cliffs. Road wet with springs welling from granite. Bough tangle overhead green world. Rain spots cool temperature, thin waterproof masks fresh morning breeze. Easy ride. Occasional passing car. A couple of cyclists on their Sunday ride. The road drops to a valley, a village high on a near vertical hill. I prepare for the climb. A roundabout signed Morlaix. Around a bend reveals the town. No climb.

Shopping streets sleep on Sunday. Captive boats bright mix of maritime colour. Hulls mirror dancing reflection across calm sunny water.

Estuary road follows tight contour of cliff. Low tide leaves deep lock gates of 7m (20ft) exposed and visible. Mud bank ooze in steepened V flows a narrow channel seaward. Cliff recedes letting in light, opposite bank further away. Estuary open view across a creek to riverside houses. The village of Loquénolé. Boats forgotten, bleached wood rots broken. Half skeleton cracked ribs and rusted heart of an engine grows seaweed on a beach. Mooring ropes tight tether boats waiting for the lift of tide. Views and smell of a nearing coast. Far white lines of sand bright against breezy primary blue sea. Cumulus cloud tops flux swirl. Rock islets support navigation lights, stone fortifications line the passage inland to Morlaix. The estuary mouth guarded central by pale yellow granite block Chateau du Taureau. Hilltop roof shine betrays the nestled presence of Carentec. Clustered houses watch from the opposite estuary bank. Out to sea a large ferry stationary waits to enter the headland port sheltered from westerly gales and Atlantic swells.

Road climbs inland, estuary between fields and trees. Carantec makes a pleasant detour. Sited on a peninsular cutting the near shore Baie de Morlaix in two giving only part appreciation of its true size. The little village bright with fresh white walls in breezy sunshine. People wander in Sunday stupor.

Low rolling fields turned in corduroy furrow, patient crops wait for harvest. Tree black outline seaward to a flattening land. Road rises to maritime industry, boat yard on top of a hill. Dropping to the River Pense. High bridge over neat lines of moored boats out of sight around the river bend. Main road splits for St-Pol-de-Leon. A campsite on estuary sand between trees. Granite buildings, Town row of closed Sunday shops. The dominant tall spire of delicate sculpted stone was once a Cathedral. Yellow granite street, another large church. Juddering granite cobble direction signed Roscoff.

Town ends in roadside houses and a quiet muddied farm entrance. Roundabout back road to Roscoff. Sign for camping. Following a walled edge to a sand and mud sheltered bay in strong cold wind. The sand blown entrance to Le Pouldu. Point de Perhariday campsite. The sign on the Accueil door 'Ouvert 4pm.'

A lane ends in a glaring white sandy beach. Rocks offer shelter from blustery wind. Voices of a family arriving for a swim, shrieks entering cold windy water swimming into deepening blue. Two scuba divers. Spear guns and wetsuits disappear toward the nearest of many rock islands filling the bay. Large white sails cross the horizon. Colourful round spinnakers pull yachts downwind. Sheltered bay holds day boat sails heeled over reaching back and forth, waves sliced by the hull break into spray. I leave the swimmers to their shrieking and laughter. Back to the campsite in cold strong wind.

A French family and a German couple wait. The Patron arrives making unhurried greeting with everyone before administration. The tent is pitched sheltered by a hedge. A shower warms. Anything not required for sleep is packed.

Alarm set for 5.30am. Tomorrow the morning ferry.

Nighttime wind increase, incessant banging comes from a farm building door. Flapping metal roofing sheets in responsive crash to each hard gust.

72 km

I am woken by the sound of rain hitting the tent. Strong wind all night metal roof rattle and banging door tells of a weather front moving in. There will be rain, then heavy rain. Weather patterns of home return to memory. My watch says 4.45am in the blackness. The only things to pack are the sleeping bag, mat and tent.

Fifteen minutes to freewheeling around the campsite barrier on a pitch black ride towards Roscoff. The dim front light of the bike gives pathetic illumination. Fighting sharp gusts of wind, the road follows the shallow bay. Through dark and drizzle tethered apparitions of boats shaking on moorings loom spectral from a windy black choppy void. Waves slap the roadside stone wall in saltwater spit.

Black silhouette sleeping streets unlit. The front light dies, wheels hit a speed bump. Bike weight slips sideways, wheel scuffs the kerb throwing the steering. I can't get my hands to the brake levers, foot goes out to balance against the path covered in grit. Slipping struggling to hold the heavy unbalanced weight, ending in an unglorified heap under the bike. I pull my leg out. Wet grit dirty clothes, a gravelled knee bleed and somehow a cut across my nose. I check the bike. No damage. The chain is off. The hook end of a bungee cord loops it back over the sprocket.

Sleeping commerce to harbourside lights. Little boats

bounced elastic on a windblown night, a few yellow street lights throw long oversized shadow. I dodge anything looking like a puddle, pothole or metal cover on a wet shining road. The bin lorry crew already at work. "Bonjour."

I leave the sleeping town floral roundabout arriving at a closed 'Gare Maritime' blurred through a heavy rain shower. The only place to stand is an unlit glass bus shelter without a seat. I hide in the corner from wind and rain lash. Body gets colder and colder. I do the jump up and down on the spot with the arms flapping dance. Then a hands tucked up the armpits bounce trying to make some warmth within. Scraped scratched knees are sore. Down my leg blood makes a trickle, cleaning myself up with a cloth. Wanting it to stop before I face the smart dressed ferry reception.

Headlights quietly arrive to stop in the car park. Welcomed dawn light pales a brooding sky. The single headlight of a motorcycle rides up and down looking for something. Slowing to the bus shelter.

"Where are the boarding lanes?

"No one is here and nothing is open yet.

6.20am. Staff start to arrive and the building illuminates.

A couple walk by with a great Irish wolfhound and tell me the place will be open any minute.

Leaning the bike. In past the shuttered booking desk making for the loos to clean myself to a presentable state. The loo attendant bids a happy. "Bonjour."

Everyone so polite. Always people give a moment of their time.

A patch up cleaned appearance not to frighten with blood and grime. Waiting out time on a comfortable seat in the warm.

Rain streaks the window, sky lightens to full summer grey raining daylight.

The booking desk opens. Smiling ladies dressed suit jacketed with silk neckchiefs.

"Bonjour." Is genuine, without corporate imposed formality.

A couple outside stop to look at the bike. Pointing and discussing.

At 7.15am queued cars are in motion towards the boarding lanes. A waiting area with seats and a coffee machine. The motorcyclist appears. I buy him a coffee. We sit, observing other motorbikes arriving along with a couple of cyclists.

Mick is on his way back from securing a deposit on a place to rent in Western France.

"I have had enough of England. People in France are polite and there is plenty of space. It is like going back to the 50's and 60's. People say hello, they help each other. A better quality of life."

Pushing my bike onto the ferry. Tying the bike to the rail, up the stairs to the restaurant. Breakfast uses loose change. In the lounge I bump into Mick again. We sit and discuss the differences observed between the two countries. Not elevating one and putting the other down, just the differences. It was interesting to note the observations from two people in different parts of the country were the same, time after time.

A kind Welshman introduces himself asking about my bike. Where did I get the panniers and the water carriers? Then about my journey, interested in my experiences.

I do not idealise the journey, just how it is. He sees the photos and we discuss travel, the three of us.

He tells me I have inspired him and that he will do

something similar himself.

I tell him to do it at his own level, in his own time and follow his own route.

The ferry nears Plymouth. Grey coast outline through a rain splashed window. Detail of Plymouth Sound. Inside the breakwater, familiar rain blurred grey hills surround Milbay docks. Ship engine's idle, a great rumble shakes the crockery and cutlery as the ship berths. Engines cease.

The noise of hydraulics opening the front of the ship signal a dash for the passengers to the car decks. Panic subsides. Down the stairs to the bike and untie it. A Dutch lady unties a part electric bike loaded for a journey.

She tells me she is "Travelling North. Tonight. I stay at university."

I ask if she knows direction? She does not. I offer to take her there. I am going nearby to the train station.

Customs booths. Out of the ferry terminal. Busy wet roads and roundabouts. Riding the opposite side of the road from this morning requires thought and over concentration. City shopfronts. City underpass. The University. The lady finds her address. I bid her a good trip to Scotland and leave.

The front door of home opens to a junk mail carpet. Familiar sights of furniture, the view to the garden. It is nice to be back, but it is nicer to travel. Every day. Different places, different people. The white line ticking by under sunshine. Always moving, always new.

3816 km
2290 miles.

THE SECOND TRIP

The Return: Bretagne Finistére

The English summer remained amphibious. The gold's of autumn blown away and frozen out by icy gales of winter. Easterly wind howls across all of Northern Europe well into the New Year. March does not yield to deliver any glimmer of a softer approaching season. The cold continues through April and by the start of May the season is more than a month behind. In the middle of May the bitter winds and wet weather forge the catalyst to go south. It takes five days to get everything in order. Quit work. Making sure the monthly money sacrifices to banks, leaching utility companies and local government monoped bureaucracy are in place averting paper threat by faceless paper people. Nearly a year of saving will release me from the financial ball and chain. Buying weeks of freedom.

Mick the motorcyclist and his lovely lady Gill left for a new life in France back in November. I helped with furniture removals loading an old horsebox with their worldly necessities.

I have better maps for this trip having purchased a Michelin road atlas taking only the pages needed. The detail shows everything including many greenways. I have marked municipal campsites on the map cancelling need of a guide book. In my idle hours I have made panniers for the front of the bike stabilising the carried load, not to increase it. One luxury addition. A folding stool for the option something to sit on other than the floor.

The ferry company answers the phone and I am booked on the evenings sailing from Plymouth. The house is shut up, the key is turned in the door. No band plays on my departure, no flags or bunting, no one waves me off because no one knows I am going. I leave as I like. To disappear as smoke.

Plymouth is empty. Shoppers an hour gone and too early for the revellers shift. Through city streets, the green space famous Hoe bathed in weakening sunshine. Dog walkers, rollerbladers and skateboarders. The view across Plymouth sound of sailing boats healed over, sunny dark blue sea choppy. Strong evening breeze, contrasted colour on sails tinted gold by evening sun. I stand with Francis Drake. In the company of memorial cannon, all face to the horizon. No Armada today, just the approaching large white ferry slipping into the dock. Cue to amble down past the corner alcoholics purple faced and shaking. The quayside patient queue totals five waiting cars. Maritime silence broken by departing cars, rumbling haulage, motorbikes and the wobbling country lane nemesis. The caravan. All in an eager race for Devon and beyond. The symphony of a thousand engines cease. The gentle sound of deep green oily dockside water lapping against the old stone pier.

Empty docks have new lines of black steel piles driven far into the mud below deep water. Tops look as giant pointed upended novelty pencils ready to receive floating pontoons. Each given the imaginative painted name of 'A' or 'C' etc. Developers are moving in. Billboard image promises apartments of glass with balconied views over tethered bobbing dream yachts and palatial motor cruisers. It is destined to become another coastal floating graveyard of mid-life middle class vanities. The strange static world of the marina.

The queue moves through the booths, passport details and picture arrive on a screen before I hand over the document. There seems no real need of the passport or human communication.

'I exist in binary. Therefore I am.' Postmodernist border philosophy.

The customs shed resembles an MOT station. A car is being pulled to bits, emptied and everything examined. I am waved through, pedalling along the allotted lane number arriving outside the little café. Closed high gates bar entry to the pier tethered towering ferry, bow open high in the air. From inside. Metallic booming noises from internal deck ramp hydraulics. The routine preparation for loading.

I open the café door, sitting down as the sole occupant watching the gathering vehicles. Indoor warmth is welcomed from the cool evening breeze sharpened by lowering sun. Industrial hill puts the dock in early shade.

"Boarding in five minutes."

Stepping out to the smell of exhaust fumes of a hundred engine chorus. Motorcycles, cars, vans. Eager anticipation watches for the opening of the chain link steel gate. Six loaded bicycles have appeared. There are a couple on city commuter bikes. Two youths on mountain bikes. A man in his mid twenties on a steel roadbike and a newly retired chap on a new touring bike doing his first trip down the west coast and into Spain. Picking up the Santander ferry return. He has allowed a month to get there. I tell him that is plenty of time. He will be at the Spanish border in a fortnight easily. Gates swing. People green fluorescent with radios communicate holding the traffic's full attention with canine command. 'Stay! Wait.' With a raised hand. 'Walk'. Cyclists are told to walk to the side ramp. Obedient cars waved lane by lane. Under raised bow jaw, all disappear as

Jonah deep amongst steel ribs.

Routine of sleeping bag and bike tethering. Stair flight exodus. Handle of the porthole door opens to ambient lounge calm. Familiar noise of stacking crockery. Staff voices speaking velvet tones of French language.

Ship engines rumble to life. The nighttime lights of Plymouth pass the window. The ferry turns to the view of Cornwall burning in dusk embers. Receding Rame Head, Dodman Point, distant grey Roseland Peninsular. The Devon side looks to Plymouth's Mew stone, the headlands of Bolt Tail, Bolt Head and Prawle Point merge black in coastal outline. Ships speed increase. Engines settle to their night's work of timed deliverance across the flat Channel of La Manche.

Dawn light through the windows tint soft pink glow to blue grey haze emptiness. Mist veils the separation of sky and sea. Only the white foam ship's wake gives a visual reference point to the horizontal on this mirror calm maritime dawn. The ship hums a quiet contented song, gliding to its destination seemingly without effort. Ahead an island floats in the air. Golden ribbon sands, the Islé de Batz. The eyes adjust to it and the brain works out its position putting it on the horizon. Coastal detail on oily smooth reflection. Black spires of St. Pol de Leon pierce the sky. The ship noses into the port of Roscoff. Repetitive seagull squawk, smell of fish and marine diesel. The atmosphere of a busy fishing port. The taste of coastal salt air wakens early morning watering eyes with one deep inhalation.

The procession from within the ship to customs. Bicycles are directed to wait against a stone wall until called by a portly little man in a booth who appears to be permanently flustered. I go to the booth window signalled by him with my vehicle of two wheels. The booth window is shut. He cannot be bothered to open it. "Non, non, a droite! A droite."

So I go around to the right.

"Non, non! Pas avec votre velo." Not with your bike.

Bouncing up and down on his plastic chair, face screwed up. A tortured soul in a kiosk bubble. I just hand the sweaty little man the passport. He looks at it through his thick round glasses, handing it back sulking without looking up. I am trying not to laugh.

Familiarity. Tranquil Roscoff. Whitewashed chapel looks across the harbour to the square granite lighthouse. I sit on a bench. The outdoor breakfast baguette with jam, enjoying the early morning sleeping little town. Cool breeze. Ropes drum metallic against dinghy spars. Gulls squawk swoop and soar. Lone delivery vehicle speeds behind. I watch it drive along the length of the harbourside disappearing from view. The cycling couple from the ferry appear. A minute's conversation wishing a good journey.

An English voice next to me. The retired man on his touring bike wanting to know where he can get some breakfast.

"There will be a boulangerie somewhere." Pointing him into the town streets. I give him the estuary route to Morlaix as an option.

He will take the old railway route out of Morlaix following the canal running from Brest to Nantes. Then the west coast.

Harbourside cream granite stone. Coloured window shutters frame patterned lace. Out of town billboard for a restaurant. Stylised lady in a bikini and sunhat gazes across sand and sea to 'Le Chalet.'

D58 main road countryside. The River Pense. No Route National ride this time. Climbing between fields without hedges, estuary of wide expanse hazed golden sand broken to islands by deep channels. Warm sun turns brown mudflat silver. Wading birds noisy in call silhouetted black nose low tide banks. Large building with a tall round tower. Next to it a crabber of pale blue beached leaning makes a perch for gulls. A green woodland field. Lone red kite perched on a new rolled bale watches cut yellow field stubble, scanning its larder in deep concentration.

The breeze in coast confinement. Up river not a leaf moves. Haze has burned to bright sunshine. Estuary ride passes fine houses high walled, built for merchants by tobacco. Road narrows, bends under grey shade cliff. Lock gate permanent high tide for many boats captive in Morlaix town harbour.

Sweet Patisserie smells, cakes and tartlets fill shelves. The etiquette for buying in France returns, differing from England. It is not just entering the shop saying what you want, paying and leaving. It is polite to greet everyone in the shop with a collective 'Bonjour' spending a little time looking around unhurried before choice.

Through town. D9 to Plougonven across the Monts d'Aree to today's destination of Callac. Road climb. Fields wild. Tall grass wave with flower. Soft cloud shade island. Sun warmed day. Livestock grazing moments gaze. Farm buildings above trees, the slated roofs of Plougonven.

Amongst the buildings to the church where an example of Finistére history tells stories in carved stone. The Calvary.

Plougonven was the first village to create a pictorial story told by granite statues on an octagonal pillar. Walking round tells the story, some of the figures almost cartoon caricatures. Serpent monsters, the devil complete with hoofs, newborn Jesus in the manger. The characters look as if they will turn their heads to follow and leap out at any moment. There was no need to be able to read to understand the stories told. It has been here since 1554. Other examples were made in Pleyben, Guimilliau, Plougastel Daolas and St. Thegonnec.

Monts d'Aree. Lanneanou. High hill pasture becomes wild moorland and fir forestery. The only meeting is with four cows on an island triangular field by the roadside. No cars. Silence. Twisting rise, ancient hedge. Gnarled tree green mossed bough. Bracken fights with bluebell for ground space under shading broad leaf. A cuckoo. Grey fast flutter dart across into woodland. Road crests, descending fast. Thoughts of the campsite. The first night of tent accommodation. Campsite sign appears. Self congratulation on navigating a perfect ride, freewheeling past new houses and a hotel still to be landscaped. Wooded lake of deep green tree reflection. A few people walk around in relaxation. Through a building site to a lakeside campsite overlooked by brand new housing. I cycle to the gates. Closed by thick chain and heavy rusted padlock.

My appreciation of Callac evaporates. I could lift the gate off the hinges and sneak in later. Too many windows overlook the site and it will be patrolled by evening strollers with dogs. Out with the map. Sun needles prickle the neck, sweat runs into the eyes. Squealing metallic noise of caterpillar tracks rumbles by arm's length garnishing with the dust of construction and oily exhaust fume heat. The only option I can see is tomorrow's destination. Guerlédan 50km. Unless somewhere else appears. Food fuel down the throat. Squashing the whining mind voice complaining. "It's too far away." D787 direction toward Carhaix. Traffic travels fast. River. Railway line. Easy ride speed. Steep cleave woodland rise, tree mass sunny hillside flattening for fields. Sign for Lochrist. D23 slow country amble.

Winding climb under shading trees, muddy gurgling streams. Peopleless agriculture, earth clod ground into the road. Little lane cuts a corner off the map. Sleeping Trébrivan. Mael Carhaix. Veloroute 6 invites. The old railway line from Morlaix winding through the Bretagne countryside joining the canal to the city of Nantes on La Loire.

Diving into sunny woodland. Railway cutting banked in wild flowering pink campion, large daisies, buttercups. Purple bell foxgloves nod under wild growing tree. The old line rises straight.

Through a woodland tree tunnel I spook a red kite imprisoned by its speed under the enclosing bough. Looking back in bird of prey frown. Tail fanned, chestnut wings in rhythmic beat. A flick of tail. Upward escape to open sky back to hunting territory.

I push the pedals, dodge the winter wash out. An afternoon of farmland herds, new crops sprout green lines of parallel ploughed geometry. Woodland ends in busy Route National traffic. Industrial shapes, an out of town supermarket. Half a litre of water beckons the fuel up.

Under busy Route National, along a field, behind a housing estate. Wood fence, washing, the noise of television, barking dogs. Squabbling children in theatrical cry, sounds of people's daily living. Bumpy track re unites the old railway line into soft green countryside. Bridge view over a slow flowing canal river through a large open park. Town roofs under stone pointed spire. Platform terminus without tracks. Sign above the station building. 'Gite,'

A lady standing outside the door. "Bonjour."

I return the greeting. Asking the way to the canal.

Tranquil streets. The Nantes Brest canal silent in watery glide. 'Camping.' Arrow direction to the old towpath. Moored river craft. The welcomed appearance of a few motorhomes, caravans and tents.

Camping Municipal Gouareac gives a happy welcome unlocking the office.

Paperwork formalities are dealt with. I am told to use the

awning of a caravan if the weather turns bad. There has been a lot of flooding in France these last few weeks. Part of the strange weather cycle experienced everywhere this year.

The tent is up, a welcomed shower. Evening meal wash up. Welcome back to routine. In stillness, distant rumbling thunder.

I walk across the site with my washed pot and plate. A man outside of his motorhome adjusts a satellite dish on a pole. His wife leans out of the rear window in charge of TV picture quality control. It is not going well. I give a "Bonsoir."

The couple are English. Complaints about the trees blocking the signal. The hi tech world slain by delicate branches of a weeping willow. The thought to move to a more open part of the large empty campsite is yet to surface.

He tells me of La Loire flooding, campsites washed away. More flooding plus terrible landslides and devastation claiming many towns in the Pyrenees.

I am asked. "Where are you headed?"

I reply. "La Loire and the Pyrenees."

I wish them both a pleasant evening. I imagine will be of conversation and light hearted card games. Or darkened tense mortified silence of televisual deprivation.

I walk the canal. Fish pool the surface hunting insects. The slow moving current. Old houses with rickety roofs reflect. Willow overhang windless mirrored surface upside down world. People enjoy an evening walk. Couples leisurely cycle the canal path. Distant rumble, not a leaf stirs in evening humidity. With the fading of light I wander back to the tent and go to bed.
120 km.

Bretagne
Cotes D'Amor
Veloroute 6

Stormy rumbles throughout the night never make the campsite. A lazy waking. Dew drop silvers everything under hanging haze. The stove boils. Sun burns the mist to reveal overhead sky clear. The thundercloud gang wait on the horizon breakfasting off warm sunshine.

Conversation with the English couple and a Frenchman cleaning his barbecue, replenishing charcoal in anticipation of lunchtime culinary delight.

Wooden bridge to a lane. Three people engrossed in gossip hold morning's shopping. Over their heads flower the last of spring blossom. Hanging shade. Main street. View down upon a watermill ruin half sunk in a water lilied pond overlooked by a lawned garden. Trees reflect green admiring themselves. Thoughts of Claude Monet's paintings.

Bag of food return. Buildings dark slate grey and brown, floral display softens the eye. The church elevated commands the town. The lane to the campsite. Conversation continues between the unmoved three.

A nod mid sentence. "Bonjour."

Mid morning. Waves of goodbye. Towpath ride crosses a

road to follow the Nantes Brest canal. Cycle ride sunny green woodland captive between water mirror and rock rough hill. People walk, jog and cycle the tranquil towpath. Bends to a steepened gorge of purple heather. Yellow broom splash brightness across cliffside. Overhanging tree branch brushes the water. Valley bend. A keeper's house above a stillwater lock next to weir thunder. Arches of old stone across the canalised river. Path end on a roadside bend. Café relaxation under parasol shade. Pleasant coffee and aperatif view built to exchange cargo between La Loire and the Atlantic port of Brest. Sealed by blockade courtesy of the British Navy. Taking forty years to build it ran very well until the railway took the trade.

I cross the bridge. Leaning old dwellings flank a hill. Canal path resumes passing a stately ruin half roofed. A majestic stone skeleton of tall chimney stacks and high pointed gable elevations. 'L' Abbey de Bonne Repose'. Founded in the 11th century. Not in favour during the revolution was burned.

A family picnic, all are involved, busy in preparation. Under deep woodland the path ends at a sign. Only randonneurs are allowed further. Bikes 'Interdit.'

Dejeuner at Lac Du Guerdélan under tree shade. Pleasure boat loads diners on a lunch cruise around the lake. Seated views from white cloth and cut glass floral tables. I find mine tied on top of the front panniers. I arrange my lunch. The boat sets off. Two ladies of age raise their glasses to me in amusement. I return the salutation, raising a tin mug. They have the boat for a midday banquette garnished with marine diesel fumes. I have the lake with a few buzzing flies. The boat chugs smog across the water. Noise diminishes, going out of sight. Only the little waves from its wake lapping the shore tell of its existence.

Surrounding steep hillside and forest tumble reflect the water's edge. The manmade lake was the end for the Nantes

Brest canal's chance for a revival. Chopping it with a concrete dam further east. Fate sealed by hydroelectricity. On the hillside, a quarry crushing rock rises a skyward dust cloud.

Up through shattered rock, broom flowers bright. Fragrance amongst small growing pines. Two bikes, one tows a trailer, speed downhill in greeting.

Quarry entrance signs of caution. Wide dusty wheel tracks made by big fat tyres follow the road. The directed path joins a disused railway line. Veloroute trail high above the lake, panoramic view. Blue water. Surrounding steep slopes cling black fir, broken patch green woodland. Thunderclouds grow as afternoon hour's progress.

The old railway drops into Mur de Bretagne. Street zig zag, bike hire shops, a ride along a narrow path. Nantes Brest canal runs south. I head east on a line running for miles. Agricultural peace, cuttings of green tunnel woodland, over wild embankments. Countryside beauty. Town roofs of Loudac. Route signposts direct through suburbs under lowering sky. Steely dark blue, slow swirl. Wind warm change to a breeze of ice. Heavy air. A thick flash of lightning. Thunder rumble over roofs. I navigate the town, railway lines and traffic light junctions. The old railway route whisks away from habitation on a secret countryside straight line ride.

Storm clouds outrun bicycle pace, releasing wrath. I am not stopping. Waterproof is testing how long the new jacket will stand a beating. Thick woodland half shelter from heavy rain hard pelt. Pushing the pace, lightning flash low overhead. Hiss followed by static violence. Overhead pylon sinister buzz in half darkness. Strong gusts warm then cold. Cloud electrical bombardment without respite. Rain soaked figure shelters in a railway hut. Bike pulled half covered from the drenching. I cannot chance loss of time. Needing to reach campsite destination. Merdrignac.

Village huddle against deep charged sky. Storm cloud moves away to give somewhere else a beating. Steady pouring rain subdues all view. Long gentle climb, washout dodge. Grit path clogs the tyres, filling mudguards, building up over the brakes and getting stuck in the chain. Grinding the bikes moving parts with every turn of the crank.

Through the raining veil, a house converted from a railway station. Lit windows glow cosy in half-light. Into saturated woodland, a clearing. Station without tracks, grey loom through the rain. 'Café.' Sign on the locked door. 'Fermé.'

Long woodland climb, above valley treetops. Below flows a river rumble foaming white turbulent over blackness. Through rain half dark, blued light throws darkened shadow. Thundery gust roar through thousands of saturated leaves. Black wet streaked boughs spidery finger dripping branch. Road chops the railway path. Entrance to a large quarry. Articulated dump truck crossing. Bulbous fat tyred wheels cause me to look upward as they roll past loaded with black boulders to feed crusher hoppers. Conveyors suspended on girdered gantries feed broken stone high over black puddled dirt. Long spidery shadows thrown by rainy arc light beam. I cross to the woodland ride, opening to fenced fields. Cows huddle for shelter motionless under a tree worried miserable in their drenching. There is the one, separate to the herd. Munching oblivious to the weather.

Open hilly field. Chapel solitary, tiny in the landscape. A single bell hung under the shelter of a little pointed slate roof. Dripping woodland path delivers the entrance of the campsite.

Merdrignac. A big outdoor music event is happening next door in pouring rain. Many people through the entrance barriers. All I want is the campsite. I bump into the Patron who is coming out of the closed barrier.

I tell him I would like a pitch for the night.

He informs me the Accueil is closed and wants to keep my passport.

I won't hand it over to a person in a crowd.

Does he want the money right now?

In the rain he tells me there is a music event next to the campsite, it will be noisy. So for the inconvenience there will be no charge. He points to the direction of the pitches telling me I am welcome to attend the evening's entertainment. It is only a few euros.

I thank him.

My attention given to find a pitch that will not flood, sheltered from the wind and has somewhere to lock the bike.

Pitching in the rain under a hedge I stuff dry clothes in a carrier bag and head for the showers. Rain and sweat soggy clothes peel from my skin to land sodden on the floor. Eager to thaw under steaming hot water to the sounds of the first band.

Dry clothed, warm. Blood hums the muscles of the body tired relaxed. Stomach hungry, the snug of the sleeping bag. Heavy rain pelt incessant, lightning return. Music accompanied by thunder. People battle wind gusts fighting to put up tents in the storm. Music plays throughout the stormy evening to near midnight. Some of the bands are excellent. The soaked audience applaude and sing along.

Of veloroute 6, the old railway line. It is excellent. Well signed, the views beautiful. But better to travel it in dry weather.
80 km.

Illé et Vilaine

6am. Everything packed but the tent. Background sky deep red. Dark yellow haze darkens to overhead black. Air heavy, without breeze.

Unpegging the tent, thunder is accompanied by heavy rain. I hole up dozing on the cold bare groundsheet. Rain subsides at 8am. Birds start to sing, rumbles banished further distant.

Campsite morning silence. Revellers asleep in puddled battered pop up tents sorry from the storm drenching. Early morning boulangerie opens its doors to a queue of three people who look me up and down with an inquisitive. "Bonjour."

Warmth, noise and fresh smells inside an early morning bakery. Waiting people collect orders. Unhurried time to select breakfast. I leave with sweet fuel for the legs on a short ride to Illifaut to visit Mick and Gill.

Street lights and housing end. Undulating countryside broken by bouquets of woodland. Barns centuries old, built of red brown mud cobb. Protective lime wash eroded, birds have dug holes for nests on the north side. Rusted red roofs of corrugated iron contrast a dark charged sky set over subdued green low rolling landscape. The occasional large rain spot in the face. Rumbling displeasure, flash of lightning. Lowering static swirl, oppressive stillness.

Small villages mark map progress. Blackened sky ride into

little Illifaut, nearly out the other side. I double back to the church. The stone spire styled in floral shape openings make it look lace patterned, delicate.

A look for the address is without luck. Rain resumes. Village square holds a 'bus cabine' where a street map shows the address. Sky opens, raining in sheets. In the bus shelter dry by luck.

Rain lashes everything, bouncing back up off of the road in widening pool. Half a dozen French cyclists charge into the shelter on their Saturday morning ride.

I say. "Bonjour."

The Mt. Ventoux sticker on the panniers is spotted.

Bus shelter is now a clubhouse. Atmosphere friendly and happy, not one under fifty five. Cigarette smoke rises. Slipping on waterproofs amongst jokes and laughter. Together they still retain the fun and mischief of youth in lifelong friendship.

Rain eases.

"Au revoir" and "Salut!" They are gone.

Into warm lit colour of the boulangerie. Buying a couple of cakes as gifts.

The address is an old worn house standing on its own. Ideal in proportion and symmetry as a child would draw a house. Square windows either side of the door finished with a steep gable end. I knock. No answer. Hanging around outside, before being spied.

I am welcomed in by Mick. Learning of enduring dodgy places rented, paying a deposit for a house arriving to be put in a dung pungent stable converted by a mad English woman living beyond her means. Double renting, pocketing the deposits. Short term accommodation near the Gironde before finding this little house where life happens slow paced, barely waking.

My wet clothes are washed and hung out to dry on the

edge of a long field of growing cereal crops. Clouds dissipate to sunshine. A day of conversation and village wanderings. A few glasses of wine and a bed to sleep in.
12 km.

My head will not lift from the pillow in the tranquil sleepy village. What could be 6am is 9.30am. I am the first to surface. I let the welcoming tail wagging dog out of the back door, taking in the first deep inhalation of Bretagne morning country air. Gazing across a sunny waving field. Countryside to the horizon. Leaning on the doorframe I think about today's leaving.

The bike was a complete mess covered in sand from the railway velo route. Grit grinding paste for the moving parts. It took a couple of hour's labour of Mick and myself scrubbing with petrol and washing with soapy water to remove the menace. A bike clean and oiled. With no tent to pack a pristine bike leans against the garage wall ready to go.

Gill cooks a breakfast of poached eggs. Boulangerie walk buying bread and ham required for their lunch in thanks of hospitality. Riding up the road, a look back wave. Two figures get smaller in the broadening picture.

Town square sign points for Mauron. Flat rolling roads open countryside, roadside rough oak fence posts. Buildings of red sandstone blend to the land. Modern hard edge houses. Into Mauron. One way system through cobbled streets rotate around a large squat square church holy roundabout. D2 agricultural soft green rolling low hills into Concoret.

Two fields lead from a farmyard, five donkeys in single file follow a year's trodden animal path. The leading animal stops, watching. The others stop. It looks back at them continuing. Others obediently follow. Last, the youngest. One third the size of the adults.

A sign for Paimpont. An abbey on the edge of a lake surrounded by forest. I stop and walk under old trees of beech and oak to the lake of Arthurian legend. The abbey a small palace. Coachload hoards wander the grounds.

D38, 'Le Foret de Paimpont.' Giant trees of oak and beech. Ancient thick boughs seal the sky in green leaf. Sun spear rays between. Illuminated pattern pools light the road. Mossed tree trunk ancient roots brushed by bracken furl carpet the forest floor in vibrant green glow.

Forest ends in sunshine. A short hill. Le Plélan le Grand. Closed for the afternoon. Map guides through Maxent and Maure-de-Bretagne. Signs for Redon, Rennes and Dinard. Pretty woodland ride, field hedgerow descent to a river. I cross the Vilaine on its way to join La Loire. The other side a railway crossing. Camping sign points past Bar Tabac. A few tents. Riverside bar, riverside caravans. The Patron friendly. "Pitch where you want."

Fish ripple the windless river. Boats moored opposite bank. Numerous fishing rods set up fishing the river without anyone fishing. Where are the fishermen? At the bar. The rods do the fishing. Fishermen do the drinking.

The evening gives orange reflection to the water. Insect buzz flits gold, evening summer song of the blackbird. The riverbank opposite is in Bretagne. This side, Loire Atlantic at Beslé. Tomorrow sometime should re unite acquaintance with the mighty wild river of France. La Loire.

Two touring bikes laden roll in.

"Bonsoir."

The lady replies. The man stares, looks worried and says nothing. Definitely English.

75 km.

Loire Atlantic

Pattering drizzle. Echoing woodland birdsong of a cuckoo and the sweet singing song thrush whose complicated song never repetitive, never out of key. I go back to sleep to be woken by the horn blast of a long rumbling train.

Green river water ooze silent under bridge shadow. The cyclists from England gone. A friendly wave to the accueil. Bar Tabac signs are placed outside the door. Uphill to a crazy house. Everything odd, windows of different sizes none in line. Odd shaped doors of different sizes with half a stone spiral stairway to a first floor flat area. A round chimney in contrasting white quartz stone corbels out of the corner of the building is built to resemble a perched owl whose round stone eyes follow. More stairs lead to a main entrance door in the roof. Frames and handrails painted bright blue. The crazy fairytale house raises a smile. I ride into the village of Beslé where a great dominating church out of proportion to the village serves secondary as a traffic island one way system.

D129 farmland drizzle. The town of Conquerieuill. Retired men in the latest team colours ride carbon race machines with tiny rock hard slick tyres.

360 degree farmland. Outbuilding sat lonely, fields of silage bales, cattle land. The first cut of hay waiting to be baled will not be rolled and wrapped today. Rain fingers drag across the

countryside. Faraway hill grey blur, trees black fuzzed outline.

Marzac sur Don. Boarded up house, panes broken, panes missing look over a lake. Lilly pad yellow flowers on green leaf islands, soft rain pools radiating circles across liquid black.

Field grass hangs heavy under the weight of incessant rain drip dripping. Every stem sobs in drizzled tear.

Nozay town buzz busy. Shops' bright lit windows shine across a rainsoaked pavement. Shops open early afternoon!

Pasta. Fresh red shining peppers. Oranges, apricots bananas fuel the ride. Bottom of town. D121 away from commerce. Straight line progress rise and drop. Saffré. Road of crucifixes made of iron, made of stone differ in size. Names carved of the families who subscribed the money for their building. The opposite side of the road boasts a crucifix 5m (15ft) high. Jesus is nailed to the cross looking as happy as the weather on top of a grotto of ornamental rocks. Putting it higher than anybody else's. I stop pedalling. Gazing in rain induced boredom, turning my head to keep observing the spectacle. The bike goes onto the roadside verge. I hit a bush and fall off sideways. My fruit lays in the road. I pick half of it up, stepping to the verge as a large truck keeping its line and speed runs over my shopping. I pick the bike up. The panniers have taken all the scraping. I peel an orange, lean on the bike gazing at my squashed fruit now part of the road surface from twenty tonnes of juice pressing.

Norte-sur-Edre one-way busy town ends downhill. Cycle lane over the river rides a wood decked bridge. Downstream motor cruisers moored on a watery expanse. I can't be too far from La Loire. Uphill Bar Tabac and a pizza takeaway. The floor scrubbed with soap. Bubbles run from the doorway joining the rain in downhill gutter journey. Busy road, main road. Speeding haulage. Country D25 should quietly run all the way to Ancenis.

St Géreon direction signs to La Loire. Downhill to a stadium. Camping municipal is in parkland with river frontage. Outside the Accueil a bike and single wheeled trailer. I lean my bike in the hedge opening the door to dry warmth.

"Bonjour!"

The pitch in an area reserved for Loire a velo route. Thoughtful use of a large enclosed gazebo containing long benches and chairs. Two hours of sleep woken by the stomach to cook. The trailered bike is next to the opposite tent. The owner appears from the gazebo hanging her towel and waterproofs to dry.

'Bonsoir.' Is followed by conversation with the lady whose appearance is of a mass of curly permed hair coloured deep loud pink. In her nose a studded jewel. She is quiet spoken and personable. Her journey started from Rennes riding to Samur on to Angers and will use the Nantes Brest canal to go down as far as Blain then Redon via country lanes before returning to Rennes.

A holiday from work in computing. She grew up in Brest where her family still live, residing in Rennes because the work is there. She tells me of the beautiful coastal rides and places to visit. Information on travelled routes is shared, conversation ends at 10pm.

77 km

Maine et Loire

8am pack up. Low cloud grey, all surroundings saturated in silver dew droplets. The lady cyclist from Rennes nearly ready to depart. A large drybag on the single wheeled trailer is sealed and the tent is being rolled and compressed. She walks over mentioning 'café.'

I pack a soggy tent, joining her in the Gazebo making hot black coffee. I produce a teabag.

"The English and their tea!" Stereotypical amusement.

Conversation. Studying maps, talk of Finistére.

The café finished. I tell her I am off to the patisserie. Cakes and pastries for breakfast.

I am told. "It is very bad! I will become very fat, there is too much sugar!" Cheeks are blown out and her arms give an impression of the size I am to become.

"You should be eating fruit, nuts and fresh pain du campagne."

Au revoir.

The lady rides downstream, her pink hair flowing, following Loire a velo. Sustained by fresh fruit and a bag of dried squirrel food.

Cobbled hill leads to a shop window full of sinful sugar. Calorie jackpot!!

Crossing suspension bridge ironwork in drizzling murk.

Through little town Liné. D751 climbs away from the river. Cast iron crucifix icon, pink roses, red poppies. Livestock and meadow replaced by first encountered neat wired rows of hillside vines. New stems supple, green leaf sprout from the gnarled knotted scar from years of pruning.

A group of team colour roadriders tell me the Loire a velo route is back down the hill.

I tell them I prefer the road and hills.

I receive a nod of collective approval.

Through countryside. Villages of size. Moments of daily life.

"Bonjour."

A steep pinch snakes around buildings. A spherical lady of eighty is waddling downhill with a full bag of shopping. Baguettes expertly placed on the top longways.

"Grimp! Grimp! Grimpeur!" She exclaims in encouragement to help me up the hill and to give the enjoyment of saying it.

Downhill. Vineyards. Wet winding bends. St.Florent-le-Veil town on the river. Long road straight ride above the river full and fast. Tinted brown floodwater, moving mass menace. Levee land protection. Woodland half drowned in swamp meadow. Floodwater field reflects boughs, trunks and shimmering green. Cows graze the edge of the levee. Ground churned by their heavy wanderings turn meadow meal to inedible mud.

Wind kindly propels upstream, rain ceases. Cloud lightens breaking to unmask a sunny world. Fresnet-sur-Loire continued flooded views to the sleepy quayside habitation of Montjean-sur-Loire. Loire a velo route familiar from last year. Road narrows through near vertical woodland. Strange ruin tower amongst roofless stone. Part military fort, part industrial relic. The coal hauler/loader no longer receives barges. Metal bridge revisit to Le Bas Isle agricultural isle of La Loire. The road winds through farm mas pocket woodland and garden fields. Traffic sounds, bridge connection to Charlonnes-sur-Loire. Chalkboard sign for a patisserie, alleyway to river moments, cobble ride. Sunshine lunch. Loire sailing boat tied against the quay. Chateau's riverside command waves the tri colours.

River ride under an avenue of plane trees. Empty closed lunchtime town, upstream road climbing bends. Church of white tufa stone, semicircular arch door. Two towers, caricatures of ugly faces, kings, animals and monsters. The place once important no longer seems used, gradually falling into disrepair.

Roadrider at speed downhill. Racing colours and sunglasses. Shout of "Allez!"

Vineyards. Rochefort-sur-Loire. Quiet town of Dene. Along the banks of the wide river. A bridge crosses La Loire into the city of Angers. I stay this side of the river. Amongst town streets, a side turning, signposted only for the opposite flow of traffic.

At the junction four boys wait. Without lighthearted personalities of their peers. They wait the same as working men. Folded arms, standing solid and unmoving, dressed not as teenagers of France. Waiting gaze concentrated for someone. A minute's ride takes me past a traveller's site and it all makes sense who they were. Working lives from birth.

Saturnin. Old buildings lean and roll with the countryside. Ancient trees solitary wait out seasons counted over centuries. Flowering hedgerows hold meadowland lush green. The village of St. Sulpice mass floral bloom. Gardens, walls, planters, house fronts. Road verge burst and spill growing colour. A select village, commutable from Angers. Rural climb and fall to Blaison Gohier. The few hang around bored in the dust waiting for nothing. Flatland woodland deep shade ride to crossroads.

Through St. Remy la Varenne. Riverside road under gaze of Abbey de St. Maur. Houses of rose bloom look across La Loire to last year's campsite. Port-St-Maur. The place in silence. River declines to contribute a sound. Far view forested edge of the river sweeps a curve. Hazed spire points skyward reflected black across the windless watery mirror. Riverbank woodland green obscures until Le Thoureil. An old port. Climbing roses of deep red and pale orange cover house fronts. Flowerbeds full of manicured bloom brush the narrow road. Low stone walls and slipways. River craft float on cloud reflection. Mooring ropes taught, boats face the flow.

Gennes. Campsite sign directs through rows of parked coaches. Boule tournament. Serious players. Faces without mercy, posture of dedication. Strategy of intent to knock out the opponent. I did not see any blood. It will only be a matter of time. Death by petit conchon. More than a hundred play. Spectators outnumber players. Announcer gives the names of people through to the next round in scratchy P.A system echo. Outbreaks of applause from each game.

Booking formalities buys a pitch near the river's edge. Tin mug of Loire Rosé, watching the river. Evening swallows and martens perform acrobatic display swoop low over the water. Cyclists arrive until dark. Church bell chimes the hour. Every hour.

98 km

I gain consciousness at 8am. Getting out of the tent the view upward is of a lowering sky, the morning getting darker instead of lighter. The view across the campsite is less pleasant. There is a half naked German, not naked from the waist up. Standing still, hands on hips frowning at anyone who catches sight of him. An imbecile. Obviously not born with the brains to put his pants on. Airing your saddle sores sir? Why do it?

To the sanitaires for a wash, finding laundry machines on the way back. Steady rain. I may as well make the best use of the day.

Rain heavier and heavier. Into town finds an épicerie.

I pay for another night's accommodation and spend the rainy afternoon lazing, eating and looking at tomorrow's route through Samur. Wondering whether to follow the River Vienne or the River Indre toward the Massif Central.

Rain fades, sun makes an appearance late afternoon drying everything by early evening. The wine finished sat outside. Evening hours lengthen the chimes of the church bell, Sandbanks and river current in orange burn of downstream setting sun.

Vienne

Weak sunlight reflects over the windless river mass in flow. Softened veil shade blue, yellow and orange blend. Sky land and water fused atmospheric. A Swiss cyclist stands absorbed contemplating the moment.

He tells me of his journey from Basle to St Brevin-le-Pins the mouth of La Loire. Now on the return. Switzerland to the Atlantic and back following La Loire. Ocean escape adventure from a country of landlocked lake beauty.

The bike an upright comfortable commuter. Everything of top quality including expensive hub gears. The bike is the choice of many Dutch and Swiss cyclists. Coming from Switzerland I thought he would have a mountain bike?

He tells me he does not like hills!

Is Switzerland not famous for being crammed with snow topped mountains?

He finds my naive assumption amusing.

Packing repetition finds place and order. Thanking the Accueil I manage to leave at nine.

Riding through the empty sanded squares of the boule tournament battlefield. Pools of blood have been cleaned, sand raked. Forensics have left, boule massacre conspiracy denied by authority.

The front wheel has become beyond rough. I think it is

finished. Internal races of the hub are breaking up. Bearing grind. Grease works its way out past the hub seals. This was its last trip, the rims worn to the limit.

How to find a bike shop? A uniformed angel appears bathed in illumination on a yellow bicycle. Le Facteur, in this case 'La,' the Post lady. If she cannot tell me where there is a bike shop in town, no one can. Ten seconds of her knowledge puts me "Direction route Samur, Deuxiéme a droite. Le magasin, Cycle obsession."

The bike leant against the shop wall. Walking in to a long room full of new shining glossy carbon fibre frames finished in striking colour. Gleaming chains and sprockets, carbon wheel glint. Coloured slick tyres yet to be rubbed into the dirt of the road. Then to the utilitarian models away from window display towards the darkening depths amongst amputation and surgical repair. Flat worn out tyres, broken wheels. Rusty chains over black swarfed sprockets hang off worn dirty frames. Bits rusted, parts broken. This is where I need to be.

A lady wearing a leather waistcoat and jeans has oily black hands which she rubs on a rag while asking how she can help.

I cobble together "Je voudrais une nouvelle roue. S'il vous plait."

She wants to double check.

With a smile I tell her "C'est fini. Mort."

Under instruction I lift the front of the bike and she spins the wheel to a noise resembling gravel rattling around a biscuit tin. I am laughing.

"Ooh! C'est mal!" She says, nodding with a smile.

I am shown a selection of wheels that will fit. Buying the most solid built of what's on offer. The old wheel pulls out from the forks. In the workshop we change the tyre and tube over.

She asks of my journey. 'Where do you come from, where

are you going?' Etc. My broken French and her odd word of English manages an understood conversation. The new wheel is in.

"Au revoir!"

The road to Samur follows the river through pretty white tufa stone villages decorated in floral colour. Samur greets with a large roundabout. A bumpy potholed ride over a wooden bridge to a cycle path. New Loire a velo signs point to ride under a road bridge. Flawless direction to a riverside route.

Samur. A rich city of architecture kept with much civic pride. The Grand building of the Mairie in splendour. Flags flutter the breeze. The river kept from flood threat by thick stone walling running the length of the waterfront. Chateau palace mass commands the river high elevated in shining stone whiteness. Black slate roofs and towers reflect silver under late morning sunshine.

Houseboat of size converted from a tub to a luxury chalet on the water, connected to the riverbank by a floating pontoon. Loire punts 6m (18ft) in mimic movement of river current swirl.

Under the gaze of a large pompous circular building white stone topped with a great dome. Sculpted balustrading. Arched carved windows between fake Roman pillars.

Beaulieu. Dampierre-sur-Loire cave dwellers in their mini chateau fronted caves. A 'chic' address. A BMW convertible parks. A tall blonde lady gets out, sunglasses on head, leans over the car removing two large rectangular paper department store bags.

A smiling "Bonjour." Gliding across the narrow road to an electric gated residence.

Mini turrets, steep pointed roofs gothic arched windows and little battlements all behind tall iron gates guarded by sentry potted bay trees.

Farmhouse and outbuildings elevated amongst marshland creek in frog croak. More cave houses plainer in detail. Lone window in the face of a cliff, on the top a chimney surrounded by trees. Subterranean village hangs half out of a cliff. Above sits a windmill. Vines parallel to the roadside. Signs invite wine tasting and purchase.

Montsereau. Block stone fortress peppered with bullet and shell holes from not too distant conflict commands the river surrounded in tranquil manicured gardens overrun by tourists shooting the building with cameras. Steps to the river. Dejeuner sat admiring the view.

"Hello!" The Swiss cyclist from Gennes.

Wishing a good ride home to Switzerland. He is gone.

Vintage French roadster cars. 1920s-early 1930s outside a restaurant. In the sunshine long bonnets, polished brass radiators. Gleaming deep reflection of gloss polished wings. Spoke wheels, black tyre paint, cracked red leather seats. Varnished wood steering wheel.

Beautiful Candes-St Martin narrow street white tufa stone. Climbing red roses, multicolour flower baskets, the village crawling with tourists. People lunch at open air tables in the square watched by the church resembling a fortress. Only the row of carved saintly figures lining the front facade give the place spiritual feel. A large vaulted ceiling entrance is supported by a central pillar. Saints watch over busy eaters. I hear a boring loud monotone middle England accent droning.

Broken clock under empty battlements no longer gives time.

La Loire is joined by the Vienne. I say a temporary farewell to La Loire, promising to meet again above Le Puy-en-velay. Whenever I get there.

Last year's campsite entrance below. D751. Boatbuilders yard at St.Germain-sur-Vienne. New boats in different stages of construction. Traditional flat bottomed river craft of wood needing no depth in the water able to negotiate shallows of the river. The upward curve of the flat fronted bow is being shaped. Large cabin midway finished. Areas of glass, a bedroom of comfy accommodation.

Woodland to Chinon St. Jacques. Long tall plane tree avenue leads to a supermarket.

The Vienne moves silent under defender's shadow. Towers at the ends of great high thick stone walls centre guarded by a white fortress chateau. Thick round tower wears a witch's hat of slate.

Busy town of white stone, arched windows and ornate black painted ironwork look across tall shading green riverside walk. Canoe group mid-stream under instruction.

Lines of growing vines, old tumbling agricultural buildings in wine country. Groups of people tension wires for the pruned vine to spread new growth under warming sun. A dusty track. Old Citroen 2CV van is parked. Pale blue faded, rust stains run from the corners of the corrugated roof, the sides of the vehicle decorated with mud. The rear door swung open. Much used hand tools for the field lay upon an old blanket. The owner, a man with many years of experience is bent over working between the vines in rolled shirt sleeves and overalls.

Bridge for an opposite riverbank town. D760 to the village of Trouges. Sign for camping. A village sliced by main road. A long hill skyward to nowhere, opposite empty village streets. Camping will be out of town. Hilltop views to the river valley across fields and woodland. Downhill. Two flags flutter, a model of a chateau advertises. 'Chateau camping. Welcome.'

Long lane to a lawned entrance Chateau. The smell of fresh

cut grass accompanied by the noise of a busy ride on mower. The mower stops, the owner of the chateau gets off and wanders over with a greeting and opens up the Accueil booking me in for the night and ordering fresh bread for the morning. I am attentively shown a comfortable grassy pitch. The place very clean and peaceful.

I talk to an Englishman who invites me over to the sound of a boiling kettle. He is a retired ships pilot from Kent who has been allowed a couple of week's marriage parole. A returning visitor to the chateau for a number of years. Spending a couple of days cycling before driving to Puy de Dome for more cycle exploration.

Caravans opposite. Cars return to them in the evening. Dutch plates. People avoid eye contact or greeting.

77 km

A waking to singing birds in a chateau garden. Overhanging trees stillness, no background traffic buzz. Natural sound. Happy campers are yet to wake.

The chateau illuminated by the new risen sun compliments building's proportion. Not overly large or pompous, a fine house, stairs sweep centrally up to the front door set in a semicircular arch of white tufa stone. First floor stone balcony tall full length opening windows framed by blocks of cut stone. A mansard roof. Windows of perfect symmetry. A circular driveway. Entrance steps rise. Fountain cascade chiming tumble surrounded by suede green lawn. A great fir spreads protective boughs over beds of red rose petal bloom.

Fresh warm bread 8am arrival. Farewell to Kent's cycling ships pilot. The Accueil signed 'Fermé.' From the basement depths appears the charming lady who runs the place with her husband. I thank her for the pleasant stay. I am told to wait calling her husband who comes out of a store in his work clothes. A few pleasantries and I ask him of the history of Chateau Rolandiére. He tells me their chateau is quite modern built 1880 in the style of Napoleon 111 on the site of an older chateau destroyed during the revolution of the 1600's. A separate ruin of a tower is the only remnant of the original chateau. He is delighted to tell the history of the building.

D750 ends at Noyant de Touraine. D58 farmland. Little riverside Pouzay. Boulangerie sells overflowing baguettes of juicy chicken and salad. The Vienne oozes under the bridge. D18 upstream amongst long waving crops and singing birds in morning sunny breeze. Little road wanders through long history villages Marcilly-sur-Vienne, Ports Vienne. A little girl dressed equestrian crosses to the gate of her house while her mother gathers things from the parked car.

She wishes me a serious "Bonjour."

I reply in equal formality to Mademoiselle.

Sunshine flat road to Pussigny. A large canvas of cherubs pulling back curtains advertise an open air art exhibition arranged throughout the village. Streets empty of people, but full of large 4m (12ft) long canvas paintings of many different subjects, abstracts of the countryside, fantasy art, graffiti art. A villlage of canvas colour. Sentry figures made from domestic scrap look down over tall yellow stone walls. Out of the village fields deep of waving corn. Wild flower smother spill from the road verge. A yellow field shared with red poppies, thin blue flower haze quarter covers the field. Dangé St. Romaine spans the river. Old town bridge. Wide shop lined street traffic busy. Yellow of La Poste deposits cards. Closed dejeuner town. Human presence solitary sat outside the bar in company of a glass. Cycling sun narrow streets. Moments from open windows, radio voice and food smells of dejeuner. Crossing the Vienne upstream D1. Same road changed number. Empty country road, river in and out of sight. Large ponds. People fishing. Elaborate tents, many rods. Fishing for several days. Village of Antan.

Industrial tin warehouse, windowless corrugated units. Potholed worn beginnings of Chatelleraut. Tired houses, ramshackle small business. Car repairs and builders stores parallel with the river. Rail bridge. Riverside houses. A stocky man in a string vest with a cigarette smoking between his knuckles leans out of his downstairs window and shouts a sandpaper. "Bon courage!"

Old bridge guarding circular stone towers no longer collect tolls for privileged crossing. Old town jumble downstream. Modern functional upstream pokes ugly municipal shapes above riverside roofline. Stone track follows the riverbank, a couple sit on a bench looking over the water. The noise and controlling weir of brick hydroelectric ugliness has generated clean power for years. A bench with smooth river views invites a stop.

Across the river fine individual houses peer between tree lined riverbank gardens. People arrive to fish optimistic. Track ends modern in architectural mistake. Cold four storey cubed monotony. Rectangular concrete surrounded by green grass square multiplied over and over. Main road grid crossroads again and again. Populated by African people and students. Token abandoned car wreck, the only focal point. Block pattern D749 will run south.

Long hill ascending, large houses. Manicured lawns behind long gated driveways. Hilltop countryside, arterial busy. Undulating agriculture, main road landscape, straight line ride. Woodland sweeps conceals the Vienne. The small village of Girardiére chopped by the road. Road chopped Ribes.

Downward river view. Steep hillside trees, noise roar from a weir. Old yellow stone, ancient tile roof sag. Spire command amongst the roof jumble. Green and red painted riveted iron crosses the river. The suspension bridge rich gloss 19th century colours. The village of Bonneuil-Matours.

Narrow street old stone, narrow maze corners. Steps to the church in cooling open door invite. I lean the bike and enter. Interior brings relief from brightness and heated exertion. Hard wooden pugh rest soaks up the silence looking a half dome apse. The decorated ceiling picks up light from stained glass windows illuminating fading blue paint. Jesus amongst plaster cracks wears a peeling halo in gold leaf and green. A circle of fading gold leaf surrounds, eyes upon the seated. Windows of saints. Complicated patterned illuminated art. Glass colour across a plain stone floor. Artisan genius of century's gone.

Cool dark calm into sun brightness. A little girl is on a tricycle going around and around her grandmother. The Grandfather arrives with a small furry terrier on a lead that wants to join in with the circular fun spinning around and around in leg tangle.

"Bonjour."

Narrow lane maze. Rumble of a weir serving old hydroelectric. A converted watermill. The first hydroelectric plant on the River Vienne generating power since 1910. Over a hundred years of electricity. Signed information for the electrical tourist.

A fisherman sets up two rods. One to fish on the bottom of the river and another for spinning with a lure. The first is baited, cast and left. The spinning rod is cast. Reel ratchet tick, spool winds the line. Narrow village street. Big plastic motorhome stuck, motorcycles rev behind. I squeeze past, over the suspension bridge. D749 follows the river. Crossing to Bonnes.

Crumbly old walls, an ancient church. Camping municipal directs through the window gaze of suburban housing. The little Accueil open. A student doing a summer job is sat behind the desk revising between moments of administration. I am given a pitch number to hunt. Fine river frontage for a few euros. The only people on the site are two families cooking a barbeque together and a Dutch couple with a caravan. My sleeping bag and mat air in warm evening sunshine, washed clothes hang. A wander to the river. The Vienne in silent flow. Un-rippled perfect reflection of opposite trees. Stone arched bridge inverted in liquid form. A splash. Fish break the mirror, widening ripples over sky orange water take the insect. Many fish without a fisherman. Constant cuckoo call. Deepening sky colour brings the mosquito arrival. I make a retreat.

Talk with the Dutchman. He and his wife have come to this part of France on abandoning a cycling holiday in East Germany because of the bad weather. Experiencing landslides and areas of mass flooding.

"A bad winter for all of Europe." he tells me.

South of the Loire the weather should improve. I go to bed. The cuckoo still calling. According to the cuckoo it is 150 o'clock.

72 km

Indre

Damn frogs! Hundreds of them croaking all night. Thankfully my pitch nearer to the road than the river. 'Do not camp next to a slow flowing river.' Retained for future wisdom. The cockerel tries to shout the frogs down at dawn. Joined on mass by the dawn chorus lullaby. Return to sleep broken by a natural waking.

Fragmented mass cloud drifts above, its convection makes a gentle breeze stirring the trees to whisper. Sun glow behind the hill painting clouds yellow signalling the cuckoo to start repetitive calling.

Cold water wakes the eyes. I meet the Dutchman on the return to my tent. He asks if I enjoyed the frogs. Telling me. "It is the same every night."

I reply that he may enjoy them all. I am leaving.

His recommend is to visit Chauvigny. A fortress cité. The first town on today's route. A dry pack up without dew. Goodbye to the Dutchman. Thanking student Patron for the stay. Into commerce looking for the boulangerie.

Old village timeless narrow streets. Bulging masonry, paths of worn stone from centuries of traipsing feet. I add mine to the boulangerie pushing the door stepping into the bakery. The smell of cooking crusty bread rises from a low doorway to busy backroom ovens.

A lady is before me. "Bonjour."

Taking time to look. Behind the counter a pricelist and menu for filled baguettes.

The door opens. "Bonjour."

Everyone replies.

I am still deciding and ask if the lady would like to go first. She is happy to wait.

"Je voudrais le Jambon buerre baguette, s'il vous plait."

The lady disappears down into the bakery and returns with nothing.

"Desole. Je n'ai pas Jambon. "

The lady next to me suggests. " Paté de campagne."

The lady behind the counter joins in "Paté de fois."

I ask the lady beside me. "Vous recommand paté de campagne? C'est bein?"

Both ladies tell me. "C'est bein."

"Paté de campagne."

The lady smiles smug her recommendation accepted.

A baguette full of paté and four big cookies the size of a hand. "Au revoir."

Bar Tabac places a sign advertising. 'Smoke good fags.' Ahead rides man on a mountain bike a wood box lashed to the back rattling garden tools.

Past the campsite south on a road without number. Through Bourgueil. Hedged fields, riverside sunshine. Flowering riverweed flow sway. Old house alone under bowing tree. Clustered buildings of work worn farms. Woodland road sharp climb. Green branch tunnel into the bright.

Sun, heat. Waving crops pale yellow ripe for harvest, amongst the dry swaying mass red splash poppies. Road snakes the fields. The character riding the mountain bike stops, gets off and is going up into a small field full of vines. A large cherry tree sits in the middle loaded heavily with deep red ripe fruit. As I pass I lift my hand to say hello and he waves for me to stop.

Where are you from? Your route so far? Where do you go? I do my best to answer.

I ask questions of him.

He has lived all his life in this area and this little field is his. I am invited me to his much cared for garden to help myself to the fruit of their years labour for free. He tells me Chauvigny is a beautiful town at the bottom of the hill.

I wish him well with the garden and ride off thinking how clever an uncluttered life with a mini Eden. This man has a few vines, a tree full of fruit to sit under shaded. Many people would look on him as a failure. Having no big car ambition, no chasing finance. No swimming pool patio dream.

Tall crops to a view south. Distant giant makes clouds cooling nuclear rods. Future generations can work out what to do with nuclear leftover's seven thousand year lifespan. Right now people need microwave ovens, 24hr T.V. and phone chargers to watch internet cute cats.

Chauvigny rooftops across the river. Castellated walls, sun bleached stone turret rock hill hard against the primary blue sky. I cross the Vienne.

Town square cafés and blackboard menus. Shining metal chairs are placed around tables by waist coated waiters black trouser white aproned, ready to serve smartly dressed families leaving church after Sunday mass. People fill the square for the Sunday social post service converse. Dejeuner surrounded by ornamental trees placed to frame gushing town square fountains. Friends and family. Voice tone and laughter.

Signs for 'Medieval cité.' Point to narrow back streets. High crumbled towers look double height built on solid cliff. Lower part in silent ruin. Black crows soar into the blue from empty tower windows. Roosts amongst great pale yellow stone blocks of solid fortification. Higher walls of windows glazed and slated roofs speak of modern habitation rising further from view.

Street maze. Old millhouse. Millpond. Blue green water, floating lily in slow spin. Busy traffic buzz climbs a steep hill. High terrace old buildings nod 'south' in their style. A viewing area over the town across the medieval cité. Further fortress walls. A great rectangular half tower half castle with a steep gabled roof of stone. Military strategic thick wall defence. A great church amongst fortified dwellings. The far end of the cité protected by a solid block fortress.

The top of the hill parts from the Vienne. Gone is the white building stone, the flatland green, the wet climate. The River Vienne is a beautiful river overshadowed by La Loire to which it gives itself. The Vienne has chateaus, fortresses. An old medieval city. Ancient villages of beauty, fine people. Fine country views over a beautiful river un-trampled by the tourist and is underestimated. Maybe I should continue with the Vienne. But it is east I travel.

Big area farming, cereal crop sunshine wave, the first cicada buzz. Long road, pocket woodland, red kite in spiral soar. The small village of Paizy-le-sec asleep on sunny Sunday. Brakes grip flying down a winding hill. Alternative old road steep, straight through a tunnel.

St. Savin. Huge abbey building commands town and river. One end part ruined, windows without glass, greyed wood rafters bleach weathered without slates. Long main building in restored architectural splendour attached to a high piercing spire. Part of a huge Romanesque style church building. Large squat square bell tower sits astride main nave roof. Windows watch the riverside terrace. Balustrade arcade, stone staircase, lined pollarded plane trees. Town square thick trunks shade cobbles with heavy bough. People sit parasol shaded. Café table aperatif.

Shaded street maze, an épicerie find. I hurry to buy, escaping the closing roller shutter. Large bridge crosses smooth River Gartempe. River bend abbey view enjoyment. Downstream old stone bridge rises to the middle carried across the river by five ancient arches. Between the arches rounded abutments, strength against the current. Either side of the bridge quaint square aged houses built over the water's edge with pleasing hipped roofs. Long garden lawn, weeping willow reflection, the water's edge. Beyond houses thick woodland privacy hides the riverbank curve.

Climbing from the river into agriculture. Sign for industrial Montlucon. Avoid.

Speeding over fields fly two birds of prey too big for sparrow hawks. Mid-sized, brown in colour at distance. Wings angled back, long straight tails. Slight lean, precision turn. Masters of speed without effort. Harriers. A privileged moment.

No traffic on main road Sunday. Freewheeling into Le Blanc. A town kept apart by the River Creuse.

Over the bridge walking a riverside footpath under shading trees to eat lunch and enjoy the water reflecting chateau. Next to it a large church squeezed under conical square slated tower. Below the governing chateau, a row of large houses. Roof tiles reflect a deep red contrasting the green tree surround. The riverbank long path. People stroll, sit on benches or fish. Martens and swifts dart above the water. Underside momentary touch the surface to take the insect. A butterfly tries to evade. Bird spins a tight arc, catching without slowing. Speed and agility of an acrobat. Shrill monotone songs on the wing are not abrasive to the ear. They are songs of work.

People with poles catch fish no bigger than sardines.

Buckets captive fish gasp. Gills open, part suffocating in warm un-oxygenated water. A bucketful for a pie. Mass expressionless eyes to gaze at the diner.

People have changed, the sophistication and peacock fashion of La Loire has gone. People live in working clothes. Better ones for the weekend. No pretense. I comment on a half filling bucket of fish. The reply polite. The voice gravel raw. Straight talk.

D951 along the river. Municipal campsite next to the sports complex. Flat road ride. Companion to the river following to an old railway line used for walking and cycling. The road is faster. Up through the gears pushes 35 to 40kmph constant. River gone from view, the railway route companion threads woodland. Sometimes level, sometimes above the road. Parts look rough, perfect for cycle amble. Above the trees two buzzards wheel thermal current, betrayed by their 'pee-eww' cry.

Large chateau looms its presence descending past industrial noises coming from a hillside. St-Gaultier. Campsite signs tempt an end to the day. Municipal camping points to a large empty site near the river. The place as big as a park holds one motorhome resident on German plates. The Accueil is closed. I sit for a while at a bench of concrete. Shower. Slow lazy shave. No one is here. I pitch the tent, do some laundry hanging it in the sun. The Patron arrives at 4.40pm producing a trail of blue smoke from a cigarette puffing away. I book in. He finishes his cigarette and immediately lights up another to continue the blue haze bliss in which he must live. Happily immersed in his hobby.

Riverside field ends over rotting concrete bridge. Steps rise to town through back streets. A weir tumble next to abandoned hydroelectricity. Rotting windows. Trees grow from deep cracked walls. The building half way falling to the river. Teenage boys fish from the building on a concrete wall.

"Bonjour." Spoken direct, polite. Dialect does not sing.

This working area has never seen a share of the money history has lavished throughout the Loire valley.

I speak to the German couple with a travelling cat. They like it here commenting on how cheap it is.

We are the two opposite ends of travel. They have power inverted satellite T.V. Fridge, generator, sun awning, patio table, deck chairs, shower, loo, kitchen and air conditioned lounge with separate bedroom and electric blinds. I have a small tent, one saucepan, one knife fork and spoon, and a single ring stove. My bike with its panniers, one sleeping bag, towel and my little stool to sit on. For electrical technology a very small torch and a pocket radio. But no cat. Observed from the campsite register, there is no difference. We both stay here tonight.

In the fading of evening light, I see the first little green lizard scurry through the grass in a nervous rustle. A woodpecker rattles a tree and crickets chirp about the warm evening.

75 km

Industrial hill noise throughout the night. I wake to crashing metal. Dawn signals the cockerel who is joined by the shrill laugh of the green woodpecker. A cuckoo makes the most perfect cuckoo call. The woodpecker responds rattling a tree.

People walk and cycle the old railway elevated across the river on a black iron girder bridge disappearing to woodland.

Motorhome electric blinds are closed as I leave the empty but one campsite. The Patron comes out from the Accueil bleary eyed, scratching a bulging belly through his string vest. Pulling a lighter from his sagging jeans pocket, lovingly lighting up a cigarette. In a blue cloud of bliss I am wished a muffled. 'Au revoir' mid inhalation accompanied by a wave of the hand.

Main street Monday. The place closed. Children make their way to the school where the noise of a hundred children talking laughing and squealing wait for the voice of the teacher to call silence on the shrieking babble. A road opens to a square. Boulangerie closed. Town wanderings. I spy a woman with a baguette. I stop outside a boulangerie/patisserie. Squeezed queue waits to buy. Downhill crosses the river on a bridge laden with tended flower boxes.

Flat green meadow view to the campsite. Weir thunders. Washed down tree has thrown a bough anchor refusing the tumble. A splendid chateau and church are sat above the river. Slated spire shines silver in sunlight. Riverbank giant willows hang ornate reflection over windless water. Background dark woodland mass under blue clear morning sky.

Little flat road, gardens of houses. Disused railway tracks bisect the tarmac. Woodland ride. D48 back to the River Creuse. River edge campsite busy under trees at St-Marcel. Junction for Argenton-sur-Creuse. Over a bridge into a busy town full of traffic noise. Shops and corner cafés, couples sat. Sunglasses, a black coffee and golden croissant next to a narrow tall glass of sun coloured fruit juice. Lone tabled men sit absorbing the print of broadsheet, an arm reaches for the cup.

Food purchased for the day already eaten. Boulangerie visit buys more. Funds in the pocket run low. I lock the bike and cross the road to a cash machine. On the way back, a young man with a dog is setting up a blanket outside one of the financial establishments in the hope of hassling a few euro's from the passing public without getting off his backside. He has a view of every cashpoint and every bank entrance. A vantage point of strategy. I have been clocked. I walk past him with a nod. He gets up to follow me having made the important eye contact then stops dead on seeing me unchain my bicycle. His facial expression of oops! He gives me a sheepish thumbs up and a low nod returning to his blanket. I know he is thinking that I am worse off than he considers himself to be! A laugh as I cycle past, he returns a smile and a wave. Double bluff.

Back street shadow follows the river. D48 under railway arch leaves traffic and social buzz. Suburb detached identical living. Hedge trimmers and pressure washers. D48a climbs away from the river. Le Pechereau. Little chapel on the corner of meeting roads. I stop for a drink. Last look to the tops of trees part obscuring the silver thread river accompanied in town hum.

A couple on mountain bikes huff and puff the gradient. Legs spin the little gears, skin glazed from exertion. I follow up the steep hill, they turn for signed Les Chaumes.

Road climb ease to tumble down farms lashed together with twine, wire and muddy rusting corrugated iron. Roses grow amongst gnarled orchard trees, lined washing hangs colour under sunshine. Fields bordered with tall wild hedge change to flat hilltop expanse. Large transmitter mast announces the summit. High field landscape, lone water tower. Views far away over many miles ridden. No travelled landmark recognised. Masses of land 360 degrees forever, blending with vague horizon. Direction told only by sun and compass.

I start to lose height. Fast freewheel through empty Malicornay populated by a solitary barking dog. Changed lands unroll. The end of the flat. Semicircular hills surround, some are pasture. Others wooded all under blue summer haze. Road wanders fields and hedgerows flowering pink and white. On the slow climb, the buzzing bee, flies, singing birds, scurries in the undergrowth. On the downhill. Green blur speed generates cooling breeze.

Cows under tree shade unmoving. Flick of a tail, the twitch

and shake to rid the annoying swarm plaguing their heads crawling into their ears and eyes. Overgrown bramble and nettle field. Lone orange rusty shed in half smother. Old car roof sinking swallowed in thorny green. D54 climb under sun bake into pristine Cluis. In the middle of the village the back tyre turns pudding, then flat. A puncture is never convenient. I get out the pump grab a spare tube and tyre lever, lay down the bike to remove the wheel. The hot sun cooking has me leaking, sweat stings the eyes. The tube has a split, no cause visible in the tyre. Back on the road leaving the silent village, straight line up and down though endless fields.

An obscurity in the agriculture. An impressive disused high long white stone viaduct cuts across the landscape serving nothing going nowhere.

Ahead rises an oasis amongst agriculture. Fougerolles.

Old fashioned épicerie selling everything at a price. The place smells old, produce of obscure brands. The man running the place is from Morocco. Nut brown skin wizened and a grey white moustache of Edwardian proportion. I buy some things for my evening meal along with cola to keep me going for a few more miles.

He has lived in France for many years, arriving from sunny Agadir.

I pay. Telling him not to bother giving the 5 cent change. Thank him and leave.

He comes out with a couple of bananas. "For strength!"

It is very good of him, he waves me off. A kindly gent.

Junction between two houses. Sign screwed to a wall old. Blue enamel flaked and hardly noticeable. The road nothing more than a narrow lane squeezes between walls, dropping behind the village. Woodland shade. Light pierces trees, everything dappled by sunlight. It could be a Renior painting.

Bumpy lane upward twist. I am overtaken by a Citroen panel van, the exhaust is broken and the whole van is so rusted I can see right through the side for half its length.

Country silence. A dilemma. The road splits without signage. Map without clue to which fork is correct. Both roads have the same amount of use, giving no indication of main route. The lanes have been so winding a decision could not be made. I trust the compass for guidance. 'S' bends at the edge of a forest will arrive somewhere. Dropping through commune lanes not on the map. Stillwater green ponds lead to climb steep hedged hills. Tarmac melt. Hot shining black liquid beads stick to the tyres. Uphill reflecting heat drains without a breeze, it must be 30 degrees. Climb twists steep, cows docile under shade from the heat shimmer. Downhill into map marked Chassignoles. I only want to find the main road. Navigation up a long farmland drag to La Cour. Twisting climb ended by D951.

It is so humid. It has to thunder. No air, nothing stirs in the heat. Yawning. Stomach feels tired. Clothes stuck to the body. Sweat stinging eyes fed by the dripping brow of my hat. Drop down speed generates breeze. Crossing the little River Couarde leaves a steep climb on the granny gear in oppressive heat. I stop under the only shading tree. Tepid drink without relief. I feel beat.

Plod ends at L'Embranchament. Busy speeding D940 crests the hill. Speed generates wind waking the eyes and head searching for energy. Fun downhill must be paid for by long uphill granny gear plod without hurry conserves dwindling energy. The climbing and the distance does not get me, just the humidity. Air. So heavy to breathe with the added heat from strong sun and tarmac reflection. At the top of the hill a tall sign. The shape of a service station gets bigger. The place without a sugary drinks chiller offers only oil, petrol and spanners. Road flattens to roll downwards. D54. Turning signed St-Sévere-sur-Indre. The destination.

Tent and caravan sign. I follow. Downhill breeze cools the body. Freewheeling rest. Sign for a golf course, sign for a lake. Road flattens. Un-enthusiastic pedalling. Downhill again, braking through bends under woodland to the little River Indre. Over a bridge looking up at a hilltop village. An old municipal camping sign ahead reads camping 100m. As I get closer the last 0 is missing. The sign should read 1000m. . . Up. Most sites are near the river out of town. Not this one.

The last climb for today. Around the side of a hill, village windows watch slowed progress. A poor attempt of a mini stone chateau. In a garden at a table sits a little frowning fat man with a grey bushy beard hammering a piece of wood. Without his shirt he resembles a hairy overgrown gnome with a toy hammer. Road climb curve follows the hill. The start of the village greets with a large sign of a red background proclaiming 'St-Sevére. Le Pays de Jour de Fete. Un Film de Jacques Tati.'

Hill gradient eases. Into a village of many half-timbered buildings. Shops display poster sized still images from the film. A sign for 'camping car.' A moment of alarm. Welcomed sign points to municipal camping. The entrance at the top of the hill. The very highest point of the village. Riding into the site finds a cycling couple busy assembling the poles of their tent and a randonneur hammering the last of his pegs.

Friendly people. "Bonjour" with smiles.

I sit at a bench for ten minutes and do nothing.

The lady rider comments on how oppressive the weather has been today for cycling. I am in total agreement.

Making a joke about the 100m sign at the bottom of the hill of which she finds funny after experiencing it herself.

No Patron. No one has seen anyone. I put up the tent and

get a welcomed shower feeling tired. I boil a mug of tea, trying to find some enthusiasm to cook, tempting the taste buds with fresh apricots. I talk to the randonneur, then to the couple who are interested in the panniers and want them for their bikes.

Rumbles of thunder overhead, clouds build. Plastic groundsheet covers the tent threading eyelets over guy ropes pulled tight. The cycling couple want one for their tent.

"Bein pour graille." Good for hail.

"Un Euro." My reply.

Opposite the campsite. The farm home to the loudest donkey. The thing sounds old. Starting low, building to the longest out of tune bray collective of flat tune car horns. Causing amusement amongst us. Sitting and chatting until dark.

75 km

The randonneur has gone. The French couple pack fast. A municipal van pulls in to their grumbling. Not wanting to pay the few euros for the accommodation. The van drives out again. Grumble changes to whoops of joy.

A quick "Au revoir" and they split.

Leaving me the only resident. I get some change ready to pay for my stay, do some washing waiting for the van return. Nothing.

Clean clothes. Walking to the village, famous for being the setting of the French comedy film. 'Jour de Fete.' The entire village was used, everything still recognisable from the film. The village flagpole, old market hall, buildings of the village square. A travelling caravan of the fairground people contains a film poster exhibition. There is a building. 'Maison Jour de Fete' housing an exhibition to the film. I try the large glass door. It is locked, movement from inside. A lady comes to the door.

"Closed until 2.30pm. It has been booked up by a school."

Wandering back streets ends at the superette.

The small people with round faces again. Last year many in Montlucon. Generations of a people native to the area.

My campsite return announced with tuneless fanfare from my companion in the stable. I clean and oil the bike.

The municipal van returns, a lady gets out.

"Bonjour."

She is the cleaner. Telling me she does not deal with the Accueil.

The sanitairs are already spotless. She cleans what is clean and leaves.

Through the streets to 'Maison Jour de Fete' on time. Opening the door going to the counter, to be told.

"Come back in half an hour."

Another party of school children have taken the place over. Wandering around the village brings scene recognition playing over in the mind finding myself back outside the glass exhibition doors.

The film was made in 1947. The country trying to emerge from for six years of burning, fear, destruction and death. Given the laundered historical timeline title of. 'Post war.' It bought a welcomed distraction when filming started, involving local people. The village square makes a natural film set as do other streets with the old houses built around small open yard areas.

The film is about a travelling fair coming to the village, inadvertently sealing the fate of the local postman. The travelling cinema shows the villagers' a newsreel film of modern American efficiency. Francois le facteur has a bicycle and a postbag for his rural round that happens with much humanity of daily routine at rural pace. The Americans have postmen on Harley Davidsons jumping hoops of fire, postmen descending from helicopters, postmen in aeroplanes and the 'Mr. Universe' postmen. The villagers treat their postman with contempt in comparison with the American film.

He decides to speed up his postal round with his own idiosyncratic version of American efficiency, ending disastrous in many slapstick results involving his bicycle transport.

I finally go in at 3pm, amongst thirty happy bouncing shouting children exiting the door. The exhibition is made up of in situ studio film sets. A cinema and village model theatre presentation documents the films making, village participation and the prosperity it has bought to St-Sevére over the years. The walk through the bar film set amongst lighting equipment and cinematic cameras is atmospheric. The tour bought to a close by a film in 3D exiting in the foyer. It is enjoyable, well presented with much warm humanity. I buy memorabilia postcards amongst the many offered souvenirs they are all I can carry. I thank the lady at the counter and leave, calling at the boulangerie for bread, enough for today and tomorrows breakfast on the road.

Still no takers for the money. No letterbox to post money for my nights of lodging.

A big calorie fuel up, packing for tomorrow's long journey to Menat-le-pont. The evening is spent in my personal free campsite with tuneless donkey serenade between beats of grumpy door kickings.

Creuse. Into the Massif Central: Gorges de la Sioule.

It starts with the low groan of metal pulled across metal in much need grease ascending in pitch to a woeful wail breaking to full out of tune bray accompanied by out of time kicks. It is the middle of the night in blackness. Could I kill a donkey? This is the nearest in contemplation that I will come. Too tired to perform the bare handed deed. How will I do it?. . . I fall back to sleep.

6am alarm. A single deep inhalation. Out of the gate before 7am. The town yet to wake in the silence of new morning. Into the square for a last fond look at the stage for the theatrical antics of Francois the postman. As if in his honour, or for some secret ritual. La Poste vans are lined up, doors open. Eager to receive daily letters for distribution. The last thoughts are from yesterday's cinema. Francois's postal advice. "Rapidity! Rapidity!" I cycle out of St-Sevére in Francois style.

A small bridge crosses the little meandering River Indre ascending along country hillside road. Leaving as the end moments of the film. Looking back to the hilltop village framed by trees, the church spire and half crumbled round tower pointing to the sky.

Black cat gives a guilty look back stare. Front paw raised, ears up. Waiting silent on the edge of bushes knowing I know it is contemplating small murder. The top of the St-Sevére road. D917 climbing slow. Ripe fields' primary yellow surround. Orange grown patches glow near iridescent. Threatening sky darkened steel sheet. High castles white hang dense, motionless. Over the ground yellow tinted mist silhouettes trees soft focus. The occasional car in haste. Between occasional rural commuters, arable rural silence.

White whirring giants swoosh blades through electrical charged air. Roadside pull in offers the rarity of somewhere to lean the bike. In the company of turbines I breakfast. Slow blade spin without wind.

Humidity intensifies. Progress laboured. Raindrop splash, cold on hot skin. Road mist. Smell of wet tarmac. Deep engine noise, approaching lorry. Overtaking at speed, large empty tipper rattles down the road. The engine noise slow to fade after the tail lights disappear into the mist shroud. 'Paté de Camion.'

Height squander into Boussac town serving outlying villages. Brown rendered buildings old under red tiled roofs. Cobbled square with a round towered house. The newer side of town. Unloved supermarket behind a petrol station. It opens at 9am. Twenty minutes to wait joining subdued pensioners leaning on trolleys in drizzle beside the recycling bins. A pile of flattened cardboard boxes change formed state from corrugated to coagulated mush.

I buy enough for a long day including custard pastries. English accents. A couple walk to their vehicle in work clothes driving off in a battered English builders van.

The town patched up, the surrounding ancient villages behind the photogenic quirky and quaint are stuck in poverty of permanent rural decay from centuries of being lived in without spare money to make proper repair.

D997 climb. La Rousille. A collection of houses amongst agricultural workshops. The back tyre is losing air rolling off the rim. I spy a few bikes for sale outside a lawnmower garage shop. In the depths of the garage a man living amongst the body parts of garden machinery is busy with spanners. I ask if he could inflate the tyre. I am told to bring the bike in. A couple of squeezes from the air gun and the tyre is perfect.

"C'est combien. Monsieur?"

He waves his hand and will not take any money. He is more interested in 'Where have you come from? Where are you going today?' and the next couple of weeks?

Today, Gorges de la Sioule. He tells me it is a long way with a lot of hills.

I tell him I will be travelling through the Massif Central.

He goes into a dream. Explaining all the beautiful places of where I must visit. I offer him a pastry as he will not take any money. Declining, wishing me. "Bon route."

The upward plod, road splits, D917. Small river meander. Humidity. Effort to breathe, big spots of rain require the waterproof. Rain on the outside, sweat drip on the inside. Which is the worse? Railway crosses the road, rusting tracks disused. Lauvaufranche overgrown tracks tell of no trains today. Houses empty. Boarded up doors, long time closed shuttered windows, rusted gates to gardens gone wild. Pathways drown under long grass and meadowland flower. The next village of Soumans. Poor repeat abandonment.

Harsh noise hard revved engines, speeding tyre roar Route National. Rain hammers. I stop under sheltering grey concrete. Overhead a ba-bang of each passing vehicle. Sound made from violent velocity. Ba-bang. Nothing. Ba-bang ba-bang ba-bang. Nothing. Ba-bang ba-bang. Nothing. It is indiscriminate, an intrusive sinister proliferation on the natural surroundings.

Pastries taste strange. I wash it off my teeth, swallow the water. Rain soaked green countryside hills, green hedges, crops of yellow and cows. Long hill plod brings a bellow. Repetitive for attention. A white cow looks straight at me pacing my progress. Bellowing. I leave the field behind, the cow has its head over the hedge still bellowing. The herd stands quietly behind. All focus on me.

Downhill ride hedged road with singing birds. A van coming towards me increases its speed. As it nears it veers head on. Driver is looking straight at me, a fifty year old face's expressionless stare. Foot flat on the accelerator. He veers away sharply back onto his side of the road in the last few seconds. I take action by giving him a big ol' finger. It is not enough to make him stop.

Why would someone do that purposely? My question is sort of answered with a look at the map. I am at the closest to Montlucon. The first time, the first trip, this repeat on the second trip. Montlucon. Dirty land of ignorance.

Speeding articulated haulage does not slow or leave much space, covering me in spray deliberate, cutting off the road in front without a damn. I reach the village of Lépaud, a tidy place, feeling happier than the preceding holes. Things are brightening up! The bellowing cow back in the field may have been pleading for escape. Road descends to climb sharp. New land view.

I am above a gorge. Hearing but unable to see a roaring river through treetops. White painted cloud evaporation floating above the snaking path of an obscured river. Forest cling to steep gorge sides travelling far out of view. Downward road twist vertical views to tumbling brown waters. The beautiful roar of an echoing gorge.

A heron on the far bank motionless, focused on deep brown pool movement next to a rumbling weir. Trees rise steep. Rain sodden leaves, intensified dark colour. Rusting steam boiler has cast iron drive wheels to work belts for machinery, piled up firewood waits nearby. Nineteenth century technology still in use, but not today. Charred remains of a large burned out riverside stone building. Hydroelectric spin. Rooftops of a town.

Green descent. Chambon-sur-Voueize. Empty one way street the wrong way. Tall brown stone houses. Shops dejeuner closed, lights off roller shutters down. Heavy rain. Riding the shining cobble rattle. Tree shelter. Large brown grey stone church. An arched door under a tall square tower built plain but strong. Short wood pillars hold the bells, a steep sided roof goes to a point. Main walls buttressed, another tower. Further wings of connected buildings.

A woman runs across the road in a blouse and skirt mid downpour holding a shoulder bag over her head in one hand, the other held for balance over the cobbles. She disappears into a doorway, the very final noise of a door hurriedly closed. Rain stops after ten minutes. End of the road, a large square. Remnants of the morning market finish packing after the soaking. The church just one facade of a great abbey. Round towers dwarf all surrounding buildings in imposed religious mass. I cross brown swollen floodwater. River ride cliffs rise into woodland. Thunder reverberates along rock valley, overhead sky steel blue and electrical. Charged to bombard.

Flat road big gear through cliffside bends. From behind the warning horn of haulage. Deep rumbling engine is getting closer. I squeeze over the white line. The cab door and front wheel alongside, engine hard and loud, darkening long passing shadow blowing diesel fumes. More wheels to a painted trailer.

Articulated axles pull another silent trailer behind. A fairground road train, carriages without tracks tethered obedient around bends. Haulage repeat deep engine breathes over my shoulder. A straight. I wave for the lorry to go, squeezing brakes to slow. Not much room to pass and nowhere to go. The long length tows a high articulated trailer pulling a long caravan, diminished space arm's length to the roadside ditch. A queue of cars patiently follow the slow moving road train out of sight. Silent exhaust linger hangs through steep green woodland.

A place to stop. I take a bite out of the last of my Boussac pastries. It tastes foul! Inside tall green grown hairy mould fills the pastry. I throw it in disgust washing my mouth and spitting the water. Cola wash down, hoping the acid in the drink will kill the swallowed foulness. Sold mould in Boussac. Flakey green souvenirs.

Long climb, rumbling humidity, granny gear hot plod. Lungs work hard for the oxygen grab. Under dripping trees. Dark charged sky gloom. Cars overtake running out of revs, changing down with a wheeze of engine protest to a lower gear. The top of the hill ends with a graveyard. Welcome to Evaux-le-Bains!

The place feels poor, desperate. People stare and say nothing. Men hobble and limp up the street, bodies worn and bent by hard work. Others born a chromosome short mutter to no one. Checked shirts, chainsaws and shovels. The place tired from endless years of manual work. Hard lives here end early, earning a plot at the top of the hill. Through the closed lunchtime little town, adverts for camping. WW2 army trucks rust at the side of the road. Oily garage yard full of old rusting car wrecks and a forecourt of battered pickup trucks. The oily smell of wet day scrapyard.

D915. Out of town views across a wide valley. Hanging

line of mist above domed semicircular hills. Horizon black with forested higher lands. Paler sky. Thundercloud absence. Road drop ride. I start to boil up, the body heats and sweats, for a few moments feel light headed, then sick. I stop and drink down cola to bombard the swallowed mould with acid. The feeling of sickness subsides. Cola so bad, kills anything. The traveller's doctor. A farm mas. Brown stone, large buildings ancient, it could be a thousand years old. Pasture border steep woodland rise, domed horizon. Noise of a busy running river behind wild trees, overgrown bushes in wetland. Current flows opposite direction, secret valley ride. Mist hang above trees, sun tries a burn through. Fields lit in soft pools of green.

A bend, a bridge. Sign announces the stream is the River Cher. This river supports towns, industrial cities and the majestic chateau palace of Chennonceaux. Today babbling in infancy, flowing past a few old houses of brown stone with shutters. The pretty hamlet of Chambonchard. Flowering gardens, above the rooftops dense woodland rises to the pine. Valley narrows, empty boarded up village. A sign says it has been purchased by the Allier/Auvergne council. Only the far end of the village inhabited. A dog runs to the edge of its garden in barking furious snarl. Bark fades with distance echoing the narrowing woodland valley. Spruce timberland climb.

Overhead fearless heavy spread wings. Whirl and whirl buzzard swirl, riding the thermal breeze. Drawing circles radiating. Territorial glide patrol. Through the trunks, coniferous valley, steep hillside rocky, darkened land of fir. Resinous smells rise from the half-light carpet of brown needles. Open daylight ascends into a peaceful village of St-Marcellat en Combraille. Closed for a nap.

D1089 freewheel Small River Bouron seems an ideal place to stop. Rumbling stomach now fully recovered, treated by doctor cola. Fifteen minutes of salad and paté baguette enjoyment sat on the bridge wall watching the water tumble.

Long hill open fields. Rise without respite. Overgrown sinking house abandoned. A large crack across the front is big enough to get an arm through. The climb straight line. Roadside boundary stone. I cross from the Allier into Puy de Dome. Big hill country. Now the climbing starts.

A warm draught of wind from above, dark charged clouds massing. Back tyre goes flat.

The puncture ritual almost religious. Saying a few words not to be repeated. Slowly laying down the bike. Kneeling in front of it. Removing the wheel, stripping the tyre from the rim. The tube abraded by an anti-puncture strip carefully fitted to the inside of the tyre. The irony of two punctures caused by a product proclaiming. 'No more punctures!' Useless. Where did I purchase the plastic menace in a moment of weakness? At the big national chainstore selling car accessories and bikes made with a 500 mile lifespan from cheap junk components. My own fault for walking through the store's disappointing doorway. I pump the tyre to something reasonable and re fit the back wheel. The chain has done some amazing knot work whilst I was not looking. Hands covered in wet oily grime getting the links straight running smooth over sprockets. A rag and drinking water cleans my hands. Sweat drips in increasing humidity. I bow to the bike in closing puncture ceremony. Dragging it upright.

I am observed over an electric fence by a stocky pure white horse with a red patch on its nose. It is friendly, eyes big black pools look at me, ears forward, body language relaxed it likes to be talked to softly. I have nothing to give. It just stays for the company and sweetens my mood. You should be with your Camargue relatives galloping wild through the marshes.

Downward to Pionsat around the neat little white building town, leaving over a small river. Green valley view steep into black, tall fir covers high hills. I stop at a picnic area. Concrete bench and concrete table warm to the skin. The body craves energy. Chocolate chocolate. A chocolate mind mirage to combat humidity drain. All I find is half of yesterday's rubber baguette and half a pot of jam. I eat the two spooning the jam and scraping the inside of the jar spotless. Washing the bread down with the last dregs of warmed flat cola. Fifteen minutes dozing at the table, head in folded arms. From unconsciousness I vaguely hear a car pass.

Cold wind followed by warm rushing air stirs me to my feet. White thundercloud castles have followed and found me. Steel blue bases tinted with deep orange in silent movement. Warm updraughts feed the storm cloud. Cold downdraughts from the high ice tops blow down. Unstable air, unstable temperatures, positives and negatives. Cumulonimbus is leaning into its direction of travel. Cloud versus valley will clash, ending in tears after hailstones.

Climbing wide green meadow. Part open inflatable battery chicken farm. La Cellette village. A pretty church. Roadside farm machinery waits in tall grass. Herds peacefully graze captive behind orange plastic stake's charged wire. Climb steepens, gears drop to easy, cows shrink further in the valley the higher I climb. Forest spruce and fir close, invisible birds sing from within the tops of hundreds of tree trunks. Breeze stir, treetop soft roar lifts dust fir fragrant. I taste the forest with every lungful it takes to get up the hill. It is a beautiful ride. Road snake forest world constricted to the next bend. Gradient ease opening daylight. Font Nanaud 739m (2400ft).

Forest green surroundings open. Long freeride, a few waving people. Signs for gites, isolated houses half way through renovation. Advertisements for lake fishing and camping. Long speeding drop. Crossroads village. Gouttiéres. Climb resumes patient on the granny gear for energy conservation. Long drag through dramatic coniferous hilly land contrasts the morning's flat rolling unending agriculture. Gradient grind, winding road. Sign for a village. Rooftops through branched green. Donkeys graze on the lower side of the hill, up above a couple of horses. One neighs, running down to the edge of the fence with its head up high, ears back shaking from side to side and showing its teeth, eyes wild, stamping the ground. I should have bought a gun, or wave an empty carrier bag at it.

The climb into St-Gervais-d-Auvergne long and drawn, steepening to the crest. Rusted railway lines cross the road. Overgrown tracks terminate. Platform abandonment, station decay amongst disused buildings. Tumbled barn, roof caved. Upper rotted floor fallen, slowly consumed by bramble tendril creep. Habited village narrow street rise.

D900 around the village. A sign. D227 Chateauneuf-les-Bains. Familiarity. Knowing the days ride will have an end.

Sunshine across near green fields. Uninterrupted view across valley and gorge forest lands to a blue coloured rising mass. The 'Chaine des Puys' great burned out volcanoes tower above all surroundings. The ruling defiant spike of Puy de Dome. Further away more volcano mountains. Monts Dore. Hazed beyond snow covered horizon ridge. Maybe the Cantal Mountains.

It feels good to be back in the Auvergne. A scene of beauty looking south. But now it is downhill to a little remaining pocket of Eden.

Freewheeling drop, steepening bends. Pines and broad leafed woodland climb to the sky. Rocks grow to cliffs spouting sweet yellow broom scent. Streams of crystal echo rush ancient cleaved worn gouge in hurry down to join the valley river. Sunshine land soft, life sheltered. The Gorges de la Sioule. Cliffs of pink and brown rock, spikey pine. Wide flowing river sometimes deep green, other times clear shallow noisy over brown stone foaming white.

Spa building hotel holds a few cars. Road follows the riverbank curve, into the village of Chateauneuf-le-Bains. Cafés, restaurants, souvenirs closed. I stop. Pedestrian bridge walk watches the smooth mirror reflecting green tumble over a weir. Long white flowering river weed sway in speeding current overlooked by old houses that have listened to the roar for centuries. Bend ride. Rock pinnacle Notre Damme de la Sioule. She holds no infant, standing with arms in open welcome. Painted white cast iron blessing given to all who pass. A few houses under towering green. 'Le Pont, Menat.' Directed over the bridge. A fisherman wades the knee deep boulders casting a fly to deep channel fast flow. Back and forth with the line. Graceful arc settles the fly on the water.

Road rises steep gorge side. A few houses, steep fields give up to rock and deep forest. High climb far down views. Tree filled twisting gorge echoes the roar. Isolated tree covered sharp grey rock tower vertical defiant in the river flow. Farm buildings lost. Patchwork little fields. Steep woodland road cut into the twists and turns of near vertical hillside. Cascading streams under the road tumble through rich green forest. My return watched by Chateau Rocher high and vertical. Walls to the edge of cliff. Stone tower window stare.

Descent to the River Sioule flowing past the front of Camping Tarteaux, Menat le Pont. Caravans, sun chairs. Smoke of a barbecue ascends straight through trees. Colourful tents spread along the riverbank. A picture of leisure. The little hamlet cluster around the roman bridge's cobbled crossing.

Two retired men walk mid-way over in conversation. I wait unhurried enjoying the sound and smells of gorge view taking a tepid drink from the waterbottle.

"Bonsoir."

"Bonsoir."

Asking. "Combien kilometres ajourd hui?" How many km today.

"Cent dix." 120.

A surprised "Bien!" Making a little amusing fun about being thirsty work.

I reply hungry work also.

They laugh. Leaving with a smiling nod.

"Bon soiree Messieurs."

"Bon Soiree."

Bike push over rounded bone shaking cobbles. Fishermen immersed up to their waists use spinners, reeling the line slow steady pace against tugging flow. Sleepy houses, a park. The campsite Accueil. Closed until 7.15pm.

Humid road miles are washed off of my back telling the body riding for today has finished.

A car arrives on Dutch plates. Two fishermen pass by working their way up the river fly fishing. Bird swoop evening acrobatic insect feed. The Accueil opens. I book in behind a Dutchman.

"Bonsoir."

Evening meal routine. River walk, stopping to talk to the retired Dutchman. Making his way back from Corsica, stopping here the night. Tomorrow, Les Mans for the motor racing.

The sun goes quick behind the forested gorge hill. River changes mood to black water of dusk. The moon appears full over broken silhouette of Chateau Rocher. In late evening stillness fish feed on insects. A splash, another and another

leaving pooling ripples that carry downstream. The river so alive. Fishermen gone.
115 km

The first wakened consciousness. Rushing water over upstream shallows, noise captive in the steep forested rock valley. No human sound to shatter early morning magic. Low mist motionless above the water. Heavy clouds grow vertical towers broody white and grey, massing for an attack on Chateau Rocher. The makings of a later day storm.

Steep lane walk behind the campsite. Humid morning warm sticky without wind. Birdsong from the hanging bough, hundreds of tree trunks in vertical twist. Invisible scurries in the undergrowth. Woodland release to open sky. Hilltop hamlet of tiny Navoir. Flower burst through the fence. Downhill leafy lane. Fenced field of white cattle watch my pedestrian progress with bowed heads standing together in knee length green peppered yellow by meadow flower. Menat rooftop jumble of new slate and old red tile pointed gables under church tower watch. Background fields green broken by wandering lines of trees. Hilltop forest black sprawls across the horizon. Sleepy street. Boulangerie door. Oven warm bread. Crimson sugared fruit surrounded in chilled cream.

Brooding cloud lowers slow billow swirl. Crack of thunder announces bath warm rain. With nowhere to shelter I accept a soaked return walking the hill winding lane. Cows huddled together in the corner of the field under green branch shelter looking worried. Soaked through by Navoir. Warm rain saturates clothes, running through to the skin. Flowers droop weeping about the rain beating. Through the woodland heavy rain sound amplified by the mass pattering on a million leaves. Rainwater babbles across the tarmac hurrying to find a natural escape through the woodland. Back to the campsite. Municipal lawn mower seat is without the driver seeking Accueil shelter. The door opens and I am told to get dry and come in for coffee.

Hot black coffee bubbles into the cup steaming. A couple enter the Accueil. The round faced small people again. Something is not right with their chalet. They are friends with the Maire and he is going to be hearing about it. A unique people found throughout the area, maybe the descendants of the original rural population before people travelled.

Lazing and sleeping in the tent. The electrical bombardment finally runs out of anger late afternoon. Ceasefire. The air all clear. Sun appearance, skyward finger evaporation rise, washing dries on the riverside fence. Early evening anglers arrive. I have an invite to see a year's progress on the barn.

The dog greets, training me to throw a ball within thirty seconds. There has been a lot of progress. Upstairs rooms are finished and a heavy iron spiral staircase waits to replace a wood ladder. I am shown where a large window opening is to be made then taken outside to the view of river and steep cliff. The rest of the evening is spent learning about the strange instrument of the hurdy gurdy. A sound box with keys, turning a handle rhythmically rotates a wheel against strings in harmonised continuous tone. The melody is played over by depressing keys. A whole band in one instrument. Beer seems an important accompaniment to its playing and appreciation.

Gorges Chauvigny

I am told to visit Charroux. A preserved village that will extend todays ride beyond Gorges de la Sioule.

Under main road, old lane runs with the flow. Hills close, cliffs grow tall around. Road near flat, an easy ride. Bends to nature's spire rock alone wearing a cloak of clinging trees. Roadside restaurant doors open empty of people, silent houses. Cleaved road climbs above the tops of trees, a buzzard's view. Whitewater roar slams rock. Bends of blasted cliff. 'Roche Armand' rock tunnel grotto cool dark and dripping an internal curve. Hearing becomes the main sense, listening in darkness. Long shadow exit. Gorges Chauvigny weaves cliff rock. Twisted trees fissured grip, hardy heather sprout amongst rock loving alpine bloom. Sweeping freewheeling blur through the village of Chauvigny. The name once in ownership of Chateau Rocher. There is also Chauvigny on the river Vienne with its medieval cité. Maybe history once held feudal connection

'Canoe hire.' Red and yellow plastic kayaks wait on riverbank green. Away from the river climbing through yellow crop sway. Ascending shrill songs from skylark and corn bunting. Long open land rising ends far forested black. Farm buildings, stacked firewood. A huddle of houses. Sweeping bends reunite the rushing tumble. Vertical view black river cliff edge cling. Lone cuckoo call, bird of prey. Raptor glides the gorge in territorial hunt. Signs for the town of Ebreuil. Gorge steepness recedes.

Open pasture. Bright walls, windows and doors of town habitation. Main street quiet, shops closed for the afternoon. Straight road leaves Puy de Dome in boundary and landscape. Softer hill roll. Open lands, St. Bonnet de Rochefort. Grey Route National metallic roar.

Roadriders. Names on shirts 'Bordeaux.' 'Montlucon.' Club riders with numbers taped to their frames, racing. I hear riders behind. Up on the pedals to pass. I just push a little harder alongside them wishing "Bonjour."

Half loaded panniers and a sunhat versus lycra streamline carbon fibre race machine. I shift up a gear working with the overtakers through the group amongst the leading riders, holding pace to some twitchy sideways looks. They cannot push too hard if they have a long way to go because they will expend energy too quick and burn exhausted before the finish. I sit with them and cannot be dropped. Legs are used to pushing a lot of weight today has been left back at the campsite. My route signed right at a roundabout. They continue straight. I turn off. Ah, sweet amusement of a race interloper!

I have been told to visit a bridge designed by Gustave Eifel famous for the tower. Tubular ironwork holds a disused railway between stone buttressed walls. One visit is enough.

D35 to Charroux. Long gradual climb, open fields, stone farms red roofed marooned amongst pale crop sway.

Narrow cobbled street, preserved masonry floral overload. People play 'pretty' to snare the euro. The place smells of tourist. Half-timbered building overhang, shops sell tat to multinational wanderers. A lot of care has gone into the village. It is nice play the wanderer, trinket souvenirs fill carrier bags. Café enticement. Smell of roasting fresh coffee drifts ancient buildings. I wander into the church. Candle lit grotto to Notre Damme, her hands together in prayer looking upward. Broad church collection box accepts all currency donation. Stained glass depictions from biblical stories. A poor soul arrow speared wears an expression of teenage apathy. Rich colours, fine detail, quality craftsmanship centuries old. I leave the rosebushes, lime pointing, old hanging signs and prettified nostalgia. Freewheeling a long open hill.

A bird of prey cuts across low, grey with black wing tips moving fast in silence. Small head scans the ground for movement, gliding a field in grid slalom waiting for the timid to break cover. Male Hen Harrier. Small. Fearsome.

Ebreuil has woken yawning from an afternoon nap. Supermarket stop, back to the gorge for return journey perspective. Gorges de Chauvigny. Tunnel ride release into the Gorges de la Sioule. Path leads to a pebble beach. Fast flow shallows over washed rounded stones and boulders. Cliffs vertical from deep channel running smooth translucent brown to black. Silent mirror, tree overhang. Cliff tower rock many times the height of the tree canopy. A pool of shallow water near my feet runs back eddy to the river current. Waterboatman skate surface tension waiting for opportunist food. Tiny fish fry scatter at the slightest ground vibration from my giant's footstep.

Cheese, smoked meat, tearing the fresh crust of cereal bread. Colourful salad, shining black cherries. All washed down with a beer under surrounding green enchantment. Sun illuminates riverbed copper tinted stones under riverweed smother. Birds dart in acrobatic feed out maneuvering butterflies and insects.

Campsite dusk. Packing what I can for tomorrows journey. Full moon climbs the tree line. A hanging lantern of nocturnal brightness, reflecting on an oily black river mirroring roman

arches.
68 km

Bright sunshine, fond farewells. Over the Roman bridge. Caravans, tents and fisherman lost to the climb under stony watch of Chateau Rocher. The mind grip on the place released, filed in the pages of memory. High forest ride. Through Lisseuil to Chateauneuf-les-Bains. Green clothed fishermen walk towards a day's sport. River edge ride experiences the final roars of the Gorges de la Sioule, exchanged for a long ascent through woodland to forest. Every tick of freewheel squander three days ago now repaid on the granny gear. The forest climb must be 350m (1000ft) of winding bends. Motorcycle convoy lean the cleaved forest curve in upward procession. Near the top they are stopped, maps open talking amongst themselves.

"Bonjour et bon courage!" Amused at my slow two wheeled comparative.

Cold wind St Gervais de-Auvergne. Village main street holds the road train fun fair ready to open for the evening. The village youth hang around in groups amongst music boom colourful rides, airbrushed cartoon and fantasy art guaranteeing fearful scream excitement. In contrast, for the cyclist supermarket excitement open to fuel a hilltop rollercoaster ride. I come out arms loaded throwing away packaging, fitting things in any available gap. The caloric overflow is tied across the handlebars. Much is carried. It is the weekend. Food famine into the rural unknown is likely to include Monday shop door 'Desolé Fermé.'

D531 sign 'Lac de Fades.' High farmland drops more than rises. View back into Gorges de la Sioule's forest rock sides. La Siouve. A few houses and farms. Cars in a field rot overgrown turned green by encroaching nature. An auberge displays a colourful quilt dangling out of the upstairs window. Old tractors rust brown in long grass, muddied machinery parked. A shining car. Ribbons tied for a wedding, looking out of place against the hardness of oil stained engines of agriculture.

Road drop brake squeeze, gorge view. Impressive iron framework of Viaduc de Fades supported on two great tapering stone pillars over 90m(300ft) high carrying horizontal framework of girdered diagonal bracing high over the gorge. Down halfway a junction. Narrow road crosses a barrage retaining a lake powering hydroelectric turbines. The River Sioule release at a controlled rate. Riding the top of the dam looks over a 45degree boulder mass holding captive millions of tonnes of water.

Placard information details the construction of the iron rail bridge designed by Gustave Eifel. 132m (400ft) high and a length of 468m(1400ft) made it the highest rail bridge in Europe upon past centuries completion. Wild rock contours. Across the manmade lake riding a bridge just above water level. An awkward view of calm water ending high into space. A liquid horizon of foreground.

From trees glides a black kite. Wing feather spread fingers, the bird sails upward in slow spiral. The only expended effort the movement of the tail. Higher and higher betraying the presence of three others appearing near unnoticeable black altitude dots.

Broom grows from rock fissure. Lone café empty. People in walking clothes gaze in admiration at grey water breeze. Rock lines parallel, sediment captive in the cliff face, fir trees try to grow. The bike starts to slow. I go down the gears feeling if the brakes are on. I look over the handlebars to check the brakes are not stuck, everything looks alright. A look behind shows I have been climbing. The horizontal lines in the rock strata rise with the gradient of the road. An illusion of flatness.

Coiled bend shattered granite. Tree density green climbing bends to windy hill agriculture. Breaks in toneless cloud. Sun leaks through holes lighting yellow pools of flower meadow. Young cows lay around a tree momentarily illuminated bright. St-Priest-du-Champs. Familiar farming, no one around, looking for directions to a waterfall. Main road junction. I have missed it.

D987. Going up. Going down. Going south. Road villages, great stacks of piled firewood weathers grey in cold waving green. Signs for Miremont. Main road to Pontaumur.

In a field gateway an animal with fur looking the same texture and colour of a coconut doormat. It is the size of a medium dog, squat and strong looking with short legs, small boney tusks and slab head with a pig snout. A boar. Roadkill laid on its side, all life gone. It is a wild animal belonging alongside the deer, fox and the extinct wolf. Living difficultly in the ever strangled pockets of wild land felled, turned, planted, cultivated fenced, landscaped, concreted. Ever hunted with a gun or bludgeoned by the motor vehicle and still managing to increase its number.

Dusty walled Laschamps. Downhill to unremarkable Pontaumur. A hint of the south in its simple buildings. Camping sign directs to the back of a sports complex next to the little running river Sioulet. The Accueil closed. A strange little campsite. Caravans greened by algae, a place where everybody knows each other. Conversing dull unanimated, staring at the interloper, weighing him up, but never venturing to make conversation. Hot shower. Food is cooking, laying in my sleeping bag to keep warm, outside it's getting colder. The evening in and out of sleep. Last look at the watch 11pm.

68 km

Puy de Dome Monts Dore

The cockrel's repetitive call at 6.30am sends me under the sleeping bag for two more hours. I check the closed Accueil at 9.00am. Ready to leave at 9.30am. No lights, no presence behind the glass. I cannot hang around all day. Too bad. I leave the odd feeling site riding around the town looking for La Poste to send cards back to England.

Town feels half lost, maybe because it's Sunday. The fire station displays old shining fire engines. Further down the street cars from the 1950s and 1960s lined up. Proud enthusiastic owners and admirers pointing, discussing, walking around looking. Hands behind the back peering to interiors.

Leaving town, granny gear plod rising, empty main D941. Buildings exchanged for trees, shale rock higher and higher. A small car park, rucksacks ready for a woodland walk, the couple shout a smiling. "Bon courage!"

Sunday high village asleep. Cold wind downhill ride, the outskirts of Pontgibaud under the giant dead volcanocs of Puy de Come, planetary Chaine du Puys and spiked Puy de Dome.

Peage Route National. Clemont Ferrand /Puy de Dome. Little D25 points down through woods to hidden Pontgibaud accompanied by a small babbling River Sioule. Old buildings, stone pillars. Tourist pretty and just in time for the roller shutter dropping on the last midday shop.

Country lane wander. The River Sioule accompanied by a railway line. Climbing look back views to the shrinking river followed for many miles. A few houses called Mazaye look to the Chaine du Puys. Farmland to Chapille, steep climb to the quiet village of Ceyssat. Thoughts of last year's storm. Villages and hamlets rural lonely, lost in volcanic surroundings. Clermont Ferrand city buzz the other side of Puy de Dome.

Puy de Dome lava flows look to still flow grey and gloopy through green smother forest. The weather station summit a waiting lunar rocket. Rack railway makes a helter skelter coiled scar clear defined under fleeting sun in cold blowing wind.

The great tower of volcanic rock a remnant. Only half remains after blowing up when lava solidified blocking the volcanic chimney. Internal pressure blew out the mountainside leaving the giant spike on one side and a collapsed pudding the other.

The D52 Montmeyre chateau climb. I stop to eat and admire distant snow topped Monts Dore giving determination for today. Concentration broken by an amused family walking past.

"Bon appetite."

I am caught chewing yesterday's elasticated rubber baguette, spooning on a jar of jam. A heathen cyclist meal.

Plantation forest permanent climb. No sky, no people. Branches, boughs, trunks surround. A few singing birds, roaring wind amongst high creaking fir. Wide churned tracks lead from great tree trunk stacks the size of several houses sitting at the side of the road. Pine resin smell blows all around. The climb feels to go on forever. Endless trees do not distract the mind with any view.

A stoat is running down the road in arcing bounds. Stopping for a second, examining me. I am too big for the fearsome little rodent to attack. Deciding on caution it bounds into the undergrowth. Between trees, tall forested volcano view. The cone of Puy de Monchier. I am taken around its green spherical mass tower. Into cold wind at Col de la Moreno 1065m (3100ft). There is café. Thoughts of warmth. No lights, door sign. 'Fermé'. Long downhill. Waterproof zipped, hood up. Cold hands squeeze chilling metal brake levers. Puy Laschamps great volcanic hill forested. High far panoramic views into land forever. Speeding eye watering chill, wind blows hard gusts, heavy bike resists the battering. It all ends at a roundabout stopping in map study. A couple ride a tandem. Accents English.

D216(D27) Orcival. Another freewheel. All climbing effort squandered ends crossing a stream hardly worth a look. Yesterday it took a mighty dam to hold back the millions of tons of water. Today half hour spent carrying small stones could block the re acquaintance with trickling River Sioule that will roar through a gorge before feeding the Allier and in turn La Loire.

Climbing resumes. "Bon courage!" Is shouted by a man with a newspaper under arm.

I stop for a drink, bike leaning against the door of a carpentry workshop. Windows dusted, machinery silent. Work waits for Monday or maybe Tuesday. A view journeyed shows the Chaine du Puys far. Blued without detail. A feeling of travelled distance.

Upward twisting bends, stream gurgle next to the road. Sheep with the strangest bleat graze the hillside. Land colour deepened. Grass darker, trees black coniferous, steep fields divide to small valleys. White cattle contrast against high land. Farm isolation, clustered buildings marooned lonely in deep cold landscape.

Road grips steep hillside. Strong gusts, needle rain squall

vision squint. Below road level the pretty village of Orcival. Heavy slate rooftops over black volcanic stone gables. Dominating octagonal church spire under steep deep green pasture. Pockets dark deciduous woodland, the blackness of high fir smother. Horizon domination. Towering green, rounded volcanic mountain of Puy d l'Aiguiller.

Ascending landscape altitude barren, soft tree shape lost to fir. Blue breaks intensify land colour. Overhead grey race, charging giant moving shadows across steepened landscape under bald gaze of Puy d l'Aiguiller. The road pass scars a steep hillside bending with mountain contour. Sharp heavy rain squall hits the road. I grip the bars to fight the wind's attempt to throw me off. Grey curtain rain veil. Tail end silvered in hard sunshine glare chases the squall off the mountain. Two spectacular mountain rock towers. Solidified volcanoes of grey imposition. Far down tiny silver ribbon road. Little house roofs shine wet on winding bends.

On the nearest volcanic spike two figures hardly definable near the top. I lose sight of them as I ride around a bend. Re appearing, the two insect sized figures standing on the summit giving perspective to immensity of size. Two mountain conquerors survey their rock landscape. The descent not so gracious on all fours, bouncing backsides cautiously down rock ridge precipitous narrow wet path.

Bends lead to rock woodland, road clings tight to mountainside, an imposing view of the two towers. There is a path. I leave the bike and run down to a ledge with a drop off stepping down hundreds of feet through trees and rock spikes to a distant valley. A climbers dream. Long slow overhangs, vertical stone mass steps on wooded ledge repeat. A climb of twenty church spires waits.

Bend ride. Viewing area. Roche Tuilliere to the left growing from the forest floor. A mass of long rectangular basalt pillars. Tall stacks fused together rise to make the rock mountain singular volcanic chimney. Roche Sandorie is to the right. Multi chimney volcanic peak, huge solidified vertical slabs. Lava river flow cleaves tree mass.

The conquerors four limbed retreat no longer observable. Rain returns sweeping the valley in a curving sheet painting all colour grey.

Motorcyclists ride in. Headlights dazzle, side stands. Engines stop.

Where I am from. Etc. Parting with "Bon route, et bon courage!"

Bend crests Col de Guéry 1268m (3800ft). Cold treeless green moonscape surrounds Puy Corde drifting in and out of view through swirling cloud wind silence. Lone restaurant. Grey Lac Guéry static monochrome fishermen. Snow crag black mountain summit momentarily appears through blanket swirl. Cloud fingers trail silent across the road. Ephemeral vapour grey mystery bends deliver below cloud level to a world of solid objects. Long hill descends over the compact ski town of Le Mont Dore. Domes, spires, slate roofs. 70's blocks of flats rise between. Beyond. Valley dead end upward sweep. Snow covered black mass jagged peaks of Puy de Sancy and Puy Ferrand cloaked in spectral shroud. Fleeting views to the precipitous perched ski station and cabled lift gantries stuck into the mountainside as cocktail sticks. Cold embrace windy town wet streets. Two camping options. One uphill. Municipal sign points downward. I take the lazy option coming in to a car park with a high chainlink fence running down a steep sided hill. One side tarmac, the other terraced. Motorhomes and caravans jammed. Part campsite, part refugee zone. Accueil 'Fermé.'

A pitch between tyres and towbars. Tent duties, down to the sanitaires with soap and towel finds a coded door lock. The French pensioners will not give me the number, just cold frowning looks pulling the door quickly shut. Do I pack up and go to the other site? I go up to the Accueil peering through the window for the code to find it is on the inside of the door looking out the glass at me. 369A not very imaginative. All the digits lined on the lock reflect the ambience. The door opens to the soft embrace of a heated world. Tepid shower slow warm. Outside temperature just above freezing. The blue tarpaulin groundsheet becomes a storm cover over the tent protecting from anything. In the darkness rain and wind squalls batter. I wear every layer of clothing in the sleeping bag. It's difficult to retain any warmth. Rain pelting the tent sounds solid. Sleet and snow.

68 km

Sleet squalls unrelenting. Flapping awning beat, loud crash crescendo. Tension and shivering from losing body heat. 2am. Checking the tent pegs in a lull between freezing squalls pelting the tent. Ground crunches crisp icy.

Crawling down the sleeping bag, head inside a wooly hat waiting for the night to end. I wake at 9am from many short strange dreams the nighttime mind conjures when comfort and ease are compromised.

Noises of people walking past. Daylight. Vehicles moving. Rain showers softer. I am glad the night is over. Fuzzed head and unrested stiff body need a couple of deepened breaths to motivate a pack up. Breakfast from town will save time.

Pushing the bike up the hill stopping at the Accueil. Opening the door to a wall of warmth. The place busy with several conversations in differing language at once. Waiting my turn for counter space to pay for the night's accommodation. No one had any idea I was resident. Causing a little confusion.

"Am I paying for the coming night?"

"No. For last night, now I am leaving."

"So you are not paying for this night?"

"No, for last night."

Bewilderment.

I must simplify the conversation. "How much is one night please?"

The polite lady tells me. I give the pitch number, pay and leave the motorhome shanty town of Camping municipal de Crouzets. The experience municipal functional. That's all.

Cycling wet shining roads, over a little river of no consequence. The infant River Dordogne!

Ski resort streets, concrete rises multi storey amongst black volcanic stone hotels. Ski shops out of season share window space equipping the randonneur doubling seasonal trade. Le Mont Dore is a well-kept town surrounded on three sides by snowy mountain rock to a dead-end valley from which the black volcanic rock ridges of Puy de Sancy rise with the snow covered cable station looking over. An impressive cliff top waterfall cascades freefall. Opposite ridge tall rocky needle looms high over Le Monts Dore.

Boulangerie warmth buys bread and savouries. Fruit pastried sweetness late breakfast. Next stop. Postcards and European stamps. The man behind the counter looks at me quickly, then again with sideways eyes. I pay with a 20Euro note, he gives me change from 10Euro. I point out his mistake. He feigns blankness and surprise.

"C'etait le vingt billet. Monsieur. La. Vingt." Pointing over the counter at the note given sat in the till.

"Oh!" Laughing, pretending he is away with the fairies in

his busy shop of just myself and him. Game up. Don't take me for a witless tourist.

He hands over the extra 10Euros, I leave. I have wandered around most of the town without an excuse to stay.

Main street rise. Pharmacy tells me at 11.45am the last week in June, the temperature has risen to a balmy 8 degrees C. Cascade rumble drops behind buildings. Road signs for Besse-St-Annastaise. No road number junction climbs fast high over the town. Shrinking building view, the granny gear plod. A sign proclaims. 'Tour de France' climb to 'Col de Croix St Robert.' I look away from gradient/ distance information. Road snakes steep, near vertical hillside. River tumble ends in cascade. On the steep climb my waterproof is off, as the gradient eases its back on to banish blowing chill. Aeroplane view across Puy Gros. Hairpins up through woodland. Famous roadriders names sprayed onto the tarmac. Out of the bends, winding cow pasture. The first brown horned Cantal cows in pleasant cowbell ring. Twisting road, dull grass plateau. Farm buildings alpine, roll down a hill. Behind the grazing herd land falls vertical. Across thin air. Rising black stone and snow of Puy de Sancy, dusted white peaks of Chambourguet and Le Capucin. Tree blocked view, amongst forest trunks, campsite entrance. It must have been so cold there last night in freezing cloud. I had the better option. Road pass barrier raised, snow poles yellow and black guide the roadside. With the blowing cold they may still be needed.

Above the tree line, views to the cable station surrounding rocky peaks. Cloud mood lifts swirl grip showing summit height. Cascade drops out of mountain raw and beautiful falling through black rock crevasse. Snow fingers refuse to melt. Single lonely sound, the wind blows a wavering tone. Deep cleave through great rocky cliffs fall out of sight. Above. Bare green dome austere, shared between ice and scree. Summit envelope. Speeding milky rolling silence.

A stony track fenced by grey weather worn wood posts rises mist veiled to a cabin closed up from the winter. Turquoise! Turquoise dyed sheep graze. Bright blue hillside bleat in blowing colourless mist.

No one is here. Roadriders names painted on the tarmac. 'Gesou' 'Contador' and a tribute. 'R.I.P. FIGNON.' For Laurent Fignon, twice Le Tour champion sadly gone. The road fittingly ascends straight into cloud.

Fenced roadside ascending bends. Sign on a post. Col de la Croix St. Robert 1451m (4300ft) surrounded by stubborn snow defiant of season. Tough climb delivers breathtaking views of barren height.

Through the first bend. I stop leaning the bike to drink and eat. Putting on my warm fleece ready for the freewheel chill. Waterproof top is zipped, only the eyes look out to stop heat loss. A white van slows, the driver wears blue bib and brace overalls and a beret. A weatherbeaten face looks out of the window and the farmer asks if I am ok.

I thank him.

With a wave he is gone.

Ahead. A great domed ridge barren green sweeping and rocky, twisting, running to distance fade. Piles of fallen scree streaks downward from many millenniums of snow melt and hard wind erosion. Sparse green broken by expanse of black fir forest. Small areas of light move across steep landscape. Sun pierces holes through the cloud. Rough lands illuminated by golden shafts of light. Vivid islands race the barren hillside.

Below pockets of trees, a bald domed hill. Winding road looks to disappear into thin air. Far to Lac Chambon. Lakeside Chambon-sur-Lac village surrounded by black forest. Over the lake towers a great volcano with a summit fortress built square and solid. Volcanoes and forested hills fade to lower land. Horizon rises faraway hazed. Grey hills of the Livradois.

Sweat from the climb chilled to the skin by the cold blowing wind. Bike descends many hairpins, views roll off the hillside. Air drop far to forest land below. Cold metal brake levers fast numb the fingers. The village of Moneaux under stone volcano chimney. New houses, old houses retrieved from dereliction. The village blur dropping at speed, forest and rock crag wild green steepness. Mountain stream weaves the valley. Into softened flowering meadow of alpine colour. Behind woodland and forest grows the snowy mountain of Puy de Sancy. Cathedral towers of basalt stand in receding winter's snowfield. Scant mountainside waits for sun.

Broom fragrant ride rises the side of a valley. Lone chalet restaurant feeds coachload diners. Restaurant window gawp, cutlery glint. Mouths busy chewing.

Across steepening hillside. Views back to a road travelled. Belvedere is signed. I stop, walk up to the rock viewpoint, a far down last look at this special area of raw beauty. High green desolate domed peaks, giant rock amongst forest. Three black kites ascend in spiral, wingtips outstretched.

Ninety degree road turn, deep woodland flat ride.

"Bonjour." Randonneurs out for a long day of woodland paths.

Into a different world, softer feeling protected under green bough shelter centuries old. Downward. Farming village four wheel drives. Spud tyres, ropes slung around the bumper, winches and cab spotlights. Tractors parked outside the front door, new piled firewood winter anticipation. Dropping weaving bends away from Monts Dore. Medieval cité walls of Besse-et-St-Anastaise.

Black volcanic stone block, arched town gate under octagonal heavy slated tower, the hanging bell, short spire imposing entrance. Cobbled narrow streets open to the town square. Fountain spouts a running chime. Cafés and restaurant tabled customers brave the chilly day. People wander under old grey stone and facades of render. Red floral decoration soft contrasts the dark grey. Little craft and clothing shops blend restrained. Nothing out of character amongst shuttered window shelter deep in stone. Thick oak doors arched tops, sized wide and squat from centuries past when people were smaller. A Notre Damme of stone high in a niche on the corner of a street looks upon Sunday sightseers.

A lady stops me. "Where have you come from?"

Her husband arrives wanting to know of today's journey.

D978 for Super Besse. Long climb, getting off the road for a slow rumbling coach to pass. Too hot for a fleece or waterproof, too cold in the wind for just a cycling top. Long pull eases. Flattening roll to a junction. D149. Tall snow dappled Puy Chambourguet dominates the skyline. Ski lift gantries hang, a sign for Super Besse points steep to a long hill. I decline. Plan stays south to the Cantal Mountains. The perfect round crater lake of Lac Pavin. Without signs for a lakeside camp. It's too cold in the wind for a volcano swim. Road follows river direction. Easy gradient leaves behind the climb. I have no idea where I will be stopping this evening. Words in the head say. 'Trust in the road.' Bend views to new lands.

The Cantal Mountains. High, part snow covered and too distant for today. The road drops, drops for miles, speed 50kmph constant. Campsite sign crossed out. Main road through Egliseneuve. Climbing through a village street sparse of people. Thick forest. Descending fast. Long sweeping bends pushes big gear speed. Lorry noise behind cannot get enough momentum to pass. I leave it behind on every bend. On a straight it catches me. Waving it past easing on the brakes until it has overtaken. Thanks from the driver. Fast pace green blur. Speeding past a turning for Condat. Handmade camping sign, a picture of a motorbike taped to a post. I follow it down the main road. Hard braking around a surprise roundabout.

Condat spills up a hill under black forested shelter. Sign points along a flat road out into countryside. Campsite entrance, wheeling to the door. The Patron arrives in her car, opens the Accueil and books me in. I buy chocolate causing comment amusement. The place happy and relaxed. The husband is busy getting a caravan ready for the season. Stopping work to greet me with a handshake and a smile. People naturally so friendly and happy.

I am told if the weather gets bad I am welcome to sleep in the function room. There is even a bed! Help yourself.

The place is so cheap. I have a field with soft meadow view. Horses behind a fence graze between moments of chasing play. Wild flowers, the bee buzz. Solitary tree surrounded by long grass sway. The bike leans against a handy tree. A couple nearby speaking French are English. Geology surveyors from Dorset. Here for walking, tomorrow headed for Puy Mary. If the snows allow.

Horses galloping play into the evening. Weak soft warm sunshine, many birds echo song from woodland. Underfoot, abrasive grasshoppers rasp a challenge tune. Dropping altitude brings a rising of temperature. Sleep comes easy in the cosy surroundings of Condat.

64 km

Cantal Mountains

The thumping through the ground of horses galloping and playing wakens. Daylight. Stillness. Fresh early morning air, an owl is calling from the woodland. Reasoning an owl is nocturnal I bury my head in warm comfortable sleeping bag.

Mist blanks the top of fir forested hill. Sun pools illuminate wild flower long meadow grass. Horses continue their play. From their nostrils exhaled vapour steams. Gold sun leaf shadow flicker across the tent, drying the day with soft warm breeze. Daily pack. Wheeling through the site thanking the owners for the stay. Conversation and humour leaving Camping la Boire Basse Condat.

Long street volcanic stone buildings finds daily bread. Roundabout. D697 climbs to a lake. Lac de Moines overlooked by a sleeping hotel surrounded in soft green woodland. Little gorge tumbles the River Santoire compressed between wooded cliffs. The black and white of a bird with a vibrant red crown flies between trees in dipping flight making an alarm cry. The spotted woodpecker beautiful, is not as vocal as its green relative.

Road split. D16 stone arch crossing. Rapids fall across rock slab tamed silent through deep black pools under woodland overhang. Trunks splintered lay season marooned on an island bought down in flood amongst large round worn washed boulders. Old road woodland climb. Easy gradient making height over the river. Background deep roar water echoes the valley. Into full daylight. Outcrops of granite cliff gaze down. Between rock, vibrant green new bracken curl. Broom fills the lungs with fragrance splashing the hillside in random strokes of yellow. Large flowering rock daisies glow amongst purple flowers. Buttercups hide the cricket chirp. Gentle climb, old roads made for animal powered transport moving at human pace. Not for the internal combustion engine slamming up through a speed crave gearbox.

Fields, livestock, twenty chiming cowbells of different pitch. Brown Cantal ladies stare nosey from their elevated field. Nowhere is the land level, sides of the opening valley slant topped by rolling hill. Silhouetted hilltop cable cars hang motionless out of season, supporting gantries lined cross the top of a hill. Cable pulley block resembles a waiting gibbet.

The river has lost its roar, the widened valley has tamed it slow moving tranquil. Cattle wander the bright green to drink a sky mirror pool. Magic ends in modern busy D3. Signed Murat, Puy Mary and Pas de Peyrol. Familiar names bring good feeling.

Under watchful Chapel de Valentine brown chiming cows graze. Volcano climb. Contours reveal valley village colours nestled in green alpine meadow suede. Multicoloured flower spill, harsh darkened tone snow patched rock mass. The long view valley shortens, mountain perspective change. Green sign. The road passes are open.

Behind. A panorama travelled. Rolling green domes, little buildings lost in sweeping landscape. Faraway horizon black Monts Dore white snow summit peaks.

Col d'Entremont downhill speeding ride towards Murat. Stone wall chapel lone on a hilltop, incredibly old. Roundabout layby. A path to the top of a green black volcanic hill where

Notre Damme d'Auvergne looks over a sheer drop to the grey rooftops of Murat. The white cast iron statue wears a golden crown holding the infant holding out both his arms in open welcome. Cantal Mountain spectacle. Forested domes and ridges, snow patched peak mountain range. A walk back from the windy pinnacle to the bike. Steep drop to the familiar. Past the supermarket through potholed industrial land to the tranquil river entrance of Camping municipal Stavalos.

Why here again? It is a good central base to explore the Cantal Mountains. The town beautiful has drawn me to wander its streets. A visit to the friendly Accueil. Pitching in sunshine. Chores of washing. Eating heartily soaking up the special ambiance under green mountain gaze.

39 km

Into town looking to buy a warm fleece for the cold nights, waiting for a randonneur shop to open. A compromise between thickness for warmth and thinness for storage.

A walk around the grey and black stone streets to the dominating church at the top of town. Notre Damme keeps watch from her volcanic summit. The peacefulness of the church, great canvas oil paintings, chandeliers and an altar of gold with marble pillars each side with niches. The tradition of a 'dressed doll' Notre Damme. Stained glass art more pictorial, telling a story rather than single figures and patterns of the north. Blue faced Mary holds a blue faced infant, both dressed peppermint green. Sun illuminates every window casting coloured shadows of red, blue and yellow across stone floor. A separate chapel contains a long listed name memorial of two plaques. The heading:- *A Ses Déportés Des Juin 1944.*

Twisting lane old buildings built tough. Roof slates of volcanic rock slab give cover immovable by hard winter gales.

Maison du Tourisme offers leaflet insight about the déportés. There is an exhibition on what happened. The leaflet is enough.

On the 12th June 1944 the occupying army lead a police operation on Murat, suspicious of people helping members of the resistance who the SS found living on Rue de Bonnevie. As a reprisal on the town, twelve days later Murat was encircled, many houses were burned out and looted. Three hundred inhabitants of Murat were rounded up and deported to Germany to the concentration camp Neuengamme. The town must have been emptied.

'Maison de la Faune.' A place dedicated to stuffed local wildlife, a building of round stone towers with conical witch hat roofs.

Supermarket shutters drop for dejeuner. A bag full of food and fruit for a lazy afternoon looking at tomorrow's route over the remains of Europe's super volcano. A motorhome arrives on English plates. I am watching the man attempting to plug in an electric hook up.

He comes over saying. "No..... 'Lectric... No. o. o. Lec... Tric." In a northern England accent.

I answer in English to his relief. The only thing I carry electrical is a camera charger. So we try it. Nothing. I tell him to go to the Accueil with his pitch number. He comes back and the lady from the Accueil follows with a fuse to put in the box.

"Ee we dont do it like that at 'ome."

Things are done as they are done.

"Still don't do it like that at 'ome."

I am asked to do some translating by the French lady. In simple words it is understood.

The lady returns to the Accueil. Hopefully not too

traumatised by the vocal man who is soon telling me he is from Costa del Salford and 'Born to ave it ard.'

Once the facade melts they are the kindest friendly couple. Making tea, talking and laughing about the different places visited. Narrowboat leisure exchanged for an easier managed motorhome. The lady has difficulty walking very far. The chap has not long had a heart bypass operation and keeps suffering from bouts of memory loss. Here they are in the start of southern France, having navigated all the way down to Murat on D roads. The summer to spend travelling together and unable to speak a word of French..... '& proud of it!'

The braying donkey alarm echoes over town. Cold through the tent penetrates the sleeping bag. Temperature just above freezing. The extra fleece has kept the body warm enough to sleep. Sun throws the heat switch bathing the field in glowing warmth. Beads of condensation hang on the inside sheet of the tent. A reach out to light the stove for tea, an act of self bribery to rise.

Misted campsite soft gold haze, calm newness of fresh morning will soon turn to harsh day colour. My Salford friend walks past as the tent is rolled, a few minutes of relaxed talking. Maybe they will visit Puy Mary today. They will definitely stay here for a couple of days, liking the ambience. I leave at 9am with fond farewells and a wave.

Patron wishes "Good journey." Au revoir Camping Stavalos.

Into town to the randonneur/sport shop to purchase a 'fireliner' for the sleeping bag. The place yet to open at 9.30am, still closed at 9.40am. Waiting time is up. No purchase is something less to carry.

Campsite glimpse, the English couple's motorhome shrunk in an empty field. N122 rise between forested hillsides.

Village amongst the trees, slate spire glint. Forest vertical, high imposing cliff, further forest takes the sky. Rising bare green splashed yellow under grey rock peak volcano.

Signed 'Laveissiére.' Country lane relief from harsh speeding N route traffic. Softened pace amble weaves a few houses. Fraisse-le-Bas. Two motorcycle cops have a radar gun aimed at motorists on the N122. One gets on his bike double quick with excited speech to chase after someone speeding.

Pretty Lavoisier. Campsite, an épicerie, pretty church under mass near vertical forest. Road through Fraisse-le-haut delivers back to main road traffic.

On the white line, behind when the verge widens. Road steepens, pace slows to the granny gear. Lorry overtakes slow, struggling. Engine roar, shudder and whine tries to find a gear to climb alpine forest. Cascade tumble steep over smooth brown rock, watery speeding sheet disappears under the road in a tunnel. Snow poles of altitude. Above fir. Rocky peak snow cover.

Tacky ski resort of Li-Lorian. Ski lifts silent, season finished. Empty crummy functional concrete apartment buildings to package winter fun seekers. Road tunnel swallows vehicle tail light procession through the mountain. For bicycles it is upward on a little used old road. Ski resort. Super Li-Lorian. Rows of chalets surround large closed ski station. Sharp bend climb. Cable lifts, high volcanic craggy snowed peaks. Cable rise across steep slope. Rock and melting snow, empty ski station summit. Icy whistle sliced by steel cable, empty chair wind swing.

Forest hill bends. Cleared forest grows concrete ski accommodation and spa hotel sprawl removing the joy of a wild mountaintop. Replaced with the disappointment of finding a town planning blunder squatting on a famed beauty spot. Col de Cere 1249m (3700ft). New favorable panorama unfolds.

The ski station at the summit of Super-Li-Lorian rises to the dominating mountain of Plomb du Cantal. Mountain spike of Puy Griou skyward from high steep ridge. Black fir forest roll to velvet green cling of high meadow. Sun hazed far below valley runs lush green flanked by high volcanic landscape. Lower slope villages and farms amongst flowing meadow edged in forest. Thin line road corkscrew descent.

360degree panorama of steepness. Stone hut high on a hillside, ancient shepherd shelter. Volcano dome part velvet green part forested, steep crater depression no longer spouts fire. Sides of the volcano drop sheer. Forest falls into featureless black shade. Road spiral downward. Junction reunites N122 delivering traffic from subterranean insides of the Li Lorian mountain road tunnel. New tunnel old tunnel rail tunnel keeps transit possible, bypassing season's frozen altitude.

Downward traffic procession. St-Jaques-des-Blats, looking for a turning over the volcano ridge down to Vallee de Jordanne. One road crosses the steepness. Small narrow lane, the sign faces oncoming traffic. Starting steep, crossing a stream. Turning behind the village. Sharp climb over roofs, houses shrink into big landscape. Single track ancient communication between two valleys. Harsh seasons road wear. Loose gravel makes the arduous climb interesting. Back wheel spin, pushing hard, the upward crawl. I put enough effort through outstretched legs and locked arms to repeatedly lift the front wheel, even with the front loaded. It is steep.

Sunshine illuminates. Colour warmed land. Birds chirp about the fine day. Clouds of small white puffy cumulus race stretching twisting tumbling. High mountain ridge hides the wind. Engine drone louder. Car climbs the bumpy narrow lane. I pull over, watching it disappear around a bend re appearing high above in opposite direction. The upward road reward, views back up to Plomb du Cantal. Shared with Puy Mary make the remnant periphery crags of a super volcano blowing up over ten thousand years ago. Meadow flower, chirping grasshoppers, swathes of broom send fragrant waft. Land sweeps steep to impressive pointed Puy Griou cliff summit surrounded by clinging grey tumbled scree.

Climbing on the lowest gear wishing for another, gradient refuses to ease until far above the valley floor. The company of chiming cowbells. Steep sunny green fields, crickets in flowering roadside verge. Steep wooded volcanic peak of L'Elancéze topped with a stone lava chimney. Castle ramparts to a fantasy fortress.

Ancient stone roofs of farms patched and mended overhang weathered stone livestock buildings drowning amongst the green. The diesel engine and power line the only intrusion to a scene that could be a thousand years old. Black kite draws air circles, the opportunist vulture persona. Low gear grind around the cone of L'Elancéze, new elevation view turns cone shape triangular. Woodland surround green world climb until light permeates between tree trunks. Top of the mountainous ridge. Sign 'Col des Perthus' Alt. 1309m (4500ft).

The reward for the climbing. Breathtaking valley panorama takes the whole human vision to comprehend. Big scenery high above to Puy Pere Arse, Puy Mary, Pas de Peyrol. Tiny plastic motorhome crawls under the commanding summit of Puy Mary. Crag summit and steep grey mountain cliff elevation sweep. Distant sloping velvet meadow village of Mandaillers. Surrounding mas farms lost specs in green vibrance. Mountain ridge as far as can be seen. Below runs the Vallée de la Jordanne. I leave the bike and walk a hillside footpath to sit and study the view listening to the wind carrying the cowbell chime.

A mountain bike leans against a van, the owner sat enjoying lunch. I watch him put down his plate, get up and look at my bike and its carried load. He stands there for a couple of minutes absorbed before returning to his chair. A nod in greeting.

Away through wild woodland, rock and cowbell. Steep hill, sharp bends. Brakes squeezed tight. Cables don't part! Hill gradient 20%. 30% on the bends. The bike would run out of control in a second.

Stone barns of many centuries. Heavy cut stone arched entrance on gable ends, the steep pitched roofs of red rusting corrugated iron finish ground level to cope with harsh snows.

Long hairpin ride. Bottom of the hill amongst the rooftops of Mandailles. Sign points for camping. A beautiful place to spend a few days using it as a base for cycling or walking to Puy Mary. Opposite direction Aurillac to follow the Vallée de la Jordanne. Narrow road, valley countryside, drop down returns to a level ride. Roadriders pass in opposite direction for the mountain ascent. High cliff sweeps the valley skyward rolling out of sight.

Big gears bring speed. Look back view of the Cantal Mountains. Valley turn ends the spectacle. Volcanic chimneys and cliffs lack majestic size. Sunny valley crater lake offers water's edge wagon accommodation. Village blurred at speed, bumps in the road, a bike airborne. Houses, traffic busy Aurillac.

Municipal campsite signed. Roundabout. Two minute ride. The entrance of a spacious campsite. Accueil closed until 4.30pm. Pitch and shower. Wise early day finish. Other campsites on the map too far for today. The Accueil opens. Skipping news in the local paper finds Le Meteo. The weather forecast. Fine weather, maybe rain or high humidity on Saturday.

Quiet Camping de l'Ombrade Aurillac. Sun yellowed evening. Tea boils while finches chirp from overhead bough.

Laugh of the green woodpecker betrays its flight. It is a lot warmer than Murat. Convection clouds build high cotton billow, fueled by the warmer radiating land heat of lower altitude. A man wanders by smoking a pipe in quiet contentment, the sweet aromatic smell of pipe tobacco hangs in the air. Ambling past with his waddling dog.

He bids "Bonsoir."

I am in agreement.

60 km

9am ride to the old part of town. Narrow lanes, old buildings lean against each other in aged slumber. Black oak overhang. Half-timbered ancient street. Large church is under restoration. No cars tolerated in the old part of town. A few people on their way to work. Others in unhurried conversation, baguette under the arm rolled newspaper in hand.

Further along, the music boom from a little alternative clothes shop yet to see a customer. Shops unoccupied, dusty windows. piled post on the floor. Posters pasted on windows advertise events long past.

I open a boulangerie door. Laughter between the generations exchanged between oven and counter. Fresh baking smells, radiated oven warmth fills the shop. Bread warm crisp, a few things for the day.

Next town needed, Arpajon.' Without the knowledge of how I will get there. Unhurried look for direction road number clue. Shop front ride bumper to bumper, old town changed to city, street jump of two centuries. Bustling traffic blur, tall glass reflects lines of buses. Overhead a passenger jet lines up low, the silver turbine scream rumble prepares for landing. One way systems and cycle lane squeeze under diesel din. Pedestrian and driver intent on destination, intent to time. The gain of modern efficiency stampedes over the soul of humanity. The efficient western machine runs to the gigabyte millisecond. But for what final purpose? Lives are not infinite.

I need the compass. No road numbers. Direction without clear route. I need Arpajon-sur-Cere. It does not appear. I cut across town, taxis queue in apathetic wait outside La Gare. A superette lures me through the door to stock up. Today will be a long ride into foodshop emptiness. Leaving La Gare. Away from the power lines, fenced sidings. Lines of work dirtied goods wagons with all the weeds, litter, grease and rust of a railway yard. Ring road two lane traffic cram mad merry-go-round, bumper to bumper lorries, cars, rows of traffic lights and stop lines. Watching traffic joining and lanes changing and disappearing, watching direction signs, checking the compass. Patience rewarded with 'Arpajon-sur-Cere.' Bricolage land's' painted corrugated discount heaven advertise materialistic dreams 'lowest price' plastic moulded, cardboard packaged made in China, with easy parking. Fighting family cars and delivery trucks for road space. Battling the bumpers, hands cover the brakes in anticipation for the road cut off hard brake lights and the junction pull out.

D990 side street suburban quietness, an occasional lawnmower, smells of cut grass. Square perfect trimmed hedges recede, countryside ascent to the village of Vézacto's agriculture. Road climbs valley side, returning along the other gives view of the travelled road. Steep green valley, cliff face drop into darkness. No traffic. A feeling of altitude ascending through the smart village of Carlat. Built under long volcanic cliffs, large gaping cave mouths of darkness in rock face curve. Above the village Notre Damme. Big Mary watches everything. Black volcanic stone church Romanesque design, solid wall tower, four lined bells suspended from an opening. Black stone houses will last forever. Hipped chequette dormer roofs with a graceful sweep finished in a heavy slates.

Climbing hill contour panorama across volcanic domed tree covered hills folding one into the other. The tops cleared cultivated as fields styled on a monk's head. Green volcanic chimneys amongst. Wooden sign for camping points Ronesque. Freewheeling steep bends cross a stream, road climbs to Raulhac. A hillside farming village along a wide street. Nothing much seems to be happening today in Raulhac.

Steep country lane D990 green leafed tree tunnel. Aged tree trunks survey the centuries watching planted season's growing patchwork acreage. An old tractor is busy turning the cut grass of a field for drying. Canvas cab roof in faded tatters, a rusty vertical exhaust stack puffs away blue black smoke wheezing. Up and down the field, muddied front wheels lean outward, the vehicle's appearance of being worked to death.

Hilltop flattens through weaving agriculture, a small village. Colour of the building stone changed from black to brown signaling landscape change. I must be leaving the Volcans d'Auvergne.

In a field, three tractors work. One collects the dried cut meadow grass rolling it into bales while the next picks the bale up and places it on the third tractor where the bale is wrapped in black plastic. Feed for the cattle for their winter living sheltered in the cow shed.

Hedges, trees and rolling hills very much an English countryside ideal. Weather compliments. Black cloud blots the sun. A breezy shower, smell of summer rain evaporating from the warm road mixes the aroma of wet grass.

Pace increase, pretty village of La Capelle Barrés. Fast bend drop through tall forest steep hillside blur edged vertical. The smell of pine amongst the rock. A sharp bend, a bridge, the surface potholed and breaking up rattling slows pace. Flat road to long fast descent. St-Martin-sous-Vigaroux. I stop quick.

A red kite has just made a swoop dropping like a stone into the road verge. It is out of view but I can hear it grappling with lunch. I am not noticed for a few seconds, the young bird becomes aware of me and flies upward. Long wings flap a blur of rich chestnut red, just out of arms reach. It all happens too quickly for the camera, the experience a long term imprint on the memory.

St-Martin' is a village of smart little houses, round stone towers and a Romanesque church. Advert for camping. Bridge across a stream ascends woodland. The village under high volcanic cliff forested. Granny gear plod, altitude matches the cliff view, lost to dense green. Cowbells somewhere above, light penetrates the trees. Small green grass plateau of grazing cattle chiming in sunshine. Signs point back to St-Flour. Rougher higher land drops steady into Pierrefort. Cowtown boasts its own weighbridge and handy communal cattle crush in a special layby.

Pierrefort, a very old farming centre. Small town or large village, it is hard to say. Its name taken from the rock pinnacle in the middle of the hillside. A large house resides upon the top. The only gathering in the year, a one day beef festival advertised for next April. Poster mugshots of two year old cows waiting on death row for the festival. The occupation of leisure seems to be sitting on a roadside wall watching for the chance of passing traffic. Stares as I pass. My 'Bonjour' is met unregistered with a drooling gawp. The head slowly turns, the brain does not.

Cowtown climb. Tractors parked line both sides of the street. Outside of a large workshop Hydraulic oil trickles the gutter. A smell of diesel. Large flat tyres wait for fixing. Tractors propped on blocks. Noise of busy air tools, escaping hiss of compressed air from garage darkness. Zig zag escape climb. Signs direct for Murat. Plomb du Cantal road pass open. Still climbing. Under the strangeness of an English post war council estate complete with strewn rubbish plonked in the higher altitudes of France above an abattoir. A sign for a campsite. . . No.

High landscape hill climb. A yellow Toyota pick-up truck hammers down a straight toward the bend too fast. The brakes are on, the truck leans hard half on my side of the road. Wheels on my side barely make traction, suspension the furthest it can stretch. Other side wheels compressed hard into the arch. Tyre squeal, back end slide. If it crashes it will happen behind me. I hear nothing but the squeal. Whether it made the bend, or went through the fence plummeting the rooftops I care not.

How much further to climb? I must be at 1000m. There are no hills around. I am on the top of them. Wind. Cold views, far blue horizon. A corner, a sign. 'Col du Puy de Renel 1075m' (3100ft). The Cantal Mountains are the view. Grey rain showers cloak their appreciation.

Down fast for a long time. Climbing through forested fractured volcanic cliffs looking as blackened flint. D48 climbs into Neuvéglise. People, the place busy. Countryside peace hoping to keep my height. Climbing around a valley, the side nearly vertical. Trickling wet grass long, a vivid green never seen before. Steep field Climb. A Cantal horse. Muscular, brown with a white mane is busy grazing sharing the grass with a vocal donkey braying on my passing. The field above has a bad tempered horse stretching its neck, head up. Teeth gnash, wide eyed and snorting. Sharing the field with a passive grazing cow. Saddle the cow. Eat the horse!

Road ends at the village of Lavastrie prettily decorated with flowers. A steel mock up giant penny farthing bike is decorated with bloom, hanging baskets overflow growing colour. More cycle orientated floral cascades through the well-kept stone village. Directions point. 'Barrage de Grandval.'

Fields in their first cut for cattle feed, bale stack grows in size, machinery working together in dust cloud rise. Opportunist black kites. The vulture circle. Waiting for a meal darting from the diminishing long waving island fast becoming coverless stubble.

Steep lane views into a mass black forested valley disappearing vertical. I follow the downhill cleft into the centre of the earth. 300m (900ft), tight hairpin bends, silent gite habitations of Grandval. Locked gates of an EDF building. A painted blue hydroelectric turbine is displayed. Curved blades spiral toward its hub centre. The final bend. Barrage de Granval holds back an immense lake of silence. The millpool giant of modern scale drives turbines at the bottom of a 30m (100ft) concrete wall. Turbulent spin creates propeller wash equal to a ship. The hum of generated electricity from a power plant of glass insulators, cables, pylons and weird metal behind fenced buildings adds sinister buzz sound to the dam mass intrusive in natural surroundings. The dam feeds the natural river running black through rocky cliff Gorges de la Truyére. Regaining composure from human beaver concrete interference. Winding natural through steep cliffs spotted with growing pines changing to black forest high jagged skyline.

Lake serenity of early evening. Trees grow twisted from fragmented rock outcrop. Mirror black shapes over silent lake. Two fishermen in static concentration, acrobatic birds hunt insects over the water. Lakeside water chimes a gentle lap.

Across the dam, steep weaving darkened forest. River rumble glimpse through twisting gorge. Folded valley marks progress far distant. Horseflies nip on the long climb, annoying flies pursue trying to land in my eyes as I sweat pushing the pedals propelling toward the light. Above the forest, cowbell ring. Climb ease. Farm habitation, the little village of Fridefont.

Street football between the local youths, shouts of encouragement from watching children sat on a wall and along the path. Pretty place. Municipal campsite, small and empty.

D13 for St-Flour and Faverolles climbing away from the village. Buildings disappear, downhill ride, sweeping bends to a closed restaurant elevated. Panorama across the lake and rising distant landscape. 'Belvidére de Mallet.' Standing on the edge of a drop. Tranquil evening water, this great panorama without presence of another soul. Hills around the lake rise softer. Original gorge path contrasts steep and craggy, matching the landscape after the dam's release.

The body heavy with the day's hilly mileage. Speed blur trees to lakeside beach sailing boats. Low bridge spans the water to a weaving rocky road under cliffs. A silent watersports centre. Lone motorhome is tucked away for the evening. I have lost all the climbing. Another beckons up through woodland leaving the lake. Evening song birds for company, darkened tree cover, unmoving stillness, shafts of late summer light. Bend after bend follows hill contour climb. Forest release, rock and steep rising field. A sign. '5mins to Faverolles camping,' I reckon half an hour at least for a bike. An arrival for 7pm.

Silent empty road. Steep village Auriac-de-Favorolles. Agricultural vehicles betray village identity. A view above all surrounding hills. Church spire, rooftops of a village. A sign proclaims 'FAVOROLLES 978m' (2900ft). Downhill to the village. Caravan roofs. I follow the camping municipal sign to a site entrance through road works. A door at the top of the site is a bar and not the Accueil.

A kind barman looks out of the door. "The Accueil is

closed. Try the house to see if the Maire is in. Go down and find yourself a pitch."

The site full of static homes. Caravan permanence. People's ideas of wood deck and pallet wood improvement. Amongst boat trailers and outboard motors two pitches are free. I check the Accueil and knock the house door. No reply. It is 7pm when I pitch the tent. I get a deserved shower. Clean clothes rejoin acquaintance with social normality. Thinking how beautiful the days ride has been. But how many hills, how many big 500m-1000m hills? Sleep is not difficult.

65 hillometres.

Haut Loire and
The Beast of Gevaudan

The sign on the Accueil door. 'Ouvert 8am.' 10 minutes ago. I will have a wash, pack then return. 8.30am. Still closed. The tent is down and everything packed by 9am. The Accueil lights are on. I try the door to find it is locked. I knock, ring the bell and wait. Nothing. There are a lot of km to make today. I cannot hang around any longer. I don't run the place. Collecting the money is up to them. I cycle out of the site at 9.10am.

Campsite road works look as areas being made for motorhomes. Kerbs and concrete, line them up and jam them in. It is where the money is. If you can fill a site with paid permanent annual residence, it is guaranteed income. Why bother with tent vagrants? But it goes against the original ideals of Camping Municipal. The épicerie/ boulangerie opposite is closed. No bread no breakfast. No fuel.

Faverolles. My experience. Where the lights are on but no one's home.

Descending quick. Happier every km away from the place. Thoughts of the Maire being friends with the Gendarmerie and the small matter of the nonpaying cycle freeloader.

Downward road views of the lake. Powerboats pontoon tied. White fibreglass cruisers, fishing rods, large outboard motors wait silent. Bends under trees and rock, lapping sounds against the lakeside. The imposing iron structure of Le Viaduc de Garabit gorge span. Arch ironwork. It is big.

The arch tapers from two granite piers, widening as it rises to the apex of its curve. Delicate aesthetic. Diagonal and vertical bracing cancel opposing forces, transferring the load to great granite piers. Across the top of the arch squared ironwork carries the railway. It spans the gorge supported from bedrock by vertical iron framed columns. Elegant in design. Ends of the bridge held by granite towers' sheer mass. Designed by the engineer Léon Boye and the master Gustave Eiffel. Taking four years to build, the arch built up in two halves and joined on 27th April 1884 120m (360ft) above the surface of the river that has since become the lake. The viaduct is 565m (1600ft) long taking 3250 tonnes of iron to build it and 60,000 rivets to hold it together. The granite supports throughout the structure have a total cubage of nearly 20,500m3. It was painted grey for many years, but now it has been restored to a splendid red as originally intended. At night the structure is lit and must look spectacular in lake reflection.

D909 runs south without crossing the lake. Gorge climb. Granny gear. Passing the bridge's massive bolts holding the ironwork structure to the masonry that still allow the ironwork to expand with temperature change. Very clever.

Upward plodding the bends. Hotel entrance has a man busy sweeping.

"Bonjour" with a smiling nod.

Under the ironwork, hairpins thread granite supports by tunnel. The view level across the top of the structure quantifies true size. Red ironwork contrasts lake dark blue and forest black.

D909 straight line level ride. Farm mas building huddle,

downhill Loubaresse. Into the village looking for a boulangerie. A school, La Poste and the Mairée. No shop. Do the people not eat around here?

Breakfast on the saddle. Two apricots. Pocket frisk finds a small cereal bar. Following Route National traffic drone. Contemplation, distraction, watching car missiles overtake trundling motorhomes and 45 tonnes of loaded haulage.

A speeding yellow La Poste van overtakes to disappear down a lane. A few minutes later it overtakes again. Road din ride for miles. A stop for a drink at the side of the road. Drone behind, an approaching tractor. Engine wavers with the bouncing of tyres. It is getting nearer. A glance over the shoulder. Front bucket high in the air. A dumpy bag swinging suspended from the bucket. Sticking out each side from the rear of the vehicle, flailing machinery takes up the whole width of the carriageway. The nearer it gets the more I realise the driver cannot see anything ahead. Cab vision obscured by the dangled load. I pull the bike into the grass verge off of the carriageway. The driver does not bother to look either side. The thing passes using all width including where I had stopped. The cab passes. Driver surprised at my presence wears a look of guilt. If the idiot tied the strops through the bag handles and over the back of the bucket it would have shortened the length of the load allowing him vision. In the act of leaning ready to hit the drainage ditch for cover I have discovered half a packet of peanuts in a side pocket. Jackpot! Celebrating by eating my winnings.

Route National concrete transports monotony overhead. Now viewed from the other side. I catch up Death trundling blind, overtake and keep speed using the survival chance over distance equation. 'Camping.' Advertised at St-Just. No boulangerie. Stomach grumbles an empty complaint. Countryside miles of nowhere.

Under Route National. Pine fringe, into Languedoc Rousillon. Little Albaret-Ste-Marie appears. Épicerie stop. The lady does not sell bread. The boulangerie is further along the road. Hungry purchase buys everything but bread.

Sleepy main street. Buildings older. People armed with fresh baguettes tell of boulangerie direction. The biggest baguette is tied across the bars. Pastries get eaten cycling the hill.

Roundabout direction for Mazeyrac. 'Les Six Routes.' D4 long straight country lane drop. Grey wood fence post split. Waving yellow crop behind the wire. A post to lean the bike. Out with a large 1kg pot of jam dunking pieces of fresh baguette. The view up to the Monts d'Margeride. Tops of hills obscured by low raining grey hanging dense in high forest is looking a long way away.

The last of the baguette is dunked in the final third of the jampot. A roadrider a long way down ascends the steep straight. Up on the pedals, legs in rhythm of calculated progress. I watch him nearing. He sees my cycle fuel. Broad grin from behind sunglasses wishes. "Bon appetit!"

"Merci." Holding up baguette remnant and near consumed jar of jam giving him encouragement of "Grimp! Grimp!" He looks back laughing with a nod, diminishing, gone into the long hill.

Country solitude. Black kites sail breeze waves sweeping the field searching for an unguarded lunch of rodent.

Downward under the pine. Overhanging cone filled branch twist, sweet and resinous. Rough pasture through woodland green windows. Dark trunks lean shadow over a bumpy lane pothole dodge. A walled town below. Towers, stone battlements, spires. A bridge spans a little river running through green meadow. The River Truyére destined to feed the downstream lake greedy for Kilowatts.

Le Malzieu-Ville campsite by the river holds one motorhome. Green clean and cared for without pallet wood and speedboats. Cream granite town greets with two bronze statues of a shepherd and shepherdess armed with a stick and pitchfork fending off a large wolf. The bad guy wears black standing ready for attack. Hackles raised, teeth growling snarl, tail down and ready to lunge. The folk legend of the Beast of Gevaudan. The beast certainly got about, last year it was around Langogne in the Cévennes. Here it is again. A ferocious statue looking at the alarmed lady as its lunch date.

Into a most perfect restored medieval walled town of houses lived in, shops, cobbles. Round towers guard the town gate. I have never heard of this place. Secret town. What a find! I spend time wandering century's worn cobbles. Ancient grey bleached heavy oak amongst weathered worn granite block. Defensive towers, street corners slits for firing arrows, portcullis entrance. Tall tower lean, little windows look down.

Town gate arch. Maison du Tourisme is next to the Mairée housed in a tower of granite. Old cart bright painted surrounded in tended bloom. People smile and say hello. The place radiates happiness, connected to the St. Jaques Santiago de Compostella pilgrimage route. C'est petit de beauté. Not so tourist worn as Carcassonne.

The back of the town. Lorry squeeze through narrow street opening to a D989 climb. Col de la Croix de Fau. Signed. 'Ouvert.'

Green meadow climb. Town shrinks in the green. Continuous gradient, the crank turns steady leg rhythm. Big hill views, high black forest horizon. Climbing woodland, climbing pasture. Distant Cantal Mountain view accompanied by a first cowbell. Pure white Charollais cattle graze peaceful below. Km marker. Altitude passes 1000m (3000ft). 1115m

(3350ft) is looking like the top. 1152m (3450ft) climbs into forest. Two touring bikes speed downward the riders wrapped in waterproof jackets for the long wind chilled descent. Smiles and waves. Gone.

1175m (3530ft) thick forest, stone markers on a crest each side of the road. Silence. Lone bird call. No one. A hundred thousand trees in growing patience. Snaking road flat. Rounding a bend climbs to 1195m (3800ft). Car gives a toot of encouragement. I climb out of the forest. Stone cross is unnamed. Croix du Fau. The unsigned road col 1270m (4000ft). Far away views, distant hazed snows of Monts Dore and Puy de Sancy. Featureless lands ridden five days ago. Long way below miniature Viaduc de Garabit in striking red. Single figure cold. Blasts of wind. Sign for Mont Mouchet 7km up a track. Le Puy en Velay 68km away. Downhill big gear wind whistle. Bumps shake vision, progress eats into the 68 for the day's destination. Km sign drops to 1190m (3600ft) through bends. Freewheel speed, brake squeeze caution. Fast line through bends watching for potholes, stones and gravel. Figure eight turns drop to the high altitude village of Paulhac-en-Margeride. Passing a farm, pulling in tight to a wall.

Cows are driven up the road by three people with lengths of plastic waterpipe to guide the animals with directional touch. By the side of a protective mother trots a calf barely the height of the adults belly. An elderly limping collie dog quarters right left, head down, the wolf smile, tongue hanging. Working into retirement, keeping the herd moving forward. Quietly through the open farm gate, into the yard towards a barn.

A joke about the traffic jams in the village. The farm lady laughs, closing the gate with a wave. A large sign in the village reads.

Paulhac en Margeride.
Burned by the troops of occupation
12 June 1944.

The place in the middle of agricultural nowhere. Resistance battles to slow repulse of D Day advance. Death, fire and bullets. Remembered.

The village shrinks, around the head of a valley. Running the other side, a view to the village under the hills journeyed. Flat road speed, silent hill forest, it is 2pm. Take a break.

Stopping at a pile of boulders under quarried cliff. The place crawls with big ants the size of my thumbnail. I put my finger down on a rock to say hello. An ant comes over and tries to saw a bit off. The unfriendly little beggar. I shall eat standing.

Forest road. Pockets of scant pasture. One grazing horse, a skinny donkey and a few bewildered sheep stare at nothing. New view faraway Monts du Deves, domed amongst volcanic forest cones. Leaving the Margeride fast through gravelled hairpin bends. Open land farms, barking dog challenge, too fast to worry. The road descent ends in Sauges. Randonneurs swell the streets walking the St. Jaques pilgrimage route.

Museum. 'Le Béte de Gévaudan' recalls the terrors of the wolf. This town was the centre for the wolf's national reputation in a film same titled 'Le Béte du Gevaudan.' The wolf terrorises the inhabitants. Sinister bourgeois mask murderous crimes against the local ladies adding a twist to an unanswered legend. The safest creatures were the sheep. Up through centuries old narrow streets winding through the village. I am stopped by a family who ask me.

Where am I from? Where did I start? Where today? Am I a pilgrim en route? They are walking the St Jaques route and wish me. "Bon courage!"

Old houses emit a friendly humanity from many centuries of being lived in. Iron verandah, cream granite walls. Randonneur shops, the place busy. A vibrance. People smile and wave. "Bonjour." A bar. Customers seated outside raise their glasses to me with a grin. Statues, wood and metal sculptures throughout the village. The climb out of Sauges. Notre Damme watches over the rooftops.

A car slows and a lady asks if I know of an address in Sauges?

I am on the way to Le Puy and do not know.

"Bon courage!"

Diminishing rooftops, rising moorland. Large granite boulders stuck in the landscape. The beast is here. Looking to far below Sauges. Chainsaw hewn. Standing, lowered head in menacing prowl. Sharp teeth bared, a line of hard spikes the length of its back to its tail. Sauges is out of sight. Upward through quiet countryside to a levelling road. Hill rolls to drop, steepness increases speed. Bend sweep needs a careful line, brakes holding all the carried weight. Below huge hills fold into a void, violently collapsed chasm into the centre of the earth. Volcanic chimney rise. Huge lava flow frozen amongst scree and boulder landslide. Cliff face solidified unearthly, strange sculpted molten shape. Behind the gorge rise volcanos to a strange domed land. Impenetrable folds, over and over to black distant molten hill shape. Descending the Gorges d'Allier. Cliff forest speeding drop crosses a bridge water roar. Under molten cliff, gloopy solidified overhang bulges strange, defying rules of formation. Tension and forces of gravity say the shapes cannot exist, possible only by the gorges igneous creation. Signs for camping point into the centre of the earth.

I stop to look over to the vertical chasm somewhere far below holding the River Ance tumbling to join the Allier. I can hear a million gallon rumble flowing. Too far down to see.

Road starts to rise, I feel good about it. Maybe I am headed up out of the gorge. Signs for Le Puy and Monistrol d'Allier.

Road drops fast under strange volcanic watch. Steep, long. Down into Monistrol d'Allier. River runs fast black, cliff gorge rock constriction, pine decoration. The two rivers join turbulent increasing the Allier. Steel bridge span joins Monistrol's houses split by the gorge. High under oozed cliff shape a building completely sheltered by rock overhang. Village on an elevated plateau looks across the gorge. Hydroelectricity claims advantage of vast flowing volume. I cross 'Viaduc Monistrol d'Allier' high above river thunder. La Gare. The tracks were laid by dynamite.

The gorge climb out starts. Le Puy 28km. 28 to go. Ideal campsite next to the river. A few caravans and tents enjoy the riverside. Smoke drift barbeque preparation rises through trees. Frozen lava, narrow road rock hewn. Precipitous drop. Do not fall, no second chance. Boulder fall across the road sit wedged in tree boughs waiting to plummet, or take the tree with them.

Higher and higher. Altitude payback for freewheel squander. Patient granny gear grind. Forested domes, wooded spikes. Black snake line of the Allier's echo. Lowering cloud hilltop envelope. Grey weather mist climb, sinuous road contour, folded rock. A quarry idle. Silent plant and crushing machinery at the side of the road. A group of randonneurs looking to cross the road to a steep path disappearing down into trees.

Smiles and greetings. "Bonjour." "Bon courage!"

Hilltop cloak, grey form blur shapes. Building loom. High village commmand. St-Privat-sur-Allier. Dark rectangle windows watch my crawling progress. Buildings untouchable vertiginous perch on the end of high ridge. Road arcs hillside, climb steep. Into habitation, the village built in horseshoe shape. I look across to a stone chateau fortress plain, one of the oldest buildings. A church. Houses four and six storeys. Some alpine, others look southern France almost Italian. In no order. Buildings in view competition peer over the one in front. Others lean upon the next in support to stay up. A roadside fountain. Greened brass piddles constant into a grey stone trough.

Twisting village street, walls so old, without time. Signed accommodation for randonneurs throughout St-Privat. Leaving along the side of a valley. Lookback view. Mist blurred shapes of the village chateau and spire. Background horizon featureless merge. Dark grey convoluted hill mass falls into the cleaved gorge.

Mist becomes drizzle, ascent into cloud accompanied by strengthening wind. By the side of the road. Murder.

> *To*
> *the memory*
> *of*
> *Marcel-Jean CHABUT*
> *shot by the Germans*
> *the 14-6-1944*
> *age of 19 years*
> *of Beaumont. (P.d.D)*

Forested hills drizzle rain. Out of tree cover the wind gusts. Hill above rolls back high in grey gloom. A stop for the waterproof windy sleeve fight. Wet weather altitude chill. Fruit and peanuts fuel the climb. Rising road eases to a plateau. Cold wind rain blurred hilltop surround. The wind batters, hill rolls over. Bike speed, shifting up through the gears, easy downhill momentum. Km post reads 1135m (3400ft). The highest point which must be near 1150m (3450ft).

In a windy cloud of rain vehicles speed past. Lights on, lifting clouds of spray across shining wet. 'Mont Bonnet' village. Descending faster, faster. No need to turn the pedals, black kites circle, a harrier darts low across the road buzzing a field. Nature's jet fighter at full throttle.

Rumbles of thunder distant, black towering cloud closing. Freewheel village blur, cold bites face and fingers. Thunder roll closer. Distant mass volcanos, jagged black chaotic skyline compressed under leaden sky. Through the drizzle blur, a single yellow shaft of sunshine bathes city outline far below. Le-Puy-en-Velay.

Roundabout ends the freewheel. Face to face with the Béte du Gévaudan. This time doubled wolf size, changing colour to brown, grown more muscular. Long fangs white. Raging yellow eyes void of pupils, claws tearing deep has highway priority from the left.

Freewheel speed, below cloud, the drizzle ease. Long bends, volcano hill surround. Temperature rise. The body's core remains chilled.

Sunshine over suburb rooftops. An elevated city panorama. Huge concrete statue of Joseph on a volcanic pinnacle. Right arm raised in welcoming blessing holding the infant in his left. Towering over a church. Large round towers each side of a great arched entrance under a bell tower. City views. The volcanic pinnacle Chapel-St-Michel perched high over the town. I pull the bike up on the path enjoying the panorama before joining city traffic mass movement. Memory of direction returns. Downhill city traffic flow, the campsite sign. Open gate of Camping municipal.

The Patron is busy opening up his evening pizza bar. I book in for two nights and pitch near trees on the only comfy looking piece of grass. A shower finally warms the body. I eat for a long time.

I talk to a man called Edward camped with his car nearby. He recognises the bike under my drying towel. "Hey! I have one the same at home!"

Today's ride has taken me from the Auvergne to the Languedoc Roussillon, Lozére and Haut Loire and crossed the Monts du Margeride and Monts du Deves. The pleasant evening warmth speaks the climate of the south. With the wild ride, sleep is no problem.

115 km

6am. Yellow tinted light, sun gently warms. The city yet to wake. Water boils for a mug to quench thirst. Body tells the mind to back to sleep, it is a rest day. Clothes wash hangs in sun. Sleeping bag airs in a tree after yesterday's damp transit.

Narrow pedestrian twist under pale façade gaze rises cobbled. Cathedral steps climb under sculpted high arch. Mass is underway, visitors quietly walk around the edge. Paintings hang, pillared vaulting high carved rise. The unaccompanied choir starts to sing with perfect harmonies and ascending song, filling the high roof of the building. Clever acoustics add reverberation, demonstrating the spine tingling possibilities of the human voice. The walking uninterested are frozen, voices of song have a hold over every person until the singing stops. I decide to stay, sitting at the back to witness more and look at the famous virgin statue. Doll like. Black face smiling with a crown of gold in a white gown. The infant is represented under the chest as a black head also wears a crown of gold. The design is very old. This one may or may not be the original after burning during the revolution. Conflicting stories about the statue increases the enigma. I read its original creation was a joint effort between faiths many centuries ago. Candles on chains from high overhead, each burns in a red glass suspended around the statue. The altar looks to be of marble surrounded with much ornate gold. The service ends with the church organ played through the great stack of loud pipes resonating through the whole building.

It could take all day to explore the streets of Le Puy. Narrow cobbled walkways feel so old. Low arches lead under grey aged wood beams to medieval doorways low. Icons of wood stare from corner wall niches, stone steps thousand year footstep wear. Tall buildings centuries sun bleached, cut blocks of grey volcanic stone. Eroded medieval pillar. Crumbling verandahs hang washing colours over iron rail. People sat behind talk watching the sunned street.

Narrow lane rise, cobbles worn polished. Traipsed steps, old doorway colour. The turnstile entrance for the Notre Damme du France. Her makeover only just finished and the scaffolding dropped.

Steps climb the volcanic pinnacle back and forth, every turn a better view across heat bathed city maze of orange rooftops. Cannon placed on the ascent, a reminder of material origin melted after their capture. She stands 16m (48ft) of cast iron, newly finished in a dark rich red shining wearing a crown of golden stars. The statue stands in natural graceful pose of beauty holding the infant who is giving a blessing to everyone. I expect her to move around to enjoy a different view of the city and surrounding mountain panorama, even the folds of the robe look so natural. The detail of the face to the shape and pose of the hand are so accurate. Delicately cradling the child as a mother would.

The cannons melted to make the statue were captured at the siege of Sebastopol 8th September 1855. The statue unveiled in

1860 in front of 120,000 people.

I could stay here all day enjoying the 360 degree view. It is the nearest to being a bird over the city. Down the steps, out through the old city streets. Mary and Jesus in wood behind iron bars. People arrive at café tables. Sunday dejeuner social under parasol shade. Accordion music echoes around tall Sunday closed shops.

Boulangerie visit. Sunshine walk back to the tent. Stories from Edward. His cycling exploits in France in the 1970s. Mistakenly cycling through a busy traffic mountain tunnel just making it out dizzy. The exhaust fumes nearly killing him. Then of how Le-Puy-en-Velay is very special. The friendly joyful feeling about the city found nowhere else.

The bike clean and oiled ready for tomorrow's journey across the Cévennes. A big carbo pasta tea fuels the legs for tomorrow.

The Stevenson Route: Velay

I have used the road atlas and the book 'Travels with a donkey in the Cévennes.' To map a tarmac route of Robert Louis Stevenson's weaving donkey journey. GR70 is a walking route of Stevenson's passage. A lot of the original route is on the road GR70 avoids for traffic conflict reasons, but will not affect me. Some of my journey will be above or below the GR70 walking route, wherever possible the travelled route will run true. Side by side.

7.45am. Edward is ready for a morning run, wishing me well for the journey. Supermarket door 8am waiting. Sign reads 'Fermé' until 8.30am. Notre Dame du France red iron contrasts primary blue sky. Sun pokes above Le-Puy-en-Velay increasing the burn. Traffic busy city hits rush hour joining the traffic stream of cars and heavy overtaking wheels heading for signed 'Valence,' looking for Le Monastier' direction via Coubon. The route Robert Louis Stevenson took along the side of La Loire. There is an old railway line that can be cycled.

I need Brives Charrensac. Busy main roundabout road works. Direction signs and numbers blanked. Direction cryptic. Bullied off the roundabout by an articulated chop off on the whirling carousel. Cycling an industrial hill. Car parts and plastic windows. Stone bridge carrys the disused railway line overhead. Heavy bike drag up steps to smooth new laid tarmac. Traffic noise and road paté roulette city bedlam exchanged for quiet forgotten world. The old line runs past the occasional house to railway building remnants overgrown in permanent disused silence. Sections of old track retained as memory to the once busy line. Hard grit under the wheels climbs constant gradient. Pretty tree tunnel woodland easy gear. Leafed shade listens for the ghost of a steam whistle. Height over the undulating road. Silver ribbon glare La Loire sunny through green meadow. Steepening wooded volcanic hills. Yellow crops lead to Volhac. Tractor flays the hedge, strimmer shreds undergrowth with a nod of greeting through helmet and face shield. A mother with a pushchair on her morning sunshine walk. Smells of cut grass, wild flower hedgerows. Tall crops hide grasshopper chirp.

Twists down across the main road. Coubon rooftops sun silvered. La Loire noisy through the village, river tumble granite slabs rounded worn by century's grinding flow. People busy village. Open shops, campsite adverts. Upward twist, side street walls in sun glare. A brown sign. 'Route du Monastier.' The old road. Higher countryside, climbing across a hill. Valley forest view. A village surrounding a chateau crowning a tall volcanic chimney. Behind, conical domed forested steep hills topped with rock escarpment repeat to fold over and over. Deep meandering valley marks the progress of the Loire's tumbling towards Le Puy.'

Climbing road turns with hill contour. Singing birds, chirping crickets, wild hedge, wild flower amongst meadow grass. Cliffs, rock, pinewood shade. Heat amplified smell of tree resin. Warning chatter from a squirrel high hidden.

Road crest. Green moorland. Splashed yellow broom amongst dull rock scatter. Busy lumber yard, piled fir trunks await process, smells of pinewood from rising dust. Hydraulic grabs swing long heavy trunks without effort. Machine blade strips tree bark. Ahead appears an articulated heavy truck negotiating the bend loaded with fresh cut trunks to feed the greed of the lumber machine.

Sunny Le Monastier-sur-Gazeille buildings. Feeling of meeting an acquaintance of old streets familiar. Museum doors open at the bottom of a car park. Interior coolness, paying a few euros to the student minding the place for the summer who welcomes with much politeness. He gives a booklet on the GR70 route. I am shown the large exhibition to Robert Louis Stevenson, detailing far more than his trip through the Cevénnes.

I expected only a dark corner of a room. Long spacious professional display detailing much information beginning with his first book. An Inland Voyage. Canoeing through Belgium and France along the rivers Meuse and Oise. Then to Travels with a Donkey in the Cevénnes and the important connection of Le Monastier with the book. Listings of his other works, Kidnapped, Dr. Jeykell and Mr Hyde, The Black Arrow, Treasure Island etc. Also his life journey across the world to the South Seas via America and Hawaii and his family life. All with much photographic memorabilia, showing the much care and research that has gone into the exhibition's creation.

A film about Le Monastier, the surroundings and its abbey. It is 11.50am, 10mins to Monsieur's dejeuner. Lunchtime must not be compromised. Remarking the same on leaving is met with laughter and agreement.

Quiet empty streets without vehicle noise. It could be a couple of hundred years ago. Timeless. Centuries of habitation give ancient villages a special feeling of historical humanity.

Two brothers of considerable age in blue work clothes come out of a house door to sit in the shade each carefully carry a full glass.

"Bonjour."

Barn doors battered by work, curved house walls, worn stone doorsteps. Sound of daily news from a window, small gardens of vegetables. Flower heads peer through a wire fence.

Downhill crosses the tumbling Gazeille River in hurry to join La Loire. D500 repetition. Through the hamlet of St-Victor an attentive donkey concentrates on noises and smells from a kitchen window.

Hill pasture wears a woodland bonnet. Sweeping valley view to black folding hills. Faraway man made merge of Le-Puy-en-Velay. Horizon hills faded blue under clear midday heat.

Petit Salettes D49 to follow Mr. Stevenson. Easy freewheeling through agriculture. Brown and white cattle, long straight horns turned forward end in sharp point menace. The beasts sit placid quietly chewing.

The village of St-Martin-de-Fugéres. Silent. Old. Built of dark brown rubble stone with red tile roofs. Road splits to a Romanesque church. Four bells shine polished brass over the roof, each placed in its own stone arch protected from the weather by a tiled roof. Below is a small arched window central over the main door under sculpted stone arches. A memorial to First World War victims. Short range artillery barrels black gloss amongst arranged flowers framed by artillery shells. Houses surround in 'midi' silence. Half a dozen people sit in garden peace under a shading parasol. Wine bottle glint decants to the glass. From a doorway. Plates arrive to the table amongst happy conversation and laughter.

Over the garden wall. "Bonjour."

"Et bon appétit."

Roadside cross the end of the village. Steep hill drop vertical from sight. Cattle graze steep hillside. Broken woodland, wild forest falls far beyond view. Across the valley. Hills of wild fir under mass volcanic cliffs. Oozed shapes protrude from steep dark green vertical into a rock gorge rumbling blue. Shimmering rapids blind under high sun. Green waterside field dotted with trees ends in rock and sand beach. Above the gorge, flat land panorama. Miniscule red village roofs amongst a patchwork sea of pale green fade. Distant volcanic hills black in fir forest.

Across the river on top of a wooded cone the part ruin of Chateau Beaufort. Campsite under of river and beach frontage. Hill forest and rock crag grow on the twisting descent into little red roofed Goudet.

The village dominated by a round tower having a witch's hat roof. Orange, green and red horizontal stripes are topped off with a crucifix. Rough stone leaning buildings, roof overhang. Lanes between, too narrow for modern traffic. A place almost empty of people, many buildings, closed shutters, gardens overgrown, property vacancy. Half the village 'A Vendre.' For sale. Perhaps the victim of the holiday home five minute dream. Leaving these little habitations sterile empty without continuity of family generation identity.

I am greeted with a surprised "Bonjour!" In the quiet of the place.

Pretty bend through the village delivers the river crossed by an old bridge. Trout shoal waiting for food arrival out of main channel flow. Across deep smooth water, tables and chairs await nobody. Upstream a beach. Screams of youth accompanied by splashing, diving off rocks into deep blue flow echoes joyful sound around the steep valley.

Stevenson hurried his lunch at Goudet knowing he still had a long days travel to reach destination. Riding over the bridge passes the riverside campsite. Gorge climb under watch of Chateau Beaufort at granny gear pace. Woodland surround, a road cut from rock, hillside sometimes bare. Alpine flower wet with trickling water, wild grass and bushes too steep to cultivate rise high to woodland. Below. Dense forest hides secret rush stream tumble. Opposite, forest steepened to lush wild grass beyond the grasping hand of man trapped by frozen vertical ooze solidified cliff.

Long drag, heat without breath of wind or breeze refreshment. Tarmac bubbles. Sticky melt road stone on the tyres rattle through the mudguards. Salt stinging eyes, clothes stuck in sweated heat. Mass sound crickets. A look back down the long valley climb beyond the treetops, far below rooftop Goudet. Rock contour bends, breeze whisp fills the lungs with freshness, return to stillness. Dead air climb. Last look down to Goudet. A bend. It has gone.

Woodland bough. Shade cools the blood, the agricultural approach to the village of Ussel. A waymarker cross. Stevenson's experiences were heat fatigued and beleaguered negotiating the climb with his awkward donkey spilling all possessions across the road repeatedly to spectator amusement.

Climb ends centre to the village. Ussel. Where silent roads meet in emptiness. A figure in the shade of the wood 'bus cabine' watches two rucksack carrying randonneurs reading their map. He could be Stevenson in overalls. Tall, long limbed with long fingers, hands resting on a stick, slight with a long thin face supporting a thick Edwardian moustache. His straight hair sticks to his brow under a flat cap. He offers a deep low long drawn "Bonjour." As unhurried as his day in the heat. Stevenson remarks on such a person of type in the next village, stopping a mother and son asking for direction. Type genetics perpetuated through the generations. Here sits a man born at home, born to his country.

Ussel has a grand church for its small size of few habitations. The church design as St-Martin' having three bells brilliantly polished in the simple tower. I cycle past a café. Four small parasoled tables amongst a flower filled garden edged in sun soaked agriculture.

Valley drop, a climb out to forest black hills. Red tile spire over trees, the approach to Costaros. Rooftop huddle around the church, part concealed by wood shaded pocket fields. The back way through town. Deep ochre volcanic rock, long ridges of red through cliffs. Back street ends in main busy road. N88 cuts the town in two. Busyness of life blood through traffic trade. The town is bustling.

A large man of considerable years wearing bib overalls, checked shirt and flat hat goes plodding past slow motion on a very old rusty steel racing bike that has not seen an oil can for a decade or two. He waits up the road for a gap in the traffic to cross. I look at the map for a few seconds. I look up. He has gone!

Direction to Le Bouchet-St-Nicholas starts further up the road. I find myself waiting in the same place to cross as the rusty bib and brace cyclist. Timed gap in traffic flow, direction signed 'Le Bouchet/Ceyres.' Quiet town lane. People sit on a low front wall outside of a house in conversation. Back of town buildings, industry fades to countryside. Low ancient waymarker cross details the old track where Stevenson took a wrong turning through landscape confusion. Without written signs waymarker crosses formed orienteering points of crossroads paths traversing the land. Direction feels to go away from where I need to be. Patience and trust in the road brings a junction. Sign points 'Bouchet'. Gaining distance the large blue figure pedals the squeaking old rusted bike to become smaller, absorbed in wild landscape.

Pinewood road twists. Gradual ascent, flowering broom wafts sweet scent across the road, cows graze the rough. Grasshoppers and crickets chirp happy under heat, hills of black fir set against sky blue. Fair weather cotton wool cumulus float trailing shadowed pools across the land. Road fork. Direction Lac de Bouchet forested crater lake Stevenson wanted to camp by. The other signed to the village where Stevenson ended up late of evening. An admirable mileage for a first days walking with or without a contrary donkey.

Le-Bouchet-St-Nicholas spire skyward rise behind wildflower and cereal crops. Flat land radiates, farmed to the village street. Waymarker cross directs from Costaros. The place changed little over the near century and a half since Stevenson gazed and wandered the same street. Apart from farming, the place supplements income from the Stevenson route for randonneurs with or without donkey. Auberges signed throughout the village. The place high plateau friendly desolation. Exposed siting a regional crossroads.

Aged black stone buildings tough stand hard high altitude winters. Stacked firewood throughout wide village streets. Tractors in barns, tractors up and down the flat streets, drivers raise a hand of greeting. Everybody says hello. One man comes out of his house whilst I am looking at the rough carvings of donkeys on the stone blocks of his house wall.

He tells me smiling. "Not to miss the others on his wall." A man with a rifle and a dog aimed at a rabbit.

He makes an aiming and "boom!" Laughing.

A thick tall chainsaw sculpture at the village crossroads hewn from the butt of a large pine or cedar. It is of Stevenson and his donkey Modestine entering the village. Quirky and impressive summing up the lighthearted feeling of the village. An inscription reads.

'On the 22nd of September 1878 R. L. Stevenson and Modestine made a stopover at Le Bouchet St- Nicholas.'

I sit on a bench. Tractors pass through the busy agricultural village. Centuries of repetitive work dictated by the season. Horse, Ox and cart replaced by diesel, tractor and trailer. The work is still the same, told by the workworn old buildings resisting the elements century after century. Only the generations change like rotation of the crop. Le Bouchet St-Nicholas is a good honest place for the proletariat, not so for the bourgeoisie. Surroundings without commodity glitz comfort.

Signs for 'Landos 8km' point to straight road out of the village. D35 drop. Straight telegraph pole road. Agricultural machinery scattered in the grass waits for seasonal use. A family in the middle of moving into a newly erected Yurt. A shining black chimney pokes central above the canvas. Possessions and children's toys fill boxes waiting for order of storage.

The young lady owner shouts a happy. "Bonjour!"

Busy village and heavy machinery recedes to green velvet landscape. Wide open cultivation within wild land. Low rolling hills green. Grey granite dry walls part tumbled through age, grazing cattle at peace. High hills far distant, near hills of granite tors could be at home on Dartmoor or in the Scottish Highlands. This view must have given a feeling of home familiarity to the wandering Scotsman.

Tarmac track D35 runs through a busy farm mas of large stone buildings. Noise and smell of many cows. Silage, diesel exhaust from busy tractors. The seven days a week endless work of farming, generation after generation. The next generation is walking back from school, a boy having made a cardboard shield covered in tin foil from today's history lesson. He has the look of a livestock farmer, even at the age of eight or nine years old. Stocky and strong. His decisive walk is of a working man, not the skip or meander of a town child. The boy has work to do. His genetics handed down from a long familiar lineage to him whether he likes it or not, his life already mapped out, born to this area. Life dedicated to the farm.

Depressions in the land hold bog and still black pool, muddied cows stand motionless. Road crosses flat barren plain, speeding vehicles travel acute angle, two directions join. D88 signed Landos. A campsite open is well named. 'La Prarie.'

Up through the gears. Straight road above Landos cuts the path marked by a stone cross. A long street of old houses. A place functional. That is it. I turn left up a short hill D53, a sign for 'Collége STEVENSON.' Bumpy lane passes the college on the edge of green swaying agriculture. Big feed silos, railway tracks part overgrown, along the quiet country lane, the back of Landos. A piled up car scrapyard rusting colours grows next to a field.

Swaying crops, long rolling landscape, far black forest hills. A waymarker cross of metal, its peeling white paint part smothered by orange lichen. The cross cemented into a large granite boulder marks convergence of old byways. Footways disappear away into green. Farming hillsides devoid of people, a few buildings dotted amongst vast acreage. Barking dogs know of my presence from long distance. Farm mas cut by the road, a village of mud and tractors. Le Mouteyre. Open lands slowly closed by dark fir forest.

Into Pradelles. Main street wakes the mind from country travel slumber. Traffic busy, sunny buildings half boarded up half restored, lived in. The square has a pillared arcade supporting very old buildings of four shuttered storeys casting long shadow of late afternoon. Fountain's busy bubble fills a large round stone trough. Perfect restored stone buildings amongst tumbling cobbled narrow way. Yellowing sun brings a changed ambience to last year's cold wind and rain experience. Open minimart purchases food and a couple of beers for this evening's campsite meal at Langogne.

N88. Rundown boarded up houses. The closed campsite of last year, now open. Notre Damme sits in a glass case at the side of the road. A hitch hiker with a large rucksack is not having much luck with his thumb.

"Desolé!" Pointing to the loaded back of my bike. The hitcher laughs and waves.

I cross into the Ardéche at speed, ahead something crosses the road. 'S' moves rapid for cover. A large snake. "Go snake, beat the traffic!" Making the road verge before the crush of the vehicle wheel. Ardéche to Lozére. Into Languedoc Rousillon all within a few hundred metres. Geographically crossing all three. The area covered by old names. Velay and Gevaudan. Now more simply known as The Cévennes. Elsewhere the three big areas are known in their own right. The approach to Langogne crosses the River Allier. Through town direction for the campsite. Under the railway bridge, road adjacent to the river. Familiar view municipal campsite.

La Cigale de l'Allier is open. The friendly Accueil. Go wherever you want. Tent, shower, cook meal routine. "Bonsoir" to people leisurely walking past. Maybe twenty people in residence.

A tall Dutchman comes over looking at the bike and says. "Hello."

I am asked where I am from and my route.

I reply "Bretagne, Loire, Vienne, Creuse, Puy de Dome, Puy de Sancy, Cantal, Le Puy-en-Velay this morning."

I am asked in a monotone voice. "What was the exact route?"

I give the names of a few towns passed through including Murat.

I am told "I know this area, I have cycled all roads of Cantal Mountains. Where exactly?"

I reply "Last year Puy Mary. This year, Super Li-Lorian, Plomb du Cantal, Puy Griou to Vallée de la Jordanne to Aurillac."

"That road is where your Bradley Wiggins fell breaking his collar bone. It is famous."

He then tells me how many times the places have been ridden as part of the Tour de France and who rode them.

I am hungry, my tea is cooked. I am not waiting out of politeness, I need to get the food in for tomorrow's energy, so I eat.

"Where next do you go?"

I tell him I am following the Stevenson route, from one of my favourite books.

"Were exactly is the route?"

I rattle off a few towns, mountains and the Cevennes.

"I have not been to this place"

"Where do you go?"

I reply "Corbiéres and across the Pyrenees. I did a couple of days last year starting at the Mediterranean and want to finish at the Atlantic."

"I know Pyrenees. I cycle them all. How heavy is your bike?"

With 5ltrs of water and some food, about 45kg.

"It is too heavy, mine 38kg."

I tell him it weighs what it weighs.

"Where do you buy the panniers?"

I tell him I made them, they are surviving their second trip.

"It is too heavy. What is your wheels?

"The front bought new in France. The back one was made by the local bike shop at home. It is a good one, built to stand the battering. It has the most spokes we could find."

"How many spokes?"

Thirty six.

"It is not enough. Mine has the 40."

"I know the gears on your bike. Tripple on the front, nine on the back"

I tell him I would like some more!

"No it is not possible. You will be 4kmph and fall off. It is too slow to have the more. You have been to the Ventoux. When did you do this?"

I tell him. "Last year. Have you been?

"Yes. It is a big mountain, but not as big as the Alps. I cycle the Alps on the cycling holiday. Your bike is too heavy for the Alps. The tour guide says bikes with triple gears are the pussys."

Another black mark against the bike. I ask him how did he find Ventoux?

"I go in my car."

"Are you on your bike?"

"No I am in camping car. You come drink wine with us!"

No. Too many km tomorrow. No wine.

"Ok. Bye."

I am left with an empty plate that needs washing. I cannot remember tasting any of my food. I suppose I still have a beer and some fruit left to enjoy in peace contemplating what has been pointed out as inadequate with the bike. The wheels, the gears on the back, the gears on the front, the panniers, the whole thing really.

Maybe I should just throw it all in the bushes and go home.

Cycle nerds. You have to love them…
    No you don't.
80 km

The Stevenson Route: Gevaudan

Peaceful spacious uncommercial camping municipal. Two resident donkeys are friendly. I have a couple of peaches dripping ripe and after removing the stones from the fruit give one to each donkey. The campsite an official 'Accueil des Ánes.' Donkey station for pack donkeys traversing the GR70 Stevenson route.

Thanks to the jovial Patron. Under the railway bridge through back streets finds La Poste to purchase stamps. Into an office full of boxes there is no one. Five minutes later a lady comes in behind me and asks if anyone is serving. I tell her not yet. I only want stamps for my postcards. She tells me this office is for business users. I must go next door.

Stamps, cards and daily bread. Town market. Stalls fill the road. People crowd, collective ambling surge.

Busy climbing N88. A view to a waymarker cross, a lane appearing as a path along a valley above a little river named Langouyrou. Sunshine plod, manmade Lac Naussac. Forested black fir fills steep hillsides around the dark blue breezy lake. Forest lands yesterday travelled.

Lake ends, forest road rising steep, a junction before the climb. D71 St-Flour-de-Mercoire, wooded lane of chirping crickets weaving through stone walled habitation.

A lady crosses the narrow road. Smiling "Bonjour."

This road will miss the hamlet of Fouzillac further along the main N88 down a dead end.

Fouzillac exchanged for old working hill farms, a running roadside fountain, L'Herm old stone houses quiet in the sunshine. Downward into trees. Valley river noisy under forested cover. A far view into the Forest de Mercoire. Hill upon hill of green forest folding, many hills to a horizon. Too many to count. Against blue sky atomic bomb thunder clouds fast build fueled by warming land. Wind direction moves the bulking heavyweights away east.

Twisting roadside shading pine, broad leafed green illumination. Light dances pools across the winding forest road. Rustlings in crispy undergrowth. Flash of green lizard scurry from my approach. A climb through mossed granite boulders, gnarled trunks grow a coat of green velvet. Tree shadow damp shade, ancient boulder walls. Boulders too big to lift sit waiting to be moved by geological time from the mossed fairy hollow.

Loubarnés few dwellings look across a deep valley. The river in the most agreeable roar magnified in echo around dense forested hillside. I stop on the top of a winding bend absorbing the view of a child's drawn ideal of rolly hill and valley. A black weaving thread makes its way down the hillside in and out of view to end under small red roofs and chimneys of Cheylard-l'Evique.

The brake release twisting to the river. A half round tower of block granite forms half of the first dwelling of a neat row of houses. The Mairé is a restored stone building with an arched entrance door. Stone built chapel has two bells suspended in a little stone arched tower over the gable. Central in the gable a circular stained glass window, underneath is the entrance stone archway. The inside plain of simple beauty, windows of deep colour thick stained glass depict wheat, grapes and fire. Orange red purple yellow and green thrown across stone flag floor by bright sunshine. Plain wood pughs, the altar, illuminated Notre Damme surrounded by flowers. The roof timbers exposed, the ceiling of long plain wood boards.

Out from cool church interior hit by the heat of the day. Across the road, the auberge. Tables and chairs empty. On the wall an ironwork outline image depicts Stevenson and Modestine the donkey. Garden flowering red geraniums spill over tubs and fill an old wooden barrel.

Outside of the auberge a 'Solex' bike. Two stroke petrol cycle motor over the front wheel controlled by a lever to engage a roller onto the front tyre and a throttle from the handlebars controlled by a cable to the motor. A triangular sprung saddle, handlebar end brakes. Simple fun transport of France. Sadly no longer produced.

Just myself in the village. No traffic, no people. The only sound, the running river.

Stevenson was well received at Cheylard l'Eveque. Cared for at the lunch table, treated with much hospitality and receiving freely given advice on loading his donkey before setting out for Luc across barren hill wild land.

'Luc' sign points out of the village. On the granny gear, steep twisting road climbs rising valley flanked steep. My companion a babbling roadside stream gurgling a waterworn gully. Either side, hills covered in deep green grass patched yellow with flowering broom. Wild pine trunks twisted against blue sky. The occasional white cloud quietly going somewhere. A look far back down to the village. A few rooftops, remaining Cheylard' hidden behind trees. Over the village, a chapel with a bell either side of a Notre Damme over maybe the graveyard that has served the village for centuries. If it is, then it will most likely be the last village home for the polite people who gave hospitality to Mr. Stevenson in 1879.

Long climb ends in flower filled meadow surrounded by fir forest. A stack of felled pine trunks greyed with age, thick trunks split with shrinkage of drying. Horizon black of vast fir plantations.

Road drops as steep as the climb. Brakes firmly gripped, straight line ride, wind from the speed roars in my ears. Wide basin of long meadow carpeted in white and purple swathes of flower amongst pale green and yellow swaying grass. A shallow river runs through the valley bottom. Clear water riverbed golden stones. Cobbled jewels of nature. The bridge is a large pipe overlaid by the road. Climbing across hillside, river sounds locked by forested surround. Steep climb through spruce woods under high sun, welcomed breeze along valley stirs trees sending a swaying wave through the far below meadow. Butterflies all around in chase. Small delicate orange and black dotted, others green tinted cream and a species completely black winged. It takes my mind off of the climb. One lonely butterfly decides to end it all through the spokes.

Trees give up to rock. Grey granite amongst scree tumble, coarse clumps of tough growing grass, stunted pine wood above. Heather softens purple pink serenaded by mass humming of bees in their thousands.

Flower perfumed air, sunny hill top. The sounds of man. A busy farm greets with the noise of the modern farm slave. The diesel engine. Livestock sheds, barbed wire fencing, concrete yards, muddy tyre tracks sun baked solid. Barking farm dogs tell of my intrusion in their agriculture world.

Road fork. Both seem to go nearly the same direction. Paint fading sign reads 'Luc' pointing right. The road ascends gentle gradient, I must be near the highest altitude of immediate land. Contour obscured by black mass fir forest all direction. Cleared islands grow cereal crops and meadow breaking the grip of growing timber. Breeze blows, trees respond a soft roar. Green meadow waves break far inland, washing against a timber shoreline.

Hilltop wild land. Green topped spruce backed by blue sky, resin smells shared with the fragrance of abundant yellow broom lighting forest clearings. Young trees in a growing competition for light. Path from the forest parallel with the road. Granite post marks its crossing back amongst darkened trunks. A randonneur appears in a T shirt and sunhat carrying a large rucksack. "Bonjour!"

Downward snaking single track weaves the steepening hillside. The footpath descends straight line crossing the zig zagging road numerous times. Sounds from within the forest of diesel plant. Large bulldozers and articulated dumper trucks are making a dirt road through the forest to harvest the timber crop. Dust rises a yellow cloud hanging over trees visible from chance view high across steep surrounding hillsides blue hazed in heat. Wide sandbanks in a valley mark the course of a running river meeting out of view with the River Allier. Far below, the ruined castle of Luc white Notre Damme looks from a square stone tower over village rooftops. Further steep forest broken by sun parched crops. Many hills rise from the deep cleaved course of the River Allier.

Out of the forest. Lane runs to the ruin chateau. I leave the bike on a slope against a tree and walk the path leading to the tower. Behind, the sound of the bike falling over. It can stay in a heap.

I walk to the base of the tower. Over the roof the Notre Damme stands in bright white on a stone plinth looking in thought skyward, hands together in prayer complete with lightning conductor. An information board connecting Stevenson with the Notre Damme detailing the visit to Luc along with a few lines quoted from the book. I lift the bike upright pushing it up to the road, the randonneur carrying the rucksack appears from forest shade.

Down to the village of Luc. Greeting with snarling dogs running along barking the other side of a fence. Barking continues after I have disappeared into the village. Silent streets, old stone houses modest, homely. A road elevated behind the church built of grey granite with a simple wall tower hanging bells between arches.

A person comes out of their house and looks twice as if... "Oooh Stranger in our village!" The figure sits on the window cill having a sideways nosey at the stranger in town. I cycle along the narrow road flanked by houses.

"Bonjour." To the lady now looking away busy picking dead skin off of her feet.

"Bonjour" Watching me go down the road. Chiropody habits detract from Stevenson's description of the handsome woman host of Luc.

Village ends at the junction. D906 signed La Bastide Puylaurent. I wait for a passing car. Two roadriders coming up the road still a distance behind. Easy gear along the flat road running opposite the River Allier. An ancient 6WD army truck rust red from years of the outdoors has a starting handle, winged mudguards, broken headlights. Homemade doors. A sheet of galvanised bent makes a square roof with a cut out for rear vision. Used for lumber hauling. Standing silent next to a large woodpile.

The approaching noise on my back wheel. The first of the two roadriders coming past on a brand new shining red carbon fibre framed machine. Rider dressed to match the bike in full race lycra with sunglasses passes elbows length away.

"Bonjour."

He puts his nose in the air, looks the other way cutting across tight on my front wheel giving a view of lycra nappy backside. A 'Monsieur Alpha.' Here comes the next, up alongside.

"Bonjour."

A repeat of ignorance. I watch them go on fighting against the bike, not in rhythm with the road. They do not ride smooth, burning unnecessary energy. Their legs are sticks. Pretenders. I look around. There is no one on the road, not a person or vehicle in sight. They carry on up the flat road slowly gaining distance away. You know what? I am not happy. Time to teach some manners.

Ahead is a moderate incline through a rocky part of the road and a slight downhill before it. This is where I make my speed. Tour de France pretenders will feel the attack as they hit the hill. I go up through the gears catching the lards of lycra exactly on the hill, coming past tail end Charlie up level with the front rider. He springs up on the pedals, I just push harder and start to close off the road pushing him slowly into the ditch. You either accelerate or drop out. The rider gives twitchy sideways worried looks. "Quarante cinq kilos monsieur! Quarante cinq kilos!" As the vocal attack ("45kilos!") He can't shake me, I hold him over the verge line now about to feel the rocks and stones under his high pressure tyres that will pitch him over the bars and into the rocky drainage ditch. He pushes, I match him. He pushes, I will not be dropped. His red face is twitching uncomfortable with the situation. Then I start laughing and put on the brakes. They race on ahead away from the foreign nutter.

"You can buy all the gear. You have to earn the legs!!"

Still chuckling, rounding a corner under a bridge into La

Bastide'.

The little River Allier flows peaceful behind houses. The narrowed street rises around a corner. Opposite the church, an épicerie. Still open. Cold meat is stored under the sleeping bag for insulation against heat. The fruit can stay on the front of the bike, a chilled bottle of cola drops into the carriers and I leave the shop Patron to discuss his friends new shining sports motorcycle parked outside.

A look skyward shows the line of a weather front in the high altitude running across the whole sky. The solid line trails cloud fingers to a paled streak haze. Signifying weather change. A junction climb behind the village into forest. The accompaniment of swarming flies. Some bite others dance around my ears and eyes. A judgement sent from the roadriders. Sneaky horseflies land gently, a slap dispatches, distraction from uphill effort. The persistent insects will not go away, I cannot get the ones that bite my back. At the end of the long straight uphill a turning at a roadside shrine. Stone carved Notre Damme is protected by an arch. Inscription under translates as.

> *You are all beauty*
> *O Mary,*
> *You are the reflection*
> *of the heart of God...*

I ride down persisted by the flies trying to scatter them with my hat. On observation I must look a deranged madman for the second time today. In this episode observed battling nothing, cursing thin air with a sweat soggy hat. The road to the Trappe de Notre Damme des Neiges. The Monastery of Our Lady of the Snows.

Stevenson stayed with the monastery brothers. Walking

with a childlike fear down this road with Modestine to meet a cloaked figure constructing the road shovel by shovel. Father Appollinaris with his barrow and stones. The trees making the woodland were not long planted. Now they are mature with many descendants of the 1870's.

The flies suddenly disappear in sight of monastic buildings. Signs direct, pushing my bike up to the Accueil. At the door I am met and greeted by a monk of considerable years who is the most naturally gracious, polite, humorous person. Making me feel most welcome. He asks. "Where have I travelled from?"

Looking at the bike. Asking. "Where is the motor?"

"No motor? Bien! Bien! Bien!"

Did I cross La Manche on the thing?

"Yes, it is a boating lake pedalo. It took a while."

Things have changed since Stevenson's visit. I am shown to a cinema where a film is run detailing the daily routine of monastic life, the daily industry and the history of the place with its expanding connections around the world. One of the monks went to Morocco to set up a monastery ending up getting killed.

After the film, he takes the time for conversation, open with no pretense. I thank him for his time and kind welcome given. I am told to spend as much time as I want around the place. As I walk toward the church another customer arrives.

The church interior austere, white walls have art reflecting the surrounding land, one piece details the monk of Morocco. Thick deep coloured stained glass windows throw light colours into the arched roofed nave, an altar of stone has to the side a wood crucifix. The place functional without distraction as its purpose. It is possible to stay at Our Lady of the Snows, the monks have a hotel and make their own wine.

In the grounds two donkeys graze. Fur worn, bald patches

from carrying the pack saddle. One animal grey around the eyes, weather worn from probably many crossings and could do with a fatten up.

A monk in a hurry comes along the path. "Bonjour!" He exclaims.

The flies have been waiting for me. Their annoying bombardment retracing my journey to La Bastide-Puylauent. Flies start to disappear as speed increases, the most athletic fall after reaching 20kmph. Speed doubled until the village junction.

The motorcycle outside of the épicerie has gone. D6 follows railway and little river through a valley. A campsite looks inviting. The little river turned to a lake by a weir. The river now a stream weaving the bottom of fields trickling between stones and around trees. Cattle stoop to drink from the shallow trickle River Allier. Its source rises puddled across the above hill. Flies return on a slowed climb. I have to put up with them until the flattening road enables enough speed to leave the horrid swarm. The approach to Chasserades. La Gare. Downhill. A bend. Camping municipal sign directs to a gate opening to wild land campsite. The Patron should arrive later, one of the residents tells me to camp wherever I like. The place is at an altitude over 1170m (3500ft) feeling as high moorland. Coarse grass, scant broom and rough trees surrounded by fir forest. I get a shower and eat. Paying for my night's accommodation. A relaxed 'do what you want' place. I like it. Flies crawl across the outside of the tent. It seems wherever there is high woodland there are 'Les Mouches.'

Last year I left Langogne and flew down the road to Villefort by 2pm. Today following Mr. Stevenson's meandering progress I arrived in Chasserades at 5.30pm and will not reach Le Bleymard until tomorrow. It has been a day of contrast, a day

of beauty. Tomorrow should be a day of green mountain lands.
57 km

The Stevenson Route: Crossing Mt. Goulet and Mt. Lozére.

Heavy rain in the blackness. I get under the sleeping bag in the warm drifting away until 5am. "Hey bourgeois, c'est cinq heures!" Was the waking call to Stevenson sharing a room with surveyors plotting the railway through rocky hilltop land. Tent ripples in strengthening wind roar amplified through surrounding pines. Great deeds of an early start are annulled in favour of cozy dozing.

8am. Cool grey morning. Wind noise through the trees lessened by daylight hours. Hills forested black. Surrounding mass of fir sliced by slow swirl cloud. Rising painted white wisps of evaporating mist. Ascending remnants of last night's rainfall. I leave pleasant campsite of 'Chasserades Source d'Allier' down to a centuries old stone village. One little épicerie boulangerie. Narrow alley maze streets, shadowed doorways. Time worn stone and rendered buildings lean in old age centuries defiant of hard winters. Worn slate roofs, half the village of closed shutters, paint fades, worn by the elements. A lot of people would not survive here. Missing daily expected material convenience. 'Auberge Modestine' named after the donkey. Bright nylon randonnueurs appear ready for the trail.

They travel light, equipped for day walking.

I ride up to the church poking squat square sombre stone tower over the village. Bells peer through open double arches. Its shallow pitched heavy slate hip roof has been throwing off winters for centuries. The tough built church spreads in all direction. Rough black masonry. A once fallen elevation rebuilt, brown heavy stone yet to weather dark. Proportion simple, squat, near windowless. Old white tombs and leaning crosses against background steep dark green to blackened forest. Montagne du Goulet sliced by grey mass static cloud. The randonneur group walk along the lane signed GR70. Direction Mirandol.

Street meander. Stone troughed water laverie weather protected under arched open ended building. Protected spiritually by an alcove Notre Damme above the keystone. The shopkeeper is busy filling large plastic cans with spring water tumble.

He nods. "Are you wanting to buy anything?"

"I am just enjoying looking around the village."

He frowns, telling me. "It is very cold here in the long winter."

"Bien sur, Chasserades est tres haut. A coté de la montagne. Au revoir Monsieur." It is high. Next to the mountain.

"Au revoir."

D6 drop. Railway rise. Long timber snow sheds keep snowdrifts from the rails. Roadside wall, steep rocky cliff, tree top wooded gorge. Chassezac tumbles toward the Mediterranean Ardeche via vast Gorges du Chassezac. A railway viaduct at Mirandol. Village split by river cleave, joined by a bridge. Houses tumble twists grey cliff.

Natural rock garden bloom, flowering plants rock anchored fed constant by chiming crystal trickle.

D120 Le Bleymard 14km, via L'Estampe crossing Montagne du Goulet. Over the Chassezac gurgle. Part moorland, part cliff, part field. Through a dark dripping tunnel wide enough for one. Daylight reveals the farming village of L'Estampe. Making height, zig zag road climbs chimneys and village rooftops. Three cats retreat to the road verge lowering flat to the ground looking out through grass blade cover. Eyes wide, cautious watch of my uphill progress. Road climb straight. Farm collie sheepdog is sat in the middle of the narrow road, watching my approach. I talk to the dog as I get nearer and stop a little way from it. The dog grey around the eyes. Tail caked in crusted cow dung and has a muddied nose. It gets up taking much effort to stand. Stiff in its back legs, silently walking over with the wisdom of age to receive a butter biscuit of which it unhurriedly takes. Head bowed eyes looking up, wandering back to the same spot, standing motionless biscuit in mouth watching me disappear around the bend.

Battered by countless hours of work a green tractor 'John Deere' spattered by its mud caked wheels is parked on the steep road verge attached to a beaten up muddied trailer. Smells of hot oil and diesel. 'Ting ting' from the silent oil dirtied engine cooling. Village shrinks into scant green the higher I climb. Rolling barren hills hide below noise of a train in two beat rhythm running over tracks under load. Single carriage appears plodding from right to left climbing the gradient in monotone grumble. Disappearing behind a hill, re appearing distant chugging across a rising viaduct.

Forest roofed bright green deciduous. Heavy timber bough tangle closes the sky. Busy stream gurgle through a thousand trunks is looking for the Chassezac. Road steep, granny gear plod, higher and higher. Coniferous smother, standing wet black trunks. Roadside orange snow pole guides misted glow against mass darkening of unmoving trees. Around a bend, the mist shrouded spectacle of a great turd standing upright defiant in the centre of the road. Whatever made it, I don't want to meet it. The strong territorial statement says. 'This place is mine.'

Temperature drop, wetted thick blowing envelope. Gradient ease, dull blurred light between mass forest trunks, I must be getting near the top. The GR70 horizontal white red white band painted on a tree, path weaves the trunks. I pass flat cleared areas, earth thick, black water pool depressions amongst fallen trunks consumed smothered by wild grass. 'Forét domaine du Goulet.' D20. Bleymard 6km. Somewhere I have passed the unmarked road col 1413m (4340ft). Welling on the forest hillside, the source of the River Lot flowing to the Garonne and the Atlantic Ocean.

Swirling mist blur, background forest grey. Natural wild pine amongst imposed dense fir interlopers. Dropping road, waterproof jacket blocks out cold grabbing cloud vapour. Speed needs full concentration. The view blur, both brakes squeezed, stone dodge, pothole weave. Temperature warms with altitude loss. An approaching battered white Renault van has a weatherbeaten face topped with a beret peering over the steering wheel in an expression of surprise. Forest gloom release, steep bare hill drop. Le Bleymard.

Unpleasant modern chalet housing. Scattered rusting farm machinery and rotting trailers sinking into wild roadside wasteland. The River Lot in babbling infancy. Carrefour supermarket electric door. Welcoming lights. Heat and bakery smells. In no hurry to leave until I have warmed through, spending time selecting food for this evening's meal and re filling the snack fuel supply. The supermarket has a section dedicated for the traveller as well stocked as a camping shop. The happy shop assistant comments on how cold it is today.

Three pick-up trucks full of logs pull up opposite the café. Chainsaw teeth above the log filled truck butt. Out get forestry workers dressed in chainsaw overalls, harnesses around waists, brushing themselves woodchip free making jokes amongst themselves disappearing through the café door. Dejeuner Bleymard. Empty. Narrow alley. Shuttered closed up windows, ancient dwellings. A little wire haired terrier on a chain is sat outside a flower decked house watching the day. The dog comes over dragging its metallic tether. I give a cookie in two halves. The small animal has a fat piggy belly and short legs. Wearing a permanent frown under coarse grey and white whiskers. Not much taller than a cat.

I stand in the square. The church central. A square tower. Terraced houses on three sides include the Mairé. A lonely lane climbs behind the church. Brown stone houses lean on each other. Heavy slated roofs bow timbers under centuries of weight. Chimneys pop through the roofs anywhere of differing heights. Some wear a slab with a small boulder stopping it all blowing away. Crossing little River Lot signs point Le Parc National des Cévennes. Mont Lozére and Le Pont de Montvert.

D20 narrows. Houses lean over the road toward each other. Old blue enamel sign blisters rust. 'Route du Mt. Lozére.' A new world of countryside. Meadow diminishes under steep forest hill. A bridge favourable for lunch. Watching water race over the rocks. My fresh baguette still warm, adding savoury paté and creamy Cantal cheese looking up at forested hills masking higher gradients to climb.

'Col de Finiels' on a blue sign. The information sign missing does not say it is closed. Pinewood fringe hill cleaved road. Ascending narrow hill contour. From rock bursts yellow broom, cascading heather pink and purple fall down the face. Buttercups and cow parsley amongst wild grass along edge verge drop. Little tumbling river dropping clear over boulders, foaming white under a backdrop of dark hill forest. Many mixed trees fight for footing and light on a steep rise. Pocket steep pastureland supports grazing herds. Glimpses through trees. Secret waterfall betrayed by roaring noise. Grass areas swallowed by forest the higher I climb. Joining hills run into each other away to high black forest horizon's ghosting mist shroud.

Twist and turn climb. High bald hill tops momentarily exposed by misted vapour lift. An approaching vehicle. I let a pickup truck overtake disappearing around a corner, appearing after a minute high above. Forest weave release. Scant grass, raw boulder wild ground.

A view back down the snaking sinuous ascent framed by overhanging trees. Below rock face splashed in wild floral decoration. The farm mas of Malaveille below the road starts with dog pounds. Hunting dogs pick up my scent, their eyes focus upward on the stranger moving on the dogworld outer space vehicle of a bicycle. Dogs do not comprehend the physical appearance of the bicycle. Let the barking commence. From behind the chainlink they offer annoyance as opposed to open ground threat. Numerous hounds climb over each other standing on their back legs to get the best bark of enjoyed pantomime rehearsed for every traveller outside of a vehicle. Vehicles do not disperse slow bountiful release of human scent. In the dogs mind they bark, it goes away. Works every time, in the brain of a dog.

A separate pound for puppies growing to youth. Father and young son walk down a path toward them. Puppies are at the fence on their back legs clambering over each other in anticipation for the visit. Excited squeals and yips already well practiced in the manners of their elders.

Sheds of rusting corrugated iron, doors decayed rusted hinges improvised shut by the leaning weight of bulk timber. Worn out tractor tyre holds bent dented roofing sheets. Amongst the weeds an old upturned bath, iron legs in the air. Rusting wheelbarrow is tangled in fencing wire. The road turns above the collection of agricultural dwellings. One has a caved roof. Lone gable in seasonal erosion. Living continues in the other half, smoke curl rises from the chimney. Other dwellings very old all share a precarious spectacular view.

Back into forest. Rooftop silhouette of abandoned chalets under reclamation by nature's creeping branch and tendril coil smothering at seasonal pace. Galvanised towers hold cables. Ski lifts carry no one. Flat plateau café windows of warm occupation filled by the contents of three parked cars grey swept in vapour waves.

At the turn of the twentieth century a two storey building then old, of summer refuge known as the Baraque de Secours with earth floors dispensing abrupt and rude hospitality.

The immediate 'Station de Ski du Bleymard. Mont Lozére. 1400m (4250ft)' is closed. Ski lift wheels unmoving, chairs sway empty. Lonely whistle of mist grey wind cut by heavy cables dropping into cloud blankness. 'Ski-Location-VTT' today is not sportif. It is abandoned bleak. Under the canopy I peer through dusted window to internal blackness taking a drink and eating snacks to top up leg energy. Steepness needs straight leg strength levering the handlebars to ascend into enveloping heavenly cloudscape.

The view is not far, all colour subdued monochrome. Sombre silhouettes of rock and bush motionless loom from grey white fog. I read that it is possible to see the Alps from Mont Lozére. Stevenson commented from the summit people claimed to have seen ships in the Mediterranean. The person

I believe is the Le Bleymard inhabitant of a hundred years ago who said. "To see the Alps?!! Hah! The mountain is always misted. There is more chance in seeing the Beast of Gevaudan!"

I like the realist, using present experience I am swayed toward his definition as truth. The slog of mountain ascent continues in nothingness. I put the lights on knowing no one can see them. Bright beam instantly absorbed.

The surreal emptiness of fog gives knowledge through memory of a visual world continuing outside of the cloud. But inside the vapour world, travel is through nothing to an immediate nowhere and is taking a lot of effort to achieve it on the lowest gear. I would welcome a couple more. The drawn monotone voice of the Langogne Dutchman arrives into my head telling me about my gears.

"No, eet iz not pozzible to have ze more. Vour kmph, It vil be too slow."

Road levels. Ghosted shape gallows appear through the blowing cloud world holding static creaking ski lifts. Gallows for a Dutchman.

Road vision increases. Trees beyond the visual immediate. Light increases, cloud lifts enough to see eye level and below. Scrubby trees, grass and scree drop wild barren. Back into mist, blowing wind speeds the cloud. Breaks in the tumbling vapour. Stumpy tree bald boulder moorland. Dense fog disorientation, steep gradient maximum effort. Dark shape smooth roar. Forest. A sign against dense fir trees. 'Col de Finiels alt 1541m' (4620ft). The end of hard climbing. A fight with the waterproof coat to find the sleeves in blowing wind. Over my wet sweated top in anticipation of fast cooling descent.

We meet again Mr Stevenson. No night sleeping under pines in the company of the stars. But I share the noise experience of massing wind in raw rude empty landscape.

Visibility nothing across the summit of Mont Lozére. Bike lights stay on in the half-light. Slow descent roll across barren moorland. Somewhere not too far away across a hilltop, maybe in the next valley, the source of the great River Tarn.

Around a corner, road rolls to a drop. Country bigger with every wheel rotation. Rude raw granite boulder strewn land. Thick mist stone monster shapes loom blurred from background drab. Perfect weather to experience Mont Lozére. I feel much at home in the granite strewn moorland. I can imagine Stevenson feeling the same from experience of high Scotland. Mazed boulders do not make for easy donkey walking.

Tumbled tors, shattered cliff. Rubble stone cabins in various states of wear and dereliction, atmospheric in thinning mist tumble. Thick granite lintel over deep set doorway supports shallow granite gable. Dead turf roof fallen, caved greyed timber supporting laths rot, broken rafter grey bleached. Rusted corrugated iron cabin roof. A red rectangle colour challenge to sombre green grey blowing dominance.

Mist breaks a few seconds of view. Steep deep valley. Far away stone ridge in shattered tumble. Fast drop along a curving hillside. Sharp bends. The hamlet of Finiels. A stream, stone dwellings, stone outbuildings, granite rubble wall enclosures. Small moorland campsite in cold rolling bleakness. Raw landscape steep. Descending narrow weave, edge drop off.

Into a vast deepening valley. Hill after folding hill cleaved deep, planetary. Water runs from above rocky crag through thin green. Scoured ditch flows full around mossed granite boulder channelled under the road. Waterworn passage through many land folds joining, rushing to form busy flow.

Rough road, travelling at speed. Open weathered pothole, stone gravelled bends. Centuries trod paths, wild hillside ramble traverses stony ridge. Birch woodland in the depths of sheltered valley spreads the further I descend. Areas of steep cultivated pasture grazed by young sand brown bullocks. The road. A narrowed lane cleaved from rough cliff under growing overhang. Tree cling, steep rock. Over a bridge, pulling the brake levers. Rocky cascade falling from above. A sheet of water under the bridge freefalls to foam white over great slabs of smooth rounded grey granite. Water bubbles through deep pools black tranquil smooth. Dropping over domed boulder rock in speed tumble. From the thundering waters, cool freshening vapours rise. Surrounding ash woodland. Leaves bright in summer colour. The thin branch nod from breeze generated by the thundering tumble.

Speed descent green leaf canopy blur. Out over steep drop grey slate rooftop Le Pont-de-Montvert nestled deep in the valley floor astride a convergence of rivers.

Lane of ancient houses. Simple chapel with a single bell. Riverside road, a few shops, a restaurant. The medieval high arc bridge under square tower guard. The rock and boulder strewn River Tarn rumble.

Camping municipal points to cross the river. Streets of stone houses look back to the main town. Rows of large dwellings on high riverbank bedrock. Church spire rise behind.

Pont de Montvert is famous for torture, murder and the catalyst for religious war. The torture was perpetrated by the Catholic Archpriest of the Cévennes against the staunch protestant Cévennes people to convince them to renounce their faith and convert. Banned from leaving the area the resistance against the intolerance grew. Ending in a march on the town by psalm singing armed Protestants breaking into the Archpriest Du-Chayla's house. Setting free captives from basement torture dungeons under gun fire before burning the house forcing the inhabitants to climb from the window and escape across the river. Du Chayla fell, breaking his hip and was dragged into the town and stabbed by many whose families had suffered by his tortures. He died of fifty two stab wounds. The crowd went on a night of murdering vengeance resulting in the war of the Camisards. The state and Vatican hunting the Protestant guerilla forces, who in turn hunted Catholics and government dragoons using many places of hiding spread across the whole wilderness Cévennes. Which house was Du Cheyla's residence?

The knowledge of these macabre events learned from the book of Stevenson's travels.

Camping municipal sits at the base of Montagne du Bougés. Steep hill views surround the town reaching back to Mont Lozére. High hills of green, scree and rock strewn tors littered boulders bigger than houses wait out time for the soil to erode to slide and tumble. Terraces scratched from the steep hillside built up on little rocky walls make horizontal areas generations old that have cultivated vegetables and fruit from collected scant rocky soil hauled up in buckets. Lower scrubby trees in turn are smothered by full woodland wild sprawl along the valley sides to the river edge amongst the rock. The height of the hills make for a small sky. A feeling of shelter from barren altitude. Shelter and water, the basic necessities for human survival have made this place an agreeable choice for centuries of habitation.

Into the Accueil, paying the polite lady for a night's accommodation. I am to pitch in an area for randonneurs containing one tent.

The pole snaps. I fix it using a hacksawed half round tent peg wrapped in tape to splint the break. The tape is tough and needs a lot of pressure to cut with the knife. The knife slips and I stab myself deep between the knuckles of my thumb, just the once. A fitting accident to honour town history. I hope that is the end of role play, binding my thumb with pink plasters that fast turn crimson. Wrapping it all with insulation tape. After half an hour blood ceases to run.

My randonneur neighbour is English. Arriving by train to Chasseradés a couple of days ago travelling from Clermont Ferrand. He is walking part of the Stevenson route to Florac. Then further down the Gorges du Tarn to meet his girlfriend and father who are at a campsite holidaying.

I shower with my thumb in the air, eat thumbs up and converse with Richard on the experiences of landscape travelled. We are both in agreement about crossing both Montagne du Goulet and Mont Lozére in mist and fog was a blessing. Not having to endure brilliant hot windless sunshine to dehydrate the body over the climbs. Plus the mist and fog made the adventure more atmospheric. We discuss the beauty of the forest and the appreciation of desolate Mont Lozére.

I comment on how I felt at home amongst the mist and granite.

Richard had not experienced high boulder strewn lands with fog. Coming from less dramatic landscape above the Midlands of England. It was a relief to get below cloud level.

How differing perception of a single place is judged against experience of faraway native land.

He had camped last night at Le Bleymard on his own in the empty municipal campsite next to the River Lot. Nobody arrived for the money. So he left it jammed in the Accueil door. After discussing the Stevenson book we decided to go into town to try and find Du Chayla's house.

A walk crosses a tumbling river feeding the Tarn. Old stone habitation, steps up to doorways with slabbed landings to mount a horse or load a cart. A walk over the bridge to pollarded trees. The restaurant too late in the evening to serve a meal. A few people sit talking, drinks on the table. Thirty people amble the sleepy town to the background river rush echoing the steep valley. I recognise the bright nylon randonneurs from Chasseradés. Not fatigued. They must be travelling between villages by car.

River Rieumalet has tumbled the long valley from Mont Lozére arriving over boulders between houses on cliffside rock. Water roar feeds the Tarn. Through streets to the church topped with a slate spire. A large monument iron cross of hearts depicting the crucifixion looks down in the fading light of evening. Alleyways lead to the river. Which was the house? Richard informs me it was pulled down because of its unpleasant history. Others say the torture dungeon was the bridge tower. Stevenson said it was a house. A large house backs onto the river with terraced gardens near the bridge, not far from the church. Maybe this was the place? We nominate it. Idle entertainment satisfied, even if it isn't.

Looking back at the terrace wall from the river's edge. Escape would give good chance of survival. The river full of large smooth washed boulders as big as a man, the opposite bank tree covered through rough dry channel ground would give good odds against the musket ball. Also it was night. The only illumination would have come from the flames of the burning house.

Back to the campsite I am given a demonstration of a hobo stove made from a cat food tin burning meths. The small tin can has holes punched around the top. Meths' poured a third inside is lit and the saucepan boils hotter than a gas stove. Alcool á brulant is available at nearly all supermarkets and hardware shops. The days of carrying spare gas cylinders are over. Small to pack, light to carry. Ingenious. From gas I am converted.

The wild sky of dusk grows dark blue signaling night's approach. Dramatic clouds driven by strong wind blow as

black billowing smoke rolling tumbling across the tops of black mass hill silhouette. Sheltered below, huddle the little yellow lit windows of Le Pont de Montvert gazing across the river tumble.
42 km

The Stevenson Route: The Valley of the Tarn

Hard showers amplified by night blackness, I wake fully at 6.30am. Moody sky broken to blue, sun splashed rocky high tors in new day gold. Shaded Le Pont de Montvert will not feel the warming sun until the great fireball climbs surrounding hills. I have a coffee for breakfast with some leftover cookies finishing a half full carton of night chilled fresh milk to save carriage. Free camera charging is courtesy from a working electric point next to an unused caravan.

A sizeable lump moves under the groundsheet, removing the inside of the tent reveals a frowning toad, puffed up and indignant upon disturbance. The cold blooded creature was enjoying the warmth from my body under the groundsheet. Au revoir.' The freeloading reptile heads for the bushes in lumbering grumbling pace.

Richard is packed and wants to walk along the road to Florac instead of going over the hill on the GR70. Stevenson took the narrow road then new. There is the modern problem of encountering traffic. The map shows possibility of many blind bends. I will use the presence of the bike to improve our visibility to passing drivers.

Boulangerie door opens. Fresh baking smells served by a

polite smiling lady. Breakfast on the hoof crossing the shallow rushing river to the guarding tower. D998 signed Florac. Past our nominated house of Du Chayla following the River Tarn in downstream direction. Under the spired church, a road lined with old houses, river views between. A cross painted on a blue door reads 'Culte Protestant.' All the murdering and persecution centuries past has led to both religious pathways quietly biding together on the same street.

Above the rooftops. Into the green twist turning with the land. The view back to Le Pont de Montvert. Its appealing grey jumble bathed in sunshine under green sprawling valley. Bald steepened hillsides ridged with splintered rock glow green suede. River silver between boulder filled channels, the pointed medieval town bridge. Every feature in view holds lengthened shadow of early morning sun. Bright woodland, opens reflecting sky blue Tarn pools. Le Pont de Montvert has gone.

Waterfalls, fine built stone bridges. Water tumbles rocky steps through trees. Opposite slopes of Montagne du Bougés rise scant high over our mid valley wander. Over treetops of oak, glimpses to silvering river pools. Above our heads moss covered granite boulders the size of a car sit half buried in steepened woodland. Trees grow from fissured rock. Dancing road shadows shorten. Sun's climb matches the rising hand of the clock marking progress against the hour.

We are in discussion of what the broken old trees are? They grow from half rotten splintered trunks and boughs new sweet green branches with long waxed pale green leaves, edges serrated. The branch ends with a bloom of long delicate hanging yellow covered in fine white blossom similar in shape to the flower of a palm. Their offspring of healthy young trees grow the same, the more we look the more we see. These individuals relish steep slopes and vertiginous rooting. They are the Spanish chestnut trees once revered. The nut harvest was a major income and food source for the Cévennes. This was as far as Mr. Stevenson managed from Le Pont de Montvert before making his camp somewhere above us up on the steep hillside.

Rocky woodland road, pleasant river roar valley reverberation. Opposite steep forested hillside under cloud empty cosmos. Richard walks, I either walk or lazily sit freewheeling alongside without a turn of the crank. Verge stop for the occasional passing vehicle. Cliff bend reveals a far unfolding view south towards destination. Large curved hillside folds neatly behind large curved hillside again and again. River passage defined by zig zag black line. Distant valley terminates rudely. Blocked by towering hard rock escarpment running horizontal as natures fortress wall topped off by rolling suede horizon. The Causse Mejean. Beyond, Languedoc hills fall to Mediterranean coastal flatland.

Views into the river. Deep channels of green submerged brown tinted rounded boulders, silver shimmer turbulence. Speeding current plunge from smooth worn slab changes to rapids. Dry bleached boulders stranded high until winter flood. Quiet deep pools, sand shallows form white beaches fringed by bright green young woodland.

Surrounding hills steep sub mountainous define southern landscape. River size doubled since Le Pont de Montvert. Rare areas of pasture already harvested, cut and rolled. Yellow aftermath stubble bleaches under the burn. Small fields too poor to harvest left fallow. A small village. Vernéde chapel with a single bell on a plateau. Above the village, paths crisscross terraced. Steepened background becomes Montagne du Bougés.

The roof of a chateau through the green. Imposing brown

stone tower watches our pedestrian progress from small square windows commanding river and road. Military austere of purpose. Unlike northern relatives slumbering gold leaf pomp. The rear of the building has a round defensive tower guarding its elevated plateau watching the road. Our passage away from the Tarn wanders woodland. Small river in a hurry tumbling from steep long valley. High climbing rocky hills stack up again and again, rugged topped castellated tors. Chance glimpse of surrounding wild landscape.

A bridge, junction signed 'Rúnes.' Geology change from granite to brown cliff shattered rectangles. Hard bands of white quartz run through broken strata. Rock flowers, strange cacti relatives hold in cracks. Road follows the river through 90 degrees. Wilder lands. A rocky gorge.

Across the river wild pines grow sparse, tall thin matchstick woodland clings steep, brown rock rising high to towers of vertical cliff. River smooth across white and brown riverbed slab, flowing blue green tint deepening colour over darkened pools. We spend time looking standing on the bend. I notice a path through the undergrowth. Richard disappears following its passage to come back a couple of minutes later telling me it looks to run all the way down to Eden.

Narrow path undergrowth weave. Stony track clamber under leafy bough smother, climbing over rock. Increasing noise of water rush reveals bright white pebble beach. River wider, deeper than viewed from the road. Upstream smooth granite worn by ceaseless flow has sculpted bowls and holes eroded from trapped rattling stones forming nature's ancient modern art.

I walk, clamber and jump across sun warmed slabs to the river bend until I can progress no more. Boulder rapids roar, river wide and shallow runs boiling, composing itself to flow tranquil glass over underwater flat shelf browned by growing algae. Slabs channel the river to a narrowing. Constriction increases speed. Fast current smooth standing wavelets stepping down to deep roaring flow. I jump and climb over rock, downstream beach of white sand is held in a rock cove. The river calms before narrowing rock squeezes the water broiling through a spout roaring a waterfall drop onto rock opening to full valley width. Further fast calm, noisy turbulent, deepening black flow in sun shimmer under hard cliff. Sparse riverside wood softens green to a gorge of dark stone. Cliff sides rise high from the river forested, the far bank coniferous. Stone crag height looks down. The nearside gorge softer. Fir, pine and conifer slopes bright green in full summer leaf amongst tumbling rockscape. The above cleaved road, steep rock rolls high out of view.

I have an exit point. The channel runs deep over submerged boulders. I can come out of the current before the waterfall. Sliding down the rock into the freshening river. The current grab, speeding the channel. Rock dodge water boil. Fast strokes head for the beach. Water shallows, current release, toes grip the sand. I get out laughing before the current grab for death's rock plummet waterfall.

Upstream over the rock slabs for a repeat. The power of the current, hundreds of tons of speeding water. Swept downstream impossible to fight. Temperature fresh, blood cooled. I have a repeat run underwater. Open eyes see opaque colours, blue green, the flash of boulders. To the surface, the fast approach of the beach.

The primal joy of water immersion. Dressed, refreshed, a water invigorated body. Drying sun warms the skin. This is how to bathe in Eden.

"You have to do it Richard!"

A moment later he races with the current and heads to the beach, getting out with a broad smile and a laugh of excitement, running to repeat the fun.

"This place is breathtaking. A corner of Eden!"

He replies. "What a place to camp!"

"What a place and all the tourists are miles away downstream."

Laughter.

All praise to Robert Louis!! He has bought us here today by his wonderful written words.

We sit and eat noticing detail, soaking up the scenery. Talking about the place, the good feeling of Le Pont de Montvert, the Travels with a donkey book. Listening to descriptions by Richard of the Gorges du Tarn he has visited many times. He must get there tomorrow to keep to his schedule, then catch a flight back to England.

It is time to move. To leave a rare place where daily repetition of a visit would never become tiresome. A place to learn the seasonal moods. We are witness to the change between spring and summer, have read the description of Stevenson's autumn. Wrapped in the warm of winter clothes it would be good to marvel at the rivers winter consuming violence. It must be powerful if it can move boulders the length of a man and stack them high on the riverbank at will. We cannot stay. Instead to be driven by the enslavement of schedule, but also by the traveller's curiosity of what lies around the next bend.

Rocky climb up through bushes, the consuming roar diminishing with distance, reducing to quietened background sound shared with birdsong. Chestnut trees overhang the road, landscape grows vertical closing the valley with high castellated crags natural broken battlements. Road bend and river twist sharpen.

The village of Cocourés detour keeps to the old road wandering through narrow pedestrian shaded lanes between old stone bulge deep doorway shadow. Twisted chimney stack above overhang of heavy ragged slate. Ancient dwellings individual, living accommodation over rooms for livestock. Cart animal half buried low entrances from the hilly lane. Narrows rise to twist on a crest, dropping to a little square. Small church hang a brightly polished bell under arch protection. Small blue Notre Damme behind glass in a wood shrine looks from above the doorway. A group of people sit on a low wall in conversation, voice echo captive from surrounding windowed walls.

A pause to greet. Polite. "Bonjour."

Winding lane deposits back to the Florac road.

Downhill sweet fragrant fresh cut pine. Lumber yard processes piled trunks next to a growing heap of sweet smelling woodchips. Abrasive whine of blades ripping timber drowns smooth river roar.

A church looks as if it had the design changed daily as it grew higher. Square tower brown stone over an arched door. Above are long arched windows, a round window. Above, large stone Notre Damme under a sculpted overhang. Above, square bell tower and a tall pointed slate spire. A top heavy cake of too many tiers. Joined to the tower, a fortress complete with battlements. The thing stands alone. Behind sit the spire and village rooftops of Bédoues.

Old stone bridge has pinned iron through ties bolted under tension, keeping the structure together. The Tarn tamed tranquil to a pond of deep brown gold. Reflection without ripple, rich tree overhang, bright white boulder and pebble beach. Beyond returns turbulent. Views tree hidden. Steep forested hills lush colour against clear blue afternoon horizon high escarpment.

Scant brown green, part rock. The Gorges du Tarn.

A couple arrive from Bédoues recognising Richard having met yesterday on the trail. They have just crossed the steep high hills of the GR70, walking from Le Pont de Montvert under cloudless sunny sky. Richard explains how we followed Stevenson along the slowly descending road route. A few minutes of happy conversation and they head for their accommodation this side of Florac.

Short hill drops us at the entrance to a campsite. We are not too sure if it is the municipal site. The only clue I can remember is that it has the word 'pont' in its title. 'Smiling happycamperland' is popular with holidaying families. It will do.

The tent is pitched. Deciding to visit Florac to escape from barbeques, screaming children and the very large wall T.V showing sport watched by fat bellied men sunburned in shorts. Their idea of sport participation is visual. Involving numerous monoped sprints from table to bar, returning with a refilled glass and a campsite burger and 'frites.'

The River Tarnon runs through a valley of woodland. Opposite high slopes rise to vertical cliffs 500m (1500ft) making the Causse Méjean. A mind absorbing view. The Causses shaped towers of rock stand singular in skyward sweep, dwarfing the rooftops of Florac.

Houses and shops share town street. Yellowing soft evening sunlight, long shadows thrown across walls. Town square busy. Plane tree shade. Covered areas, tables set for evening meals. Tall building long windowed balconies look over the street. Occupants sit people watching. Presence betrayed when called to by friends from below. An evening meal. Watching the people of the town watching the people of the town.

Many little shops open to browse. Street walls in people

echo. Sun reddens to a fading glow behind high cliffs.

Changed lands. The Highlands of France have been left up the valley. The air breathed has a warmed fragrance that belongs to the south.

20 km

The Stevenson Route: Valley of the Mimente Crossing the Desert In Search of Modestine

6.15am. Peace of early morning, a tent free of morning dew. No hurry waiting out time for shop doors to open for food and funds. Water boil chatters tea ritual. Richard packs his tent and rucksack needing as much time as he can to complete a 32km walk. Clear sky promises him a hot day. He must cross the river and follow the Tarn downstream. The map offers a narrow lane route into the gorge to meet with his girlfriend and father. Today we travel opposite direction. Farewell fellow traveller. Et bon route!

I wheel out as people surface. Florac cashpoint. Supermarket stock up. 9.30am. Shaded pharmacy reads 24 degrees and rising.

The other end of town, Camping Pont Neuf. Municipal looking site along the edge of the Tarnon. That was the name in memory.

Road junction reads N106. Proclaimed 'Vallee de la Cévenols.' Following the pretty River Tarnon full of sizeable trout waiting out of the main current for petit déjeuner to arrive. I travel against the flow, road pulls a gentle incline.

Nature's castle rock rise. Henry Moore giants' sculpted. Tall freestanding pinnacles. Catherdal flying buttresses hold the Cause Mejean from collapse. Giants weathered, too big to contemplate fashioned by the hand of man.

The Tarnon shallower than yesterday's Tarn. Calm pool reflects steep wooded hills green to the summit. Road leaves the river. Bends weave new views. Red brown mountainous rock wear scant hardy pine. Mountainous splintered cliff mass claims the sky. Road twist, the base of high craggy rockscape between full sun and cast blanket shadow. Sweet roar given by River Mimente. Chestnut and birch splash bright green amongst dark dry pine and coarse tuft yellowed grass. Into the valley of the Mimente, opening enough to house an opposite hamlet under black chateau ruin reached by a little bridge spanning the trickle. I stop to eat, enjoying the view to the old ruin wondering how much stone has been taken from the chateau to build and maintain surrounding houses. Post revolution.

Contrast between sides of the river. Opposite bank rockscape. This side rich green woodland. Lane winds a hill. Stream tumble chimes through woodland to the Mimente.

Through overgrown woodland cleave, a disused stone bridge crosses the stream. Narrow road no longer used reclaimed by nature's smother. Wading stinging nettle and thorny bramble crossing the bridge in tendril grip over which one man and his donkey would have crossed. A little bit of history. Helping to keep the journey as authentic as modern day allows. N106. Stone walls along the inner edge older than the two way widened. This side very much authentic in footstep and hoof.

The valley hospitable, dramatic cliff mellows to steep hill cultivation amongst wild growing bush and scrubby tree. Across the river runs an old railway line disused of many years part overgrown. Bridges and stone walls follow the valley, its path hewn by dynamite, sledgehammer and shovel. Road drops between steep hillside to crossroads. Sign directs Cassagnes. Single track. Above disused fields, fallow grass and thicket. Boundary post grey rotting gnarled, leaning holding remnant wire rust. Clumps of trees mark the way of a stream descending the hillside. Background spartan green, topped by fallen tors. Lower hillside overgrown, stone walled terrace layered steep. Earth no longer grows a tended crop in modern supermarket world where food appears full grown vaccum wrapped scrubbed harvested from articulated chiller transport.

Hillside arc, slate roof silver dazzle. Road rise, long curved house terrace shuttered closed. Road to a little church. The village once burned and destroyed in the religious wars by the state. Its hills hiding the Camisards in above secret caves. The huddled sleeping village guarded by one barking fluffy terrier defending open door territory. I ride out the way I came in.

Crossing main road buzz. Zig zag under tree cover to river noise. A hidden railway station with an old iron riveted water tower no longer replenishes steam engines. The centuries roll by. Stevenson boarded overnight back at Chasserades with survey engineers for the proposed Cévennes railway. 1870's efficient superhighway travel. Horse plod replaced by steam pressure. Superseded by the highway of a thousand daily cars. Past ingenuity joins the obsolete. Pathways left to walk or cycle. The only daily steam from an installed coffee machine. Industrial buildings used for refreshment in pursuit of idle leisure.

I cross the Mimente over a clattering iron bridge. A closed up house, river tumbles between rock slab and boulders. Sounds of woodland singing birds. Direction split. D162 woodland climb. Steep sided valley reverberates below rushing water. Streams trickle green hillside in crystal chime and gurgle. Up through green tint illumination of a thousand tree trunks gripping sheer side hill observing my granny gear progress. Luminous bracken pale green, yellow and orange yellow butterflies dance. Waterfall cleave dries barren. Sun floods, trees thin to reveal the summit of Plan de Font Mort. A battleground in the Camisard war. A memorial stands tall made of stone in celebration of peace.

> *150th ANNIVERSARY*
> *The edicit of tolerance*
> *OF THE MARTYRS*
> *OF THE "DESERT"*
> *Le Protestants of France*
> *Museum of the Desert 1937.*

For the efforts of the 300m (900ft) climb I am rewarded with a fantastic panorama of the wild Cévennes. Far away rocky mountains bathed in blue. Folded jumbled compressed, sharp ragged shapes, arid, unnavigable. A place to be lost in forever. 'Le Desert.' The hiding place of the guerillas of the 1700's. Being without roads the state dragoons would have felt very vulnerable under watched terrain. Cut off at the next turning. Roads were built, to patrol and ruthlessly subvert the villages wiping out the protestant occupants from above with cannon, fire and sabre. Modern day, the roads serve as ways to cover this beautifully strange part of France. Coiled road threads back and forth weave in and out of view through the immense area. The brakes are off, up through the gears. Speed, speed. Out into the sunshine. 'Le Desert' downward rock and scrub ride, the cicada buzz. Aeroplane view tiny roofs of farm buildings lost in vast blue land. Far below miniscule buildings on edge drop offs. This is nature's big rock engineering project. Brakes, leaning 'S' bends. Hairpin drop through rude raw land. Houses built into rock above and below the narrow road cling to the hillside. 'Nougaret.' Left without inhabitants. The rusting steel shutters of an empty municipal building swing open banging against the wall throughout four seasons. Broken windows, empty. Bare wires trail bare boards. The building becoming a victim to the ingress of all weathers nearing dilapidation. The opposite dwellings empty for years. The sound of people laughing rises. A rooftop near vertically down has a terrace where people sit relaxing and conversing. Occupied habitation maybe seasonal. But it is habitation.

Road bend. The cicada mechanical unison pulse. Heated shimmer. Deep open valley, rising far rock hills. Farm mas perch on the edge of vertical running ridge. Dwelling of isolation high above. Ribbon road zig zag threads barren scrub weaving rock and cliff. A way out.

Clifftop sharp bends. Panoramic views for miles under blue sky force a stop. The beauty of consuming emptiness. An area of natural silence, the sound of wilderness. Unusual for the 21st century. So important connecting the past with the moment. Not a century past, but unmolested ten thousand years plus. The roads built and land depopulated by history cannot be changed. It needs leaving alone to the people that live here, born to the area and no one else. Including far away big brother restriction of committee decision. Un-fenced, un-prettified, empty. Raw.

Unhindered seasons rotate in timeless silence. Butterflies never seen before flit their dance looking for nectar of the flower. A sharp bite through my sweated clothing breaks concentration of the moment. The horsefly a monster. Telling me clear off. Or give blood.

Speed through endless bends, a deep gully in the hill, the road has collapsed to a long drop. Temporarily repaired by the silent machine parked in shade of narrow road. Signed St.Germaine-de-Calberte. A track on a bend. Bearded young counter culture waves smiling greeting. Below in a perfect fit with the shape of the hill a Yurt tent with shining black metal chimney surrounded by piles of firewood for the full four seasons. Wild living free subsistence for free thinkers comes complete with front porch aeroplane views.

Through Mazel Rosade. Old clinging houses huddled together occupied. Laverie against a cliff. Rock welling spring feeds the trough protected by an arched stone cabin. Water to wash and for the colder months water protected from the elements. Bend after bend tarmac ribbon through natures rock garden fringed in twisted pine. Purple and pink heather, weathered rock, steep ground pine cone littered. The distance descended measured against height of the hills closing around do nothing to subdue the vertiginous edge drop. Far down little rooftops are industrial farm buildings in big land agriculture.

The road turns about a ridge. Hillside of chestnut explode pale yellow blossom waiting for pollenating insects to start the fruit cycle. Trees massive, split in half continue new branch growth. Ancient split wood forms ornate twisting pattern, new trees together in bushy youth battle for light dominance. Others pollarded years past by tending hands. Amongst the chestnut, cherry trees hold deep red and black ripe fruit swell waiting to be picked, this whole area once an important cultivated garden of nuts and fruit. The gutter of the road full of chestnuts of past season uncollected amongst the husks, all gone to waste. Horseflies return. I have stopped for only a minute. At the bottom of the hill the road to St.Germain-de-Calberte. Square spire above the slated jumble old houses rise to old stone wall cultivation terraced to above rocky pine forest covering the village dwarfing hill. Stevenson stayed a night here after a long day's journey arriving after dark from the Valley of the Mimente. A considerable achievement of distance over unfriendly walking terrain. It is also the final resting place for the Archpriest Du Cheyla being bought here from Le Pont de Montvert.

Persued even when dead. His funeral raided by the Camisard guerillas. The priest and congregation scattered leaving the dead man in the church.

The road signed for St Etienne-Vallee-Francais. Dropping to a wave of heat. Birds compete with the buzz of the cicada. Road bend, new bridge crosses River Gardonne. Pebble beach, river channel in quiet flow. Altitude touchdown.

Accommodation advertised 'Gite Stevenson' and 'Mas Stevenson.' The legend of the journey revered, albeit in commercial venture. Road climb gentle, tall walls into the village of St. Etienne-Vallée-Francaise. Narrow walled medieval part of the village fortified. Accessed through archways once gated. Living accommodation above, no windows below. The later additions to the village outside the walled centre are still very old. Leaning up the hill against each other. The tiny square dominated by the church. The door is open. Dim lit interior cool, musty smell from skin clinging damp. Stained glass window art, Notre Damme naturally lit cleverly from above. The statue has flowers at her feet. All glowing in half-light. Oil paintings of antiquity hang from plain walls.

The bleach of full sun brightness. A cross of iron depicts sacred hearts and sun rays. Facades of buildings mass floral display. St. Etienne-Vallée-Francaise holds the smell of money. The only wealthy place I have journeyed through in the Cévennes. Desirable residence commutable from St. Jean du Gard.

Downhill past cafés and restaurants. Fragrant blooms

decorate to entice the euro. A waitress looks up, giving a smiling "Bonjour."

Road straight descends, accelerating speed. Young counter culture sticks out a thumb.

A wave and a "Bonjour."

River reappearance has gained size. Flowing around a large pinnacle of rock holding a few pines. 12km to St. Jean du Gard. Bridge crosses a tributaries. Pleasant riverside stop. Views shared with a restaurant. I stop and get out a hunk of Cantal cheese and half a baguette to eat on the riverbank watching the flow around the rocks. A cloud of midges surround and descend to feast, landing in my eyes and mouth, choking. Stinking things. Late lunch never started. Back to the bike. The following insect cloud.

The start of a gorge. River Gardon de Mialet gathering size. Joining rivers feed the pleasing roar. Shallow and rapids tamed to deep green clear water. Colour intensified by white glow pebbles. Bright sandbank beaches fringed lush green with woodland. With every road turn rock cliff changes to sub mountain. Spartan pine isolated thin silhouettes on high barren ridge against primary blue Mediterranean bake. Where the pine tree's water supply has dried up, trees stand grey dead and branchless. Telegraph skeletons on tombstone ridge.

Pointed summit. More determined pines, trunk twist from rock fissure growth strains to vertical. Offspring in precarious mimic. The River Gardon de Mialet flows deep green and wide through impressive landscape.

Road leaves the river and the wild Lozére to enter the Gard. My watch tells me it is 3.45pm. Within a minute a loud bray from a donkey echoes the hillsides. Sounded across the border. How fitting for the moment. Or is it the ghost of Modestine?

Tight narrow bend climb. Traffic dodge skills. I have hardly encountered a vehicle for hours. Upward through woodland to a crest, down through smells of cut pine. Fringe habitation, road end at traffic light junction. The mind takes a few moments to adjust to town vehicle blur.

Green light descent. Aged terraced town. St. Jean du Gard. Traffic noise, pedestrians. Moped cloud of blue two stroke. Everybody hurrying somewhere. Even chic shoppers rush a pace. Caution in traffic. Upward glance, blue plaque street name. By luck. 'GRAND RUE.'

Corner displays shining stock of a hardware shop on the path. Street old narrow, high facade loom. The number needed. 125. Watching the numbers climb in favour. Many closed doors in narrow street shade echo. Dwellings amongst shops. Three storeys, five. Dusty window display, roller shutter closed. Names for the post box. Names for the doorbell. Homes for many generations. Wire crisscross high between buildings. Numbers lead to an address next door to a wine shop. A large fading green bottle cut out, a black painted label 'PINET.' There is no need to knock on a door. Everything is outside.

125 Grand Rue has a very old iron hitching ring on the door reveal. This is where Modestine was hitched after Stevenson sold her. I am standing in the road astride the bike looking at the accompanying sign.

The 4.10.1878
R.L.STEVENSON
tethered "Modestine"
his female donkey.

An arrow points to the hitching ring.

Noises from behind as a couple arrive at the address. Opening the door, struggling laden with shopping.

"Bonjour."

They guess I have stopped to see the ring in the wall.

I ask if I may take a photo.

"Of course!" The lady adds proudly. "Stevenson sold the donkey in this house."

I thank them adding. "I am not the first to find my way to this address?"

They laugh and tell me. "There have been many."

The door closes. I lean my bike against the wall, a couple of photos and flick the hitching ring with my fore and index fingers. The iron hoop chimes against the masonry.

I cycle down the street.

This is where the Travels with a donkey in the Cévennes ends. To the doorstep. 'The Stevenson route GR70' continues on to Alés. Stevenson travelled there by coach, post book. 125 Grand' Rue is the closure.

I like the spin the owner of the house has just put on the end of the story. The book details notes post story saying different. But she has it handed down by word of mouth from owner to owner. How things over time mythologise, facts become part blurred. No one knows the exact route apart from the detailed old roads and drovers routes. The rest of the route has been nominated by vague memory interpreted by reasoned supposition or handed down the same as I have just experienced. To become an enigma can only add romance to the journey and the more romance the better.

Chapeau a vous Monsieur Stevenson!
Voyageur d' avant-garde!

I ride around the streets of St. Jean du Gard. A beautiful high arched stone bridge crosses blue tranquil river. Framed by steep dark green wooded hills falling to valleys meeting the riverflow in sun softened haze of late afternoon.

I buy postcards, find my way back out of town. Passing Grand Rue re unites traffic lights. Turning for lands west. Signs for 'Corniche des Cévennes.' Tomorrows route.

Road split. D907 and corniche D260. Under sits a campsite. The Accueil between the two roads at a farmhouse. The campsite across the road on the riverside where the petit River Gardon de St-Jean flows. I book in for one night.

"Pitch wherever you please."

Elevated at the river's edge with a water invite. Narrow deep flow gently around large boulders lapping sand and pebble beach. Opposite bank overhangs tree branches full leafed. Down to the water's edge. Pleasant cool extinguishes the body's road worn heat. Underwater my head is cooled.

Clambering the riverside boulders. The routine of shower, then eat. Sat outside of the tent watching tranquil flow. My neighbours for the evening so pleasant. I lend a lighter to a Frenchman struggling to light his barbeque with duff matches. A large Dutch family is busy arranging an outdoor banquet to feed the many while I sit in happy repose with a cold beer lifted to Mr. Stevenson, reflecting on another perfect days travelling. The peaceful ambience of the river is looked over by a tall forested spike. Colouring changes from dark green to black. Shadows lengthen with the falling sun under an orange sky.

69 km

Corniche Des Cévennes

The Gardon-St-Jean peaceably runs below my humble nylon abode. The happy contentment of greeting a new world born every day to those who wake outdoors. Another idealistic place to camp. Simple and beautiful. Sun's shielded appearance sends an orange glow across clear blue hitting spike summit, firing treetops from black to burning orange. Glowing warmth lowering with sun climb.

The ground dry, without morning dew to muddy the dust, not a leaf to stir. The Gardon presence of shaded noise upstream busy in small tumble regains composure to flow silent in fear of waking the campsite from contented slumber. Pools clear deep, looking into a mirror of shaded hill orange reflection. A hole through the middle of the world. Only trout stir the flowing glass. Insects taken, surface ripple radiates journeying downstream silent.

I wonder whether to stay for another night, but to leave a place in part longing remains fresh and good in memory. A compromise by not being in a hurry. Breakfast is slow, packing at half speed routine is a simple pleasure overlooked. Camera batteries get extra charge, stove busily boils happy chatter.

I am ready to leave at 9.30am. Waiting was a good idea as a small problem has been solved. The arrival of a white boulangerer's van selling fresh bread and pastries. The lady serving does a busy trade from a forming queue. Bread for the day and water capacity full I am saved from a St. Jean du Gard return.

'Au revoir' to the courteous French people on the next pitch and wave to the Dutch family. One of the children has an armful of fresh baguettes for the breakfast table. I cycle the slope, opposite the 'Corniche des Cévennes.' Col sign. 'Ouvert.'

Climbing. Hairpin bends, forest and rock. Clear sky temperature races through numbers beyond thirty. Hillside trees without density without number. Spaced and spindly, shade scant is welcomed where it shadows the road. Zig zag, the side of one hill. Zig zag, climbs the side of a valley. Sweated effort rewards fine views across great space. Barren scrub mountain peaks. Falling vertical sweep, many creased valleys. A long way to this morning's starting altitude. Glass windscreen glint on a bend coming from a gaping black mouth tunnel of two lanes cut through the base of rock mountain.

The morning sneaky squadron of horseflies return. The bite spurs the upward pace to escape the creepy insects. I am battling one noble insect that will not be swatted and will not give in. All others have given up the speeding chase. Looking behind for the biting offender's next assault I notice a roadrider. The fly quietly settles on my thigh, once the fly concentrates to bite, they do not look for the fatal swat that with practice comes quick and sweet.

The roadrider pulls alongside "Bonjour."

Between breathes saying. I was hard to catch up the hill.

I tell him. I was trying to escape le mouches, the flies. "Je horreur les mouches!"

He laughs and asks me where am I from?

England. Starting in France at Bretagne.

"I am from Anduze."

I passed near the town last year from Pont du Gard.

"This is the third day of proper summer this year, you bring the good weather with you!"

The rider is full of conversation. We get to Col de St-Pierre and stop, waiting for his friend to catch up.

I get information on the route and how beautiful this place is.

I mention places visited.

Knowing my route from Mont Lozére and rides last year near to Spain.

His friend arrives. A moment for breath. They are willing to ride with me. I tell them not to wait. My loaded pace will be slower.

"A la prochain!"

By the time I reach their coffee stop, they will be long gone. Distance grows, riders lost to trees around stony bends.

A hundred photo opportunities. Many visual moments. Gazing through trees windows to the vastness of 'Le Desert' Cévennes. Horseflies. One strange big yellow and black fly's stinging bite earns a dispatch, not before inflicting a widening crimson pool soaking my glove.

Panoramas of yesterday's downward trip. Road thread disappears in wild hill weave. Behind dusted rock hills, ridge upon ridge sharp edged and raw. The famous blue of the Cévennes. Waiting a year to experience the plunging rocky crags. It needs time to visually and mentally focus to accept and appreciate the size. A farm mas on a crag sat on a tiny arable plateau. A minute model on an island cut off by a surrounding world of vertiginous rock dotted with arid scrub falls sharp from the heat pulse into darkened chasm shade.

Road crest. Ridge road view Cévennes wonderment. A sharp bend, a rocky crag, a viewpoint. 180 degree panorama.

Uncountable maze from Massive Aigoual in the south around to the far away ridges above Gorges du Chassezac. Spine ridge multiplied reaching for Mont Lozere. It is difficult to conceive size. The roadrider understated the earthly barren beauty.

Twisting ribbon road drop. Speed speed, woodland blur. Chestnut trees, some perfect, others split grey half dead still produce supple branches growing new leaf, sprouting yellow blossom fountain. Motorcycles enjoy this road, there is no chance of wearing a tyre square negotiating endless bends. Behind I hear a homely familiar sound of twin purring pistons of classic British engineering. Two Triumph Meridan 650 Tigers roar past on French plates. Ideal roads for the low end power of the Great British parallel twin.

Long climb open sky heat. I drink. It is equalled by the amount pouring from my skin. A climb. The plod to another viewing area, the old road. The new safely cleaved road away from the drop off. A near 360 degree panorama.

Along a ridge top path, making extra noise through the ground with heavy feet warns sunbathing adders of my approach. Sun heated slate pokes through flowering heather and dry scrub bush. Quickening slope falls from sight through undergrowth tangle. The view is for many miles, I must have climbed 700m (2100ft). Heat shimmer silence. Long way down, tiny ribbon track road. Occasional rooftop lost consumed in vastness. I wonder how I crossed it yesterday. It looks unnavigable.

Poor soil crumbles to dry dusty powder under each footstep. I stop to look close up at the different flowers that happily thrive. A large white rock daisy, the hardy heathers. Conquerors of all climates and altitudes. A plant with fleshy points for leaves spiralling up a thick stem ending in many buds opening to yellow thin petals eight to a flower, it looks almost a cacti. Its name I have no idea. Blue bursts on the end of a thin stalk. Beautiful vibrant violet coloured flowers of five petals as delicate as butterfly wings. Wild encroaching dog rose throws white and pink petals. Bees provide ground level music with songs of work. Many butterflies flit open bloom.

In a tree a strange nest or cocoon. There is no obvious entrance to be the nest of a bird. A giant spider? It is the cocoon probably of the silk worm once farmed by the Cevenol people. Pieces of natural evolved engineering. Intricate, impenetrable.

Le Pompidou. First habitation since St. Jean du Gard arrives through trees and fields held on a small plateau. Little village, a few houses and two churches. One in part disrepair with a square bell tower topped with a slate roof. The other pristine with a gleaming polished bell suspended in an arch. Above the arch a trumpeting angel with a halo doubles for rifle practice full of bullet holes. Sport for the evangelical huntsman.

Village street climb. The immaculate Mairée hanging rose bloom over painted grey ornate railings. Road edge laverie trough of four levels tumbles a pleasant trickle.

Steep grind, sweat sting eyes. Car way above marks D9 climb. Brown rock rise to a hairpin bend. Up again needing full lungful's to grab oxygen from hot dry air. Cliffs of pale schist, the shape of the hill less angular. Steepness remains, white rock hill roll replaces sharp edge brown crag. 360 degree crest panorama. Half is of the Cevennes parched maze of blue ridge haze. Beyond. Flatter lands heat hazed shimmer melts with the sky. Other side grows Montagne du Bouges looked over by Mont Lozére. Further away the high brown plateau of Causse Mejean rises rock cathedral towers from naked underpinning cliff.

Flat road straight. Bleached pasture waits for baling. The phenomenon of will o' the whisp spinning cut hay on thermal currents rising from the field edge cliff drop. Hay spirals the air for fifteen seconds before falling back to earth. The twister appears further along the field repeating mischief across neatly turned lines of cut hay. Wild land. Boulder strewn. Rock rises rude across rough ground. Wild flower butterfly proliferation. Wild pine stunted, tinder dry heat shimmer. Resinous smell ready to combust.

Col du Faisses 1026m (3070ft). Hill rolls the road downward. Hot generated breeze. Ticking freewheel, sounds of riding without effort. Causse Mejean suede covered tops of great cliffs white streaked grey. Below stumpy forest eases into lands of chequered cultivation.

I am high up. On a ridge rising towards the Causses. Land drop holds plateaus. Small havens marooned on plummeting forest valleys falling to blackness. Old farm buildings crisp under heat slide down the steepness. Freewheel speed hard on the brakes, wheel cooling stop at St-Laurent-des-Treves. Dinosaur bones advertised. Tumbledown stone houses hold onto the rock, battered from the seasons' winds. Dusty doorway crispy paint. Bleached wood. Little windows peer vast area views. The Causse Mejean. The further Causse Sauveterre. A great white rock cone stands solitary. The edge of Mont Lozére. Land behind darkening the horizon marks the ending of the wetter Margeride.

The D9 now D983 speeding hot tarmac bends. Sunny wildflower aroma. Dry Causse overhead sculptured rock towers. Nature's giant figure sculptures over forested hills dropping to valleys guiding rivers on their way to the downstream Tarn gorge. The Tarnon gently flows deep green pools edged with piled white pebble banks. Wild growing greenery. Tree black shade.

Woodland hill climb, a junction. The road busy in slavish

imposed daily clock routine. Wild free lands are left behind. Down alongside the Tarnon. People sit at the water's edge. Children laughing jump into deep running pools. Families shaded picnic repose.

Florac buildings lengthened shadow of late afternoon. Supermarket stop buys too much, squeezing things that will not burst amongst clothes and the sleeping bag. Squashable objects over the handlebars. I carry more weight, it does not matter. The next part of the journey should be flat.

Crossing the Tarnon leaves Florac. N106. Signs for Le Pont de Montvert. Direction points 'Gorges du Tarn.' Two Gendarmes watch the road. I wear my road halo. D9078. Widened flowing River Tarn under growing cliff mass. Busy village of Ispagnac. Soulless commercial feel serves coach herd and car visitor. Campsite icon points to cross stone bridge to Quezac. Restored village narrowed walls hang flower basket colour. Camp sign. A one field site. Le Vieille Moulin. The Old Mill. Decades established, relaxed. I am shown a pitch by an elegant gracious lady Patron of considerable years. She selects a place of "Not too much sun and somewhere to lean your bike."

I am asked of today's journey and then of the week's journey?

After I compliment the Cévennes, she tells me "Once I rode across the Lozére on a horse." With a very proud look in here eye.

An admirable achievement!

The site is very quaint, paced humanity. Lacking garish big screen sport and 'frites.' The evening's entertainment. Noise of rushing river and evening summer blackbird song.

64 km

Gorges Du Tarn

Background river tumble. Sun lights the top of the hill working colour through the trees warming the quiet little field and its dozen occupants asleep in caravan and tent dwellings. I call at the Accueil looking to say thank you and goodbye. The door open, the place empty.

Pretty stone village tidied beyond reality. Every shining new car has its own parking space fronting manicured flower beds, roses and ornamented floral basket display. People play 'village.' This place could give the manicured rivals of La Loire a run for money salivation. An industrial bottling plant keeps the equilibrium.

Single road, navigation easy. Stone towers. Giants' chimney stacks. I enter nature's massive engineering erosion programme. The river wearing through the stone has create a great gorge valley breaching the two Causses, Mejean and Sauveterre. Done on geological timescale too big for the human being to comprehend change in a lifetime. Impressive cliff scenery grows as the road follows the flow. Road rise to freewheeling drops subtle and sedate.

Blajoux is a moneymaker. New compressed village gite development cuboid glare sucks the euro. Sharp angular double glazed above the real village looking softly into the river. Across the water a great concave water gouged cliff hangs curved.

Tower vertical rise, fringed tops dark in woodland. Bird of prey steady glide against blue clear morning.

Vines grow neat wherever a piece of ground can hold the tethered green branch sprout. The ground smells of rock, flavouring the grape.

Windows peer into the deep bottle green smooth translucence. Village tumbles up a white and grey cliff. Houses shaped to fit onto whatever rock foundation can be found. Trees soften growing colour against hard rockscape. Tall smooth rock pinnacle high over the village is topped with a chateau ruin. Woodland clambers skyward through rock tower steep gorge.

Prades village cherry tree laden. Dark ripe fruit shines asking to be picked. High sculpted stone mushroom towers. Tourist village of St. Enimie. Riverside canoe station. Racks of coloured plastic kayaks wait to take willing participants on a downstream gorge journey. Motorhomes. Twenty motorcycles parked gleaming in line. Street jammed visitors. Shop bustle. The whole village resonates human voice and cash register ring busy as a weekend bargain market. I join the boulangerie queue. Compressed into the shop, served pizza on a moving human conveyor belt ejected through process back outside amongst the people clogged part goldmine part village.

Three arches of yellow stone cross to an island. Houses survey from rocky river perch. Yellow plastic paddles beneath. Laughter from the adventure seeking.

Tunnel through rock controlled by traffic lights. Temporary cool darkness to emerge in squinting brightness to a quietened rocky world.

"Bonjour" from a sauntering roadrider.

The ride easy. Tall crags smoothed and curved no longer feel the cool rush of water against rock marooned high feeling only the wind. Waiting for a splash of rain to evoke underwater memory of fish hiding amongst the safety of waving weed. Trees find a footing shading the rock from hot bleaching sun. Crag tops once little islands have grown a fringe of pinewood. A river countless centuries older continues the millennial clock in of twenty four hour eroding work.

Junction from the main road lost to a tunnel appearing over a single high arch connecting St. Chély-du-Tarn. Stone house jumble twist, road weaves secret up amongst trees to Causse Mejean. A cascade splashes over rock to plunge into the Tarn. Canoes and kayaks venture behind and get within the spray. Paddlers laugh and scream at the fun of a hot summer's day soaking. Pougnadoires. Islands stand high above the village river eroded into fantastical overhanging shapes. Tunnels, rock towers, the buzzing of cicadas, singing birds. Shrieks of paddle splashing laughter continue. A pretty village on the opposite side of the gorge named Haut Riverec is built of ancient houses some habited others empty stone shells guard the terraced steep hillside to dead end towering rock.

Downward into La Maléne where many low racing and roll caged rally cars are parked. Bonnets raised, people bent over working on the engine. Enthusiast wander, the sunglasses pose. Pointing out parts of a vehicle. Talked up knowledge gains association. The meeting is to race up a steep hill climb to the Causse Mejean. I leave La Maléne to the sound of loud revving and crackling exhausts warming for a speeding ascent against the clock.

Overhanging cliffs darken the road in imposing shadow. Road splits to one way tight under a succession of convex overhangs defying gravity in smooth worn rounded form. Rock sculpt covers the width of the road and beyond. The Cirque des Baumes. A ride under impressive high rock towers solid straight smooth. Cliff face hundreds of feet high. Tunnel shade to sunshine.

Freewheel through souvenir land, roadside shops. Stalls, trinkets and cards. A few houses, rock tunnel ride, flattening road, the gorge vertical. Sub mountainous.

Big wings circle. Gliding effortless spiral, riding thermal breeze. Smooth easy swoop gains speed. One is joined by others. Sign reads 'Belvidere des Vultures.' Big black shape. Feathers fingered on square end wings. The birds fly too high to make out the head. One disappears into a horizontal crack with a ledge, sheltered by high overhang. I witness more gliding Cirque de Marcellin.

Junction. Millau. Left for Le Rozier. Persuasive campsite icon in hot afternoon burn void of breeze. I book into Camping Brudy and pitch the tent. River path signed from the campsite. Pebble bank at the end of trees, families sit and people swim with the current. Cooling River Tarn extinguishes dusty road heat. The swim experience without wild excitement of the high Tarn, but neither would I want it after energies expelled riding the beautiful gorge.

The tent pole repeats the persona of a broken limb having quietly snapped. I patch it with another cut down peg wrapped in insulation tape and push it back into the sleeve.

The couple opposite have spent ten weeks living in a van travelling as far east as Croatia, the Dolomites and Alps. Tales of landslides and enough snowfall to enable winter ski runs to reopen. Escaping flooding in Eastern Europe, this has been the best weather experienced. The man a climber, having the appearance of being made completely of thin rubber and sinew. He goes off for a hike and climb up a high peak to watch the vultures.

Across the gorge valley a helicopter is hovering above a cliff, a rescue for somebody.

Sun glows gold, then to deep orange turning the rock towers burning red. Fading to black block mass silhouette under night time starry sky.
55 km

Aveyron. Languedoc. Haut Languedoc.

Mellow campsite, kept in sleep until 8am. Slow waking. The eyes open, the body too lazy to move. A Frenchman stops me halfway through packing. Interested in my journey and the places.

Replying. "Bien! Bein! Bein!"

Wanting to repeat it himself. He packs his barbeque and deckchairs to move on.

The van couple surface. I give the lady a sachet of caramel chocolate powder. She is jumping up and down with the thought of hot chocolate. Her husband slips rock climbing shoes on for the high peaks. I am gifted a little pot of surgical alcohol to soothe mosquito bites.

Pushing the bike out of the campsite waving to the Frenchman and his wife midway through tying their bikes across the back of their motorhome.

Le Rozier for fresh bread. The village situated under the meeting of the Causse de Sauveterre, Causse Mejean and Causse Noir on the joining of two rivers, the Tarn and the River Jonte. Important intersecting crossing points between rivers and land traversed. A place with a long history of habitation, the oldest square tower elevated on rock security. Church built into rock, walls semicircular, octagonal tower Notre Damme prays over the village. House surround under rock peak. Strategic in defence elevated on rock foundation. Towering behind, the peaks of the Causses. Rocky summit pious iron cross leaning. Mini chateau stone crumbling tower guards the bridge.

Horn blare. Engine roar. Porsche 4x4 overtakes too fast on the narrow bridge towing a caravan. People watch it squeal around the floral roundabout, caravan wheels leave the ground. Disappearing in direction of Millau. I follow at bicycle pace expecting to meet it upside down smoking dead in a ditch.

The river hot morning hazed. Upstream bridge ruin. Rock and pebble bank island marooned in bottle green depth. An inverted 'V' of ripples, the only disturbance to the mirror flat. Fish break the surface drifting with the silent current. Trees lean in water reflection, steep rocky forest grows to above tall cliffs. Causse Mejean block tower pinnacle horizon. Sky empty blue, morning bright heat. Smooth water serenity.

Road meanders the river sometimes in temporary parting. Canoe access reads. 'Interdit!' Makes me want to go down there.

Red squirrel runs along the road chirping a warning. Indecisive running a few hops one way and then the other. Red fur tufts grow past its ears and the bright brown red of its tail follows its arcing antics bounding every direction. Deciding to run back into roadside from exactly where it emerged. Wasted energies. From the bushes chirps shout angered disapproval.

Gorge opens. Fortress chateau alone on a rock pinnacle. Vultures hang in the sky. Slow wheel above dark ruin tower walls. Black feather sail trimmed rides invisible thermal waves ascending clear blue. Bald head, hook beak, long coiled neck sunk into body blackness. The griffon vulture projects a strange sinister character. The persona of a flying undertaker. It patrols radiating circles, looking for a customer to silently descend over.

Overhanging cherry tree's branches bend full of black ripe fruit. I help myself to cherry sweetness, relieving the branches of their heavy burden enjoying the raptor flight display.

The little town of Riviéres-sur-Tarn. More functional than the prettified villages in the gorge. Landscape change. Rock platforms run between hills individual. Areas of fields and pockets of planted vines standing green lined waist high above black pruned trunks. Fast easy ride, in and out through St. Paulhe. I have missed a turning to cross the river for a country lane that would have ambled all the way into Millau. Road wide. Dual carriageway downhill speed. Famous Viaduc de Millau in its entire length. Rectangles move along the structure, the largest of articulated container lorries lost behind wind deflecting rails of engineering wonderment. From this distance the bridge rises high behind Millau dominating the wide valley between the end of the Causse Sauveterre and the southern Causse Larzac. A delicate structure of seven thin pillars of concrete tapering outward. Each pillar splits in two reaching the bridge deck reversing to taper into one. Cable fan holds the bridge deck. Long white steel strands give appearance of triangular ship sails. Somehow the modern bridge fits gracefully into surrounding landscape.

Suburban road busy traffic, roundabout fight, traffic jam land. Campsite sign to motorhome lines. Big wheel dodge, 'zone industrial.' Crossing the River Tarn. Downward view supermarket. Leaning the bike against the building. A pavement display of strewn empty bottles compliments a rising fragrance of sun baked urine. A doorway to air conditioned cool politely raises the hygiene standard.

Signs for St. Affrique D992 toward the famous bridge and out of town. There is a cycle way wide and separate from the main road looking down on an industrialised River Tarn. Hill climbs to a very old village. Pretty church, terraced old dwellings long arcade verandah view overlooks the river. The village smothered by suburban development. Industrial colour tin box buildings shimmer under sun bake. Traffic light release. Downhill to more steel 'bricoler land' rising from dusty graded earth. Big advert commodities to feed materialistic happiness. Emptied pocket buys short term joy.

Building materials, new tarmac road bubbles under oppressive heat. No breeze day under full solar burn. Road climb. Straight line, the inside white line on the granny gear. Heat reflected blast from new black tarmac sends sticky stones around under the mudguards with a rattle and a 'pop' going for another round. Long windless climb bakes without shade, oven dial turned up full. My body is starting to overheat no matter what I drink. The sun hard, air devoid of oxygen. Lungs work hard grabbing what they can. A sign. 750m to the top. It's a long time arriving, passing under the great bridge structure near level with Causse height. A sign 'Expo info Millau Viaduc' and a favourite word. 'Gratuit' = free.

Coasting the car park, sweat soaked dripping dizzy from effort. Spindly tree promises shade. I sit under spartan branch shelter to eat, drink and rest the body tremble to calm.

English motorcyclists look at the bridge amongst a dozen cars parked. The number stays roughly the same, only the vehicles change as the inquisitive come and go taking a break from the journey.

Cooler. The body composed, walking into air conditioned respite. How hot I was I do not know. Now I can see straight without muscle trembles.

A scale model of the bridge. Cutaway section shows the clever construction. Concrete pillars hold towers of steel that support cables holding the enclosed framework of the steel deck over which the traffic flows. Simple in explanation, genius in the engineered design making it all work, the longest supporting pillar is 325m (1075ft) from the ground. Everything lines up and all forces equalled transferred vertical back through the pillars into bedrock.

There is a paragraph about the design architect, Norman Foster. A paragraph about Gustave Eiffel and one about the inventor of reinforced concrete and the patent rights of 1928 for the real bridge nerd. I could buy a bridge T shirt, bridge table mat set, a model of the bridge, a commemorative bridge plate, or just a postcard. Three ladies are dressed similar to air hostesses. Two look official staring solemn in screen trance, the other deals in taking money for the tat. I add my couple of euros returning to the heat blast.

Many crossing vehicles high above. The top of the tower holds fanning cables to the bridge deck. Future modern shaped delicate symmetry radiates cables from tapered supports looks quite art deco, a fashion of one hundred years ago.

Two German motorcyclists walk over intrigued with my bike and its panniers. Where have I come from? One wants to photograph the bike.

I am not running on full energy. The hill and the heat has got me. The body demands a problem child's hyperactive menu. Half a bar of chocolate, biscuits, bread and jam drinking plenty of cola. Such a foul cocktail should make a stomach turn in sugared convulsion. The body greedily absorbs all looking for more.

D992. Bridge panorama of slender pillar rise. A last view of the great structure at its deepest point crosses the River Tarn. Downhill squanders height. Cooling minutes of freewheel breeze. Little St. Georges-de-Luzencon. Leaves the popular places, back into working land. No campsites at every village. Transitory country, a means to travel south. Where shall I head? St. Affrique. Too lazy to navigate all I need do is keep on the road number.

Small River Cernon, a railway line. Good signs for easy travelling. Landscape Causse tower crags. Distance between widens, isolating the rocky tops. Rome-St.Cernon. Zig zag crossroads town, surroundings grow crops. Steady climb to Lauras. D999. A decorated roundabout. Statues of sheep covered in mirror tiles, shining around a rusting sheepdog and shepherd. Roquefort-s Soulzon junction advertising the famous cheese. The area cavernous. Caves host a special mould that grows on the cheese. Fissures in the caves keep air movement giving the maturing cheese special flavour.

Road drop. Speed speed. Up through the gears pushes flat out. Passing cars accelerate hard to make it. Sunbathed town far below. Pale yellow walls under a mass of orange tile roofs surrounded by forest hills. Centre to the town an impressive spire. Sign informs St. Africa. Secondary translation. 'St. Affrique.' Direction centre ville or ride on? I look at the map. The Monts du Lacaune are too far for today. Campsite gamble ends with a municipal campsite icon. The hallelujah chorus with full orchestra plays a verse in a tired head. Direction past a college. The back of a sports stadium to a perfectly kept municipal site under old trees.

The Accueil a wood chalet. The Patron friendly. Price municipal cheap. I am told to fill bottles with cold drinking water. The lady will put them in the freezer to make an ice cold drink at no cost. The kind touch of uncommercial camping municipal.

A dozen friendly people in tents and caravans. Buzzing cicadas turn their mechanical noise on and off. Heavy thundercloud is part hid behind a veil of grey. Rumbles from surrounding hills. A peel of thunder runs the valley, a few cup sized spots of rain. Nothing. The air so thick. Evening hour advance brings effort to breathe. Lightning. Long silence to nightfall. I stretch the groundsheet over the tent for protection and go to bed. Midnight. Winds roar different temperatures, minutes of stillness. Lightning without thunder. Tense air silence.

56 km

Haut Languedoc

A night of storm threat ends in sunny morning. Air heavy to breathe.

The Accueil holds two dogs, one is a very small ball of barking candy floss, the other poodle derived, sat comfortably on a chair silent moving only its eyes. I collect my two frozen bottles leaving with much genuine thanks. The simple kind thoughtfulness to freeze some water will serve well on today's hot journey.

Boulangerie stop. D999 signed Albi hugging a river. The good sign of roadriders in race colours means easy route for a while. Good speed gains distance over time. Roadriders no longer around, town traffic dies. Climb into agriculture, river further and further distant. Crops parched yellow, rolled silage bales bake dry under sun. Red rock, red soil. The colour of the Languedoc.

On the road, slow moving combine harvesters take a lane and a half. An escort car warns oncoming traffic. Heat intense. Land of dusty red rolling fields, open landscape climb under barren blue. Long plod, windless heat, the top. Crossroad agriculture.

Viewing area shade. Sun warmed concrete benches and tables under welcomed tree shadow. Iced water melted. The bottle held between the wrists cools the blood, wiping sweat sting from the eyes. Folding the map. D32 will run through Belmont-sur-Rance to a little road running next to a river trickle following a valley. Then up across the Monts du Lacaune to a lake.

From shading branches of unmoving leaves, rolling hills steepen to forest blued hill horizon adorned with tiny versions of childrens' stick windmills. Faraway wind turbines asleep under heat burn.

Downhill D32 in bike made breeze. Outcrops of dark sandy stone. The hill bottoms out, a long slow climb without shade. Steep pinch crests amongst new houses. Belmont-sur-Rance appears unexpectedly after a bend. Church dominates in dark ruddy brown Languedoc stone from the top of a hill. Tall spire, flying buttress support, surrounded by connected wings smother the top of the little town. Under church control little brown tiled roofs huddle jumbled down the hillside in all direction. Narrow cobbled ways negotiate an upward climb. Overhanging roofs, old buildings display floral rich color to sombre brown stone. A town hidden sited at the meeting of several regional routes.

The D113 circular hill drops into farmed countryside. Trees smother the valley, the road single track. Farmland pasture trapped between slow running River Rance and steepened wood hillside. Farm machinery returns to the farmhouse. Land quietens for dejeurner.

Under heat bake not one cloud floats across the sky to challenge high sun. An old building with an overhanging roof on the roadside throws short road verge shade. I stop and get out the seat, drinking water dozing with my hat pulled over my eyes. My back against the cool wall, legs take the sun bake. A car passes while I am seated. Half an hour later it returns, my posture unchanged. A stretch tells the body to wake.

Road accompanies the River Rance flow. Isolated farms, a green world climbing and dropping. Hills become cliffs. Brown fragmented rectangular stone overhanging. Narrowing valley. Stumpy twisted oaks climb cliffscape. Trees dancing shadows over tarmac. Shimmering leaf, wisp of breeze, river noise. Little cascade tumbles white, clearing through glass pools. Vibrant green life glows under sun glare. Colourful jay glides between trees. A look up through overhanging boughs to heighted rock crag. Green woodpecker in dipping flight utters a half laughing alarm. Road bend, pockets of sloping pasture terraced. A smallholding. A bridge where rivers meet. D51 points for Mounes' leaving the most pleasant road from Belmont-sur-Rance that has never been too steep. Fine views with a traffic count of two cars.

Mounes' rises the lower slopes of a valley numbering maybe forty dwellings and a Romanesque church above. Steep field tree surround, the place silent. A large farm mas, formidable red stone barn of three storeys. Archways under hide a stone vaulted ceiling. Modern mud covered diesel machinery stands next to a light blue painted old wood cart with wooden wheels. Equine muscle exchange for oily horsepower. Washing hangs colourful to dry crisp clean in bright Languedoc sun. I sit on a little bridge in the shade of moss covered trees. Busy river tumble races under the road. A place to cool and eat to fuel up for the impending climb.

Granny gear plod conserves energy. Steepened patient grind, still leaf overhang. When shade disappears heat is hard, sun burns strong. Wheels sink into melting tarmac bubbling shiny black, the comic 'zzip' of road stone sticky on the tyre rolling through the mudguards. Above. Steep managed forest of fir cool in its dark interior emits resin fragrance. Below. Sounds of cowbells. I am watched by three cows. Solemn stare fixed on my slow passing progress. Three heads slowly follow around from right to left, ears attentive. I am their day's excitement, no doubt their evening's main talking point.

Welcomed woodland overhangs the road, cooling respite from heat burn. High above the valley, twenty 30m high wind turbines making the slowest of turns from a bare rock strewn hill. The white towers on the horizon viewed from the bench.

Noises of haulage. A short lorry passes before a bend. The lorry collecting dead livestock is full. The smell of dead flesh gassing with every heated bounce. I climb the tree covered road, the offensive smell lingers captive without breeze to move. Lungful after foul lungful tasted on the slow ascent.

Hills converge to crest. A junction. Road signed 'Moulin Mage' D62. A car pulls out, droning cooling fan works overtime. The woman driver leans out of the window and shouts "Bon courage!"

I seem to be at the highest part of the hilly land with only a couple of distant fir covered spikes challenging for altitude. One has a monument on the summit, the other a meteo station covered in masts and ariels. Both are black horizon silhouettes above a convoluted panorama.

Through the village of Barre flying. Speed speed speed! Out of gears through Gos surprising two individuals standing in the middle of the silent road looking at a house. Speed generates breeze refreshment, a feeling of progress after slowness of the climb.

Moulin Mage. Craving an ice cold drink. The café Patron locks the dusty door behind him. Nothing moves in Moulin Mage, not a dog not a cat, everything gone to sleep. The only waking creatures are roadside crickets joyfully chirping about the afternoon heat. I stop to top up the waterbottles from my reserves. The remains of this morning's frozen refreshment warmed tepid. Plastic taste without refreshment.

Signs for Lac Laouzas. Woodland descent. The village of Nages full of floral display. Restored chateau pours wine and fresh coffee under parasols for the well dressed. Old cart painted, filled full of red bloom in front of field yellow aftermath stubble. The village has made a big attempt to pull visitor revenue keeping the financial arteries going, prolonging habitation's ancient existence. Rusting horse pulled plough folklore advertises farm produce. Bridge shade starts a lake. Adverts for camping follow lakeside road, junction steep. 'Camping village hotel.'

On a glass fronted sign board outside of the entrance a menu offers a hot dog for what I would pay for a night's accommodation. I do not read the next line. A place of manicured emptiness. Polished executive cars parked outside hotel glass. The image void of hospitality for a traveller.

Back to the bridge. Uphill woodland, fields drop to a roundabout above the barrage. A look at the map for camping possibilities. The only one is across the Monts de Espinouse on tomorrow's schedule. The plan. If I come across a campsite on the way. Stop. Roads ahead are guaranteed steep. I am resigned to a long day's ride. Water supply is low, consuming over four litres today.

Bends hug the lake. Little Villelongue parched fields yellow frame last views of lake blue. Sunny sails slow, moving across the water. Woodland ascent, echoing birdsong, dense shading trees, steep hillside back on the granny gear. I could do with more.

Long plod crests a col of 957m (2900ft) dropping on a winding bumpy wild woodland lane. Below, rooftop appearance. Bungalow shanty village becomes the proud 'village fleur' of Fraise-sur-Agout. Manicured, tidied, full of bright rich multicoloured floral displays to attract people.

Motorhomes line the river. Nothing signed for tent dwellers. A sign for toilets, waterbottles ready at the basin tap. My thumb covers the spout, turning the tap. It sprays. Yipee! Mains pressure and not oozing bacteria tank water. Bottles fill clear cool joy between stolen cold gulps. A face wash and neck cool banish sweat, dust and grime. The village has been of some use, although not what the Maire intended. People amble prettied streets pumping euros into veins of rural habitation. Sign for Olargues. A church, climbing over the village. D14 farmland.

Fields of cut dried grass are being baled. Four farm dogs are playing, running around together on this sunny evening. I am spied by one bravely running to the fence directing a bark tail in the air. Others arrive to see what the alarm call is for. Two do not notice, the third looks up, then back at the barking hound as if to say. "Is that it?" Walking back to watch the baling for the fun of chasing rodents trapped in the diminishing harvest island.

Gold early evening sun saturates all colour adding lengthening shadow to every object. Above grows forestry. Trunks at the roadside warmed deep ruddy gold contrast permanent black interior. Thick needle covered branches glow deep vibrant green from uninterrupted sun. Bends, woodland, pasture. All rise to meet Col de la Fontfroide 971m (2900ft).

Two flagpoles fly the tricolours of France over a sobering memorial in the middle of nowhere. It is a large monument to the resistance and to the many deportees of the Languedoc shipped to death camps in Germany, Czechoslovakia and Poland. A sealed container houses mind chilling barbed wire fragments and ashes collected from Auswitz and Sachsenhausen death camps. To the left on the memorial stands a large resistance cross of metal painted black.

A poem. 'The Wagon' written by Albert Simon who was one of the deportees details the rounding up of Langudocians and their cramming one hundred at a time into the rail goods and livestock wagons telling of the long journey taking days. Suffering without food. No drink. No toilet. Leaving the occupants all ages including children crammed suffocating degraded in their own filth with the knowledge of an awful awaiting fate of. 'The final solution.'

Up here by myself, sweated out, tired in the surrounding silence and without stepping out from air conditioned cocooned comfort. The memorial is emotionally moving. It feels profound in my freedom to exist in the moment. A polished stone reads.

> *THOSE WHO WANT TO*
> *IGNORE THE PAST*
> *ARE CONDEMNED TO A REVIVAL*

I leave the memorial to behold views of biblical proportion. Evening gold panorama of endless heavy bare rock mountainous crag and summit running away into haze. I have reached the Monts de Espinouse. Coming out on top of them. Thoughts of crossing the long ridges falling into vertical darkness cut by summit block repeating layer after layer brings raw wild excitement of being alive.

Far away in hazed fade small blocks of pale colour. Mediterranean towns and big city cube sprawl faraway somewhere. Snake black thread coils rock ridge, another further away. The road.

I remove my wet sweated top. Evening banishes the sting from the sun, land releases a day's retained heat. The brakes are off. New world fast dropping, wind dries sunned skin.

Mediterranean warmth, hairpin twist. Sign. 8% average, down. Tiny roofs held in large black shade long way lost in distant valley bottom. Rising towers of white limestone rock. High summits of hard ancient grey granite from the birth of the world. Matchbox village nestled between ridges watched by a giant peak. Village reached by cotton strand cut rock connection. I stop several times to relish silent panoramic awe dropping to Col du Poirier 602m(1800ft). Expecting a climb. The road keeps dropping. Bend twist into wild pine. Giant trunks sentinel, maybe ancient cedar. Deep vertical ridged bark trunks taper church tower skyward.

Helter skelter, bends bends bends. Rockscape, scrub. Rooftops, houses. Stop.. The main road east of Olargues. Cars, people, valley world soft. Left D908 looking for a campsite sign. If this proves nothing, there is always St. Pons long distance. Olargues is signed as; 'One of the most lovely villages of France.' Municipal camping sign points main road. The village separated by a river. A high single span medieval footbridge link. The older part of the village built over a rocky hill ending in a square stone ancient tower sheltered under a pointed roof. Curving valley road. Through trees caravans and tents riverside roar. Bridge entrance, the site.

The Accueil is the busy bar. I pay the friendly Patron for two nights and a beer, the place costs next to nothing. Good feeling radiates.

The Patron asks. "Where have you come from today?"

"Je commence St. Affrique."

"St. Affrique! C'est trop loin! Non." That is too far!

"Oui. St. Affrique." Finishing my beer and asking for cold frosted repeat.

I pitch under dry trees on warm parched yellow ground. A big pasta meal, finished with a beer. Surrounding cliffs lose their pink evening glow to the onset of darkness. The sounds of happy people and a babbling river in echo along the wooded valley. Sleep comes without effort.

97 hillometres

No need to get up, no plan for anything. Slow breakfast steam rise ritual of the chattering mug. A day for washing. Remnants of wash gel empty, clothing finished by soap bar lather. Everything hangs to dry. Mystery of the odd sock. The other escaped. Fellow campers are out for the day. The site in motorhome and bright tent silence.

Air cools, cicadas stop their buzz, crickets cease chirping. Only the acrobatic swift and swallow continues ariel work. A few large spots of rain fall from smothering thundercloud's rumbling creep. I join the ground dwelling creatures by crawling into the tent falling asleep under humid heat. Waking to breaking blue.

My feet tread the worn cobble step rise. 'Chemin St. Jaques.' Stone wall icon and old iron crucifix signal ancient way. Under a town gate too narrow for a vehicle. Ancient niche central over ancient arch. Medieval Notre Damme holds the sculpted infant. Strange naive representation dictated by church rule.

Ancient lean. Rising street. Crooked house stone bulge. Worn render terrace under sun heat glare. Three and four storeys. Bleached wood, heavy shutters faded hang open. A swaying cat sat on a window cill next to a box of growing flowers watches the world. Little shop in survival struggle. Dusty windows interior empty. Workshop corner scratches a living. Steep narrow cobbled twist, roof overhang, archways secretive. Overflowing bloom escapes walled high gardens. Iron verandah over narrow lane, palm tree peer over stone wall. Parasol next to a single chair compliments an open doorway.

Streets to the old bridge. Parapet stone, central apex arch simple and beautiful straddles the slumbering river in lethargic summer mood. Flowing channel surrounded by pebble bank, a beach of sand below. Scrap wood and roped drum raft dragged above the flow waits to be the vehicle of children's afternoon fun. Alleyways to parkland, fine bridge view. Behind rise high peak Monts de Espinouse. Somewhere up there lives the wild man of Languedoc with his sheepdog, garden, bike and climbing ropes. Noise of laughter and talk, a café of many seated enjoy a long lunch into mid afternoon. Épicerie 'ouvert.'

The old fashioned grocery store void of corporate colour. Stock piled homemade shelves strain in bend, stacked crates decant daily necessity. My arms hold a box full for the evening feast and tomorrows ride fuel.

Laundry duty complete. Lazing eating fruit. "Bonjour" to passing people. Background rumbles from hazed mountain altitude.

8.15am. Farewell Camping Municipal Olargues. The cycle route along the old railway line east should end at Mons. A tree lined path remembered from last year's ride. Into a little village, snacks from the épicerie. Stalls assembled, vans emptied of stock for display under sun. The place looks like Mons, but I am not sure. The place unnamed. New cycle route carries on further, I follow uneasy. Farms and streams under tall impassable hills. The magnificent Gorges de l'Heric. Majestic skyward cliff pinnacles tower over craggy ridge. Signed announcement. This is the new extended cycle route. I stop and turn around. I was right. The village was Mons. Back I must go. Doubled journey, wasted miles. Consolation of the beautiful morning low sun exaggerating white rock peaks. The downside is lost time of precious early morning coolness.

Unmarked Mons. Stalls full of clothes, hand forged knives. Fruit jams and local honey surrounded by gregarious bargain hunter's mauling paws. Downhill short ride, painted suspension bridge crosses the flowing River Orb. D14 bend lookback view rises to the Monts de Espinouse.

Watery mirror weave in gorge reflection. Growing forest black cling on high rock hills, areas of planted vines grow on scant earth pocket. Changing river. Changing mood. Steep crag weave, silver thread flow reflects bare blue morning sky roaring white over stone shallows.

Ridge summit fortress tower, battlements alone. Road weaves the river bend, 180 degrees reveals the tower's watch over yellow stone Vieussan. Roofs orange in sunshine, house lean huddle under fortress protection.

Bends easy, freewheeling sun drenched scenery. Roadrider group's morning ride. Team colours, carbon frame glint. The easy route through the Languedoc. Gently down, views to a deepening river. Vine row planted, the opposite bank long thin fields amongst rock. Iron winches fixed at the side of the road hold cables suspended across the river connecting to vineyards. Amongst rusted abandoned, iron shines greased black cogs in perfect working use. The means of sending produce across the river.

Rocky bend climb. River weave path. Dropping fast ride, vineyard blur. Wide flat boulder strewn beach sun bleached, nothing grows amongst the highest round boulder height of swollen winter flood. Unexpected Roquebrun, advertised as a 'Mediterranean garden.' A town of size. River widens, bridge crossing views back to multicoloured houses terraced steep. A square fortress high over the little town on a rock pinnacle. Different pastel colour rendered buildings, little windows painted summer blue. Four, five storey individuality. Top of hill church lost amongst many buildings. Behind Roquebrun towers a large barren domed triangular hill naming the town. Riverbank weeping willows, rich green trees, large palms. Rafts of riverweed submerged sway. Red and yellow kayaks drift. Families enjoy the wide flat beach river bend. Winter floodwater channels become summer shallow pools of play.

Camping municipal on the way out of the town. If yesterday had not been a rest day I would stay here. A place worth spending time in.

Hot climb out of town semicircles the valley. The idyllic town pretty on the river. Roquebrun equals any coastal town of the Cote Vermeille.

It seems a long way to the top of the hill. Full day heat under clear sky, tarmac radiation throws back the burn. I stay on the granny gear, conserving energy. Stopping the body overheating. There will be a top to the hill, there always is. Noises from behind. A roadrider up on the pedals, face screwed up, sweating, panting, grabbing oxygen from void hot still air.

Nodding an exhaling. "Bonjour!"

He stays up on the pedals of his carbon race bike, pulling on the handlebars, body muscles in twisting strain, mind focussed on the crest. I am a minute behind arriving. The art of distance cycling. Minimum effort for maximum gain will get you far.

Brown dry rockscape panorama. Long dusty downhill pushes the big gears. Warm breeze roar, speed blur, sunshine cicada buzz. Plateau vineyards leave the River Orb and its beauty to flow on through Béziers, weaving flatland to the Mediterranean Sea.

D20 signed St. Chinian. Slow climb amongst endless sweeping lined vines. Fruiting round green grape heavy swell in bunches shaded under vibrant leaf growing from dust. River runs companion to the road to vanish into dry countryside.

Views back to journeyed blue hilled Languedoc. Roadside habitation into St. Chinian town tree shade. Large central square busy with human and vehicle traffic. A convoy of painted up cars on Dutch plates drive through the town, horn blare passenger wave. Locals look on amused, others indifferent.

Welcomed shaded bench invites a stop to cool and watch the town. People dark haired with the olive skin of the Catalans. There is much difference between their northern countrymen. Old country exists within new borders. People remain unchanged, born to a land and not to a dividing line decided on paper.

Old town street. Terraced houses high. Window shutter bright colour, every window wears a flyscreen. Noises of lunchtime drift from open window. Buildings hardly make shadow in midday heat. D177 out of town, smallholding farm, pocket vineyard. I climb strange land fragmented white cliffs. Boulder remains shattered cubed. Black flame conifer tall amongst rock, desert plants abound. Across lower slopes a chapel on a high rock ridge. Notre Damme du Nazareth. Upward in the heat. The company of chirping crickets and cicada buzz. Block crumbling bands of limestone schist cliff horizontal, natures dry stone wall naturally form terraces on which rough scrub bush grow amongst bleached coarse grass. Climbing push. Windless heat. Crumbling white crag contrasts primary blue clear sky. Shadeless bends, cultivated vine. Solitary overhanging tree shade island respite. I stop. Water runs out of my skin pores as fast as I can drink. Last gulp, a single hint of breeze welcomed. Temperature burn hot soaked skin. Road climbs rockscape weave. Granny gear push crests wildscape views to far hills.

The place holds a feeling of desert. Flat plateau radiates all direction. Scrub, stone, withered tree. Dried stillness. 360

degree sunburn view standing on a rockpile looking across wild land haze silence. Intense rising heat shimmer illusion. Remoteness. Dusty desolate beauty so old, outside of time.

A sign points to Assignan. Half hidden rooftops bake crisp under heat. Uphill signed D178 Villespassans. Breathing heat cooks lungs from the inside. Dusty climb through scrub to a crest. Hot wind freeride through the village. Little orange coloured sagging tiled roofs. Flat topped square church tower, two bells burn in an ironwork frame. Overhead acrobatic martens and swallows swoop and twist catching lunch on the wing in blue cloudless backdrop.

Road switches to D20. Wild sub desert crispy scrub. Rock outcrops, pocket vineyard neat heat shimmering rows. Dried up white pebble riverbed random puddles of bright green. Edged brown dead, algae bleached white by the great blowtorch in the sky. Vines irrigated by arcs of mechanical spray. Pumped life from the subterranean.

Mediterranean twisted pine, resin ooze smell, tinderbox heat. Land devoid of moisture feeling about to combust. The hotter it gets the more cicadas buzz in their thousands. A deafening mass rhythmic engine pulse hidden in stillness. Land undulates, road follows dried riverbed. Collective dwellings tend the vine. Aigues Vives. In the square the dried up drinking fountain blows dust. A sign. 'Eau non potable.' No Occitan 'Aigue,' and no 'vive' in Aigues Vives.

The little place silent. Closed. I sit on a wall in welcomed corner shade, and drink, cooling. Distant diesel hum gets louder appearing in dust as the school coach, ejecting thirty energetic young souls bringing the place to life with laughs and screams. I leave the youth to their village square and ride through dry streets, every building shuttered down to the dust for the afternoon.

More desert rockscape, buzzing and vines amongst brown rock. Wine born from moonscape land, the road to Aigne. Proclaiming '1000 years of history!' A thousand years of bent over tending the vine amongst blowing dust, turning the press, rolling filling and storing barrels. Many generations make perfection decanted without thought into an everyday glass. Without wine industry these places would perish.

Long easy downhill, withered tree. Rock strewn wild dry scrub dust. Change of lowering altitude softer feel. Beaufort bursts colour of displayed flowers. Neat church surrounded by tidied houses. Behind the village a horizon of blue hills hazed featureless through heat shimmer. Road drops speeding past acres of green nurtured vines sharing landscape with crops. Everything flattens ending in roundabout on the outskirts of Olonzac. Painted carts loaded with old wine barrels burst with floral display. Supermarket on the edge of new 'bricoler land' is open.

Air conditioned interior feels satisfyingly polar to the skin compared to outside heat. Cool relaxes the body. I am in no hurry to leave. I buy water having drunk my five litre capacity today and the mileage yet to finish. A handful of people wander long cooled aisles. I saunter to the unhindered checkout. The electric door return into bright barbecued heat.

D52e points Lezignan Corbiéres. Empty D11 crosses the Canal du Midi. A hire boat chugs from under the road bridge. Sunbathing passengers, a steering wheel, chrome levers. Navigating the liquid glide, bow wake pushing warm pea soup. Journeying under overhanging green shade upstream towards Carcassonne. Two cyclists with loaded panniers amble a bumpy towpath under shade. Seed thoughts of future travel.

The D611 crosses a rushing canal feed weir where a long thick trunk has become stuck between walls. The spidery shape collects debris in precarious hang.

Two bikes, one with a child trailer are stopped at the side of the road, a young family are touring. Dad has the panniers and loaded tent, mum pulls the toddler in the trailer. Smiles and waves as I pass.

Low roll hill crests revealing rows of green growing stripes of planted vines in every direction accompanied by the buzzing cicada pulse.

Sky ahead no longer tranquil. A great thundercloud sits thick. Forward lilt, sucking life from rising land heat as it travels. The dark unstable tower of bedlam is miles across. The hotter the land surface, the further the cloud can rise. The more vapour mass it can store, the more violent it can become. When its heat can no longer rise, the top iced at its maximum growth can only spread outward in forward compressed lean. This one has an anvil top fully formed. The cumulonimbus storm cell. Inside the cloud millions of vapour droplets are blown up and down melting freezing melting freezing. Supercooled. Liquid on the inside frozen on the outside creating static charge. Polarities inside of the cloud split. The lower above freezing is charged negative, the higher altitude below freezing becomes positive. All the ingredients for the cloud to become a thunder cell. Once the electrical tension reaches one million volts pm2, it is ready to release its wrath. Today across sun heated charged ground. I watch the giant cloud track diagonal across direction of travel. Will we meet in violence or passively miss in differing direction?

Lezignan-Corbiéres old streets radiate from the centre. Old stone church terminal crack whole height of the tower. Buildings added around its base over different centuries add quirky marvel. Shops open. People living daily routine. I cycle a circular road one way system ending modern municipal.

'Toutes directions' guesswork. La Gare to industrial land running on a fork road joining a busy arterial route. Every vehicle on a straight line blast out of town. Compass reveals wrong direction. Large sign. 'Narbonne.' 180 degree gap dash. Heading back to town.

Across flat wide land cumulonimbus turns sunny countryside into dark storm battlefield. Hurrying its pace looking for me. Spots of heavy rain hit the skin stinging an iced temperature. Cold wind strengthens. The impending thunder cell rage. Building shapes of shelter ahead, nearly back to town. Watching the road, pushing the pace. Sideways glance at the blackness. Lightning within the cloud, thick flashes stab the ground rumbling its approach. I reach part shelter of a boulangerie/wine shop with a slatted wood canopy half missing and jam myself against a large window of a closed dusty store. Waterproof is on. The storm hits the other side of the building in deluge lash. Sunny day instant late evening. Wind near gale, chairs tumble across the car park. Wild thrashed branches break from a tree. Overhead canopy rattles and flaps resisting in half dereliction. Busy traffic submission slowed. Headlights. Wipers unable to clear the deluge from the windscreen. Vicious lightning superheated air expanding hiss. Ground shaking crack, electrical discharge across the sky. A million volts per m2 goes to ground nearby. Railway sidings opposite. I am looking at the main feed substation powering the rail network via many overhead cables. I could have picked a better place to stop than next to the biggest lightning magnet for miles! Visibility a few metres. Through the window across the room, the opposite window battered by a torrent. I feel the different air pressures push and pull the glass. Tighter against the window. Rain bounces off the path, water creeps over the dust towards my feet widening a deepening flood.

Main road traffic at walking pace. All I can do is patiently wait. The storm violence enjoyable. Most welcomed after the last few days of hair dryer heat. An hour of beating, the storm moves on. Soft pattering rain changes to a mist of drizzle before stopping. The fresh smell of rain evaporation steams off tarmac. A tree opposite is minus a limb and a few small branches. A man in a white apron appears from the boulangerie retrieving plastic chairs strewn across the car park. He walks to the road verge standing up a sign.

I ride off dry. How did the young cycling family manage? I hope they reached shelter in town or missed the storm completely.

Big slow rain spots. Roadside gurgle clears the running water. Weak sun appears to start the evaporation. Spent remains of hanging flat cloud. Behind grows the thunder cell queue. Without the heat fuelled muscle of their violent forebears they will have to find heat energy to grow from somewhere else or perish in the cooling temperature of night. The magnificent storm cloud reduced to fill a dirty roaring culvert in seaward haste back from where it came.

D611 direction Ferrals les Corbiéres where there will be a municipal campsite with hot shower municipal comforts. Road busy in work end commute. Out of town car sales, industrial corrugated business parks. I hold my road at a roundabout, fighting from being pushed down the first exit. The car behind impatient honk. I clear the roundabout in a few seconds. The road holds water atomised to spray soak by speeding vehicles. Truck scream past empty on the depot run. Black tyre tracks sun silvered road. The wet wind blast nearly sends me upside down in a dirty flowing drainage ditch. Centre lane signed Ferrals les Corbiéres, pushing through the traffic. D106. Streaming tarmac vehicle spray. Tired and dirtied into a quiet town just finished a drenching. Downpipe gurgle feeds gutter rivulets. Wet road silver ribbon, long shadow old streets sun yellowed in evening. Sign for the municipal campsite, following through town buildings. Downward slope finds the barrier locked, the long grass Accueil shut up from winter. I scoot around the barrier finding overgrown pitches out of sight from overlooking town windows. Mains water is still on and it is warmed in the pipe from ground temperature. I cycle no further today.

The tent is up out of view, bike is stashed in the hedge. The lid of the pannier box makes a bath washing the sweat and road grime from tired skin. A cook up fills the belly and the pot is washed.

A footpath runs behind the overgrown hedge, I hear people walking along. A dog picks up my scent. It does not have time to look, the thing pulled away by its owner. A little arriving drizzle puts me inside the tent. Misted rain patters gently on the green nylon while far away rumbles of thunder roll the hills. It is not often I welcome darkness, but this evening the sooner the better. The residents of Ferrals les Corbiéres will be at home and my tent lost to nighttime.

Broken sleep from barking dogs kenneled outside. When they subside their lonely howling and yips a donkey starts up sounding to be the most woeful animal ever to have been born. Weeping a tuneless lament all night.

120 km

Corbiéres

6am. Hoopoe birds. "Hoo-po hoo-po." Calling to each other. Sleeping bag slumber, the body yet to move. Pink morning glow, sun yet to threaten its fiery appearance. Dogs and donkey are silent, mist hangs above the ground. Nobody stirs in Ferrals-les-Corbiéres as the freeloader rides out.

7am crossing pretty River Orbieu. The bridge ornate, iron lamps decorated with floral overflow. Riverbank willows long lazy water stroke reflect a sky mirror pink liquid void hole through the world. Into uptown, climbing easy through the main street. Amongst the sleeeping houses. Shopkeeper carry's his morning delivery.

Wishing a hearty. "Bonjour!"

This is the only habitant of Ferrals-les-Corbiéres I have met and on his jolly salutation I base my opinion of the friendly place. I thank the town for its private spacious accommodation provided at the best possible price.

D106 signed Durban-Corbiéres. Fast downhill through open vine country oranged by a rising misted sun. Thézan-des-Corbiéres snores in extended dawn. The epicerié preparing for the day contains the only human movement. Sweeping hill of vines. One car passes, hills grow craggy, land closes. Low sun shaded behind steepening land keeps fresh temperature to early morning. Vines grow anywhere cultivatable. Three roadriders are out for their early morning ride.

Friendly "Bonjour."

Breakfast at the roadside under shaded wild rock shape. A sign for St. Victor Ermitage, points to a coiled lane.

Direction 'Durban-Corbiéres.' Rock tunnel ride to a secret gorge world. Fantastical eroded fairy grotto castellated shapes. Scrub holds between white rock and trees along the cool deep blue of calm river. Someone is trying their luck fishing in a large clear flowing pool. A couple close the door of their car. Rolled towels under the arm walking a rocky path for a morning swim.

Sun breaks over hills riding into Durban-Corbiéres. Supermarket stop waits for the door to open. The attached boulangerie already busy, people leave armed with red hot baguettes.

Roadside old houses, entrances on the street. Open shutters, sun bleached façade. Long dusty shadows of early morning.

River flows quiet between heaped pebble banks. Cathar chateau ruin guards the town. Square broken walls and rounded crumbling tower craggy rock hilltop command. Blue backlit and hazed under brightness of sun. Lone flag limp on the castle top asleep in windless Mediterranean heat.

Climb above the river leaves town. Widening rocky valley, pebble islands grow reeds. Winter scoured channels away from the main flow reduced to green algae trickling pools. Climbing road looks over a drying river. Shoals of fish struggle to get to the main channel. Fish shoal near marooned in deep pools, probably bought down by the thunderstorms of last night. If there are no more storms to bring water to carry them downstream between the pools they will become stuck. Doomed to a suffocating death as the temperature rise starves oxygen from their fast evaporating world of pooled warm water. I could scramble down and help myself without a problem. But they have enough trouble to deal with without my adding trauma to their frail future, existence measured possibly in hours. I think of the fisherman this morning, upstream in the gorge attentive and enthusiastic hoping for a catch one. The fish are all here. Stuck.

The smallest flat piece of ground between rock is home to the vine. Rows and rows ripened, near bursting fruit hangs heavy. A mass of strong green colour against bleached scrub hanging onto existence over sterile rock.

Two roadriders pass on a downward ride. "Bonjour!"

I crest the little Col d'Extréme 251m (750ft) the smallest col with the biggest name. Dramatic lands. Ridges sub mountainous look impassable in distance perspective.

The ruin of Cathar Chateau de Aguilar. Part tumbled walls centuries baked under heat. A dust wreck of once fine fortress. Huge stone wall towers, a central square fortress building stands on solid rock top hill. Defensive walls part tumbled. A large blockhouse alone on a rock pinnacle. Cliff strategic protection to side elevations. All under haze. The place as large as a village. Not easy to attack, neither to escape. After many centuries alone in the silence of nowhere it remains imposing on the landscape. The scourge of kings and popes all centuries dead and gone. Their work completed with the Cathar people longtime exterminated. All the human effort of building the structure, the history of murder and blood ends as a focal point of pleasure in the landscape for thoughtful ponder from the humble bicycle.

Cicadas announce the rising morning temperature starting up the mechanical heat engine buzz. Downhill rolling into Tuchan. Tight streets, worn tall facades pastel colour. Shaded side road glimpse to high glaring rock ridge behind the town. The place used busy holds happy feeling. Town square plane tree shade, one way circular route. The only two way road is blocked by a tractor reversing a trailer into the garage under a house. The traffic jam is dealt with in laughter. I cycle between the queuing cars, under shaded cool walls leaving Tuchan in hard sunshine. A taxi gives a friendly toot racing up the road lifting dust.

D14. The planted vine grows from long beds of small stone. The smell of limestone rock will flavour the grape. Rough land boulder strewn. Nothing grows tall or abundant apart from the tended crop to service the bottle.

Great overhead ridge opens to a deep plunging valley. Cliffside angled rise, rock holed round bigger than any cathedral window. Dropping bends, hoping not to disappear into the gorge cleave deep below in black shade. Abandoned vineyard twisted stump deadwood baking in lines evokes cowboy film dusty graveyard. Hills close high, road squeezed upward. Gorge compress surrounding cliff tower, sheer slab thrust half mountain. River roar rumble around a hundred cliff boulder chunks that have pelted the river from high crumbling crag. Tumbling water echo from rock tower sides. Abandoned buildings open stone ruin halfway to the river part overgrown by scrub, only one retains a holed and slipping orange tiled roof.

The thundering accompaniment of the river. Flying along a corniche road cut from rock, moments of shade thrown by cliff giant overhang. Downhill meets roaring turbulence crossing a stone bridge. Dynamited cleave delivers softness. Quiet composed flow along sandy beaches under overhanging tree shade surrounded by high rock ridge.

Lunchtime Padern. The only sign of activity is dejeuner parasol table preparation. One person arranges chairs, another brings the glint of cutlery to surround the cold bottle. Above the sleepy village, a ruin Cathar chateau grown from solid rock pinnacle, too steep to climb and too hot to contemplate attack.

Battlement mass stone wall. Window openings half tumbled, broken ruins bake under clear blue. The castle small compared to its mighty neighbours a few miles away. Flat ride. Three hoopoe birds dart a moment of flying colour. Pink sandy bodies, black and white striped wingtips in rapid dash toward the river.

High rock ridges blue in heat. The back of Plat du St. Paul. Solitary black cypress, an expression of Cézanne or Van Gogh. Valley view of distant Chateau de Peyrepertuse dwarfed on top of its huge rock tower presiding over surroundings.

The little road bends its way to Cucugnan sited over a rocky hill. Maison du Tourisme finds welcomed shade. Car stop visitors in transit.

A 1960s convertible. Long, white. Engine in the rear. Cooling louvered vents between tail light fins. The top is down. 'Caravelle' chrome letters glint. A restored Renault. The couple in the car crane their necks eyeing Maison du Tourisme on a slow drive past. The lady passenger in 60's red headscarf and horned sunglasses consults the map. The car accelerates, pulling at the dust, taking the dead end to Cucugnan.

Climb re visit plods the granny gear. Twisting rocky bends. The imposing block fortress of Chateau de Quéribus defiant on its rock pinnacle.

The hill panorama of sun drenched ridges. Patchwork valleys rise distant snowed mountain blue to Spain. Below ribbon road ends in matchbox sized Maury lost in vast area haze softened. The quality of high atmospheric silence from Grau de Maury.

Brake release. Momentum. Quick shift through the gears. Effortless freewheel through rock ridge to lower land. Town building cut through. Quiet shade streets. Main road junction.

Voices from the dark interior of Bar Tabac. Articulated thundering truck blur vibrates the ground and lifts dust from the road. Time to wake from scenery stupor needing focus of main road wits.

D117 toward St. Paul-de-Fenouillet. Long hot drag. White line distance from passing vehicle speed. Uphill heated plod. The mind absorbed with spectacular rock ridges running parallel both sides.

A toot from the taxi from Tuchan on its return journey. I wave.

Different view of spinal Plat de St-Paul rising. Opposite, ridges and mountainous rock peaks tower behind hot misty blue. St.Paul-de-Fenouillet mix of old buildings closes in tight surround. Distant dusty road climbs stone hill disappearing into last year's Gorges de Galamus.

Flat road busy, traffic speed dropping tone of the Doppler Effect. Castel-Fizel, ruin on a pinnacle perch. Narrow road Caudies-de-Fenouillédes. Block shade buildings, sounds of living echo the walls. High blue heat hazed silhouette. Lapradelle village under protective watch by the towers and battlements. Chateau Puilaurens high on vertical ridge built to rock parameter extremes looking untouchable. Long climb through forest and shattered slate. Col Camperie 534m (1630ft) earns a freewheel in breeze. The return to the River Aude roaring cold and turbulent blue.

The campsite busier than last year. Plus it is the weekend. Activity minibus collects 'canyoning' participants. Barbeque smoke rise between vehicle and tent jam. The plunge into fake blue chlorinated pool in crowded sun lounger surround.

My heart is sinking opening the door of a noisy Accuiel. A Dutchman is asking for stamps in English to the French lady behind the counter. It does not register with her vocabulary.

Why should it?

The Dutchman repeats it louder.

"Ztampz!" and again,"Ztampz!"

This time with a comedy mime with his tongue out licking his thumb and pushing into his palm.

The lady delivers a cool reply.

"Les Timbres. Monsieur. Nous ne vendons pas les timbres. La Poste en ville."

Pointing imaginary dismissive towards the town post office.

He is standing there not getting what he wanted. Professionally frozen out with no further eye contact for his impoliteness. I am next in the queue.

"Bonjour Madame."

"Bonjour Monsieur."

"Vous avez un emplacement pour le nuit? S'il vous plait.

C'est pour une personne avec tent en velo."

"Oui pour un nuit. Vous avez la carte d'identité?"

"Passport. Voici."

"D'accord."

I pay for the night and am given a pitch number and given direction.

"Merci, Madame."

"Merci á vous Monsieur."

I wheel the bike to a pitch without grass. Tyre ruts and dust. Tree roots over the ground. I squeeze the tent onto a flat corner. Pegs resist baked stony ground. Car wheels spit gravel arms length away lifting clouded dust over everything.

The tent is up. I walk a few paces to the river's edge immersing a pair of boiling feet. The chill of fast-flowing iced mountain water. Toes grip cold river pebbles. Blood cools rapid. Cupped cold water goes over my head. Ice bucket Pyrenean water baptism renews mountain vows shocking the breath. Repetitive head washings leave a body calm. Cold water runs chilled over my soaked shirt.

Inflatable boats full of wetsuited waving participants on a whitewater rapid ride. Downstream shouts, screams and laughter consumed by the noise of river roar. I am back under the towering cliff gorge. It is very beautiful, later in busy season and must be accepted as so. I am surrounded by Dutch people who in a large group behave no different from the English. I get a shower and hang some washing. No one speaks to the invisible man.

Cicadas have tough late night competition from the 10pm cheesy music 1970s disco in timewarp parallel universe. The nightmare intends to bring down the cliffs of the gorge with a seismic boob tube glitterball flared pulse, finally giving up the attempt at 1am. I could have camped on waste ground at the back of a city nightclub. There would have been no difference.
98 km

Crossing the Pyrenees

7am. Sandpapered eyeballs compliment a fuzzy head from only five hours sleep. Electric hookup spare socket charges my camera batteries. Leaving little Holland and its package holiday hungover residents. Out of the gate before 9am with a feeling of bland indifference to the tranquil place turned sardine 'happycamperland'. No 'Bonjour,' no eye contact. How I missed the French people, the velvet language and formalities of politeness. Outside of the gate the fruit stall is yet to remove shutters.

Across the road leads to Axat, Gorges St. George and last year's mountain road. A detour to Quillan and the repeat experience of riding through the impressive Defile de Pierre-Lys.

Rock towers close vertical, the River Aude turbulent turning up the volume as the road runs fast through rock tunnels, overhangs and towering sheer cliff. Easy downhill all the way into Quillan busy with a market filled car park. Traffic light side street delivers the town square. People sit enjoying coffee. Petit dejeuner digests the broadsheet.

"Bonjour." With a smile.

Busy boulangerie sells thick oozing pizza fuel for later. Tempting seed bread and cream fruited pastries for now.

The main D117. Traffic light tight corner ascent leaves

townscape living for suburban detached dwelling. Granny gear patience, climb, climb, climb. Breath in rhythm. Snaking road. Every turn watches shrinking Quillan gradually swallowed in a block shaded gorge. The silver ribbon river hidden hazed shaded. Climbing above hill giants. Opened country of blue jagged ridge maze.

Altitude. Col du Portel 602m (1800ft) proclaiming 'La Route des Cols'. A junction. Steep bend ascent. It is a return to patiently watch Quillan digested into vast Corbiéres spiked confusion.

Climbing through a farm hamlet. The Corbiéres have gone.

Land greener, climbing through Courdons. Farm dog bark. Blue overalled figure has his head under the bonnet of a muddied 4WD pick up clanking spanners, faithful dog laid under the vehicle panting in shade. Downward speed two roadriders, shouting "Allez!" The sound of the freewheel gear frenetic ticking a noise blur over speeding tyre hum. In a second they are gone.

Col de Courdons 883m (2700ft) road gently falls through rich green land proudly advertising the growing of potatoes! Yesterday wine, dust and desert. Today rich green. Sounds of cowbell meadow. The buzzard 'mew' from dense green woodland. The difference of land and climate within a cycled hour is near incomprehensible. Signs point to a side lane for a celebrity hideout. 'Belvis.'

Straight line speed through green land. Distant altitude views. Snow covered peak over black conical hills. The Pyrenees mountain horizon.

Fields cut. Rolled bales for winter feed. Aftermath field bright yellow baking under sunshine. Road splits for Estagel. The village épicerie. Patron carrys the box displayed stock inside. I pick a few things from the chiller buzz, leaving with the sound of the roller shutter being pulled. A village of wide streets, a few old cars parked. Nothing happens. Ritual silence of dejeurner. Pedalling out of the village. Solitary barking dog, a passing car.

Marshals direct roadriders on an amateur race. The first to arrive are directed through the sleeping village. I travel opposite direction signed for Belcaire. Straight road agricultural climb, gradient increase. Belcaire arrives under a pollarded plane tree avenue. Roadriders fly through the town in file, all numbered. Many competitors in varying states from passive to red faced oxygen grabbing and the few focused super fit determined.

Belcaire steep between sun bright white walls. A marshal for the cycle race is sat in the shade, half asleep on a chair tapping at his phone oblivious to the world.

Roadrider groups keep coming. I climb 'S' bends. A place to stop under a shading tree. I get out my pizza digesting the race and how cyclists negotiate the sharp bend. Some weave in brake squeal, others carve a curve smooth without speed loss. More riders. The tail end wobble are not as professional as the first bunch.

Bend climb under trees makes altitude. Two girl roadriders speed down the hill delivering a happy "Bonjour!"

Sweet smelling pine, the crest of a hill. A marshal is surprised to see my appearance. Brown sign Col de Sept Fréres 1253m(3750ft). Lands ahead roll alpine green. A village named Montaillon sits inside of a hill amongst lush pasture topped with a small ruin fortress. Road follows hillside contour, land rolls green. Two touring bikes laden, one tows a trailer. Waves and inaudible greeting. Pace slows ascending humid to Camurac. From the other side of a hill, baritone rumble. Cloud top pokes over ridge, blue black mass follows. I watch it slowly moving away acute. Thunder rumble increases the pace, road steepens in still heat.

A brass lion steadily streams water from its mouth flowing music into a stone trough. The sign. 'Eau potable.' I scoop some in my hands and let it run down my face ice cold. Colder than the River Aude. Catching the breath. Under thirty degree heat the water feels just above freezing. More scoops poured over my head and neck. I take my empty waterbottle filling it. It is the most quenching drink ever experienced. PURE. The true experienced meaning to the word. Ice cold filtered from mountain rock without chemical tamper. So cold. It cannot be gulped. I feel every swallow through my body left and right cooling my insides. I have found gold on this hot day. Tepid tap water remnants empty to the road verge. Bottles fill chilling the hands with over splash.

Climb climb back and forth. From far ahead, deep baritone thunder roll. Cold draughts blow strong rushing hillside woodland in roar. Col de Marmaré 1361m (4000ft).

Black mountains, snow cover. Frozen escarpment enveloped in cloud swirl. Battlefield rage, cumulonimbus unleashes heavy artillery. Road straightens, gradient ease. Col de Chioula 1431m (4200ft). Black smoke cloud rising, thick violent lightning spears opposite mountain range. The strength of the electrical discharge releases a pressure wave reverberating through my body. Leaning the bike on the col sign I walk amongst empty restaurant tables to watch. The storm stuck in a mountain valley unable to move raging in worsened temper. Fingers of lightning flash across the sky overhead. The storm is not coming this way, intent on attacking Andorra followed up by a grey sheet of rain.

Spike summits and long falling ridges one behind the other monochrome through the rumbling veil. Mountain wonderment. Black peak, escarpment and ice. In no hurry to descend through storms raining remnants. Air clears revealing cable lifts rising steeply across opposite valley mountainside. Main road runs the valley floor. Its passage shut from view by a rising escarpment.

I climb on the bike to start the steep descent. Brakes alternately squeezed, wheel rims overheating could burst the inner tubes. Descending wooded rock land, steep snaking lane drops fast down the hillside. A camping sign directs for Sorgeat. Vertiginous valley floor faraway below. Little town roofs, tiny vehicles along cotton thread arterial road below the gaze of 2000m (6000ft) snowcapped peaks. Sorgeat direction greets with a climb. A long time patient, pedals turn the granny gear. Slowly, the appearance of an old village. Sorgeat stone buildings have seen a few hundred winters. Piled firewood sits in long rich green grass, a tradition as old as the houses. Dripping green overhang, roadside babbles water flow. A campsite thankfully open.

I book in and buy a can of beer frosted running in cold beads. The pitch is next to a little stream flanked by thick spongy grass. The long welcomed shower of red hot cleanse. Rain starts a gentle patter on the tent. A temperature half of yesterday. At the top of Col de Chioula the restaurant said 22 degrees. Numbers further cascade throughout the evening.

A Dawes Galaxy touring bike arrives, the rider probably English. I am dozing in the sleeping bag lullabied by rain's soft patter. Background gurgle stream accompanies perfect temperature of evening. Quillan was at 289m (870ft) the last col was 1431m (4200ft). It has been a great ride, the view paid for by the effort taken. The spectacle well earned.

68 km

I awake to green. It has been a couple of weeks without its colour dominance. Moss sponge soft, rich grass wet cool to touch. Shading broad leaf shimmer, thermal breeze rises from the valley. Clear mountain peak views across panoramic valley. Forest reach to white snow laying thick over black stone of mountain against blue morning sky. Yesterday's dying storm re born rises as long evaporation fingers re uniting with the clouds.

I start the pack. The touring bike rider wanders over. He is English, coming to France also using the Plymouth to Roscoff ferry. Taking the flat route down the West Coast. Riding over the Pyrenees, unable to cross the famous Tourmalet mountain because huge landslides have destroyed long sections of the road making it all impassable. The road will be out for months. This is not good news. The top can be reached, but it is a return downward on the same road with a long detour around the valley routes.

I am told the N20 I want to ride along today is fast, very dangerous, crammed with speeding vehicles and lorries nearly blowing him into the ditch. Too dangerous for bikes and I am not to attempt it.

He also tells me that all the shops will be shut today because it is a public holiday. If I want bread I won't find any. I should have ordered it from the local épicerié in the village yesterday on my arrival. He may go down the coast into Spain via the Cote Vermeille to chase a woman met on the West Coast.

I finish packing. Walking the bike past as he is clips bags onto the rack of the beautiful old steel Dawes Galaxy tourer. I wish him a good trip and he replies the same. Thanks the Patron, a smile and a wave freewheeling under bright green.

Tarmac lane to the village. The épicerie open and selling to anyone. I buy a few snacks and a baguette, possibly the one belonging to Mr. Dawes. As I ride out of the village I see the English rider and wave. I am gone. Switchback ride arrives over the roofs of Ax-le-Thermes. Main road junction crossing into the crammed bustle. A town full of sightseers and shoppers. The épicerie open. Fueling up with ripe fruit, chocolate, milk and a bottle of coke. Breakfast sat on the street corner wall under bright warming sun watching the world go by dressed stylish. Unlike myself, dressed sweaty.

Green traffic light release. N20 toward Tarascon-sur-Ariége. The main route for Andorra and Spain busy bumper to bumper. Alternative lanes wander through villages above the valley running parallel, but this road is fast and covers km quickly. High sub mountain solid rock towers over running River Ariége. Sun heat reflects. Engine and tyre noise, heat and speed pass close. Montagne de Tabe over 2000m (6000ft) looks over hillside villages above the river guarded by ruined chateau Urs. Towering peaks of 1700m-1800m (4400ft). Dual carriageway speeds busy traffic. I am passed by stone face Monsieur Alpha le roadrider. His hallowed presence a good sign of being allowed to cycle this road. All vehicle taillights light up applying the brakes for a roundabout.

Leaving busy arterial noise, climbing steep rock mountain footing. Tree covered steepness is shared with industry. Rusting grot scrapyards contained by steel roadside fencing. Hydroelectric satanic buzz feeds off large black steel pipes descending vertical cliff face. D8 green hemmed steep. Roaring river, vapour rise. Thundering liquid noise batters through rock cleave. Adverts for cave paintings, 'Parc Prehistory.' Chateau gaze over quiet climbing road surrounded by forest steepness to Vicdessos. A quiet village of singing birds, flower spill. Tumbling river, a campsite, along a sunny narrow street. A minibus is being loaded with bikes after a cycle ride. I am wished "Bon courage!" and a minute later find out why.

The road climbs stupid steep out of Vicdessos for as far

up as I can see on a narrow lane surrounded by trees. D18 eases at the turning for Sentenac. Steep grind. Suc-et-Sentenac rooftops poking silver above the greenery. Tree hidden river fills the rising valley with sweet hum. Sweat pours on the climb, gradient settles to mountain road. Shade island roadside trees soften a heated climb.

Road becomes D15 rising over 1000m(3000ft) to high steep vertical forested hills part masking great snowed frontier peaks. The climb difficult, gradient unrelenting in and out of shade. Crystal stream bubbles the gutter. Cupped hands catch cold clear water scooping it over my head and neck cooling the blood. New views, mountainous land. Higher and higher I climb. Closed up stone dwellings sink wild overgrown. Steep 's' bends.

Large house. A barking dog regards me as afternoon sport following my progress with canine vocal encouragement running along the front of the house's garden and back again. As the road hairpins above the rooftop, the dog appears along the back garden continuing the barking, making sure I disappear. In his dog mind he has victoriously sent me on my way. I was going in the direction anyway. The thought not occurring to dog brain.

Switchbacks, straight line grind. Cycling uphill with the brakes stuck sums up mountain roads. Slow plod, woodland thins, above forest line. River speeds in tumble under the road. Thundering noise reveals an impressive cascade. White roar. Wet shining sharp black rock, long rich grass. Tree anchor deep fissure next to the vertical river drop. Consuming noise. Rising atomised invigorating vapour kills the heat. So much water tumbles.

Green bald land. High summit rock surround. Road grind bend on bend, views better with every turn of hill contour. Sun obscured solid by cloud line. Brown sign. Port de Lers 1517m (4500ft). A rest from the saddle walking across the road. Below view of the tarmac snake followed coiling outcrops and steep hillsides climbing the head of the valley. Far below mountainous hills rise dark forested from obscured valley village of Vicdessos. Escarpment horizon jagged half cloud hidden.

Coloured nylon figures slow wander across scant hillside, walking the GR10. The ancient way traversing the Pyrenees. Lone tree's defiant survival, stubborn snow companion refuses to melt. River tumble through rock and scree between two bald round rocky hills form the roadside cascade. Cloud decapitates snow dappled hill keeping summit height secret.

Sun obscured, sweated dripping clothes cooled enough to want to move. Road drops. Speed welcomed, altitude loss is not. Dropping through rocky moorland, two youths stand next to a van shouting "Bein, bein!" Tower mountain dominates. 'Pic de Montbéas' rises above all. Long dropping valley view falls to civilisation hazed.

Cars parked alongside the verge, people watch paragliding. Colourful parachute foils glide backward and forward looking for thermal updraught from the valley. Wind whistles the paraglider cords. The seated pilot sails by.

Downward bends, weather worn building makes a café. A lake lined with white parked motorhomes. Bridge to broken boulders. Shattered rock valley climb, rough grass, scrappy bush. Struggling forest cling steep sides sweeping to high ridge. Road coil high climb beyond view.

White cattle cowbell music adds sound to barren landscape. Cloud swirl silent, obscuring rocky tops at will. Broken road dead end valley. Snow patches refuse to give up, blanketing grass and tumbled scree. Land of rock. Enduring slabs of strength look over rock shattered by ice expansion. The lake far below shows the twisted travelled road. More bends, uphill grind, patience. Far ahead a sign on a post sits under a rock spike of the most pleasing shape. A mini mountain sweeping steep to tall triangular stone peak against a centre tall narrow spike. Closer and closer, zig-zag bends. Wandering cattle obscure the sign. 'Col d'Agnes.' 1570m (4700ft). New found energy pushes the pedals. Last bend. The road pass crest guarded passive by a chewing white cow with sharp horns.

I receive the payout for my afternoons work. A view into high mountains over the frontier into Spain. The vast panorama of many black peaks step back covered with snow. Vast descending escarpment. Snow filled ravine black shade. Near mountain cloaked moody, the furthest rise high gleaming sun shined ridges. Spike form of mountain summit. Snow enhances rock contours laying deep between steep slopes. Lower mountainside vertical black fir forest deep monochrome shaded by slow swirling dark mass cloud. Warmed whisp evaporation twists slowly upward to join mass cooling cloud instability. Air sharp as sea. Stormy day fresh. A mountain of grey rock under blanketing grey cloud sends wild water tumbling in freefall cascade through forest fir. Baritone echoes bounce from dead end valley.

Thunder rolls the mountains. The endless cycle of warmed evaporation from decaying snowfields joins the daily vapour rise meeting freezing sky temperature. Cumulus towers form growing unstable, setting up the thunder cell discharging many lightning strikes until the storm rains out and dies. Re starting the evaporation cycle.

D8 descent fast and steep. Full use of brakes. Straight bend straight. Dripping muddied solid ice shapeless blocks feed roadside streams. From a footpath appear randonneurs released from mountainside dark forest paths after day on the

GR10.

Downward for five minutes. Stopping to feel the wheel rims with the back of the hand. Cooking near skin burn from hard braking. I must wait for the cooling or I will lose the tubes to melting punctures. Ten minutes at the side of the road amongst thousands of green overhanging trees. Birdsong serenade over roaring far below river. Another five minute ride, both brakes held firm keep the bike under control in precipitous descent. Bends roll steeper. Empty freefall edge. Another halt. Wheels rims burning require a patient wait. Five repeated stops earns an easing mountain valley. The rooftops of Aulus-les-Bains spa town with a minimart and Presse. Restaurants and old noble fronted hotels. Campsite signs direct down a long straight road into a tidy site with a friendly Accueil.

Thick grassy pitches. A large undercover area laid out with tables and benches for anyone to use. Hot water flowing over the body relaxes and warms muscles. I sit looking up at steep forest surround, towering peaks in and out of vapour veil watch over the town. Nearing darkness, gentle rain falls to background mountain rumble.

78 km

6.30am. A randonneur is sat under the covered awning at a bench. Mini jet stove boils dehydrated breakfast. Rucksack packing in methodical order, contents laid across the table.

"Bonjour."

7.30am he walks off carrying a loaded rucksack, arms rhythmic in pace holding walking poles bound for the GR10. Straight out of town to a mountain valley climb of forest, the great cascade and rocky beyond.

Overhead cloud swirl cuts mountain top view. Humid, peaceful pleasant in stillness. Tent hangs to dry. Packing while the stove chatters for tea.

A couple are camped across the site travelling on mountain bikes. They are travelling across the Pyrenees to the Atlantic. Their journey started in Italy.

Day brightens, temperature rise. Sun begins its burn. Soaked tent releases vapour in steaming rise to join the afternoon cloud mass.

Goodbye to the couple, a parting thank you the Accueil. The town offers two options for food. One overpriced, the other not so bad for a mountain town. A few things not to add weight to the little carried. D32 following a river speeding rapid. Growing along a slow descending valley.

Mist banished by burn. Sunshine ride, widened valley crops and pasture. Street of buildings lining the road make a village named Ercé ending with a very old Romanesque chapel. Walls of ancient masonry bulge, simple arch bell tower under a metal cross. Cattle graze amongst long grass and meadow flower. Hills rise forested, rock pokes through high valley sides. A look back to Aulus-les-Bains. Black stone mountains ending high in dappled snow.

The River Garbett runs through Vallee du Garbet. An alternative road climbs to Ustou descending to Seix. This road goes to Seix fast on a big gear, speeding bumpy rattling road gently rolls with the river. A bridge of tree shade invites a stop hiding from morning heat enjoying the speeding river slamming into boulders, rushing around slick rock slab in ice blue turbulence.

Easy ride to Oust. Half full colourful campsites. River crossing. D3 upstream into the start of Seix. A town built over the meeting of two rivers. Buildings grab a footing in the flow. White painted render, summer blue shutters. Bursting flower filled baskets colour a busy town of narrow street bustle.

Shoppers, people sat under rainbow parasols talking, drink coffee, enjoy an aperatif.

Car horns, blue moped smoke one way system through the narrowest echoing streets. Signs for 'Col de la Core.' Town noise fade, steady climb concentration, steep pinch. The upward road. Sun glare without wind. Surrounding mountains hard edge against blue morning sky. Woodland ascent going skyward. Half an hour of slow grind gives a view down to tiny town little red roofs and ribbon streets making Seix. The town surrounded by great wooded hills. Valley flows a silver strand.

Shade islands from roadside trees, open sun glare. Water gulped runs back out of the skin, soaked clothes drip, gloves saturated. Salted sweat drip, vision sting. Horseflies nip the skin through clothes, bare legs bitten. Annoying pretenders rarely draw blood compared to their Cevénnes cousins of doubled size and ferocity.

Green forest sweep to mountain peaks. Rising ridge, high snow cover. Grey white curtain ascension through the blue. Dense cloud crown across a snow topped giant. Climb grind slog, bend after bend. Patient turn of the pedals earns slow change view over three hours. Great mountain spine ridge forested. Rock tower. Blue hazed massive beauty, low valleys roll so far, lost from sight. Roadrider passes slow pedalling carbon fibre.

"Bonjour!" Laboured breaths.

We both grin and nod. Unspoken climbing conversation of raised eyebrows followed by a nod. Breath too precious to waste talking. Slowly ahead. Slipping distance from his wheel, around bends, further and further away. A toiling figure absorbed into the mountain.

Rare shade earns a stop to let the body cool. Patience delivers Col de la Core and its 1395m (4200ft) of hot grind.

I am soaked as sat clothed in a bath, peeling my soggy clinging top off to let the mountain cool breeze dry the skin. A clean top feels soft to the body. I am so tired, the heat drain has used three litres of water. Stomach grinds empty, the want of food. Looking back to the long climb. Traceable ascending wooded mountainside, long thread constant gradient. Behind far down, the large forested hill where the hidden road drops to far out of sight Seix. High above, the peaks of Cap Ner, Tuc de Quer Ner and Mont Valier 2838m (8500ft) possible to walk to via a refuge hut.

I do not take one step. Laying out on a picnic bench, eyes closed. I don't care about anything. Not wanting to move. Not intending to move.

Temperature cools, slow swirl blocks sun turning everything dull sombre. Shaded laying snow tinted grey transformed to white frozen sparkling islands where sun burns holes through dulling cloud grip. Highlighted illumination's slow sweep. Glowing patch sun soaked in detail.

A monument at Col de la Core of solid granite with a black marble plaque. My rough understood translation:

> *To the memory &*
> *honour who passed from*
> *France to Spain*
> *1940 1944. The confined*
> *of Castillon, Oust, St. Girons.*
> *The 'Path of Liberty.'*

Dangerous work in desperate times. I observe this landscape in its friendliest mood of the four seasons. Local knowledge risking life helping others from certain death.

The body calm and lazy. Yawning walking towards the bike.

A Frenchman asks me. "What direction have I come from today?"

He is a little difficult to understand as his Pyreneen accent sounds part Spanish spoken rapid. Tone rises at the end of each sentence completely different from his Languedoc neighbour's slow paced drawn dialect.

"Je commence Aulus les Bains et fin Castillon avec le chance un place pour le camping."

He relays the conversation to his wife and friends sat in an attentive line on a blanket. As I set off they wish a smiling "Bon courage!"

"Merci, au revior."

Brakes are eased. Steep around a green hill, villages far away distant, specs bathed in sunshine. Vertical drop, the tarmac thread weave hidden, appearing, running through far away forested valley floor. Mountains rise not so precipitous. Great angled ridge fold, one behind the other. Hard edged rock roots suck at the valley floor. Far detail misted to haze block shape, cloud dense over mountains builds afternoon towers.

The hot wheel rim stop. Wild panorama detail, river valley glint. Shaped lowland forest hills, mountainside contour rise. Smaller peaks hidden within giant's shadow. Rumbles high of no concern. Any wind thermal travels vertical to the mountains. Thunderstorms remain stationary. Air mass orographic storms. Unstable air fuelled by evaporation over the mountain. Away from the mountain the air more stable in temperature, insufficient in charging electrical Frankenstein.

Five minutes of braked freewheel before another stop is required for cooling. The daily wheel cooling, the daily cloud building. The storm cycle, familiar routine. If any were missing the day would feel incomplete. Temperature warms with altitude loss. Flattening land, softened world. Through a couple of villages. 'OURS NON!' written on the road in large painted yellow letters (no bears!) again and again.

A fine old church over steep dropping valley. The gable end becomes the tower holding two bells under a slated platform, a higher bell central in its own arch. The tower wall ends in convex concave patterns to a circular central opening with decorative finials. Three crosses point to the sky. The design evokes Spain.

'OURS NON!' 'S' bends, junction. Downhill into Castillon. Town shops end finding the town plan for camping direction. Corner supermarket sells plenty, the campsite tucked down behind town. I pay the lady for a night's accommodation, putting me out to graze my purchased carrier bag in a field away from the organised sardine packed caravans.

Full season occupants unmoved until the winter. T.V. ariels, satellite dishes, cables. Gossip over plastic fencing, sun chairs, loud T.V's from caravan windows. The field of tussock grass guaranteed full of mosquitos and midges. But it has space. The nearest neighbour is at shouting distance. The noise of a little river under trees comes from the bottom of the site. Tent, shower routine. The needed washing of sweated clothes. White soap bubbles dark grey, many rinses clear the water. A dripping bundle to peg. Air thick humid, nothing dries. A great peel of thunder rolls across the sky followed by another. Large splashes hit the tent as stones, then….. nothing. Humidity hangs. Rumbles bounce between mountain surround. Sleep comes before dark.

54 km

Heavy air. Everything hangs warm damp. 10.30am. Enough waiting. Tent wet and heavy is bundled in the bag. Clothes are tied over the pannier box and socks are threaded through the front panniers to dry on the road. I should have done this earlier.

"Thank you." To the Accueil. I am wished a smiling "Bon route."

Main street jam. No vehicle traffic on busy market day. Stalls line the road, frenetic shoppers. Silk scarfs, clothes, crepes, hardware. Drool worthy spiced smell of Moroccan food permeates. I push the bike past saucepans and knives, jeans and belts. Chicken slowly spins flamed crispy golden brown. Tempting food smell and human traffic cease on a green road ride turning down a straight D618.

Countryside crops and birdsong, views across to a long valley ends yesterday's mountains. Morning vapour transported skyward. Stormy white castles thicken early over mountain direction halfway grown unstable.

Pretty valley running river. The road its happy companion, meandering together through hamlet and village. Vegetable garden ripeness, fine house gardens burst bloom, rose garden flowers to the river's edge. Neat stacked firewood, farm buildings, dogs sunbathe in docile pant. Valley rise narrow, streets of St. Lary.

'Mew' call betrays the buzzard. Thick rounded wings, outstretched fingers glide drawing circles higher and higher in bright morning sky. How farmland and the buzzard are so connected, the opportunist aviator who works the field.

Uphill, road graffiti. "Ours Non!" Underneath in pink, "Elephants Oui!" The humour lasts into the village of Portlet d'Aspet, hot in bright high sun. Three working men sit in the shade of the bus shelter eating lunch. "Bon courage."

Notre Damme sits watching from a pillar. Switchback height over rooftops. Roadside chapel icon, singing woodland. The steep pinch ascent easier than the last two days. Bends cut from cliff, tree overhang. Opposite falls from view. High blue hazed silhouette rock ridge closer. Roadside buildings, sign offers camping. The unexpected arrival at Col de Portet d'Aspet 1069m (3200ft). I stop for lunch enjoying views to new mountain peaks forested looked over by frontier high snow altitude. Cloud envelope, the mountain veil. Dense leaning thundercloud sprawl across black splintered rockscape.

Steep descent, patient wheel cool. Four Italians pass on mountain bikes bundled with camping gear.

"Bonjour!" as they pass. Whoops and shouts disappear through woodland bends. Voice fade, mountain silence.

The four have stopped at a memorial for their fellow countryman. The Tour de France rider Fabio Casartelli died here in 1995 at the age of twenty five after hitting the concrete road barriers. The memorial carved from white stone in the shape of a wheel, the lower part covered by a sculpted draped Olympic flag, the other side changes to a wing. An inscription reads;

Fabio Casartelli
16 August 1970
To his memory and to his courage
Olympic champion 1992.

There is a sundial commemorating the time and date of his death. The memorial immaculate surrounded by flowers.

Steepening bends, a loaded touring bike making the ascent. The rider happy and red in the face followed by roadriders full of grins and greeting. Next are a group all out of the saddle pushing to climb a steep pinch. Their minibus follows towing a bike trailer. They are the pampered on an organised tour having only to carry one drink bottle, everything else catered for, from meal arrangement to a waiting bed.

A roll of deep thunder focusses attention. At the bottom of the hill the D85 will take me over Col de Menté toward the frontier. I stop and watch the mountain become fully enveloped in raincloud stabbing thick lightning. The booms and crackles of the storm will not move for a couple of hours until it exhausts itself. My punishment for leaving two and a half hours late this morning. I want to go over the col. But do I really want to be inside a thunder cell on an aluminium bike with nylon static making waterproofs in hail, rain, gales, lightning unable to see anything? No. I could wait around for two, three hours until it finishes. Not enough hours are left in the day. I can reach destination without too much detour. D618 runs parallel, climbing lower land to the valley of the Garonne following the road to Luchon and back into the high mountains. I pass the four Italians in a bus stop busy talking, sheltering and not coming out.

The road drops. Mountain river ride, big gear, woodland speeding bends end at beautiful pillared and decorated Notre Damme shrine of comforting words to the traveller, *'Mary protects us,'* although dedicated to a cholera epidemic many years ago.

Easy ride crests unnoticeable Col de Buret 599m (1800ft). Mountain splendour replaced by raining rage storm shrouding everything in grey blanket bedlam. Rain spots hit in ice sting from cloud edge steel brooding spin. Quiet Just d'Izault. Rock and woodland, climbing to fields and harvested meadow. Rolled yellow bales wait patient to be wrapped and collected. Isolated trees marooned in yellow harvest stubble, steep forest slope. Rocky Pic de Cagire summit wears a shroud of rain. Air warm. Rain spots. Not enough to wet the road, but enough to give relief of freshness climbing woodland. Steady gradient needs only a rare expelled push from the legs. A road climbing ideal. Through surrounding greenery appears a restaurant, hotel and a small appealing campsite. A sign. Col des Ares, a mere dwarf of 797m (2400ft).

Unfolding views of new lands to travel. Far below, inhabited matchbox models at the base of towering mountain. High peak haze, atmospheric observation. Nature's giant geology project older than quantifiable time and bigger than comprehension. It takes a long time to retain mountain magnificence detail. Snow glint through hazed sunshine suspended in sky. Mist evaporation lays thick isolating lower mountainside. Mystical Chinese silk painting views. Convolutions and summit outline blend to fade stepping to dissolve in softened infinite. A hard clear day will give sharper detail, distance discernible but the haze misted blue panorama promotes an atmosphere of painted dreamscape.

Freeride squander to Antichan-de-Frontignes. Above the village a ceramic orientation table from the 1920s. Detailed direction names surrounding mountains, towns and valleys to include a glacier just in view on this hot hazed afternoon.

Down through Antichan,' church domination elevated on rock surrounded lowly by village roofs. 'Route Barre 2km.' Ignored, descending sweeping bends. 'Route Barre 1km.' Steep weave against shady walls to the village of Ore. Dropping through dusted sleepy lanes to a flattening road rudely meeting N125 diesel fumed racetrack. Signs for Bagneres-de-Luchon and Espagne (Spain). A bridge crosses grey murk, shallow, noisy flowing. River Garonne. The great river to Bordeaux. Flowing out of infancy.

Railway lines parallel the river. Village ride greeted by an angry German Shepherd leaping snarling and barking behind a wall. Flat valley road next to the river, traffic background buzz.

Villages once kept busy by through traffic before the new built road now comatosed. Floral pride shared with subsiding decay. A junction at Marignac. 20km to Bagneres-de-Luchon and 18km to Espagne.

Steep forested valley hemmed tight by craggy mountain ridge. Black angry cloud joined by warmed white vapour rise. Storm builds. Air heavy, lungs suck extra hard to pull oxygen from every breath. Cierp Gaud, signs for camping. I want to hold out for Bagneres-de-Luchon, playing chance with the overhead mass. D125. Cycle lane stops and starts, wide rideable tarmac hard shoulder, good leg pace, the mind watches darkened cloud swirl. Railway tracks diagonal through the road. Guran busy in home commute. Day fades to late evening instant. Lightning hiss low overhead, a baritone of thunder.

A bend. Across bumps of railway line shine. Bus shelter empty, I pull in. The sky opens a deluge. Headlights of busy traffic whizz by, rain and spray near nil visibility. I am joined after one minute by a French roadrider, pulling my bike up tight making room.

He is straight on his phone telling home he will be late because of the storm. We talk discuss the route of my journey. He gives good tips about roads ahead and mountain beauty. His knowledge profound after living in "Luchon" since birth. His bike is white, everything carbon fibre a top of the range race machine 'Pinarello.'

I ask him. How much does it weigh?

"6 kilograms."

I reply my loaded bike is seven times heavier." Much to his amusement with a mime of a cretinous pace of turning the pedals.

I tell him. "I have the gears for the Grandma." Causing laughter.

He gives me direction to a recommended campsite. A place called Moustajon.

"Turn left at the sign for the Intermarche."

Storm subsides, rain eases to drizzle. We leave with a friendly "Au revoir." Up on the pedals sprinting around a bend into the grey.

Slow climb, valley hemmed steep. Dark forest hills, busy River Pique. Flooded campsite in submersed dereliction. Tyres cut black lines through water laying across the road in grey mirror sheet. Spray billows from passing vehicles, air still. White strokes of mist cloud slowly twist rising to black overhead brood above steep darkened forest ridge. Rumbling surroundings claustrophobic, thick still air. A couple of campsites for the motorhomed. Roundabout, sign points Moustajon. Quiet road, a village, watching for the sign. Rural road to nowhere under black forest cliff. Patience. Wet empty road, start of the campsite. The Intermarche sign as directed to the campsite gate.

The pleasant Accueil. I want to practice my French, the lady serving is so polite and welcoming, wanting to practice her English. I try my French, she replies in English. Inter language correction. I am the corrected. I find a pitch that will not flood if hammered by deluge. Tent, hot shower, supermarket buys ingredients for an all evening feast. Rumbles in the mountains, slow moving black blanket shroud. People offer a cheerful. "Bonsoir."

72 km

Thumping spots of rain hit nylon. A crawl from sleeping bag warmth. Pulling the plastic tarpaulin from under the tent, fixing it over. Staked to survive a stormy drenching. It is not long to wait. Rain comes hard while tucked up cosy. My watch says

1am. Drifting in and out of sleep, bright flashes light the back of eyelids, peels of thunder angry stuck in the valley, unable to move from the dead end. It all subsides to gentle patter by 2.30am.

The waking sense of light. 7.30am. The tent dry, air fresh. Sun yet to climb the mountain surround. Tea and sleep waking at 10am.

Bright sunshine pack, supermarket stop. Flat outskirts of Bagneres de Luchon. Admiring tall majestic dark rock peaks sugar topped in snow into Spain. Roundabout traffic busy, climbing out of town, steep against rock. Deep stormwater ditch holds fallen stone and broken boughs waiting for the wash down journey. I must not fall in. Across the valley hydroelectric pipes mountain drop powering an industrial view. Ski lift cables to Superbagnéres, sloped snowless, docile out of season. Sweat runs ascending a plod over the disappearing town. Eye stinging salt wiped from the vision. Snowed high mountain horizon already part obscured in vapour rise.

Back and forth ever up towards the village of St. Aventin. Rocky bend riding the edge of the stormwater ditch as close as I can allowing vehicles to overtake. From behind, the approach of a large diesel. It does not slow its engine tone. Horn blast, maintaining speed. The high revving drone casts a shadow overtaking blind on a bend. I see an orange truck come down the hill opposite before the overtaking coach does. The coach now a third of its length past. I stop sharp on the edge of the stormwater ditch, the coach sees the oncoming vehicle and swings back in chopping the whole road off. The long metal body nearer and nearer, elbow length away. I get ready to bail into the ditch before big wheels roll over me. Missing by a leg graze. The driver with sunglasses and a black moustache looks his tubby face into his wing mirror to see if he has squashed me. He does not slow or care, continues in denial. Kicking down a gear, the black spiraling exhaust cloud envelopes. A pathetic driving decision. Overtaking blind over the oncoming carriageway on a steep mountain bend. . . with a coach. It is local, battered and probably the bus.

St. Aventin is glued to a vertical hill. Buildings have rooms overhanging into high nothing dramatizing the perch. Garin gets very steep. Maximum push creates maximum water to run from my pores in skin soaking grind. Steepness ease. A stop for a drink and a body cool.

Seated glazed roadriders share the pain with an oxygen grabbing "Bonjour."

I get a silent thumbs up from one of them. It is all his energy can spare.

Climb ease, a turning for Oó and Lac d'Oó. Maybe named after the view. The lake a blue mountain pool surrounded by rich green and slender black peaks. Another steep pinch into green alpine mountain beauty. Signs advertise a ski station.

A group of roadriders slowly catch me on carbon fibre feathers.

"Bonjour. Vous avez les beers dans la boite?" Making a joke of my carrying panniers.

I reply. "Oui. Et pizza et les glacés." They laugh.

I add in a low voice. "Et pour les cyclists EPO, Tour de France stéroids, de America! Je vend au Col de Peyresourde. D'accord?" Laughter.

In English, I am wished "Good luck. Good trip!" They ride on.

Under a summit of green, ascending across steep mountain slope. Determined snow resists sun, cowbell chime far below. A village in a valley bowl. Pointed spire, little roofs surround, winding tarmac ribbon green picture alpine ideal.

Ever climbing. Eyes follow road progress far ahead. Steep line rise to stacked 'S' bends retained by stone walls. Big yellow letters. 'OCCITANIA.' Proud regional graffiti.

I stop to cool. Sun obscured, air sharp, fresh to breathe. Mountain silence challenged by a solitary cowbell. One warbling bird sings out to a big green mountain dead end.

Boulder ooze from the landscape moved by frozen nature's erosion programme working the winter ice shift under slow gravitation.

My shading hat has fallen from the handlebars somewhere. I am not going back.

Dead end escarpment claims the sky. Stream trickle beneath the road. Passing roadrider. Legs and lungs in rhythm nodding a greeting, pace mapped time/energy to ascend the col. On the second bend I stop, make a sandwich and sit on the wall watching a tiny coloured rectangle of a car making its way up the long climbing road. Pounding up the hill is a distant roadrider absorbed into the great green high landscape. I watch him round the top of the valley to appear below on the first of the hairpin bends disappearing out of view under where I sit eating. Here he comes! A sixty year old crazy man looking aggressive with the world. He stares down at the road, face screwed up growling, pounding the pedals. I christen him 'Carbon madman!' For his crazed expression, frenetic pace and race machine.

Three roadriders appear over the brow of the hill speeding downward banking hard on the corner pedalling as fast as possible for a maximum downhill speed race shouting. "Allez!" Coloured shapes get smaller in the landscape. Tiny coloured crouched rectangles, blistering two wheeled speed racing the grey line to vanish around the bend.

I crest the Col de Peyresourde 1563m (4700ft) with new

views crossing from the Haut Garonne to the Haut Pyrenees. The green mountain hides areas of rough rock snow escarpment and black skyward summit. Steaming cloud rises across high black towering rockscape as smoke rising from cooling new world creation. High background horizon white icy glacial spiked mass contrasting far below soft rolling green.

The High Pyrenees. A vertical abyss far out of sight. Foreground suffers from ski station outbreak. Six storey seasonal apartments built in collective blot. Concrete tacky repetition grows along the plateau edge. Paths of worn winter fun end under deserted lifts waiting for season's return of the powder sportif. Lower slope wooded ridge road runs precarious, the other side plummets into a void big enough to hide a city.

Vertical cliff swallows a large portion of sky horizon. White smouldering cloud fingers rise pulled upward from convoluted ridge summit. Vapour swirls meet angry grey steel brooding above 3000m (9000ft) black rock snowcapped frontier.

A wood café glows dim yellow illumination through condensation window run. The establishment not busy. Two vehicles silent loiter in the parking area.

Clouded col temperature has plummeted. Lungful's of crisp cold air refreshment. Road falls. Fast blur through green bald land. Ice cold stream tumble through velvet green valley chattering over stone meeting the road. Above. Hillside cattle graze in cowbell symphony. Above the cattle, a stone building so old somehow continues to stand in lone resistance on a high altitude perch.

Great mountains come into view. A mass of rock, peaks triangular. Jagged tooth summit. Shy neighbours veil themselves with dense swirl grey. Road hugs near vertical mountain. A bend to aeroplane view. Far below floor sweeps infinite to peaks and jagged high rock shape. To the north. Mountains diminish to forested peaks fading to hills greener in soft land merge. Beneath. A lake sends a silver ribbon connecting valley villages, running away to haze, I squeeze the levers, brakes struggle to slow carried weight. Wheel rims need to cool. Cloud unveils far away high snow peak views.

The bike runs away without a turn of the pedal, lone roadrider pounds at the mountain. 'Carbon Madman!' The return. Standing on the pedals looking down at the road, face screwed up. Angry as ever! Carbon Madman is gone in twisted growling gargoyle caricature racing the clock, determined to beat a personal best.

Wheel cooling stops enable listening to mountain silence. Peaks taller with descent increase their landscape dominance. Louderville, through Estarveille blurred speed alongside quick flowing River Lauron. Fast big gear pothole dodge weave, bouncing over ridges. Road fun ends in roundabout for Arreau.

A group of motorcyclists at the side of the road map busy. I follow the river, into Arreau town bustle. Fine half-timbered history, stone fronted shops, a place so alive. Many shops dedicated to the randonneur and the souvenir hunter. Maison du Tourisme, shows camping municipal at the edge of a river.

Rear main street buildings overhang speeding water rush. Behind the town forested peaks conical, sharp, claim the sky, sheltering Arreau. Over a bridge. The busy covered market, stone pillared buildings of hundreds of years. Bottom of town, flowing rivers meet. D19. Sign for camping, municipal depot. Gendarmerie ride to riverside pleasant Camping municipal.

The tent is pitched to resist a storm on sponge green comfort near river edge flow. Speeding water slams boulders, standing waves mark underwater obstacles unmoving amid frantic turbulence. Not a place to fall or contemplate a paddle. Water speeds the milky blue tint common to mountain rivers.

Guaranteed frigid in temperature. Far bank low solid rock disappears around a bend. Woodland dense hides overhead noise of a road. Steep wooded mountainside climbs into vapour shroud privacy.

Screams and laughing whoops. From the upstream bend a rubber boat appears laden with laughing people on a wildwater downstream bounce and paddle. The steersman at the back of the boat digs frantic to avoid a large rock bringing the boat centre to the river, speeding fast past the campsite with continued laughs and screams. A second boat flies through the turbulence around the river bend ploughing straight into the rock. Energies of the sudden stop transferred from boat to paddlers launches all. Limbs grab at nothing flung high out of the boat. Frantic scrabbling bodies are helped back in. Everything at the mercy of the flowing current. One person is swept away disappearing underwater spinning in the flow, appearing, plunged under racing whitewater, void of density for buoyancy. Frantic downstream paddling, toward the helpless individual. The last viewed facial expression is gasping panic. Flapping arms grab nothing spun and bounced around boulders. Going under again. The boat catches him, pulling him up by the shoulders and backside face first into the bottom of the boat, going out of sight with a pair of wet suited legs stuck vertical in the air. Two more boats appear full of shrieking laughter waving on downstream adventure.

I walk the side of the river getting some low light motion blur camera shots of the flow. Signs detail emergency procedures for flash flood and earthquake tremors. The place on a fault line. Mountain creation over geological time continues.

Evening light fade brings soft rain. Washing my one saucepan and dish at the bac á vassille a dozen Spanish students eat a meal under cover. A dozen smiles, happy faced giggles.

Rain hard. Lightning flash, overhead hiss followed by ground shaking rolling thunder half drowned in river roar. Snug in the tent sleeping on a fault line.

40 km

Stormy wild flashes, closed eyelids lit blood red, blinded white on opening. The tent stays dry through hard pelting rain. I fall back into sleep. Static electrical artillery continues bombardment ceasing fire after a couple of hours dragging the mind in and out of sleep. Enjoyment of nighttime storms now part of nocturnal routine.

Tree stillness, white noise river roar. Gold top forest peaks painted by morning sun, thin gilded vapour rises into windless blue. The tent shake displaces small pools caught in the nylon folds, silver beads speedily run the sides joining dew covered soft wet grass. Washing hangs on a fence in anticipation of the first drying sun rays. The tent hangs in hope of reducing soggy carried weight for today's climbing. Breakfast in map ponder of the day's route. Sun arrives casting joyful radiance splashing gold to the river roar. Evaporation steams from drying clothes. The tent dries in minutes. I pack.

Town clock points 10am. Street jam stalls, market atmosphere. Tables laden with stock outside shopfronts entice a browse. Ambient bustle ends crossing stone bridge river roar.

D929. Hydroelectric siphons river water captive in black still pool feeding spinning turbines. Fishermen lean on a parapet of stone intent to entice a salmon.

D918 rides quiet green. Blue col sign. 'Col d'Aspin. Ouvert.'

Snack fuel up anticipates a long climbing morning. A man pushes his wheelbarrow mountain of weeds, and brambles up a driveway making conversation commenting on last night's weather.

Telling me "Col d'Aspin is a steep climb."

I reply. "They all are!"

He wishes "Bon chance."

I tell him. Follow behind. First man 'jardin sportif' with a wheelbarrow over the col.

Country ride woodland flank, stream rush secret hollow, everywhere so green. Morning shadow long. Valley fresh mist smell. Sun yet to turn up the heat dial for cooking. Road climb, Arreau rooftop shrink. Silver path morning river runs under dark cast forest mountain shade. Above, green sunsoaked mountain scarred by thin line rising. Tiny rectangle creeps upward progressing, sun reflected glass glint. The vehicle nears the top.

Steep road mountain hug. Panorama expands, forested summit darkened contrast against horizon cliff mountain spike. Clear day morning sun lights every contour and detail. Folds, scree slides, escarpment. Snow cling in deep vertical crevasse hiding dark beyond illuminated reach of climbing sun. Valley green suede pasture bright softened in full sunshine of low land soft living. Behind the mountains the never ending cloud towers. Heated land builds a giant to rain out over and over, keeping the spectacular mountain landscape lush forested. Beautifully raw.

Hard steep full straight leg strength. Lone tree green leaf parasol stop. A sweated body cools. Winding bend rise, granny gear plod. Pace of patience.

Two roadriders on a downward run. "The Tourmalet is closed. The roads is gone, it is impassable. It's a detour all the way to Lourdes."

I reply. "I heard it has been closed for a while. Still it is worth a go?"

"I went up from this side all the way to the col and came

back down again."

I am thinking about the returning down the same route as going up, on a ride that is meant to go from the Mediterranean to the Atlantic in one way of constant progress. Ending up back at square one is against traveller's instinct.

"Is the café at the top still open? I ask.

"No idea. I am doing the 100hour across the Pyrenees, no time to stop. Anyway how much does that bike weigh?"

"My bike loaded is around 42kg. I am travelling light today." Laughing.

They are finding the hills tough on their featherweight carbon machines. One complains of the muscles in the bottom of his back hurting. There there.

"How do you get it up these mountain roads?" Shaking his head.

I do a hand mime of turning the pedals, telling them "Low gears and determined grunt. Nothing too technical."

They are headed the way I have journeyed on an organised pamper package where everything is carried in a minibus. Their ride is timed 100 hours on the road to complete from West to East ending at the Mediterranean.

I tell them. "You will do it. Nine hours riding over eleven days. On those bikes, no problem. Good trip!" and they are gone.

The road busy with bikes. Roadriders up, roadriders down. Some friendly, others maintain stone faced Alpha male superiority hiding behind sunglasses.

Bend bend turn, bend bend turn. A pace of crawl along sheer mountain claws height. Narrow opening between two steep hilltops. No road higher. Maybe the col. Road eases in chilled freshness. Winter gales have flattened a large area of trees. Roots poke at the air, trunks flat face the same way pointing down steep hillside stamped by a giant. Slow appearing sign reads Col d'Aspin 1489m (4500ft).

Ringing bell cows munch rich green. One stands nodding. Eyes shut, ears alert. Protecting her calf resting beneath. An eye opens to any small noise, returning to a protective nodding doze.

Under green bald hill and rocky ridge I look back to the morning's picturesque climb snaking progress up steep sides. Far below under two forested mountains in shrunk size. Rooftop huddle of Arreau. Winter's low sun struggle to light the town below the overpowering surroundings must keep cold season days in permanent icy dusk.

New views, new mountains. Fast downward road swallowed in thick fir forest surround. Wheel cooling stop amongst conifer bough smother. Pine resin smell, swarming buzz, birdsong. Two touring bikes loaded plod at the hill. The encouragement exchange.

Helter skelter tree trunk blur under sweeping furry needle shade. Wheel cool stop. A lady is walking her bike up the hill, mouth open, face glazed by gradient and heat.

Her American accent. "Aa'm tired, ma legs have had e-nough! This was meant to be fun. It's the last mountainn am'a gonna do. Phew! The other guys have gone on a-head. Aa'm gonna walkit!"

Pushing her gleaming roadbike, looking back she gives a wave.

The brake release. Forest blur rolls faster and faster to a river gurgle weave through a wide valley of agriculture. A hotel lost amongst rolling green. Pretty St. Marie-de-Campan. Idyllic riverside campsite bathed warm with afternoon sunshine. Road squeeze between gables. Bright walls, open doors, narrow wall echo, old village street. Many bikes lean the walls. Riders enjoy coffee and food under parasol shade to a background hum of conversation.

The sign of disappointment. 'Access á La Mongie OUVERT. Col de Tourmalet FERMÉ.'

The red sign for the Tourmalet. Thoughts of whether it is worth going up seeing as it is closed. I suppose I should go as far as I can. The map marks a campsite under half way up the mountain road. I have enough energy. Stopping there will make tomorrow's ascent quicker. With time for the ride down out of the mountains through Bagnéres de-Bigorre, Lourdes and Argelés-Gazost on an unwanted detour the long way round.

Vallée de Campan follows the river in mountain direction. The sweeping valley an easy climb. Summer dresses, shading hats. A group of ladies are out for a walk with their dogs. 'Maison á Louer.' Houses to rent summer and winter. Never homely, silent dead window gaze hopes for a week of occupation. Farm buildings. Farm machinery, half buried under long yellow grass. Petrol station holds large ex-military 4WD vehicles waiting for recovery work. The habitation of Gripp starts and finishes without notice. Climb steepens, mountain valley. Menacing thick black cloud roll decapitates dense vertical forest.

Feeling of hunger grinds the gut. Energy is fading.

Rock ride, an avalanche shelter. Water drips through the concrete roof. Into the open. Caravan roof approach to the municipal site. Road climb, cascade drop, pool broils under the road. A river compressed between steep forest rock. Side lane, half derelict activities centre. A coach collects children. Adults attempt authority in controlling the bouncing mass of juvenile energy. I cycle to high chainlink closed gates, push the flat bolt. Hinges close in metallic squeal. Accueil sign. 'Fermé.' The place full of permanent caravans, campsite shanty town. Static caravans green moulded, plastic white chairs stacked in little withered gardens. Mats hung out to dry for months, parasols blotched black with algae. Pallet remnant fences and decking, unskilled projects of retirement. An old lady in fluffy slippers shuffles across worn tarmac to the sanitaires.

"Bonjour."

I top up my water and walk back to the Accueil. Still closed.

My options. Stay in the high fenced refugee camp if there is a pitch. Or cook up here, then head up to the Col du Tourmalet and freewheel back down the mountain to St.Marie du Campan's pretty riverside campsite. I look around to see a smashed and crumpled static caravan fenced off. Wrecked by flood. The place hit explains its melancholy feel. I am not staying here one more minute than I have to.

The stove soon chatters, the last of my bread, the end scrape of jam between bits of cheese is all that's left for a quick eat followed by a mug of tea. It will have to do. I wash up and pack away. Closing the squeaking gate. Body fatigued.

Pothole lane glumness exchanged for Tourmalet grind. It is too late in the afternoon to do this.

Overhead black swirl thickens, slow engulf of high forest ridge darkness. Cloud masks the first hurdle toward the road pass. I see a lorry crawl miniscule into cloud line. River drop cascade torrent pools captive in a waterworn giant grotto.

Randonneurs in waterproofs downward from the mountain shout "Bon courage!"

Two roadriders wrapped up for the cold pass speeding in descent.

Big trucks carry stone. The high revving crawl past. Tyre bulge, loaded weight. Low gear leviathan's struggling fight with the climb.

Landslide treeless mud is being stabilised with stone filled gabion baskets. Florescent workmen and hydraulic slab arm of heavy plant swarm busy in repair to hydroelectricity. Heavy revving diesel and flashing lights amongst mud slide subside.

Into hard forest climb. A waterproof wearing roadrider on his speeding chill exit. 180 hairpin climbs to the first ski station, silent. Machinery noise passes construction repairs far below. Hillside view, valley forest. Rock roadside, dripping avalanche tunnel. Fir tree smother. Silent movement catches the eye.

Large heavy brown wings flap once. A flash of yellow. Four more incredibly large birds of prey reveal their silent selves leaving springing branches to majestically glide over steep dropping valley. Glide builds speed, soaring without effort across far forested hillside. Circling together choosing a single pine tree to all perch at the highest forested line. The birds are the biggest I have ever seen. Dark chestnut brown with a yellow tint of near iridescence to the back of the head and neck. The beak a large deadly curved tearing hook. Wings in flight are massive, curving down at broad ends with a fanning of feathers along the trailing edge of the wing. Half wing length a brown speckled band. Legs the size and thickness of a person's forearm. Clawed feet the size of an adult hand. Majestic fearsome. The Golden Eagle. Le Aigle de Roi.

All hail the real king of the mountains!

The privilege of witnessing the wild king so close renews energies within. Bald land climb, scattered rock. Housed generator lifeline for a mountain town. Dripping concrete, half-light avalanche shelter. On the roof a swing shovel clears fallen boulders, trees and debris. Caterpillar tracks, steel teeth blackboard fingernail scrape overhead. Open world daylight, rolling cold misted shroud. Block shadow building shapes evolve to dissolve through blowing cloud approaching La Mongie.

A climb into disappointment. Poor man's mini Blackpool

stuck up a mountain. Flashing lights, multi storey concrete box repetition. Irish theme bar flashes green illumination. Ski lift silence, grey blow blackens late July afternoon to November evening. Human form silhouetted through silent billow. No reason to stop. Shops selling food 'Fermé.'

Ski lift wheels, lattice steel and cables slew. Rock perch tower block ghost apartments. Darkened absorbing thick fog. I stop to put the lights on. Empty concrete and themed tat dispensaries fade in climbing silence. Visual existence the length of the bike. All senses of a world outside the cloud vanish. No riders to meet down the mountain. No vehicle travels the ink cloud soup. All sound absorbed except for hard breathing heart thump. Spots of rain hit the skin. Sounds of the waterproof zip up. Only the eyes look from under the peak. Temperature plummet. Rain turns to sleet, pelting sloshy splots become hard ice fighting with snow. I have to get off, I cannot see anything. Bare leg ice sting, shoes fill with chilled slosh numbing every footstep. Cold ice down the shorts makes a soggy iced nappy. Through freezing translucence the white line under slipping feet pushes the loaded bike toward the next guiding snow pole.

I tell the mountain "I'm not giving it up! You are going to have to freeze me then fry me! I am not giving it up!"

Slowest freewheel gear tick marks slowed walking pace.

'Splat splat' snow pelts the thin waterproof protecting body temperature from element assault.

Snow turns to sleet turns to hard rain. I stop drained and tired, remembering I have glucose. Three round soft orange flavoured tablets are greedily chewed and swallowed. Plod pace, rain ease. Calm drizzle. Back on the bike to ride the slosh. Tyre slip finds a road to grip. Rock spike loom pierces 360 degrees of vapour disorientation. Road edge ride in half-light mist roll. Cloud lift. Fantastic snow sugared black tower peaks loom concave in curve. Sharp escarpment, scree slide, creeping snowfields. Black summit frozen step back and back. Steaming vapour hangs a shroud. A million years of ice ground rubble ends green fringed in weak vegetation. Lone building high watches the road twist. A café. Clear day mountain panorama stolen in grey void. I have to get off the bike to squelch through steep slippery grey slush on a bend. Back on riding bends passing an empty car park. The crest of the road col. Shattered cliff, cleaved black rising ridge.

On top of a stone retaining wall, the large metal sculpture representing the first Tour de France rider to cross the col. Octave Lapize. Next to it, the col sign. 'Col du Tourmalet 2115m.'(6350ft).

My bike leans against the wall. The famous large metal sculpture is bigger than it looks. Sculpted face in an emotional state of wrenching toil. Knowing just how he feels. Octave Lapize, the rider who on the Aubisque shouted at the race officials "You are all murderers!"

I understand completely his expressed sentiment.

There is a plaque connecting the statue to his ordeal reading.

The 21st July 1910
The champion Octave Lapize
being the first competing cyclist
to get over the Col du Tourmalet
during the stage Luchon - Bayonne
on the 8th Tour de France.

The self-publicising Tour de France loves monuments. Many ordinary people had ridden it before. I met a couple who had ridden it on a tandem.

Peering over the edge the closed road reveals a sheer drop.

Bend twists far down swallowed by a mass of shrouding cloud. It is a road that I am disappointed about, unable to experience.

Famous café lights glow dim yellow through a misted window. The homely invite appeal after a soaked journey. I remove my waterproof and top, wiping my body dry from sweated efforts. A crisp clean top feels soft over a quick deodorised body anticipates domestic sociability.

Sign advertises the souvenir shop. I walk in to be greeted "Bonjour."

I return polite formality, wander the trinkets falling sucker to a cycling top. 'Col du Tourmalet 2115m Finisher.' I consider it the only cycling top worth having. Along with a couple of postcards with the official Col stamp for the nerdy.

I pick up a sticker for the pannier box and leave with a polite "Au revoir" to the lady who has just relieved many euros without the effort of leaving her seat.

Across the empty wet road toward the café. Through the billow of silent blowing, grey spectral shapes loom to become figures. Two muddied touring bikes appear from the closed road. Short of breath. Spattered mud grey. Relieved to reach the top.

They are from Holland. I move my bike so they can get a photo.

I ask them. "How did you get up here? The road is meant to be closed."

"From Luz. A way for just people. We must wait for construction machines and walk. It is difficult, not good."

"To make it is some achievement! Thank you for the information.

La Mongie to St. Marie de Campan is open. It is sunny down there and has a nice campsite."

"We go for coffee yes?"

"After you."

A door opens to lights and enveloping warmth. A smiling greeting behind the counter. Steaming coffee and a pastry costs me as much as a plat du jour. I would happily pay double. The few people in the place huddle around a computer screen watching the Tour de France. Wall adorned historic memorabilia hangs. Background sound frenetic commentary squeaks from a speaker.

An original 1908 racing bike of the type used in the Tour to cross the mountains hangs dusted from the wall. Fixed wheel, one rear brake, rounded drop handlebars. Comfy sprung leather saddle, two drink bottles hang from rear forks of a strong steel bracketed frame. Tough wheels count 36 spokes. A sprocket of different size each side of the rear hub gives spinaround two gear choice. The design shape of the bicycle in over a hundred years has not really changed. Only the materials of manufacture. While Carbon fibre and alloy frames are light, nothing beats steel for reliability and narrow crosswind resistance. Its bend and flex endures endless hammering abuse. Downside for the racer is weight.

1950s magazine covers. Gino Bartelli, Stan Ockers and Louison Bobet climb Pyrenees roads. I join watching 'Le Tour' happening far away. Somewhere flat, somewhere sunny. A world away. Thanking the people in the café for coffee, friendly hospitality and the free warming. I bid goodbye to the Dutch riders.

"Bon descent!" From the Patrons.

Closing the door, walking into cold clinging mist silence.

A gap in cloud steam. All around tall grey craggy peaks, snow, scree. Boulder slides amongst the birth of rivers wandering marshy beginnings. There is a silence in the high mountains. Sound absorbed. The simple noise of a footstep does not travel.

No song from a single bird, no chirp or rustle from the ground. Rude raw as the day of creation. The mountains belong only to the mountains.

I climb on the bike. Cloud billow veils all view descending a narrow empty closed road. Cleaved dynamite hewn from stone. Black sombre challenge by snow finger loom drip dripping across wet rock bends. Thick fog, guided by the white line. Without surrounding vision, if the line plummets from the edge I will follow.

Thumping rain spots, edge of road into rolling cloud. Dull sodden cliff. Steep drop narrow bends dense in fog. Many twists drop quick through the altitude. Singular hole in the cloud reveals ice, snow. Stark rock jagged mountain. Fleeting view. Shroud returns disorientating.

Cloud hovers head height across a valley. Little rivers blast angry, compressed pressurised in steep descent joining from all sides tumbling vicious. Speeding a spiteful whitewater roar. Cloud thins the lower I drop. Bike increases speed, air starts to warm. Deliverance below the vapour blanket.

Head of steep mountain valley. Vertical slopes cut by swirling blanket ascension. Creepy rising vapour fingers in ghosted silence drag at the rock.

Violent landslide. The whole side of a hill torn. Internal soft guts of mountainside has spewed huge boulders locked inside for a million years. The next layer hangs ready to drop into the turbulent dirty grey tumble boiling in scouring grind thunder. Never have I seen water so malevolent. A fall would end quick in pulverised drowning death.

Washed away road becomes muddied track. Temporary bridge over mad rage river has cleaved a deep channel through what was once a resort. Twisted mash mess splintered wood and jagged aluminium wreckage laid to waste by the lunacy of a joining river. What power is possible from the main flow?

Landslide upon landslide following the main torrent downward in dirty chaotic roar. Scars of violent damage high above the angry flow. Road patched from heaped machine scavenged boulders resist torrent grip. Rubble compacted over makes a bumpy mud sliding ride. Hundreds of stripped broken trees rammed violent into high piled boulders. Land stark, primeval, ripped bare of every soil grain. Ahead, the town of Baréges.

I ride into a warzone bombsite. A million boulders. Some half the size of a house, most are the size of a car, bought down tumbled in torrent smashed through the town. Houses hang into nothing, walls punched to part collapse. Connecting bridges boulder pounded, road undermined hangs broken. The width of boulder damage is the width of a field. The length of damage continues for miles and miles. All the time the sound of water roaring. This is after the catastrophic event.

Lone trees shredded splintered, limbs ripped off buried incomprehensible by boulder rock. Hydraulic yellow arms of the biggest swing shovel diggers work constant looking lost amongst rock wreckage, endlessly piling stone. Feeding big articulated earthmoving fifty tonne dump trucks. Large wheels and whining gears bounce across rough tracks through wreckage, tipping boulders into the torrent to divert the river from vulnerable buildings. It seems an impossible task, but the little human mammal is determined and mechanical arms never tire.

An old spa town once the bone healing hangout for the rich including Toulouse Lautrec. Buildings buried boulder filled. Rocks hanging out of windows. Town street muddied thick. Big wheel tracks slip and slide. People cannot smile. Eyes of emptiness. It is very sad. If there are deaths or bodies yet to be found it would not bring surprise.

Wreckage out of town. Destroyed campsite's crushed motorhomes. Battered gas bottles and splintered remains of chalets under pelted boulder mess. A twisted ball of crushed metal full of rocks was a car stripped and crumpled to bare steel.

'Route Barre.' Waiting for empty dump truck huge wheel procession to pass.

The bike slide. Narrow made up mud track precarious next to the speeding torrent. Standing wave vicious spit bounces higher than a man. I should not be looking up at a river. Machines drop boulders into the flow in hope of a hold for a road foundation. How much water came down here is incalculable. I wait with a couple of people for a machine to finish loading. Swinging its arm around, the revving engine slows. Driver in the cab smiles and waves us through a deep mud and rock bath. Bike tyres grip, wheels lost under mud slurry, sideways slip hard over hidden rock. Balance on the pedals, gripping the bars. Sliding close past metal caterpillar tracks. Hardworking engine heat blast sandwiched narrow next to grey roaring water. Tarmac relief. Old road solid under the wheels. Queuing boulder haulage waits. New services trenches laid. The town still running on tankered water and generator electric.

Repetition cleaved destruction runs to Luz St. Sauveur. One campsite escaped elevated from destruction is open.

The pitch a contrast of soft green. The Patron very pleasant. I explain the sad sights on the way down. She is in absolute agreement, speaking soft, respectful. Sombre in expression throughout simple discussion.

Shower is hot. Grey mud adventure spirals the plughole leaving the body clean warm tired. Blood hums a pleasant thump. The mind agrees in contentment. Mug of tea steams.

Sat outside. Surroundings in evening summer softness contrast the day's journey. Mountain peak dark blue silhouette behind a ruin hilltop tower across the valley. Long craggy ridge rises back to the Tourmalet. Under pink evening cloudscape a cascade falls from high cliff tumbling through woodland to meet the frenetic rumble softened by distance.

Across the road, 'Camping Bastan' placard names the river that has obliterated its existence. Entrance sign invite. A twisted steel shell of a crushed car amongst boulder heaps. For the people who live here throughout this valley, it is nothing but a broken picture of sadness.

66 km

A morning to get everything dry. I am so hungry. Core of the body in constant tremor. Town streets find a Carrefour supermarket spared demolition. Shelves filled with calorific joy to fill my well used 'sac souple' carrier bag.

The ground floor of many buildings buried. Walls punched through by rock and tree trunk onslaught. The river looks to have has changed course relaying surrounding landscape at will. Mowed lawn middle class suburban detached housing one side of the road. Pancaked car crushed amongst boulder grey splintered trunks on the other. A Frenchman points where the town car park and green walks were. Baréges is mentioned softly, almost hushed in conversation. Food greed walk back to the campsite shoving in the calories. Washing dried by climbed sun lighting surrounding mountains on a clear blue day.

I have to wash all the grit, mud and dirt caking the bike. The frame crusty, gear mechanisms full of grey sludge and grinding grit. As are the brakes. Sludge has got into everything. Plastic food packaging makes a bowl. I fill a plastic bottle with hot water from the sanitaires. Clothes washing gel becomes the detergent. A long patient scrub removes all grit from moving parts. The bike rinsed detergent free is left to dry ready for oiling.

A cyclist from Slovenia walks over and asks "Have you been up to the Tourmalet?"

"Yes. Down through Baréges."

He looks at my bike. "It is difficult?" Nodding to his carbon fibre roadbike gleaming. Delicate carbon wheels glint, little coloured hard slick tyres. Sat on a car boot rack.

"You will not be able to ride the broken roads. Unless you carry the bike through the rocks and the mud. It would be better to drive around to St. Marie de Campan and ride up from there. The roads are clear to the top. La Mongie is rubbish. The Col is nice."

I tell him about the cascades and the eagle experience and ask him. Where has he been riding?

"I have been to the Aubisque. Very beautiful. You must go to Gavarnie. It is not far. Through town past the supermarket and down. Just follow the road. The cascade is the biggest. You will go?"

I reply "On your recommend. I have been looking at it on the map. I will go today."

Brave words from a tired boy. The mind overrules a protesting body. You can do it!

I oil the bike. Constantly snacking fruit, cramming as much as digestion allows to feed the fuel furnace. A carton of ice cold milk devoured while packing the tent. Crisp sun-dried clothes roll tight. The Slovenian cyclist has his tent packed for a drive detour to St. Marie de Campan. Exchanged information fuels enthusiasm.

I leave with a wave. Supermarket refill includes salami for fat and energy content plus necessity beer. Both are wrapped under the sleeping bag where it always stays cool.

Neighbouring St. Sauver has not been spared. Boulder victim. Damage and buried buildings. Road swings left to follow the Gorges de St. Saveur. Slow climb companion to a river tumbling turbulent blue through a vertical gorge. Stone bridge straddles gorge cliffs in single near semicircular arch.

Railing grip. People lean, neck stretched, peering the edge. The gift shop next to the bridge informs 'Pont Napoleon.'

Slow easy climb follows pretty gorge view high to vertical cliffscape. Isolated auberge. Vacant closed campsite. Crumbly scarred concrete avalanche tunnel pelted by many winters. Opening bend to hydroelectric feed mountain vertical. Piped pressure spins the turbines. A visitor centre. Empty. Machines work the river making a flat platform to sit caterpillar tracks dragging out boulders and washed down tree trunks. Keeping turbine flow clear fed.

Vertical cliffs part revealing pretty rock valley. River tumbles stone cleave under snow topped grey mountain summit loom. Meandering bends under rock towers lead into little Gédre.

People relax. Unhurried conversation around a table. Wineglass glint catches the sun. Dejeuner appears on full plates served by a white jacket waiter to background mountain river music.

Hairpin bend, road splits. Left rises steep to 'Cirque de Tromouse.' An impressive mountain concave semicircle accessed by steep winding road. The right easier leads to Gavarnie.

Two empty campsites washed out by flooding. Road twist through house sized boulder 'Chaos de Coumély.' Thundering turbulent blue vapour rise atomised crash through the stone jumble. I breathe in airborne freshness. Gavarnie appears as slow as my upward progress. Motorhome plastic shapes poke above a wall.

Final pinch delivers shops and crowds of ice cream eating day trippers mixed with pole walking randonneurs carrying bedrolls and rucksacks. Cirque du Gavarnie and the Grand Cascade signed through a shuffling people mass in wandering trinket daze. Minimart sells fruit amongst the postcards. French fast food permeates sickly artery coagulating cooking. Riding centres hire horses and donkeys to hack to the waterfall. The campsite is over a wood sleeper bridge. Quiet crystal river forms a moat resisting the crowds.

I book at the bar for a night's accommodation. 'Pitch wherever you want.'

Steep grass slope push suddenly lightens almost self-propelling. I look around to see a grinning helping hand assisting with a laughing. "No problem!"

The campsite holds mellow ambience. From my tent a clear view to the great mountain semicircle age worn rock. Grey twisted folds hold snow ledges running to fissures. Towering jagged peaks rise to 3000m (9000ft) snow topped magnificence. A view better from distance to appreciate full panorama and size. From the left, a river plunges over the mountainside in freefall 400m (1200ft) turning to spray before hitting a rock ridge, reforming and falling out of sight.

The site on a rough terraced slope holds nowhere to lean the bike. A bleached branch with a fork fits the crossbar in improvisation. The tent assembled, finding the shower. It takes much effort to walk to the tent.

Falling asleep, waking at sunset. The moon rises a glow before magically appearing full above the mountains, Illuminating peaks. Snow glows pale blue against darkened high rockscape extending a fading twilight.

In darkness I wander to the river. The body in constant

tremor without feeling cold, face and forehead burn from a couple of days without a hat. Legs eager to ride, the body has had enough overruling the brain. No more! Tomorrow will be a rest day after riding every day since leaving the Monts d'Espinouse of the Languedoc.

The winding motor of a helicopter. Taking off creating wind blown dust sucking debris into the air. Deafening engine and rotor blade chop heads for the mountain in strobing light pulse.

A young Irishman points to signalling light from the mountain.

"There! See it, the signal! Those six flashes mean assistance is needed.

My name's Dermot. I love the mountains. Have some wine."

I have a small plastic tumbler half filled while Dermot explains.

"Different signals are for different requests, some are reply signals. Whoever is up there knows the signals. They know what they are doing... There they are again. Guiding in the helicopter."

A light flashes from the mountain. Helicopter searchlight focus. Lower, hovering before going closer and closer. Hovering still minutes before lifting away from the mountain to wait stationary.

"My girlfriend and I have been up in the snow walking the GR10. There have been some dangerous passes and tense moments. So much snow up there for this time of year."

His girlfriend finds him, comes over and hugs his arm. A petit beautiful person. Deep pool eyes and a soft spoken rich Irish accent. Dermot mentions parts of their walk to her.

She tells me. "There was so much snow and icy rock. I was not expecting it to be so dangerous. My first time up in the mountains."

They cuddle into each other watching the helicopter and sipping wine.

From behind, the noise of an engine. The headlights of a 4WD pick up loaded up bounces along the track popping stones from the tyres, headlights towards the mountains. The helicopter continues a stationary half an hour hover before getting close to the mountain. Overhead return hurried, brief. Flying back to the mountainside for a couple of minutes before flying away. Night silence broken natural by soft chattering water chiming over stones. Excitement and curiosity replaced by fatigue.

I wish Dermot and his girlfriend goodnight and a good trip. Long may they be together sharing a love for the natural order and the outdoor life.

Helicopter return briefly wakens me. Strobe and searchlight illuminates tent interior whilst landing. The engine dies, the chop and whine of the rotors slow to silence. I feel hungry falling into sleep.

23 km

Impressive lightning throughout the night brighter than burning magnesium blinds the pupils from behind closed eyelids. Thunder rolls from right to left amplified by the dead end solid Cirque. An hour of heavy rain. There is no worry. I do not bother opening my eyes. Everything will stay dry. Lightning continues silent. Nocturnal mountain moods.

I wake at 7am. Neck and shoulders have locked solid. Any movement, the muscles say No! Feeling sick I have a thirst. Body feels as if the skeleton has been stolen. Apart from my legs. They want to go, ready for another day. But I am unable to move. Making tea is strenuous. Several mugs go down my throat one after the other followed by sodium electrolyte dissolved in water to feed depleted muscles. I wake again at 10.30am. Sun turns the heat dial to oven ready. I have to get out. Morning sun attacks my face and head. Suspending the groundsheet half from the top of the tent pegging the other to the ground makes a sanctuary of cool shaded shelter. I doze in and out of sleep, muscles ease their solid grip late afternoon. The feeling of sickness subsides enough to eat. I consume two packets of noodles, my emergency carried food. Weighing nothing, noodles are full of fat and carbo energy easy to digest. Between eating I drink plenty, returning prone, happily shaded.

Slow shower and shave. Slowly into the cool bar Accueil paying for another night. Slow uphill return to sleep. Early evening woken refreshment.

I take one of my two carried T shirts and rip the back out of it making a pirate hat to soothe my head from the power of the sun. How important a hat is. A couple of days without and I am in a mess hiding from daylight! The sun's UV rays are three quarters absorbed by lowland atmosphere leaving 25% contact to the skin. Mountain altitude UV penetration intensifies to 75% of hard burn.

I make my headgear. A thin tent is assembled nearby by a randonneur.

"Bonsoir." To a man who is nut brown with gnarled skin, scraped legs skinny tough. The look of a climber.

He nods.

I add "Le vue du cascade est agreeable plus et les montagnes, le vue est extrordinaire!"

He replies "Jay swee Anglays. No comprehen-day." Waving his hand.

"Where have you been?"

"GR10. Crossing with the Spanish GR11. I have walked

from the west across the paths and snow fields staying at mountain refuges. One of them was full of Spanish scouts. I thought I was in for a night of hell. But they were good as gold. Really nice."

I ask. "Where are you going next?"

"This is the end for my trip. Tomorrow is a rest day, a shave and a tidy up. Then it is back home. Flying out in two days to Northern Ireland. It has been good."

I get to the minimart before it closes. Fruit! I have a craving for fruit. I walk past the stable where the horses are being made ready for a release to the field after their day's employment. Back at the campsite I sit in the alpine flower meadow watching the endless cascade. Many others fall around Cirque du Gavarnie. But the big one claims visual attention.

Orange mountains reflect a setting sun. I drink a litre carton of chilled milk. The sound of many hooves brisk along the stony track.

Horses appear. Knowing riverside routine. The rider behind keeps the herd moving forward. One decides to be awkward and crosses the bridge. The rider comes over, putting a rope bridal over its head and uses his horse to pull it. I does not budge, digging four strong legs into the track. He tries again. It bucks. He gets off and hits the whip onto the ground with a shout. The horse is gone wearing the slack rope cantering to join the obedient group. He mounts catching them up.

The horses must obey. If one is seen to get away with disobedience, they all will do as they please and that is too dangerous when carrying or being around crowds of people. Next plod the nodding donkeys. Indifferent to everything. Moving as an untidy bunch nosing at the bushes for a snack apathetic, following the path of the horses.

I find a sachet of coffee given to me from the Stevenson trail.

Hot coffee tastes good. Caffeine. Strength is fast returning. The pirate hat will not be leaving my head. A nod to randonneurs. I go to bed.

3am. Fully awake. The heavenly cosmos free from light pollution. Gavarnie so far away from street lit towns. The background of space held in blue cast against black spike silhouette. Landscape bathed blue in glow. Mountain spacescape holds vibrance unique. Looking into space shows the present and far back in time. The longer I look, the more infinite stars become. Although there must be a fluxing number. It is the void of space, the vacuum that is the true incalculable infinite. The forever nothing holding everything in the universe. From chained atoms forming the droplets of moisture held upon wet grass under my bare feet to chained atom form far galaxies outside of incalculable universal time, all common formed in same sequential law.

I put a bag between myself and the wet ground. The crackle of plastic as loud as thunder in nighttime silence. Breath and pulse echoes boom rhythm off the mountain. River runs in nighttime hush. Moon moved to a further valley radiates cool glow behind convoluted ridge. This hour, a similar place to this, most people will never experience. It is a quality that can never be enjoyed cocooned inside false four wall security. I sit for an hour. The movement of getting off the carrier bag deafening loud. Daytime unnoticeable. Quietly into the tent. Joining fellow mammals in nocturnal rest.

Brightness of morning. Horse hoof 'clack' along the stony track. Opening eyes, no rush to move. Slow reach to light the stove. Surfacing before the heat dial is turned up.

I talk to the Irishman. Stories of mountain climbs and snowscape walks.

"I don't climb so much these days because arthritis has got in my arms and hands. It has arrived in my knees as well. Too many years of hanging by my fingertips and wedging my hands in a rockface. Once we did a fast descent belayed on ropes with a couple of Germans in the Dolomites. We had a race.

"These mountains are not the biggest. The difference between the Pyrenees and the Alps is that you bend your neck back further to see the summits of the Alps!" Laughter.

He looks at the Cirque. "The Pyrenees are beautiful. Greener than the rock of the Alps. Beautiful."

"What was the landscape like on the walk?"

"Snowed ridges, lakes, snowfields and normal worn paths all surrounded by summits. There is a refuge tied down with chains. The place is made of aluminium. I was up there in the thunderstorm. In that tin conductor."

His tent is thin, tiny and light weighing 1kg. The cooking pots are titanium, the tent pegs titanium. A homemade cooker shield pushes into the ground to protect the feather flame of the tiny stove from the wind. A homemade pot insulator keeps heat in the food. Everything specialist keeps down carried weight.

I tell him about my breaking tent poles. The broken one is breaking again and others show fractures. I get some good advice from a lifetime's experience. When you buy a tent you pay for the quality of the poles. Advice from experience always makes obvious sense.

Waves and au revoirs to people camped around who's acquaintance has been made. The bike is walked down the slope. Tap water is sourced from the campsites own chilled mountain spring. The lady busy cleaning tells me to go into the bar.

Bottles are filled. Saying. If it is going free, a preference for beer over water. Water is all I get. Leaving the moment in smiling humour.

Busy village weave through languid wanderers, ice cream stupor and shop nosing tourist herd. People drone subsides. Downward gorge route. Notre Damme des Neiges watching over all. Back on the road. Rocky chaos rising towers spiked and snowed. I gain speed without a turn of the crank, freewheeling a road steeper than I remember on the upward journey. Road follows the tumbling blue tint around sunshine bends compressed between rock mountain. Stone bridge crossing, zig zag drop to Gédre. Slated spire in blinding hot sun reflection. Surrounding houses fresh painted, flowers colour the village. River Gavarnie tumbles the gorge, passing high pipeline hydroelectric feed.

Wild speeding river, deepened gorge roar echo. Twisting road speeds past Napoleon Bridge. Slow plod through damage. St. Sauveur. Luz St. Sauveur.

A view toward the culprit Tourmalet. Steep mountain ridge without respite. Peaks tower over 2000m (6000ft) hiding lakes and feeding meltwater cascades of altitude giving crazed power to the tumbling river. Flood warnings seen at many campsites proclaim. 'Innondation!' Pictogram person running, an arrow for directed escape. Seeing this aftermath brings realisation. There is no harbourside tidal rise for six hours. Something gives. A gigantic brimming bucket knocked over without warning obliterating everything in its path. I am enlightened from unknowing ignorance.

Supermarket stop. Across the road people talk, drink and eat sat under parasol shade.

Fuel for the day. Cold meat slides under the sleeping bag. D921. Gorges de la Luz devistation.

A long slope rising into mountain one side, rock rise sharp mountain ridge the other. Riding over raged river gaping land wounds. Road flattens, easy downward glide. Body requests food. Riverside stop. Across the grey running channel large banks of boulders have been mounded to heaps by the speedy flow. The farm opposite has lost half the width of its field the length of its farmed land. Now it has less growing capacity to support the herd through winter. Meaning a reduction of livestock numbers or buying in winter feed. A lose lose situation whichever way. The riverbank now close to the barns and farmhouse building. Not much remains between foundations and rock slab riverbank. A corrugated sheet sticks out of the riverbank in battered diamond on a new formed beach. River valley road to lost gardens. Proud long manicured striped lawn ends ragged. Ornamental trees hang the edge, roots dangle to nothing.

Traffic light slow progress. Single lane, temporary bridge. Collapsed roadside sheeted in effort to stop the subsiding road from total disintegration. Crossing the river around a bend, the road squeezed by an impressive rock gorge of towering cliffs fragmented jagged rising to high blue. Road repairs to holes. Side of the road gone, washed out undermined now propped where once was a large stone wall. New cave scour under the road, barriers stop vehicles plunging into holes the depth of a house. Everything emergency patched. There are no other roads to reach the people of St. Sauver, Baréges, Gavarnie and hillside villages. Outside of self-sufficiency this is the only feeding artery. It would be a time again for the pack donkey to cross the GR10 up the back of St. Sauver over Col de Riou at nearly 2000m (6000ft) down to Cauterets in the next valley.

Avalanche tunnels, rock netting. Boulders overhead hang suspended caught by cable weave. Rocky gorge view, speeding river. New formed islands of massed boulders packed with washed down sediment. New world brown creations pleasing.

Landscape projects designed for planting by nature.

Soulon. The first of little towns signals the ending of the gorge. River gains open distance, tall bank massed grey boulders and splintered stripped tree trunk chaotic path away to fading haze. Land opens. A feeling of space. Running ahead immense high rock cliff ridge. Heat and haze blue cast rock mass familiarity. Connection with the castle lands of the Corbiéres. Temperature increases the further away from the mountains ridden. Fresh mountain air replaced by thickened warmth of lower land.

Signs through roundabouts toward Argelés Gazost. Habitation. Traffic, nothing too busy. Houses, municipal buildings and businesses serving the occupants of the approaching town. It takes a few minutes to re adjust from the last few days of wild mountainscape which is true reality. This detached human evolved version only serves the individual with a few essentials. The rest is mass packaged commodity to occupy a flitting mind and feed the machine.

D918 appears. Sharp left climbs backward direction. Steep winding road, compressed town housing, parked vehicle mass. I climb over the town on the granny gear reaching for the waterbottle. New mountain views unfold. Back view mountain ridge falls far to the Gorges de Luz.

Open valley split by mountain growing 2000m (6000ft) to a snowcapped summit. Further peaks hold large snowfields sharing claim with grey rock mass heat hazed in blue tint.

Near valley detail obscured by a thunderstorm busy raging against all sides trapped. Thoughts of. Headed which way? I climb towards the village of Arras-en-Lavedan. Thick magnesium flashes rip the air. Dense blue black charged cloud sends block streak rain obscurement.

Arcizans-Dessus, houses without people. Sky blackens,

temperature fluctuates. Strong wind blows down the valley, thundercloud churns overhead dense. I stop and put on my waterproof, riding into deteriorating weather. No turn back, backwards is not forwards. The road will look after me. Ahead appears wooden sanctuary. A lone bus shelter. Sky opens, large splats of rain hit the road. Into the shelter. Deluge cue. Pulling the bike close to the bench, getting myself tight to the corner dry and snug. Outside the wind picks up to a howl. Pelting rain bounces back up off the heated tarmac steaming before flooding. Lightning hiss superheats air low overhead, thunder shakes the ground in body reverberation. House roofs opposite overwhelmed in gutter cascade, blowing sheets whipped by a gale. The bus shelter floor is soon under water, feet tucked up on the bench dry. More flashes and rumbles. Darkened sky. Day becomes late evening. Rain and wind deluge lasts for an hour. I sit it out, flashes and thunder from all direction. Intensity weakens, wind vanishes. Thunder rumbles moving away. Rain becomes drizzle becomes nothing.

Air mass saturated, wet tarmac shines. Smell of washed road fresh in the nostrils. Time to move up the valley before a storm repeat.

Pace quickened. Constant rhythm, legs, heart and lungs kept just below exertion. Good distance made over time. Wet shine reflection, darkened colours of countryside cloud imprisoned deep shade. Sky threat. Stormy interlude white evaporation clouds hang motionless against dark sky brood around black rock mountain. Streaks trail steel blue marking progress of rain. Dark background murk accentuates stark lightning stabbing a snow covered peak.

Two touring bikes emerge from misted vapour rise. Waterproofs cling, saturated.

"Bonjour!" Shouted through a smile.

Campsite caravans. I want to get further up the valley hopefully to Aucun for the Aubisque climb tomorrow. Heavy rain splash infrequent, above saturated moody swirl keeps the waterproof on. The village of 'Bun' dropping through lush countryside into Aucun. Two campsites signed left. Country lane leads to static caravans one side of the road. The opposite looks favourable having uninterrupted views to the long 'Vallée d'Arrens' ending in high snow covered mountain wall frontier interrupted by the continuing storm in mind bending rage.

I book in to the friendly Accueil. The lady consults her husband as to the price as I do not have a car. He overrules her charging full price. She stands staring a frown, hands on hips. It is not of much consequence, a couple of euros. He seems to be paying dearly for the atmosphere directed.

The place immaculate in every way. I pitch on flat spongy grass. Open a door to spotless sanitaires. There is a tall long faced Dutchman guarding his phone while it charges from a shaver point. Lone man hanging around toilets is never good.

"Bonsoir."

He says nothing staring at the wall. I assumed it was his phone.

The soft patter of rain on the tent. Rumbles cease, air freshens. Surrounding noise of cowbells in the meadow. Mountains revealed clear in view. Storm clouds dissipate. Soft pink cotton float over snow-topped summit. A beer from the Accueil accompanies view appreciation.

The lady serving asks. "Where have I travelled?"

She is open mouthed about the distance covered and the time taken.

She asks. "Did you cycle through the storm?"

I tell her the appearance of dry shelter found at 'bus cabine.' Outside with a beer. Pink sun has highlighted lower

mountain slopes green. Great rock towers black shining wet. Vertical escarpment contour defined. Broken craggy summit spike, shaded crevasse. Pink snow glow. At the end of long flat valley meadow sits a line of village roofs overwhelmed by mountain scale. Distant lone church bell chimes ten.
56 km

Car alarm scream, rude dawn consciousness. The Dutchman lumbers from his large Wendy house tent. Arm outstretched toward the vehicle pushing key fob to cancel the racket without success. Standing in the field a gangly dawn scarecrow silhouette moves the few paces to open the driver's door silencing the horn blare.

Why do you have to set an alarm on a sleepy little country campsite? Tin god. Precious phone. Suburban euroman has brought unnecessary fears on holiday with him. A man whose electronic technology is beyond his comprehension. Tented neighbours have appeared. Without explanation or apology, Stone face returns to his large nylon dwelling.

5.30am. Sun makes its daily rise, a consolation too good to miss. The stove purple blue flame dances around the pot, bubbles appear. Water boils. Steaming tea mug too hot to hold compliments the cool oranging new day. Sun glow rise behind black rock silhouette. First tints of snow orange summit, black shade of mountain mass. Long shadow distorts perspective across high ridge glow, accentuating size of every fold and rock crease brightened by eastern gold.

I leave at 8.30am thanking the lady Patron.

She wishes. "Bon route et bon velo!"

Tidy 'Aire de Nature. Aucun' is left early, riding through a waking village in busy bird chirp amongst countryside roll.

Superette morning delivery. Shelves sell everything,

camping spares and repairs. I buy enough food to last the day.

Mountains close the valley sky. 'Arrens Marsous' narrow street points to the climb. Pretty wooded garden, hillside ends habitation. Signed Col du Soulor and Col d'Aubisque. Slow climb, back and forth steep ascent. Overhanging trees bring welcomed pools of shade, early morning clear heat burn. Steep field rise, ascend the bends, repetitive view shrinks and falls. Slow approach clattering diesel gets louder. Tractor tows a trailer of vacant sheep to summer grazing high pasture. Large white monastery elevated on a flat ledge centre to a woodland clearing. Steep hillsides rise forested, bald green above. Mass trunks leaves and needles peer the edge of steep ascending ridge. Background vertical forest, sheer cliff slopes rise to grey mountainscape stretching far to weathered broken snow tooth crags.

Morning roadriders. Slow pass up on the pedals, lungs greedy for air, sweating with so much needed effort to overtake on this narrow empty upward lane.

Silent Monsieur Alpha. Earns my indifference.

Tree shade stop earns a drink looking back to village rooftops swallowed in green valley suede. The white monastery lost under unfolding mountain panorama from a halfway climb. Diagonal ridges fall from peaks, step backs step higher. Skyward thrust stone protrusions produced from colliding pressures of slow mighty violence of an ever moving earth's mantle. Seeing is nothing less than wonderment. Heavy planetary engineering in constant flux beyond memory of the human race.

Upward. Above the tree line, grazing cattle chime friendly comical cowbell tunes. Roadriders in slow overtake. Older riders on a mixture of featherweight carbon fibre, aluminium and trusty steel-framed machines. Questions of the weight I am pushing.

"Quaronte deux kilos plus." my reply.

The rider lets out a whistle carrying on with smiles, nods and waves.

Gradient ease, the col approach. Closed café, ski run. The only visitors are children playing on a zip wire. One pushes the other along as hard as possible sending the clinging passenger crashing into a spring rebounding along the wire, shrieks laughs and playful screams.

The col arrival. Background mountain views. 'Col du Soulor 1474m (4500ft). Riders give the thumbs up making friendly conversation. Every post or place to lean a bike is taken. I lean my bike onto the road verge and go for a stroll to look back down the climb. Then a walk over to the other side of the col for new landscape view.

Dropping fast a wide bowl of a valley opens rising to a mountain peak. Ahead rocky topped mountain ridge corniche road hugs mountain cliff cleaved rock face. Winding contours promise an aviator's view. The single track road open seasonal in daylight hours. Mandatory low speed limit. Behind towering rock, snow covered crag giants. I walk back to the bike.

A French roadrider asks if I have any oil. Between us the bone dry chain is lubed along with the gear mechanisms.

He asks of my route and is impressed. His experience of England. Once staying in Bristol with his wife.

A parting. "Bon route."

Corniche road, big drop off. High vertical view skyward out of sight. Spectacular. The most impressive cycled. Level narrow weave, mountain cliff. Vertical view, valley floor silver stream thread snakes vivid green velvet. Dots of brown chime the cowbell. Road edge knee high. Edge fallen. Step off into nothing.

Narrow rock arch famous from a sepia photo showing

Gustave Garigou on the 1911 Tour de France wearing a dirty white pullover with tyres and inner tubes crisscrossing his shoulders tucked under his arms. Lone riders self sufficient. One bike, rough roads without tarmac and no big team following on the back wheel telling how to pedal.

Under the arch, open road cliff curve. Vast space across wide valley green. Mountain road snake coils contour swallowed by block shadow.

Randonneurs greet happy "Bonjour!" Walking poles, rucksacks. IGN map hangs from a cord.

Forested hill dwarfed in vast landscape. Dripping tunnel, curve stops light penetration, short ride darkness. Wheel bump bump over uneven concrete, light ray splash across rough rock subterranean grotto into open world sunshine squint.

End of the corniche. A bend, crossing a stream noisy through rocks. Blocks of ice dirty stained in stubborn drip melt deformed of shape.

The beautiful view majestic back across the fantastic travelled route. Mountain spectacular. Castle shaped protruding crags tower above the road keep their snow.

Return view of Col du Soulor and far down yellowed pasture falls into forest drop out of sight, lessened mountain peaks green run north fading to distance. The alternative climb to Col du Soulor from a place named 'Nay' traced constant convoluted, ascending gradient.

Obscure shed sells cheese. The place empty. A young boy is sat doing nothing in the shade waiting for a customer. "Bonjour."

Woodland dense. Uphill plod. Shade respite from clear sky heat. Bike busy famous cycling road. Out of the tree line, road cleave hugs vertical cliff. Corniche unguarded vertical drop. Truth or tales of someone once sprouting angel wings not making the bend. Far reaching spectacular green mountains. Cliff rock plod around a bend. High building tops a green dome. Thin climbing zig zag ascent must be the col.

Rare shade against a cliff. Water trickles flowering rock adding ambience to the cool. Riders open mouthed sweat glazed slowed to a plod.

Patient drag up the dynamited cleave. The main distraction for the mind a huge grey slab of rock poking above the green dome. The higher I climb, the more rock spike spires appear. Under the col. Final ascent nearly, almost. A coach full of Germans swings wide chopping the road in front of my wheel. I stop. Chrome hubcaps inward sweep the long vehicle into an open car park area.

The pillared sign. Col d'Aubisque 1709m (5000ft). Panoramic fantastic. 180 degree mountain range. A world within a world.

The coach decants passengers in mass gabble filling a restaurant adorned with a hundred parked shining bikes.

A smaller café quieter. A wait to cool the body. Stone front gift café hides a trinket grotto. Shading parasol, the tabled wait for earned coffee. A young couple with their toddling child at a nearby table attentive to his attempted wanderings. The waitress crouches eye level making a fuss over the child enjoyed by the approving mother.

Across the road giant steel bikes in the colours of Le Tour de France set against green alpine rolling hills grazing white chiming cattle. Far side rolls steep freefall. Across the void grow mountain towers, horizon frontier snow giants. Hard edged dark against primary blue heaven.

Ski lift gantries roll over green suede to tumble the edge. Across a bottomless valley the biggest panoramic mountains tower. Slab Pic de Ger skyward. Folding ridge repetition vertical lean. Great scree piles beneath tumble to forest. Triangle tower rock outward lean strives skyward. Half melted snow fields, background mountain rise, convoluted ridge snowed. Grey solid rock, Vallée d'Ossau. Four towering snow dusted peaks over high mountain cliff. Further range, greater height. Ice covered high Spain. It is the most beautiful horizon set against clear sky and for this journey, the most scenic Pyrenees witnessed.

Descent. Green alpine hill winding, restaurant edge vertical drop. No turn of a pedal. Wind roar falling through the altitude, bends of concentration. Cyclists plod upward. Wheel cooling stop. River rumble somewhere in a valley hidden beneath sheer drop forest tops.

Tacky ski resort grows with every bend. Gourette apartment blots, anything of taste hidden. Dusty plate glass ski shops, concrete pillar apartments. Roaring whitewater, avalanche tunnels, forest. Water roar adds wild atmosphere to beauty. Back view towering mountains beyond proportion dominate the sky. Waterfall rock plunge through forest. Blue lake mirror reflection, forest overhang. Pebble bank symmetry, mountain giant reflection. The lake man made. Beauty created in the name of hydroelectricity.

'Eaux Bonnes.' Past era spa. Old facade of fine arches proudly announces 'CASINO.' Conjured image of dapper dressed 1920s, roadster cars. Feathered and suited for an evening's gambling to the background sound of tinny trumpet jazz. The place silent. Empty of glamour, empty of people. Deserted.

Snaking drop ends in junction. Direction Laruns and Pau. Opposite signed to 'Espagne.' Spain. Winter banished, road 'OUVERT'.

D934 valley road drop. Viewed high peaks, mass obscured by lower forest ridge. Temperature increase. Laruns half asleep cafés and shops. Road follows river, village sandwiched between river and high ridge. I turn for Bielle. 'La Route des Cols.' Dusty hot farming village. Bus cabine offers a urine odour shaded stop. The village asleep shuns afternoon heat. I feel like joining them.

D294 back and forth climbs rooftops. Full afternoon heat. Close to the village of Bilhéres the road coils clustered houses. Heavy lorry drone, high revving struggle climbs the dusty winding road. Extra effort through the pedals, legs straight push. Not to risk being caught by the lorry on the steep narrow bend. Safely on the straight. The diesel monster never arrives, turning for the village.

Long valley view across to heat hazed high ridges, forested stone spinal in blue. Sun fast drains energy, clothes soaked, dripping. Horsefly return. They bite, I swat. A stupid game without remorse from either opponent. Sign. 2km to a plateau. 'Plateau' a comforting word. Flat progress without effort.

Climb through parkland. Families sit under lush shade on green grass. Children splash in pools from a stream. Car parks. A popular place for walking and relaxing. Moorland announces the plateau trapped between high ridges. Horse riding advertised for an open countryside plod. Woodland flat ride. Energy is leaving the body, I stay on an easy gear. Out of snack fuel, the last climb of the day, the mind forces the body to respond.

Tooth shaped rocks against mountain skyline are high but not high enough to retain the snows of winter, alt.1600m (4800ft) hardly get a second look. How expectation has risen!

Woodland hides a thousand singing birds, riding under shading green. Horsefly nip. Rising forest country. Narrow clearings secret, wide deep mud churned wheel ruts. Imprints from a forest leviathan. No deep roar of powering engine. Tyre printed trail crosses from one muddied track to another. The vehicle must be the size of the Baréges quarry dump trucks. Today being Monday is a day off. Piles of tree trunks limbs amputated sit no longer to grow await collection. Coloured numbers sprayed on the chainsawed butts.

A large biting yellow striped fly the size of a hornet chooses a vein through the glove to draw blood. A good battering lets it know of my displeasure.

Forest climb green beauty. No respite from nipping flies. Road flattens, contour bends under forest, a build of speed. A roadrider out of nowhere overtakes cutting a bend nearly meeting the front of the only car in opposite direction.

A bend. 'Col de Marie Blanque.' 1035m. (3100ft) green midget amongst journeyed snow giants. Forest beauty, green walking country sings birdsong accompaniment. The big yellow striped fly is looking for me. This time bringing his gang. I do not hang around, leaving them at the col.

Road straight. Bumps in the road are hard, too fast will throw the steering. Wind roar, open road green blur. Somewhere near a river gathers strength. Sign for camping. Speed, speed, speed. The fast drop pull on the levers takes a long time to stop for hot wheel rims. Ten minute ponder resumes the speed, over the tumbling river. Road bends, little Escot snores peaceful in repose. A hump in the ground cannot be called a hill. Valley junction. Opposite railway line goes to Spain. Cliffs rise sharp, rocky chasm. N134. Opening valley tumbles the River Gave d'Aspe. Speeding an easy road through Asasp. Brown municipal camping sign. Pulling the brakes. Little road entrance, an old fashioned site next to the river obscured by reeds.

The Accueil is run by a pleasant student. I can go anywhere in the back field under the trees. The place so cheap, equalling a coffee. The pitch is flat. Rules for washing dishes are. 'Clean it to use it, then please leave it dirty for the next person.' The ambience peaceful relaxed common to municipal sites. This one with complimentary fresh washed plughole snacks for the desperate.

I say hello to two Spanish riders on moutainbikes whose wives travel with all their equipment in a van. Stormy castles grow in the sky on a pilgrimage towards the mountains. I put the groundsheet over the tent as a precaution and get to bed listening to chirping of crickets. Thoughts of. "What a ride!"
74 km

Flashes and rumbles in the blackness stirs slumber. I do not open my eyes, it is the nocturnal mountain music and without mountains do not seem complete. Thermal wind rushes toward the Pyrenees taking the deranged static charged cloud with it. The next conscious thought is of birds singing in soft warming light. I surface at 8.30am.

The Spanish riders tweak their bikes ready to leave. One comes over talking about the route. Theirs has been similar for the latter part of my journey through the mountains. I remark that they must have passed me yesterday. Today they are going over Col Bagargui to St. Jean Pied-de-Port. The weather is not looking good. Mountains enveloped in fog and black smothering cloud stillness postpone route decision. The thick swirl not looking to burn off. I need food for fuel before anything.

The Spanish riders leave with a friendly wave followed five minutes later by their wives in their VW van with a toot on the horn. The Accueil stop saying thanks. Main road leaves village life. Orolon St. Marie supermarket sign, outskirt town rooftops through trees. Car park and plate glass, the bike locked next to electric sliding doors. The two Spanish ladies appear loaded with shopping, surprised to see me so quickly. Hello and goodbye again.

Orolon St. Marie. Roundabout roundabout. All signed direction points 'Pau.' Directed west by the guiding compass. Road split. Decision time. D24 Mauléon Licharre in sunshine. D919 back into mountains sliced off by dense black cloud and fog. The best of the mountains finished yesterday. I have served my time in blackened cloud, fog and thunder. Weather choice favours sunshine.

Country valley, softened view, cereal crop expanse motionless. Background aged trees years patient heavy boughs hold green still leaf. Sliced mountain veiled solid grey. Sky heats fast in mid morning brightness. Winding countryside climb, freewheeling green into Esquiule village devoid of all living souls. A bench invites to eat sat by stream dribble. Agriculture to Barcus. The few slowly amble baguette under arm through daily life ritual. Village climb into woodland cuts the side of forested valley drop, high views across low hills to mountain sweep ends abrupt chopped grey.

Horseflies appear for the swat game, clothing fast soaked climbing under the heat. Maybe it would have been cooler in the mountains. A roadrider comes down the hill shaking his head at my chosen steep climb. This is an easy one Monsieur flat man.

Hilltop view far countryside, cluster habitation. Dotted farms, undulating Pyrenean foothills. Crops and ploughed mud geometry. Growing patchwork opposes green land domination. Beyond the green. Grey.

Long freewheel, twisting green bends. Speed blur under high sun. Strobe shimmer through a thousand overhanging branches. Cooling wind invigorates the senses, open land effortless ride drops to Mauléon Licharre straddling a river. Old bridge crossing, backstreet parallel with a walled river. A stop for dejeuner.

Steps to slow moving peaceful water. Fish pool the surface, widening circular ripples carry downstream. Mirrored gables distort in tree lean river reflection. Downstream buildings overhang the water, streams pour mini waterfalls. The background surround of steep rock forest.

This is still a mountain river. Tributaries start under the frontier with Spain. Many have joined before reaching this town. Anything remained over time grows or has been constructed elevated. Anything within grasp of river flow is on death row. Thoughts of Baréges and St. Sauveur reinforce understanding. 'Innondation' the main historical influence for the architectural engineering of this centuries old town.

Lunch is of bread, local cheese, sweet peppers, tomatoes burst in sun ripened taste. The finish of lunch rides an empty one way street into a medieval town. Cut stone splendour church and chateau. Restaurant dejeuner enjoyed in shaded town narrows. Deep discussion cutlery wave above the plate accentuates vocal opinion.

D918 appears taking me further west. Reuniting from the Aubisque, now pointing to 'Col d'Osquich.

Musculdy bright village, straight climb stopping to drink.

A lady getting into her car tells me. 'Fresh water by the Mairée office.'

Weaving road ascent void of shade. Domed green bald hill, high passage. Road steep, grinding slow plod.

Farm truck parked. Above in a steep field the sound of commands given to a sheepdog working sheep from one field to another. The dog obeys to the second the instruction given, going right, left. Cat prowl low slow movement, statue still immediate on command, mouth hangs open, tongue pant, wolf grin, ears up. Raised paw attentive in anticipation.

Grass dome traverse, the upward climb. Far reaching views north. Many rolling hills melt to hazed faraway flatter land.

Layby stop for a shiny 4WD with blacked out windows on English plates. Doors are open, tempers are frayed. Children told full vocal bellow to "Shut up!" in loud London accent. There is no one else here, the driver looks for a few seconds without communication. A moment of fine landscape view soured.

Contour weave, unremarkable 'Col d'Osquich 500m' (1500ft) marked at a car park by a very old rusting enamelled sign. Two mountain bikers have made the climb from opposite direction. Both red faced, fast breathing from exertion. Smiling a nod of greeting.

Downward speed rests the body. Fast bends, long drop straight, farmland, dotted houses, stone barn tumble, junction village 'Larceveau' under sun cooled haze. Timed negotiation of busy roundabout, wide road fast late afternoon traffic. Two lane D933 for St. Jean Pied de Port. Long climb, trees, bushes, roadside rock. White line ride fighting speeding lorry wind slam along a glass and metal strewn gutter. Main road dust. Road grime of a thousand wearing tyres dragged into the air by speeding wheels. Top of the hill Croix de Galzetaburu.

Rough carved figure on a stone medieval way marker cross, a drink in contemplation. The famous St.Jaques pilgrimage route through St. Jean de Pied de Port. A convergence of ways, the crossing point into Spain. The proud Basque region recognises no frontier or outside government imposed from the two capitals. Names of the villages and hills spoken and spelled in Basque defiant of the governing north. A different country, as are the Catalans. Strong bonded in proud identity.

Two loaded sit up and beg bikes pull in taking a rest from the long hill and busy traffic. They are Dutch and have followed one of the threads of the St. Jaques St. Diago de Compostella routes from Holland finishing at St. Jean de Pied de Port. Returning home by train. I let them put distance ahead.

Road fall, long straight soon slowed by upward progress of the two Dutch riders creeping painful progress along the verge amongst the stones, glass and metal. I stay patient on the white line, road levels passing with a wave. Roundabout points to St. Jean de Pied de Port. Ramshackle industry, ribbon development uninteresting road. An advert for camping opposite. Wide sweep through a traffic gap into a shanty site.

I am greeted by an old portly Frenchman in straining braces and a string vest.

His gravel voice tells me. "The Accueil is closed. Come back later."

Mould stained caravans and home cobbled porch additions do nothing for ambience. The place fits the area.

Simple reply of "D'accord. Merci." Buys a getaway.

Busying bend crossing a bridge. Traffic elbow through the bumpers, looking for direction, watching the compass. "Hey!"

The two Spanish riders are parked up on their bikes.

"You are here already on that bike!"

"Not the mountains. I went Orolone, Col d'Osquiche in the sunshine. How were the mountains?"

Eyes roll up. "Col Baguargui is a little road, hard work in the wet cloud. Col de Burdıncurutcheta is long. Up this way, up that way, again again again. Rain all the time, cold in the cloud. We are tired!

It is the finish of the mountains and tomorrow our last day when we make the coast and go back home to Pampalona. Where are you going?"

"Find a campsite. Then through Landes, the West Coast to Bretagne and home to the southwest of raining England." I do impressions of the rain, they laugh and reply.

"You come to live in Pampolona. Sunshine, warm. A beautiful place to live. Ride with us, the campsites are on the road to Cambo les Bains. Our phone is not working to call our wives, we do not know where they are. We cannot get an answer."

Through the town, phone box stop. A phone card is produced but the mobile phone has now gone flat, no power, no number can be produced from the memory.

I tell them. "You see the randonneur shop across the road. Well, two nice Spanish ladies went in there and bought the biggest backpacks." They look at me. I carry on pointing to the next building. "You see the bank distributeur automatic. Well, the two ladies with big empty backpacks emptied it and went to the shopping mal in Pau!"

One looks in part shock. The other laughs. "You have the cycling. They have the shopping." Laughter from all of us.

"What shall we do? Maybe try the phone in half an hour. We wait. Maybe they look for us. We will stay here in town. There is only one road."

I tell them. "I am going to find a campsite. If I see them I will tell them where you are. You have a good trip. Bye."

"Good trip! See you!"

Signs for Cambo les Bains. Campsite advertisments.

The entrance to the first, a four star rating, the next maybe miles away.

Opening the door to the Accueil. Preparing to pay double municipal site rates, expectation does not fall short. The heart starts to sink. Busy entertainment, themed evenings and a fun pool. I am given a number where my allotted rectangular piece of grass may be found and laid upon until next late morning when I must vacate or cough up for another night. A deal of resigned acceptance.

I push the bike. Throwing a leg over a saddle 'Interdit.'

Ahead are two ladies in reclined repose with a drink.

"Hello. Your husbands are in town lost, near to tears and their phone is broke. Please go to their rescue."

"Oh! Thank you!"

The van soon in spouse search.

My pitch number is unfortunately opposite the sanitaire block. The echo of slamming shower and toilet doors resonate. It could be a long night. In compensation, showers are hot, the place clean and the people happy. I eat as the van returns with two cycling husbands following obedient, laughing and waving. A retired Englishman comes over nosing at the bike asking about my journey and advice.

"I suppose just do it. A good tent, a cheap tarpaulin, a decent waterproof and granny gears. Follow your own route at your own pace without expectation." No expectation equals no disappointment.

Tired early evening half an hour nap has a midnight waking confronted by an unwashed saucepan. Bleary eyed midnight pan scrub. The occasional passing representative from the multinational union of drunks staggers past laughing at nothing. Practicing the reaching of physical postures far beyond yoga without toppling. Throughout the night the toilet door slam. Floodlight illumination. My preference for thunder storms of the natural order. I am missing the mountains.

88 km

Mountains to the Sea. Landes.

6am alarm. In the porch of the tent an information leaflet for a walled city to visit. The Englishman. He must have returned last evening for further discussion for his cycling trip and found the tent zipped and me sleeping.

Quietly past my sleeping Spanish friends, snoring families and the alcohol stewed unconscious. Throwing a leg illegally over the saddle through the campsite out around the barrier.

On the road before 7am feels good.

Morning fresh. Cloud fingers drag steep forest tops, blanket cloud smothers small mountain peak in post dawn greyness. A river to follow. Road matches downward direction. Up through the gears fast ride. Railway track weaves the far bank. No traffic.

One person walking opposite direction.

"Bonjour."

Steep green hills hem the road, D918 west.

Placard repeat. A photo of a woman. Named, words underneath read. 'Political prisoner.' Regional graffiti. 'ESKUDA!' The country I travel through. Sprayed letters 'ETA.' The outlawed separatist group. Spray paint yellow, runs end dripping letters adding poignancy to a cause. Repetition along the road.

Builders' truck rattle to work. Wide verge, my own lane to travel. Bends climb to resume downward speed. D918 split. Cambo les Bains. Favoured D932 under busy laned concrete. France has woken up and decided to drive all motor vehicles. Spinning traffic under and around roundabout land. Route National concrete. Pillared flyover overhead stretch, signed Biarritz, Plage Anglet, Centre Anglet, Ocean plages and Bayonne centre. Road focus, following the number. Multi lane junction weave around towns towards the Ardour river. Busy traffic lane change, traffic light junctions. Up onto the kerb checks map and compass for reassurance. Tyres and exhaust surround in metallic spin. Anglet, the River Ardour. Dockland, ships. Bayonne city view, tall building proliferation. Distant spire skyward strive, multi lane condensed humanity.

The river diverted on orders of Napoleon. Originally its dangerous mouth wrecked many ships at Capbreton. Now ships arrive in safety at Bayonne. Napoleon the Dude. Foreward thinking genius in moving the river created one of the finest surf spots in Europe. The Ardour now mixes waters with the original Gaves Réunis half born from the mountain sourced Gave d'Orolon. The town passed through yesterday taking its name. Orolon St. Marie.

A pavement full of runners race over the bridge. Lined spectator applause is not for me.

Crossing the river. Seaward through Boucau. Lined rail goods yards, freight depots, tall silos, waste, rust, industrial zone rubbish. Potholed streets, municipal buildings. Tarnos. Empty streets to a busy little centre of open shops bustling with business. Through an open shop door a hairdresser gabbles at her customer. Next door's fruit and veg shopkeeper enjoys a cigarette watching the street. Overhead mist haze is under burn. Sunshine arrival. Town square, traffic lights. Main road buildings of Ondres cover the top of a hill. Suburban street signed 'Piste cyclable.' The path running throughout Landes.

Bumpy rough weave, tree shade. Smooth tarmac for bikes and walkers under woodland crosses a road to Labenne. Ambling hire bike dodge. Two wheels pedalled the only traffic. A roadrider in front on a steel-framed racer from the 1970s makes good pace. I sit back a few bike lengths letting him do the riding and braking. By the speed travelled he knows the route. Pine wood dapple shade path, personal guide deals with oncoming hazards delivering me to the outskirts of Capbreton.

Town of car horn fanfare. Theatrical driver window arguments fade to soothing deep note of Atlantic Ocean breaking waves. House roofs amongst sand dunes, rising lane to a white sand beach running the whole coast to the Gironde estuary.

The beach south Capbreton is famous for its wrecked concrete mass cubes of German WW2 bunkers the size of bungalows laying rolled over across the beach. Slowly sinking in the sand along from the port entrance jetty. It is also famous as one of the best surfing beaches. 'VVF' (very very fast). Today there is the slightest onshore breeze to the blue green wave breaking over and along sandbanks from slow rollers to the famous inshore barreling dredgers sucking up the sand, enabling the rider to get covered up by the wave for a couple of seconds. Then put the foot down to accelerate out away from a mauling. The only boards for hire at the beach are soft foam boards for beginners through the surf school and would come back in pieces as would my energy depleted self. The money supply runs low and must be stretched to Bretagne. The coast sucks euros now in high season.

It is good to watch the local surfers weaving through the sandy brown dredging tunnels and best of all to watch when they do not make it out ... Slam!

Views back toward Tarnos and the River Adour under full sun of blue sea beneath hazed blue sky. White of breaking wave surges onto blinding ribbon sand blurred by hazed rising spray.

D652 main route bypasses the busy surf town of Hossegor. It ends climbing the only hill visible for miles, dropping to D152 on the way to Seignosse. A cycle way runs on a smooth tarmac path under shading pines through sandy dry heathland. Bright green bracken shared with purple flowering heather carpet.

Pine forest miles skirt the seaside resort of Viex Boucau-les-Bains. Flat path runs on tarmac under the needle topped canopy killing half the sun ray burn, shaded lines cross the path throughout the forest floor. No cars, no fumes, no need for an attentive ear. The mind half meditative, legs and lung comfortable rhythm. Little town Leon.

D652 road ride makes a change. Head down to pound the pedals north for miles and miles over flat heath marsh stabilised by man made forest. People emptiness, no name crossroads villages until the sun lowers yellow in the sky.

Campsite entrance lures a tired body. I book for one night.
The Patron asks me. "Where have you come from?"
My reply. "Ajourd hui. St. Jean de Pied de Port."
"Les Pyrenees!"
"Oui Monsieur. St Jean de Pied de Port. Vous vendez froid beer?"
"Bien sur!" I have a cold beer. Conversation with the Patron.

Pitched tent brings realisation. I have no idea where I am. Somewhere between villages near Mimizan?

The few people on the site are friendly, everyone part of the family of France. I sit out watching the sun orange away until the sky darkens to evening.

154 km

Gironde

Quiet pack. 7am on the D652. Atlantic Ocean freshness of every breath compliments windless new morning. A cockerel announces the sun has just made a gold appearance shining through a thousand pines. Small villages, through sleeping Mimizan. Town streets yet to wake.

'Military zone!' Fenced. Cycle path compulsory, separate from the carriageway slows the progress. A lake. Etang d'Aureilham. Sun climbs the top of the pine casting pale gold over windless water in black shape reflection. St. Eulalie-en-Born, road ride to Parentis-en-Born. Cycle trail weave to the middle of town. Supermarket stop fuels a long day's ride.

D46 runs straight north without deviation. Quiet Sanguinet. Straight line, head down, leg lung daily rhythm. Kilometres fall under forest flat land. Mios, a bridge crosses the calm River Eyre grassy banks and riverside café. The place busy, it has just gone 12pm. Everything stops for long sunny dejeuner. Steam rises from the coffee machine behind counter gloss, wine bottle decants to a waiting glass. Chicken slow spin golds brown, people in work clothes, suits and best summer dresses. I buy a coffee sitting by the river. Canoes unload from racked minibus trailers to take customers downstream. A long way from the Tarn or the Ardeche. Instructors are still dressed 'Extreme!' Even for slow moving pea soup. Canoes depart yellow and red, observational amusement ends, time to go. Town sign for the cycle way. Map shows it running long distance.

The path an old railway line crossing behind villages through little towns. Biganos, Audenge, Lanton stop and start, crossing many little suburban roads. Stop start drag is swapped for the faster main road. A river decants to the great water filled inlet of Bassin d'Arcachon. A foreground of many masts and colourful boats. Mass shellfishery shelter, the fresh smell of the sea cools the lungs. Views of a great bay. Far distant black tree fringed coast, white sand dune mass.

The railway path appears at Arés. Lége-Cap-Ferret exchanges human habitation for pine forest tarmac path. Pines twisted, pines tall, heathers of pink, heathers of purple. Straight line flatland forest for hours under sunshine on this beautiful cycle route. I overtake a grandfather with his two grandchildren. "Bonjour."

How many pines in this huge region?

Buildings ahead. Le Porge, A large park of tall shading trees. Pace broken earns a stop at an empty bench to eat and drink. Bells ring, accompanied shouts. Two children with the grandfather wave and laugh about overtaking my seated self.

Through town into forest country following the railway line passing the three again waving and laughing. A long hot afternoon in the saddle, so many miles roll under the wheels. Lacanau appears. A sign to Le Port. Posh hotels, large houses and a chalet village end at a small floating pontoon for yachts at the shore of large Lac de Lacanau. A small café serves drinks to the well dressed. Sweated soggy I buy a lollipop. Standing at the lakeside amongst boats looking at the view. Ice, sharp on the tongue cools the blood delivering welcomed refreshment from sun warmed tainted water.

Map options. There is the old German coastal patrol road

cutting up behind the coast, or the D3 straight from town arriving at Hourtin. The latter wins over the picturesque coastal route for distance time and remaining body energy. Luxury gated accommodation ends at the cycle way. Grandfather and grandsons have stopped and are studying the map.

"I'm lost! I need to find Le Port." the man exclaims.

I reply "Left and straight on." pointing to the direction.

"Oh good. Are you just riding in Landes?"

I tell him where I have been.

He exclaims. "The ride from the mountains, St Jean de Pied de Port! Oh! Thirty km downhill!"

His face is lit up going into dreamy memory knowing all the roads well.

"Where are you going now?" He asks.

"Hourtin, for camping"

"There opposite. It is the new cycle way running to Hourtin. 28kms straight."

Across the road new hardly ridden tarmac beckons into forest. Pines, sometimes broad leaf, but nearly always pines. Thousands of grey peeling bark trunks, broken limb scars. Growing twisting bough holds spreading branches of green needle, baking under glowing sun sucking at the marshy heath for sustenance. The sun sting lost in tinted yellow glow. Cycleway straight, never to make the vanishing point cleave between a million pines sweet resin fragrance. Straight line break weaves a farm. I am sprayed by slow moving frames of irrigation creeping mechanical along a wide flat field. Signed return resumes straight line ride. Forest fire remnants. Charred trunks stand black. The dead point skyward. Broken stump, new growth low green. Burned areas of multi football fields. Hand painted sign advertises camping. I slow in contemplation of whether to stop, but with the momentum of constant leg rhythm I have passed it.

Hourtin appears after fifteen minutes riding into a busy little town arranged around a square. I look for the town information board for camping. Nothing.

Tired and wanting a shower, thoughts of having to cycle to the coastal sites of Hourtin Plage. There is one here somewhere. Out of the main square following signs for Lac d'Hourtin. Long suburban road, adverts for camping. Two busy 'Happycamperland' sites. The first on the road junction. Peering through the chain link security fence. The place full, tents against the bulging wire. An ariel view would resemble packed contents of a sardine tin. I ride along to the neighbour boasting specialist equine themed events. I go in knowing it will be expensive and possibly hell. Out of water, out of energy. It is evening. Needing to satisfy my grinding empty stomach.

The Accueil, a colonial American mock 1800's wild west saloon. According to cowboy films, as I have ridden dusty into town a lady will remove my boots while I am in a tin tub full of bubbles relaxing with a cigar.

The reality. You will pay top price. No single person tariff, it is run like a hotel. I have to pay for two people. It's too late, I feel beat. My hands are up, they have got me. It costs me eight times municipal rates hammering the dwindling funds. Neither do I get the bubbly bath or a cigar. But the polite Accueil reads my facial bemusement finding a pitch away from 'Fun! Fun! Fun!'

If I was not so tired I would ride to the sea for a wash and sleep in the woods. There is no chance for a sneak back shower. After weeks on the road, I do not look like a two week tourist.

My pitch is under tall pines. It is impossible to get away from their branches. I do my best to put the tent away from heavy overhead boughs. If one snaps and falls, you are jam.

Showers are busy with people preparing for their evening

amongst screaming lost kids and shouting German youths. I manage to shower and shave. The mirror reveals fast decaying happiness.

Through a mass of barbeques, fat sunburned red bellies and mud eating toddlers my tent of sanctuary appears. A Dutch family on the next pitch do not speak. The whole place is just what I expected.

I eat, finishing as dusk arrives. I do the long walk to wash my dish, returning to fill my waterbottles for tomorrow. Vowing to leave early.

152 km

The seaward rumbling approach of a thunderstorm. No longer orographic stationary mountain storms. Summer heat fuelled towers move rapid greedily sucking vapour fuel from the sea. I am out of the tent to put the groundsheet over and double peg everything. Good luck to the rest of you. The wind is on its way. I go back into the sleeping bag liner that is all that is needed for comfort courtesy of captive heat's warming release from the ground.

Rumbles and flashes intensify with an arriving wind that softly purrs through the trees. Silent suspended lingering stillness. Gale roar through the pines. Needles and dust blown into the air. Tents flap hard. Magnesium flash, superheated burning air. Ground shaking crackle across the sky. Bright flashes blind through closed eyes. Bombardment commences. Big spots of rain hit the tent before pelting as an emptying gravel truck. I am tucked up snug in the dry. Rain lashes for maybe half an hour moving off with the cloud rumble. Others follow further up and down the coast. Hourtin is spared further violence. Someone's child is crying.

The alarm wakes at 6am. It takes fifteen minutes to break

comfort of slumber. Saturated ground evaporated near dry. A carton of milk goes down the throat and I manage to eat some brown bread smothered in thick jam cleaning the knife off with my tongue heathen style while packing. The bike walk through the sleeping campsite weaves sagged tents holding puddles. Others totter on collapse pulled from the ground, soggy towel and clothes lay in dirt. Overturned sun chairs amongst barbeque tumble storm victims. I walk around the barrier cycling off without seeing a soul. Cycle lane points to the path. I use the road to a silent town.

D101. Gardens advertise boats for sale. Flat countryside road north. On the map I am level with last year's campsite at Pauillac. Reckoning on about the same distance, I should reach Pointe de Grave for the ferry about 1pm.

Early morning riding through Landes is beautiful. Low pale golden sun, no wind. Empty forest roads dead straight to the vanishing point. Centre white line is ticking by. Roadside houses marooned in pine.

Crossroad Vendays Montallvet. Boulangerie shutters down. People surface for new day routine. D101 forest marsh, water drains beneath the road. Black depth still water glints under sun. Cycleway crosses the road, signs proclaim an EU funded scheme to make Landes an area devoted to car free exploration linking towns.

Ancient marshland heath, signs for Soulac-sur-mer. Grayan ends the forest. Verdon-sur-mer brings a familiar downhill twisting ride to Pointe de Grave. Arriving in time for the loading black hulled ferry. A few euros gets me on board, the bike tied. Leaving the dock to cross the Gironde estuary. Finding my way to the restaurant, joining the coffee queue. Outside to watch the receding coast behind white churn propeller wash.

A raising of the cup in quiet toast to Landes and the

Pyrenees in gracious thanks. Leaving their beauty to live on in words, pictures and revered memory.

Across the calm wide estuary the approaching town of Royan grows in size and building detail. Off the ferry into town. Thoughts of finding a campsite. The information board a little way along the people busy sea front promenade is showing many campsites. I would like a rest day.

I could have a rest day and not have to travel up through Marennes and Rochefort. The tide will be out. Remembering the muddy marshland stink. On the map. La Gare.

I follow the sea front into busy town shopping streets.

La Gare sells a ticket to Nantes via Saintes. The train leaves in an hour and a half. Time printed on the ticket 11.11 am. A speeding time from Landes! I can look forward to a rest day on the move. Nantes for this evening and then a ride up through Bretagne for a few days. I sit outside the little café next to the station. Hot dog treat and tea kills time. Slow station wander feeds the ticket in the mouth of a gnawing yellow machine.

Little 'TER' Train Regional arrives, carriage level with the platform. Electric door closes, whizzing through countryside to Saintes. A bike drag up and down stairs between platforms to wait for a connecting Inter Cite. The platforms are low. It is a struggle to get the bike up the ladder steps of the Inter Cité carriage. A helping hand pulls the front wheel up for me and I lift the rest up one step at a time. I thank the lady for her help and tie the bike to a rail.

Countryside speeding blur. Townscape, farmscape. Route National vehicles keep pace or go backwards from speeding progress. Carriage occupants nod swayed to sleep in the heat of afternoon or stare in train window trance. Speed blur fields change from yellow parched to green. Trees grow broader, floating cloud expands across the sky. Building style change, the journey plays speeding rewind crossing the expanse of La Loire slowing to the outskirts of Nantes.

Carriage empties. The platform lift does not want to work. The slow bump down the stairs wheeling along a corridor to a slope rising to the modern ticket hall main doors.

Downhill city ride. River fresh. Bright city buzz of Nantes. Around the pleasant port, colourful boats and barges, painted funnels, varnished wood houseboats for portable city living. Riverside ride. Under stone railway bridge. Grey concrete overhead humming Route National. Quietening path, the natural bank of the river. Fenced compounds and scrap piles appear, green open space. Campsite sign. 'Belle Riviére, St. Luce sur Loire' directs. Short leafy lane wheel to an Accueil camping garden. A gracious welcome, a glass of wine. Unhurried conversation.

My neighbours are cycling. "Bonsoir."

More conversation. I find I have been speaking in fair part the language, picking out key words spoken of sentence meaning. The last couple of weeks a lifted barrier for communication without realisation.

My neighbours are from Holland. A family who have cycled down La Loire from Orleans. The weather has not been good. Showery rain all day every day. The scenery still impressive. Nice people riding tall heavy upright old Dutch bikes that will last forever.

62 km

Bretagne Return

Thunderstorms return nocturnal lullaby serenade. Semi-conscious seeks deep comfort wrapped in the sleeping bag liner. Overhead loud bang rips the air, a blinding flash goes up river. Rain pelts the tent, Back to sleep not remembering anything until waking at 8am to faraway rumblings of displeasure from out to sea. Stormy castles, dark moody sky brooding bad tempered. Slow smother envelopes the river valley.

Ordered fresh bread collected. There has appeared a tent on the next pitch, the young travelling magician and juggler makes his way around Europe using money made entertaining in towns. A happy friendly person walking into Nantes with his bag of tricks.

The Dutch family are going to get the train back to Orleans because the weather forecast for today and the rest of the week for the Loire valley is bad. Guaranteed.

I take their decision as good advice. Use the train to get up into Bretagne and jump off where the weather clears.

The faraway rumble slow approach. I hurry breakfast to make a fast pack. My neighbours are busy dropping their tent pushing everything into bike panniers. Farewell. Pushing the bike to the Accueil finds it empty.

Out of the gate, the leafy lane ride back to Nantes. Lightning announces rain's return. Under the thickest trees.

The waterproof slipped on to patiently wait. Hard downpour, hiss and thunder rumble. Path floods in pools forming ponds. Half hour pelt eases travelling upstream following the thunder.

Sun glint gives the all clear. Fresh ride over wet silver. Riverside cycle path, buzzing city centre life.

La Gare people busy echoes announcement. I join the queue for a Bretagne ride. The yellow machine validates the ticket with a gnaw. Waiting for the train to come up on the board. An opportunist looks through the bins walking off with half a drink and a newspaper to digest.

Half an hour later the Dutch family arrive.

The man laughing. "How did you like the rain?"

"I got under the trees and waited."

"We took shelter in the big store selling old furniture. Have a good journey."

"Have a good trip back to Holland."

Bike bump up the stairway to the platform. Modern TER carriage level with the platform makes loading easy. The train speeds through steady rain. Dark green land, wet roofs. Shining soaked roads under grey sky through rain streaked window blur to the city of Rennes.

Change of trains, change of platform. Bike bump drag ritual, one step at a time. The carriage addition of an English couple on holiday from university riding different areas of Bretagne on their heavy laden touring bikes decants them in steady rain at St. Brieuc.

Rain streaked windows continue to Morlaix. Standing outside the station in steady rain waterproofed wet downward ride under half-timbered streets. Morlaix in its dull soaking is still easy on the eye. The main street full. Weekly market fills the town, the wet crowd shop undeterred. Covered market stalls, colourful umbrellas. Smells of cooking and trader noise selling softens a wet afternoon. Patisserie stop politely serves the finest fruit tartlets. Along the harbourside. Flower spill, boat masts. The feeling of a journey coming to a close. Rain peppers the estuary in soft hiss. Cloud hang unmoving in grey drear indifference, riverside boat brightness subdued monochrome.

Far white squares amongst tree black hillside become Carantec. Beyond in a grey blur the head of the estuary with the guarding stone mass fort on its rocky island. I climb over a hill flanked by fields and drop down to join D58 crossing the River Penzé. Rain ease. Car wheels lift traffic spray from a soaked shining road, busy roundabout points towards journey's end. Signed 'Roscoff.' Sun breaks the grey lighting pools of colour across summer countryside.

The little promontory town of Roscoff out of reach from the dense cloudbank. Buildings bathed in a warmth of late afternoon sunshine. Pretty harbourside ride. Baskets of flowers amongst pale gold granite. Chapel road ends in rocky coast. I cook my evening meal under sun warmed tones of approaching evening.

Over windless green glass, a wooden sailing lugger has dropped its sails motoring slowly past a lighthouse. Far out. A trawler cuts a black line wake across mirror sea reflection gaining in size towards the fishing port followed eagerly by many flapping white specs of gulls.

The white painted stone chapel surrounded in fiery bloom enjoys an elevated view across town and harbour. Sun lowers in orange burn scorching distant cloud fiery red. Over oily calm sea, the sound of a choir singing sea shanties on the harbourside has an audience of a listening applauding crowd.

I ride down to the ferry terminal, paying for the crossing. Reluctantly walk the bike through the open jaws of the waiting ship's shadowed steel ribs for the night boat sailing across La